NEW STATE SPACE

New State Spaces

Urban Governance and the Rescaling of Statehood

Neil Brenner

OXFORD

UNIVERSITY PRESS

OXFORD

UNIVERSITY PRESS

Great Clarendon Street, Oxford OX2 6DP

Oxford University Press is a department of the University of Oxford.
It furthers the University's objective of excellence in research, scholarship,
and education by publishing worldwide in

Oxford New York

Auckland   Cape Town Dar es Salaam   Hong Kong   Karachi
Kuala Lumpur Madrid Melbourne Mexico City   Nairobi
New Delhi Shanghai Taipei Toronto
With offices in
Argentina Austria Brazil Chile Czech Republic France Greece
Guatemala Hungary Italy Japan South Korea Poland Portugal
Singapore Switzerland Thailand Turkey Ukraine Vietnam

ISBN 978-0-19-927006-4

Printed in the United Kingdom by
Lightning Source UK Ltd., Milton Keynes

PREFACE

This book represents a synthesis of theoretical and empirical work I embarked upon in the mid-1990s. At that time, as a graduate student in political science at the University of Chicago, I became frustrated with the apparent indifference of state theorists, comparative political economists, and political sociologists to the role of territoriality, spatiality, and scale in modern political life. The translation of Henri Lefebvre's *The Production of Space* in 1991 exposed me to the conception of the state as a 'spatial framework' (Lefebvre 1991: 281) and inspired me to inquire further into the geographies of state power under modern capitalism. I subsequently slogged my way through Lefebvre's untranslated, 4-volume work *De l'État* (1976–8). Upon reading the remarkable chapter on 'Space and the State' in vol. iv of that book (recently translated as Lefebvre 2003a), with its provocative but tantalizingly incomplete analysis of 'state space' (*l'espace étatique*), I knew I had begun an intellectual journey that would preoccupy me for some time into the future. The opportunity to study in UCLA's Department of Geography during the 1995–6 academic year enabled me to explore the cutting edge of critical sociospatial theory, political-economic geography, and urban studies, and provided me with solid foundations on which to pursue my goal of developing a spatialized approach to the contemporary state. Equipped with a more thorough grasp of critical geographical political economy and a rejuvenated excitement about the possibilities for importing some of the insights of this remarkably vibrant research field into the 'non-geographical' social sciences, I returned to Chicago in the summer of 1996 and began outlining a dissertation project.

During my year at UCLA, I had written an extended research paper on the restructuring of urban governance in western European global city-regions. The paper was critical of the tendency among global cities researchers to postulate a declining role for national states under contemporary conditions. Against such assumptions, I attempted to demonstrate that western European national states had played key roles in facilitating the process of global city formation, and that they were in turn being transformed, both functionally and geographically, through this role. After leaving Los Angeles, I remained convinced that globalizing city-regions would provide fascinating sites in which to investigate such transformations of statehood more systematically. I was drawn, in particular, to the idea of comparing the interplay between global city formation and state spatial restructuring in different national and local contexts. I settled on Frankfurt and Amsterdam, two of Europe's major second-tier global city-regions, as suitable field sites and, a year later, dissertation fellowships from the Alexander von Humboldt Stiftung and the Social

Science Research Council enabled me to pursue such an inquiry. During the second half of the 1990s, debates on metropolitan institutional reform had exploded in each of these city-regions. Although efforts to install a 'Regional County' (*Regionalkreis*) in Frankfurt and a 'city province' (*stadsprovincie*) in Amsterdam ultimately failed, I found that struggles over metropolitan governance were an important expression and medium of significant changes in local, regional, and national regulatory configurations. In both city-regions, changes in state spatial organization were being justified, from a variety of ideological perspectives, as a means to enhance locally and regionally embedded socioeconomic assets, and thus to attract mobile external capital investment within an integrated European economy. And, in both city-regions, the major strategies of metropolitan institutional reform, whether of neoliberal or social democratic varieties, were premised upon a significant intensification of previous, locally focused forms of economic development policy and 'urban entrepreneurialism' (Harvey 1989*a*). My dissertation devoted considerable attention to the task of comparing the very different institutional orders, regulatory arrangements, and political alliances that underpin German and Dutch capitalism at national, regional, and local scales. One of its more surprising conclusions, however, was that broadly analogous processes of state rescaling and urban governance restructuring had unfolded in each country's most globally integrated city-region during the course of the 1990s. The research left me wondering whether similar transformations of statehood and urban governance were occurring in other city-regions as well, both within and beyond the European context. I completed my Ph.D. thesis in the summer of 1999, and then relocated to New York University, where I found a new (trans)disciplinary home in the Department of Sociology and Metropolitan Studies Program.

I had initially intended to write up my case studies of Frankfurt and Amsterdam in the form of a comparative, book-length monograph on global city formation, urban governance, and state rescaling. However, as I returned to the manuscript, I was continually distracted by a desire to work on a more abstract level, in pursuit of additional theoretical insights into the nature of contemporary rescaling processes and the associated transformation of state space. Meanwhile, as I broadened my knowledge of the European situation, I became increasingly convinced that the processes of state rescaling and urban governance restructuring I had observed in German and Dutch city-regions were not, in fact, unique to those contexts, but were unfolding in strikingly analogous, if contextually specific forms, throughout the western European city-system. A new book project thus began to take shape in my mind—one that would attempt systematically to forge appropriate theoretical categories for the study of state rescaling while delineating the broadly shared patterns of state spatial restructuring that have emerged in major western European city-regions during the last thirty years. Though they are absolved of all responsibility for the final outcome, discussions with Bob Jessop, Roger Keil, and Nik

Theodore convinced me that such a book would be viable, perhaps even valuable. I thus set aside my case studies of Frankfurt and Amsterdam, and embarked upon the new project.

A James Bryant Conant fellowship at Harvard's Center for European Studies during the 2000/1 academic year provided me with the requisite time and space, coupled with a truly superb library infrastructure, in which to embark upon this project. The vast resources of Harvard's Widener Library enabled me to explore in greater detail the trajectories of state spatial restructuring and urban policy change in Britain, France, Germany, Italy, and the Netherlands, among other European countries, since the postwar period. My year at Harvard also enabled me to reflect more systematically on the challenges of combining the key insights developed in my two favorite contributions to state theory— Henri Lefebvre's chapter on 'Space and the state' from vol. iv of *De L'État* (1978) and Bob Jessop's *State Theory* (1990a). Thanks to a Goddard Faculty Fellowship from the Faculty of Arts and Sciences at NYU, I was able to make considerable progress with the writing of this book during the summer and fall of 2002. The remainder of the writing was completed during the summer and fall of 2003.

This book thus draws together approximately eight years' reflection on state theory, state rescaling, and urban governance restructuring in western Europe. While initial formulations of some of its arguments were published in various academic journals and edited volumes during the late 1990s and early 2000s, these ideas have been reformulated completely for purposes of this book, and have been embedded within a synthetic theoretical and empirical framework. An early version of Chapter 2 has been published elsewhere (Brenner 1999a), but it has been revised and expanded extensively for inclusion here.

This book is intended as a first installment on what I hope will become a longer-term, comparative investigation of the diverse pathways of state rescaling that have crystallized across the older capitalist world since the global economic recession of the early 1970s. Whereas this book is devoted to the tasks of theorizing the process of state rescaling and explicating major pan-European trends, much work remains to be done in order to decipher, and to explain, the contextually specific forms in which state rescaling processes have unfolded in divergent national, regional, and local settings, both within and beyond western Europe. The theoretical framework and macrohistorical perspective developed in this volume are intended to serve as a foundation for this type of variation-finding comparative investigation.

As will be evident from my extensive citations to their work, my greatest intellectual debts are to radical scholars Henri Lefebvre, Bob Jessop, and Erik Swyngedouw. These authors' ideas on state spatiality, state restructuring, and rescaling processes have provided much theoretical inspiration for my own efforts. Ever since I began working on urban political economy and state theory in the mid-1990s, Margit Mayer and Roger Keil have provided invaluable critical feedback on my evolving research agenda; their mentorship, encouragement, and friendship have helped me maintain my momentum throughout the long gestation of this project. More recently, I have been extraordinarily lucky to be able to rely upon the intellectual comradeship of Bob Jessop, Martin Jones, Gordon MacLeod, and Nik Theodore. My collaborative work with these remarkably creative, diligent, and dedicated scholars has been a formative intellectual and personal experience, and it proved essential to my ability to undertake, and to complete, this book. Additionally, and often unbeknownst to them, a number of friends and colleagues have helped me grapple with various theoretical and empirical problems during the period in which I was working on this book. For this, sincerest thanks are due to Bob Beauregard, Julie-Anne Boudreau, Nitsan Chorev, Jürgen Essletzbichler, Jamie Gough, Steve Graham, Susanne Heeg, Andrea Kahn, Stefan Kipfer, Andrew Kirby, Stefan Krätke, Helga Leitner, Peter Marcuse, Andy Merrifield, Harvey Molotch, Sean O'Riain, Anssi Paasi, Jamie Peck, Allan Pred, Mark Purcell, Klaus Ronneberger, Saskia Sassen, Nathan Sayre, Christian Schmid, Jessica Sewell, Bill Sites, Neil Smith, Ngai-Ling Sum, Pieter Terhorst, Dick Walker, Danny Walkowitz, and Kevin Ward.

During my meandering foray through graduate school, I was privileged to work with a number of generous but intellectually demanding scholars—including Nick Entrikin, John Friedmann, Allen Scott, and Ed Soja at UCLA; and Gary Herrigel, Moishe Postone, Bill Sewell, and George Steinmetz at the University of Chicago—each of whom deserves my warmest, sincerest thanks. I owe a particularly massive intellectual and personal debt to my erstwhile dissertation chair, Bill Sewell, who has been a steadfast advocate, a wonderfully constructive critic, and a consistently reliable adviser ever since I first met him over a decade ago. In addition, through his embarrassingly frequent notation of 'JA' ('Jargon Alert') on more of my writings than I care to remember, Bill has been a staunch defender of clear prose, despite my often stubborn resistance to his good intentions. While I doubt that the present text will live up to his high standards, I can only hope that Bill's influence on my thinking and writing will be evident.

Since the fall of 1999, I have had the good fortune to work in the Sociology Department at New York University, which has provided a supportive, tolerant, and stimulating intellectual environment for research and teaching. NYU's Metropolitan Studies Program has been an exciting postdisciplinary space, thanks in no small way to the seemingly boundless energy, enthusiasm, and everyday cheerfulness of my tireless colleagues. Participants in my graduate seminar on 'State/Space' in NYU's Sociology Department deserve special thanks for their enthusiastic critical engagement with many of my ideas on state theory during the spring of 2002. I would also like to thank the participants in colloquia held in the Political Science Department at York University, Toronto (November 2002) and in the Geography Department at Rutgers University (February 2003) for their incisive critical reactions to some of the key arguments developed in this book.

A particularly massive thank you is due to Nitsan Chorev, Bob Jessop, Eric Klinenberg, Andy Merrifield, Nathan Sayre, and Nik Theodore, for dutifully and meticulously reading all or part of the final manuscript, at inexcusably short notice. Their detailed suggestions, questions, and criticisms helped me navigate my way through a final round of revisions in the early winter of 2004. I eagerly look forward to an opportunity to return their generosity. Of course, I assume full responsibility for all remaining errors of fact or interpretation and for any other limitations in the final text.

It has been a genuine pleasure to work with Anne Ashby of Oxford University Press, who has been a supportive, patient, and reliable editor at every stage of this project. Paul Cleal, Design Manager at OUP, likewise deserves my sincerest gratitude for grappling with the unwieldy formatting dilemmas presented by the many figures and boxes included in this book. Warmest thanks are due to Richard Malenitza of the NYU Digital Studio for expertly and patiently scanning the maps; and also to Morgan Jones and Matthew Murphy, who provided research assistance at various stages of my work.

It took me a little while to get into the groove of life in New York City. For helping me do so, and for preventing me from wandering astray in so many ways, I am deeply grateful to Nitsan Chorev, Peter Dodds, Doug Guthrie, Corinna Hawkes, Andrea Kahn, Andy Merrifield, Duncan Watts, and Liz Workman. In addition, a number of truly good friends and comrades—including Antonio Bellisario, Jeremy Bendik-Keymer, Stephen Collier, Moira Egan, Jürgen Essletzbichler, Ted Hamm, Howard Harrington, Ruth Horowitz, Eric Klinenberg, Steve Monte, Tara Murphy, Esan Rodney, Nathan Sayre, John Shovlin, Djibril Sinayoko, Sandra Smith, and Caitlin Zaloom—contributed countless good vibes and helped me keep my balance beyond the world of book-writing. Cycling wizard Chris Griffin deserves special thanks for inspiring me to ratchet up the pace. Last but not least, I am endlessly grateful to Sara Nadal for giving me so much of her *vie quotidienne*. Her young sidekick, Lula Martini, helped me stay focused, and kept me laughing, during the final push to finish this book.

Beyond New York City, I would like to thank my grandmother, Sylvia Brucker, for inspiration and encouragement. I will always be grateful to Manu Goswami for the many years in which, through her love, companionship, and laughter, she sustained me in life and in work. Deepest thanks go to my brothers and sisters—Clayton and Michael, Jill and Tracey—for remembering not to take me too seriously; and to my nephew Jonah, for bringing so much more light into my world, even from afar. I dedicate this book to my wonderful parents, Ronni and Sandy Brenner. Their unconditional love and support, through the crazy twists and turns of life, have sustained me in more ways than they will ever know.

N. B.

Brooklyn, New York
January 2004

ACKNOWLEDGEMENTS

The author and publisher are grateful for permission to reproduce the following material:

Chapter 2 From a very early version published in Theory & Society, 28, 2 (1999): 39-78: *Beyond State Centrism? Space, Territoriality and Geographical Scale in Globalization Studies* by Neil Brenner. © Kluwer Academic Publishers B.V. With kind permission of Kluwer Academic Publishers.

Map 4.1 From Robert E. Dickinson *City and Region: A Geographical Interpretation* (Routledge, London, 1964, p. 388). Reproduced with permission.

Map 4.2 From Hugh Clout *Regional Development in Western Europe* (Chichester, John Wiley & Sons, 1981, p. 27) © John Wiley & Sons Limited. Reproduced with permission.

Map 4.3 From *L'Espace Géographique*, no.4, 1973, p. 251 (article by Roger Brunet). Reproduced with permission.

Map 5.1 From DATAR Brunet: Les Villes 'Européenes', Paris: La Documentation Française, p. 79 © RECLUS 1990.

Map 5.2 From Federal Ministry for Regional Planning, Building and Urban Development, *Guidelines for Regional Planning*, Bonn, 1993, p. 5: 'Prevailing Settlement Structure'. © BfLR Bonn 1992. Reproduced with permission.

Map 5.3 From Bundesministerium für Raumordnung, Bauwesen und Städtebau, *Raumordnung in Deutschland*, Bonn, 1996, p. 19: 'Urban Networks Pilot Project' (NB The urban networks shown on the original map are only those networks that were studied with the scope of a research project commissioned by the Federal Ministry. There are also other urban networks in Germany). Reproduced with permission.

Map 5.4 From Kamerstukken Tweede Kamer 1987–1988, 20490 no.2, p. 96. Reproduced with kind permission of the Tweede Kamer der Staten-Generaal, The Netherlands. © Grafische Beeldvorming Rijksplanologische Dienst.

Map 5.5 From 'Landsplan perspektiv: Development perspective towards the year 2018' (Ministry of the Environment, Copenhagen, 1992). Reproduced with permission.

Map 5.6 From 'France, Ile-de-France: tendances et perspectives. Une contribution au debat sur l'amenagement du territoire' (Paris, Conseil Regional Ile-de-France, 1993, p. 48) © IAURIF.

Map 5.7 From Stephen Graham and Simon Marvin: Splintering Urbanism (New York and London: Routledge 2001, p. 325), adapted from D. Chevin, 'All the right connections', *Building* 19 (July 1991), 47. © *Building*, reproduced with permission.

Map 6.1 From Bas Waterhout *Polycentric development: What is behind it?'* in Andreas Faludi (ed.) European Spatial Planning (Cambridge, Mass.: Lincoln Institute of Land Policy, 2002, p. 98), reproduced with permission. © DATAR (Délégation à l'Aménagement du Territoire et à l'Action Régionale): 'Tentative pour une définition spatiale des zones d'integration mondiale périphérique' p. 101: *Aménager la France 2020*, published by the Documentation française February 2002; © AEBK, cartes et communication. Reproduced with permission.

CONTENTS

LIST OF BOXES

LIST OF FIGURES

xvi *List of Figures*

LIST OF MAPS

ABBREVIATIONS AND ACRONYMS

APEC	Asia-Pacific Economic Cooperation Conference
ASEAN	Association of South East Asian Nations
BCR	*Bestuurlijke Commissie Randstad*
CODER	*Commission de Développement économique régionale*
CPRE	Regional Economic Planning Committee
DATAR	*Délégation pour l'Aménagement du Territoire et l'Action Régionale*
DGXVI	Directorate-General for Regional Policy and Cohesion
DoE	Department of the Environment
EMU	Economic and Monetary Union
ESDP	European Spatial Development Perspective
EU	European Union
EURACOM	European Action for Mining Communities
EZ	Enterprise Zone
FINE	Fashion Industry Network
GA	*Gemeinschaftsaufgabe 'Verbesserung der regionalen Wirtschaftsstruktur'*
GATT	General Agreement on Tariffs and Trade
GLA	Greater London Authority
G8	Group of Eight (leading nations)
HRA	*Raumordnungspolitischer Handlungsrahmen*
IGO	International governmental organization
IMF	International Monetary Fund
INTERREG	Community initiative concerning border areas
IRI	Institute for Industrial Reconstruction
LDDC	London Docklands Development Corporation
LPAC	London Planning Advisory Committee
MERCOSUR	*Mercado Comun del Sur*
METREX	Network of European Metropolitan Regions and Areas
MILAN	Motor Industry Local Authority Network
NAFTA	North Atlantic Free Trade Agreement
NGO	Nongovernmental Organization
ODC	Ørestad Development Corporation
OECD	Organization for Economic Cooperation and Development
OLR	*Openbaar Lichaam Randstad*
ORA	*Raumordnungspolitischer Orientierungsrahmen*
ORI	*Overleg Ruimtelijke Investeringen*
PSEP	Provincial Socio-Economic Plan
quango	quasi-autonomous nongovernmental organization
RCSR	Rescaled Competition State Regime
RECITE	Regions and Cities for Europe
REPC	Regional Economic Planning Council
ROG	*Raumordnungsgesetz*

RoRo	Randstad Consultation on Spatial Planning
SDAURP	*Schéma Directeur d'Aménagement et d'Urbanisme de la Région Parisienne*
SDR	*Schéma Directeur Régional*
SEM	Single European Market
SEM	*Société d'Économie Mixte*
SERPLAN	London and South East Regional Planning Conference
SMP	State mode of production
SPZ	Simplified Planning Zone
TGV	*Trains á grand vitesse*
UDC	Urban Development Corporation
VINEX	Fourth Report Extra 1990
WRO	*Wet op de ruimtelijke ordening*
WTO	World Trade Organization
ZAC	*Zone d'Aménagement Concertée*
ZUP	*Zone d'Urbanisme en Priorité*

ONE

Introduction: Cities, States, and the 'Explosion of Spaces'

> we find ourselves faced with an extraordinary, little-noticed phenomenon:
> *the explosion of spaces*. Neither capitalism nor the state can maintain the
> chaotic, contradictory space they have produced...
>
> Henri Lefebvre (1979: 290)

This book is an attempt to decipher the transformation of statehood under
contemporary capitalism. In recent decades, this issue has attracted considerable attention among globalization theorists, international political economists, political sociologists, and other students of contemporary politics.
Across the political spectrum, from pro-globalization boosterists (Ohmae
1995) to anti-globalization critics (Hardt and Negri 2001; Strange 1996),
many scholars have forecast the imminent demise of national state power
due to the purportedly borderless, politically uncontrollable forces of global
economic integration. During the last decade, however, a significant strand of
political-economic research has advanced the counterargument that national
states are being qualitatively transformed, and not dismantled, under contemporary geoeconomic conditions.[1] Within this emergent interdisciplinary literature, scholars have explored the ways in which diverse arenas of national
state power, policy formation, and sociopolitical struggle are being redefined
in response to both global and domestic pressures. The new forms of statehood
that are resulting from these wide-ranging transformations have been vari-
ously characterized as competition states, workfare states, internationalized
states, catalytic states, network states, post-Fordist states, post-national states
or, more generically, as post-Keynesian states.[2]

---

[1] The literature on the restructuring of national states under conditions of contemporary globalization has grown rapidly during the last decade. Representative works include Agnew and Corbridge
1994; R. Cox 1987; Evans 1997; Gill 1995; Helleiner 1994; Jessop 2002; McMichael 1996; O'Riain
2000; Panitch 1994; Sassen 1996; Wade 1996; and Weiss 2003. A more detailed examination of state
decline arguments, and their associated epistemological assumptions, is elaborated in Ch. 2.

[2] These labels have been used pervasively in the interdisciplinary literatures on contemporary
state restructuring. See, among other sources, Ansell 2000; Boyer and Drache 1996; Hirsch 1995;
Cerny 1995; R. Cox 1987; Evans 1997; Jessop 1999a, b; Keil 1998a; Peck 2001a, b; Scholte 1997; Weiss
1998; and Whitfield 2001.

While these recent, 'transformationist' approaches have contributed valuable theoretical and empirical insights to the study of contemporary statehood, they have invariably focused upon two overarching geographical scales—the *national* and the *supranational*. For instance, scholars of contemporary state restructuring have investigated, among other institutional shifts, the crisis and reorganization of the Keynesian welfare national state, the increasing internationalization of national policy systems, the consolidation of new supranational institutional arrangements, and various putative challenges to national state power associated with geoeconomic integration. Against the background of such studies, this book is intended to broaden and deepen the geographical imagination of contemporary state theory by investigating the major role of *urban regions* as key sites of contemporary state institutional and spatial restructuring. Rather than treating cities and city-regions as mere subunits of national administrative systems, I suggest that urban policy—broadly defined to encompass all state activities oriented towards the regulation of capitalist urbanization—has become an essential political mechanism through which a profound institutional and geographical transformation of national states has been occurring. My claim is not simply that the institutional infrastructure of urban governance is being redefined but, more generally, that transformations of urban policy have figured crucially within a fundamental reworking of national statehood since the early 1970s. A geographically attuned and scale-sensitive approach to state theory is required in order to decipher the new state spaces that are being produced under contemporary capitalism.

The core of this analysis focuses upon a major realignment of urban governance and state spatial policy that has occurred across western Europe during the last three decades. During the 1960s, most western European states established relatively uniform, standardized administrative structures throughout their territories and mobilized redistributive spatial policies designed to alleviate intra-national territorial inequalities by extending urban industrial growth into underdeveloped, peripheral regions. This project of spatial Keynesianism (Martin and Sunley 1997) continued into the 1970s, but was widely abandoned during the subsequent decade, as policymakers became increasingly preoccupied with the challenges of urban industrial decline, welfare state retrenchment, European integration, and economic globalization. Subsequently, in a shift that has been famously characterized by Harvey (1989*a*) as a transition to entrepreneurial urban governance, national, regional, and local governments mobilized new, growth-oriented approaches to urban and regional policy in an effort to promote economic development from below, rather than through centrally steered programs. As of the early 1980s, national states began to introduce new, post-Keynesian spatial policies intended to reconcentrate productive capacities and specialized, high-performance infrastructural investments into the most globally competitive city-regions within their territories. Meanwhile, major urban regions were equipped with place-specific forms of state administration and special-purpose, customized regulatory arrangements, which were increasingly seen as a crucial institutional basis for enhancing global competitive advantages and attracting mobile capital investment. The highly polarized national political-economic geographies that have resulted from these realignments are characterized by the diffusion of neoliberal discourses emphasizing market-driven growth, flexibility, and locational competitiveness; by the intensification of interspatial competition between urban regions; and by a growing differentiation of national political space among distinctive urban and regional economies, each with their own unique, place-specific economic profiles, infrastructural configurations, institutional arrangements, and developmental trajectories. The postwar project of national territorial equalization and sociospatial redistribution has thus been superseded by qualitatively new national, regional, and local state strategies to position major urban economies optimally within global and supranational circuits of capital.

One of the central agendas of this book is to trace this fundamental rearticulation of urban policy and to explore its multifaceted implications for the nature of statehood in post-1970s western Europe. I argue, first, that city-regions have become key institutional sites in which a major rescaling of national state power has been unfolding. The intensified national targeting of local and regional spaces for economic (re)development strategies during the last two decades has not occurred within a fixed institutional framework, but has been enabled by, and has in turn accelerated, a fundamental transformation of state scalar configurations. The long-entrenched primacy of the national scale of political-economic regulation has been destabilized as new scalar hierarchies of state institutional organization and state regulatory activity have been forged. Within these rescaled configurations of state power, major urban regions have become important geographical targets for a variety of far-reaching institutional changes and policy realignments designed to enhance local economic growth capacities. For this reason, processes of state downscaling—the devolution or decentralization of regulatory tasks to subnational administrative tiers, coupled with a restructuring of subnational institutional configurations—are as fundamental to the contemporary remaking of political space as the forms of state upscaling that have been examined at length by international political economists (Gill 1998*a*, *b*; Mittelman 2000). Second, I argue that national state *institutions* continue to play key roles in formulating, implementing, coordinating, and supervising urban policy initiatives, even as the primacy of the national *scale* of political-economic life is decentered. From this point of view, the erosion of spatial Keynesianism has not generated a unidirectional process of Europeanization, decentralization, regionalization, or localization, in which a single scale—be it European, regional, or local—is replacing the national scale as the primary level of political-economic coordination. We are witnessing, rather, a wide-ranging recalibration of scalar hierarchies and interscalar relations throughout the state apparatus as a whole, at once on supranational, national, regional, *and* urban scales. As Peck (2002: 332; italics in original) explains, 'Contingently scaled functions [of state power], such as those associated with the national welfare state, are not simply being moved around, they are undergoing a process of qualitative transformation *through* rescaling.' Therefore, in contrast to analyses that forecast a linear denationalization of statehood—whether through the strengthening of supranational institutional blocs or due to the enhanced regionalization or localization of state regulatory capacities—this book underscores the continued importance of *spatially reconfigured* national state institutions as major animateurs and mediators of political-economic restructuring at all geographical scales. As deployed here, therefore, the notion of state rescaling is intended to characterize the transformed form of (national) statehood under contemporary capitalism, not to imply its erosion, withering, or demise.

I have attempted, as much as stylistically possible, to minimize references to 'the' state, as a singular noun. In my view, the singular concept of the state misleadingly implies that the institutions in question converge, by definitional necessity, upon a single (national) geographical scale and are subordinated to a single (national) political center. While the notions of the local state, the regional state, and the national state remain appropriate for referencing specific tiers of state power within a multiscalar institutional hierarchy, I believe that the generic concept of *the* state has become increasingly problematic. The notion of *statehood* seems to me a more precise basis for describing modern political institutions, because it does not ontologically prejudge the configuration of state scalar organization, the level of state centralization, or the degree of institutional isomorphism among state agencies.[3] While we shall see that political strategies to establish a centralized, nationalized hierarchy of state power have indeed played a key role throughout much of the twentieth century, they are today being widely superseded as a more polycentric, multiscalar, and non-isomorphic configuration of statehood is created. Consequently, new conceptual vocabularies are required in order to transcend some of the entrenched assumptions about state spatial and institutional organization that have been inherited from the Westphalian geopolitical epoch (Agnew 1994; Ruggie 1993). In the chapters that follow, I attempt to confront this task systematically by developing and deploying an explicitly historicized, spatialized, and scale-sensitive approach to the production and transformation of statehood.

---

[3] The term 'statehood' is often used to denote the goal of anti-colonial, secessionist, or national-liberationist struggles—as, for instance, in the struggle for Palestinian, Kurdish, or Kashmiri statehood. By contrast, throughout this book, the term 'statehood' is understood in its more literal sense—much like the German term *Staatlichkeit*—to connote the distinctive ensemble of social relations embodied in, and expressed through, state institutions. Chapter 3 elaborates this conceptualization in greater detail.

From the scale question to the new political economy of scale

> Epochs of world history hinge not only upon the rise and fall of great powers or the successive struggles among mobilized social groups but on the attributes of political space, whether weakened or strengthened or rescaled into larger or smaller commanding units.
>
> Charles Maier (2000: 809)

My point of departure is the proposition that historically entrenched forms of national state territoriality are being systematically unraveled and, consequently, that diverse sociopolitical struggles to reorganize the institutional geographies of capitalism are proliferating at all spatial scales. Writing in the late 1970s, the French social theorist Henri Lefebvre (1979: 290) vividly described this situation as an 'explosion of spaces' in which established geographies of industrialization, state power, urbanism, and everyday life were being thoroughly destabilized and rewoven. These trends have intensified since that period, as a transformed configuration of globalizing, neoliberalizing, and urbanizing capitalism has crystallized (Brenner and Theodore 2002a). Throughout the social sciences, the origins, contours, and implications of these shifts remain a matter of considerable controversy (for overviews, see Amin 1994; Albritton et al. 2001). Nonetheless, some initial evidence that inherited nationalized and territorialized formations of political-economic space are today being significantly reworked can be gleaned from a cursory examination of three contemporary worldwide trends.

1. *Global economic integration.* National territorial economies are becoming more permeable to supranational, continental, and global flows of investment, money, trade, and labor (Dicken 1998; Daniels and Lever 1996; Knox and Agnew 1995). During the last thirty years, the massive expansion of foreign direct investment, the development of advanced informational, communications, and transportation technologies, the dismantling of various legal constraints on cross-border financial transactions, the liberalization of trade policy, and the intensification of international labor migration have combined to generate what Castells (1996) has famously termed a 'space of flows' that appears to lie beyond the territorialized national economic systems inherited from previous phases of capitalist development. With the expansion of foreign direct investment and speculative cross-border financial transactions, new offshore economies have emerged, composed of Euromarkets, tax havens, export processing zones, free trade areas, and other virtual regulatory spaces (Cameron and Palan 1999). While considerable disagreement persists regarding the appropriate interpretation of economic globalization, most scholars would agree that we are currently living through a phase of significantly intensified geoeconomic integration that is destabilizing inherited national economic formations. Under

these conditions, as national economies become at once more permeable and more tightly intertwined on a global scale, purely territorialist models of economic life—with their rigid distinction between the 'inside' and the 'outside' of state borders—are losing intellectual plausibility (R. B. J. Walker 1993; Sassen 1996).

2. *Urban and regional resurgence.* In conjunction with the crystallization of offshore economies, the expansion of global trade relations and the worldwide integration of capital markets, localized agglomeration economies have acquired a renewed importance for major fractions of industrial, financial, and service capital (Storper 1996; Grabher 1993; Scott 2001). Precisely under conditions in which geoeconomic integration is rapidly intensifying, locally embedded economic interactions have become basic preconditions for globalized capital accumulation (Sassen 1991). Consequently, a local and regional renaissance has been unfolding as 'super-clusters of producers come into being in the shape of dense agglomerations (typically forming large metropolitan areas or world cities), tied functionally together in a global division of labor' (Scott 1996: 400). A huge literature on global cities, industrial districts, learning regions, offshore financial centers, and other new industrial spaces has proposed that these subnational territorial production complexes today represent the 'regional motors of the global economy' (Scott 1996) insofar as they harbor the socioeconomic assets, innovative capacities, technological infrastructures, specialized skills, institutional networks, and sociocultural milieux upon which the leading sectors of transnational capital depend. This resurgence of urban and regional economies cannot be adequately appreciated on the basis of state-centric models that encage economic activity into self-enclosed, nationally scaled territorial units. As debates on the contemporary 'local–global interplay' (Dunford and Kafkalas 1992) proliferate, the role of urban and regional economies as engines of industrial growth is being more widely acknowledged.

3. *The consolidation of new supranational and cross-border institutions.* The regulatory significance of supranational institutions and multistate regulatory arrangements—from the EU, NAFTA, APEC, ASEAN, and MERCOSUR to the IMF, the World Bank, the G8, and the GATT—has also been enhanced throughout the world economy (Larner and Walters 2002; Mittleman 2000). Such supranational institutions have played an instrumental role in institutionalizing neoliberal ideology and, consequently, in establishing the political preconditions for the expansion of inter- and intra-bloc trade and investment flows (Gill 2003). They have also underpinned the development of new forms of multilevel governance grounded upon dense interdependencies between various tiers of political authority, both above and beneath national state institutions (Caporaso 1997; Scharpf 1999). These trends have been articulated in conjunction with an intensification of horizontal networking, translocal linkages, and cross-border cooperation initiatives among local and regional states and other non-central governments (Perkmann and Sum 2002; Hocking

1998). Thus, new forms of institutional organization, political authority, and economic coordination appear to be proliferating above and below the national scale of state power, leading to a 'complex intertwining of institutions at all levels of the world, from the global arena to the regional level' (Boyer and Hollingsworth 1997: 470). Such developments suggest that capitalist economies no longer represent coherent, neatly self-contained geographical units, but are today being permeated by new types of vertical and horizontal linkages among diverse, multiscaled institutional forms.

As this abbreviated sketch of contemporary political-economic transformations indicates, purely territorialist, nationally focused models have become an inadequate basis for understanding the rapidly changing institutional and geographical landscapes of capitalism. Under contemporary conditions, the 'institutional arrangements that at one time were congruent at the national level are now more dispersed at multiple spatial levels'; meanwhile, a 'multifaceted causality runs in virtually all directions among the various levels of society: nations, sectors, free trade zones, international regimes, supranational regions, large cities, and even small but well-specialized localities' (Boyer and Hollingsworth 1997: 472, 470). Most crucially for the present study, these wide-ranging institutional and geographical realignments have been intimately intertwined with processes of *rescaling* through which entrenched scalar hierarchies—stretching from the urban and the regional to the national, the continental, and the global—have been destabilized and rearticulated (Swyngedouw 1992*a*). A key agenda of this book is to investigate the origins, dynamics, and consequences of such rescaling processes in contemporary western Europe, above all with reference to the rescaling of state spatial regulation and urban policy. The essential task, in this context, is to examine the dissolution of the nationally centered, Fordist-Keynesian configuration of statehood and the contested consolidation of qualitatively new scalar hierarchies of state regulatory activity across the western European political-economic landscape.

Investigations into contemporary rescaling processes pose some daunting methodological challenges. Foremost among these is the need to develop a theoretically precise yet also historically specific conceptualization of geographical scale as a key dimension of social, political, and economic life. A reification of scale appears to be built into everyday scalar terms (for instance, local, urban, regional, national, global, etc.) insofar as they represent distinctive socio-territorial processes (for instance, localization, urbanization, regionalization, nationalization, globalization, etc.) as if they were static entities frozen permanently into geographical space. Relatedly, existing scalar vocabularies are rather poorly equipped to grasp the complex, perpetually changing interconnections and interdependencies among geographical scales. For, insofar as terms such as local, urban, regional, and so forth are used to demarcate purportedly separate territorial 'islands' of social relations, they mask the profound mutual imbrication of all scales. These difficulties are exacerbated still further by the circumstance that much of the social-scientific division of labor is organized according to distinctive scalar foci—for instance, urban studies, regional studies, comparative politics, international relations, and so forth—which systematically obstruct efforts to explore the intricacies of interscalar relations. Drawing upon Lefebvre's (1976a: 67–8) terminology, I shall refer to this cluster of methodological dilemmas as the 'scale question' (Box 1.1).

Box 1.1. Approaching the scale question

> Today *the question of scale* inserts itself at the outset—at the foundation, as it were—of the analysis of texts and the interpretation of events
>
> (Lefebvre 1976a: 67–8; italics added).

Key methodological challenges:

- Conceptualizing scale as a *process* (for instance, of localization, regionalization, nationalization, or globalization) rather than as a permanently fixed, pregiven thing;
- Conceptualizing the intrinsic *relationality* of all geographical scales and their embeddedness within broader interscalar hierarchies;
- Developing *postdisciplinary* methodologies that emphasize interscalar relations and multiscalar transformations rather than ontologizing the distinct scalar foci upon which traditional disciplinary divisions of labor have been grounded.

In order to confront the scale question effectively, it is necessary to elaborate a dialectical approach to *scaling processes* under capitalism that is capable of capturing the ways in which, as Swyngedouw (1997: 141) has proposed, 'scales and their nested articulations become produced as temporary standoffs in a perpetual transformative sociospatial power struggle'. In the rapidly expanding literature on the social production of geographical scale, this task is now being directly confronted.[4] As contributors to this literature have convincingly argued, scalar hierarchies are not fixed or pregiven scaffolds of social interaction, but are themselves produced and periodically modified in and through that interaction. As Smith (1995: 60–1) explains:

Geographical scale is traditionally treated as a neutral metric of physical space: specific scales of social activity are assumed to be largely given as in the distinction between urban, regional, national and global events and processes. There is now, however, a considerable literature arguing that the geographical scales of human activity are not neutral 'givens', not fixed universals of social experience, nor are they an arbitrary methodological or conceptual choice [...] Geographical scale is socially produced as simultaneously a platform and container of certain kinds of social activity. Far from

---

[4] The literature on the social production of spatial scale has expanded rapidly during the last decade. For foundational statements, see Smith 1993, 1992, 1990; and Swyngedouw 1997, 1992a. For a detailed overview of more recent work, see Marston 2000.

neutral and fixed, therefore, geographical scales are the product of economic, political and social activities and relationships; as such they are as changeable as those relationships themselves.

The contemporary period of intensified geoeconomic integration, Europeanization, welfare state retrenchment, and accelerated urban-regional restructuring provides a dramatic illustration of this proposition, for it has arguably entailed one of the most wide-ranging and transformative rearticulations of scalar arrangements ever to have occurred in the history of capitalist development (Swyngedouw 2000*a*). I shall interpret the reworking of state space in post-1970s western Europe as an important medium, catalyst, and expression of these broader rescaling processes. I shall also have occasion, at various junctures of this study, to consider the relationship between the rescaling of state space and the rescaling of other institutional forms—in particular, capitalist economies and urban systems. Box 1.2 summarizes the conceptualization of scaling processes that underpins this analysis.

Box 1.2. Theorizing scale and rescaling processes: core propositions
(See also Brenner 2001*a*, 2000*a*, 1998*a*.)

In recent scholarship, geographical scale has been defined in a variety of ways. Representative definitions include the following:

- Scale is a 'nested hierarchy of bounded spaces of differing size' (Delaney and Leitner 1997: 93).
- Scale is 'the level of geographical resolution at which a given phenomenon is thought of, acted on or studied' (Agnew 1997: 100).
- Scale is the 'geographical organizer and expression of collective social action' (Smith 1995: 61).
- Scale is the 'geographical resolution of contradictory processes of competition and co-operation' (Smith 1993: 99).

The conceptualization of geographical scale used in this book is broadly compatible with the aforementioned definitions, but emphasizes, above all, the *hierarchization* of spaces in relation to one another. From this point of view, geographical scale—or, more precisely, the process of *scaling*—is tied intrinsically to what Collinge (1999) has termed the 'vertical ordering' of social formations. The geographical dimensions of social life consist not only in the fact that social relations assume contextually specific forms in different places, localities, or territories. In addition to this 'horizontal' or 'areal' differentiation of social practices across geographical space, there is also a 'vertical' differentiation in which social relations are embedded within a hierarchical scaffolding of nested territorial units stretching from the global, the supranational, and the national downwards to the regional, the metropolitan, the urban, the local, and the body. It is this vertical ordering of social, economic, and political practices that defines scalar organization in any social formation. A number of propositions follow from this initial conceptualization:

1. *The scaling of social processes.* Geographical scales are not static, fixed, or permanent properties of the social world or of social spatiality as such. They are best understood as socially produced, and therefore malleable, dimensions of particular social processes—

such as capitalist production, social reproduction, state regulation, and sociopolitical struggle. Insofar as any social, political, or economic process is internally differentiated into a vertical hierarchy of distinct spatial units, the problem of its scalar organization arises. As Smith (1993: 101) indicates, geographical scales provide a 'partitioned geography' within which diverse forms of social interaction unfold. At the same time, the differentiation of social processes into determinate scalar hierarchies is never accomplished once and for all, but is continually forged through everyday practices, conflicts, and struggles (Swyngedouw 1997; Jonas 1994). The scalar organization of a social process or institutional form may thus become an object of direct sociopolitical contestation and may, by consequence, be recalibrated.

2. *The relationality of scales.* Scale cannot be construed as a system of nested territorial containers defined by absolute geographic size (a 'Russian dolls' model of scales). The institutional configuration, functions, history, and dynamics of any one geographical scale can only be grasped relationally, in terms of its upwards, downwards, and transversal links to other geographical scales situated within the broader scalar order in which it is embedded (Lefebvre 1991: 85–8; Howitt 1998). Consequently, the significance of scalar terms such as global, national, regional, urban, and local is likely to differ qualitatively depending on the specific social processes or institutional forms to which they refer.

3. *Mosaics of scalar organization.* The institutional landscape of capitalism is not characterized by a single, all-encompassing scalar pyramid into which all social processes and institutional forms are neatly subsumed. This is because 'different kinds of social process have very different geographies and they do not all fit neatly into the same set of nested hierarchies' (Allen, Massey, and Cochrane 1998: 60). Insofar as every social process or institutional form may be associated with a distinctive pattern of scalar organization, the scalar configuration of capitalism as a whole may be described as a mosaic of superimposed and interpenetrating scalar hierarchies (Lefebvre 1991). Any systematic account of scaling processes under capitalism must therefore begin with an analysis of how, why, and when the social process or institution in question has been subdivided into a vertical hierarchy of separate yet intertwined geographical scales. Concomitantly, such an account must also specify the relevant spatial units within that hierarchy, their evolving role within the hierarchy and their changing relation to other units within that hierarchy.

4. *Scalar fixes.* The major large-scale institutional forms of modern capitalism—such as capitalist firms and national states—interact and evolve continually to produce certain 'nested hierarchical structures of organization' (Harvey 1982: 422) that enframe social life within provisionally solidified 'scalar fixes' (Smith 1995). Such scalar fixes are composed of temporarily stabilized geographical hierarchies in which social, economic, and political activities organized at some scales tend to predominate over others (Collinge 1999). Once established, these scalar hierarchies constitute relatively 'fixed geographical structures bounding political, economic and cultural activity in specific ways' (Smith 1995: 63). The long-run historical geography of capitalist development has been grounded upon a succession of determinate, if chronically unstable, scalar fixes through which the socioterritorial preconditions for capital accumulation have been successively secured, destabilized, junked, and remade. Throughout much of the history of capitalism, national state institutions have played a significant role in constructing, reproducing, modifying, destroying, and creating anew such scalar fixes (Brenner 1998a).

5. *Scalar transformations.* Processes of rescaling do not entail the simple replacement of one scalar configuration by another, fully formed one, or the total disappearance of

some scales as others supersede them. On the contrary, rescaling processes generally occur through a path-dependent interaction of inherited scalar arrangements with emergent, often highly experimental strategies to transform the latter. Consequently, even in the midst of intense pressures to restructure a given scalar order, inherited scalar configurations may close off certain pathways of rescaling by circumscribing the production of new scales within determinate institutional and geographical parameters. The dominant scalar orderings of one historical period may thus strongly condition and constrain the development of subsequent scalar configurations. While established patterns of interscalar relations are never permanently fixed, they are generally destabilized and transformed only in the wake of intense sociopolitical struggles.

In sum, I am concerned to explore what Jessop (2002: 179) has recently termed the 'new political economy of scale'. The new political economy of scale may be usefully contrasted to what might be termed the 'old' political economy of scale, which involved epistemological debates regarding the appropriate unit of analysis for social-scientific investigation. As Wallerstein (1991) has shown, such debates have recurred periodically within the social sciences since their institutionalization in the late nineteenth century. It is only recently, however, that social scientists have explicitly recognized the historically malleable and politically contested character of scalar organization. The new political economy of scale is thus grounded upon an explicit, reflexive concern to decode the multifarious ways in which inherited forms of scalar organization are being systematically rejigged. Box 1.3 (overleaf) summarizes the key elements of the new political economy of scale that are explored in this book.

I believe that contemporary rescaling processes pose fundamental theoretical and methodological challenges for social scientists concerned to analyze the changing institutional landscapes of contemporary capitalism. In the following chapters, I develop and deploy one particular strategy for investigating the new political economy of scale in the context of recent scholarly debates on globalization, the transformation of statehood, and the remaking of urban governance. There are, certainly, other theoretical perspectives, methodological orientations, and empirical focal points through which contemporary rescaling processes may be fruitfully investigated.[5] My analysis is thus intended as a contribution to ongoing social-scientific research on contemporary rescaling processes and their implications for social, political, and economic life under early twenty-first century capitalism.

[5] The definition of the new political economy of scale provided above is intentionally broad, and thus encompasses extremely diverse strands of political-economic research. A number of methodologically reflexive and theoretically innovative accounts of contemporary rescaling processes have been developed in the vast interdisciplinary literatures on geopolitical economy, including: Cerny 1995; K. Cox 1997; Boyer and Hollingsworth 1997; Eisenschitz and Gough 1996; Gough 2004, 2002; Heeg 2001; Herod 1997; Hollingsworth 1998; Jessop 2002; Jones 2001; Kelly 1999; Larner and Walters 2002; Leitner 2004; Leitner and Sheppard 2002; MacLeod 2001; MacLeod and Goodwin 1999; D. Newman 1999; Peck 2002; Peck and Tickell 1994; Schmitter 1999; Sheppard 2002; Smith 2004, 1995; Swyngedouw 2000a, 1997, 1996.

Box 1.3. Key elements of the new political economy of scale

There is no new privileged scale around which other levels are now being organized to ensure structured coherence within and across scales. Instead there are continuing struggles over which spatial scale should become primary and how scales should be articulated and this is reflected in a more complex nesting and interweaving of different scales as they become rearticulated [...] The new political economy of scale does not involve a pregiven set of places, spaces or scales that are merely being reordered. Instead, new places are emerging, new spaces are being created, new scales of organization are being developed and new horizons of action are being imagined...

(Jessop 2002: 179)

- Geographical scales and interscalar hierarchies are continually produced and contested as arenas and outcomes of collective social action. As such, they may be modified or transformed during the process of sociohistorical development (Smith 1995).
- Under contemporary conditions, the scalar configuration of major institutional forms and social processes—including capital accumulation, state regulation, urbanization and sociopolitical mobilization—is being destabilized. In each of these institutional arenas, we are currently witnessing a proliferation of strategies intended to dismantle inherited scalar configurations and to produce qualitatively new scalar hierarchies.
- The emergent scalar architecture of globalizing, neoliberalizing capitalism is more complex, tangled, eccentric, and volatile than the nationalized interscalar arrangements of the postwar, Fordist-Keynesian period. There is no longer a single, privileged scale of political-economic organization, and emergent scalar configurations do not overlap with one another in neatly isomorphic, congruent patterns. Consequently, 'different scales of action come to be linked in various hybrid combinations of vertical, horizontal, diagonal, centripetal, centrifugal and vortical ways' (Jessop 2002: 180).

Rescaled states, polarized territories: reworking uneven spatial development

The old bugbear of uneven development refuses to go away despite the blurring of borders and extension of transnational corporations. It keeps coming back in new forms

Richard Walker (1997: 345)

My investigation of state rescaling is centrally concerned with the regulation of capitalist urbanization and, more generally, with the changing political form and institutional mediation of uneven geographical development. In the most general terms, uneven geographical development refers to the circumstance that social, political, and economic processes under capitalism are not distributed uniformly or homogenously across the earth's surface, but are always organized within distinct sociospatial configurations—such as urban agglomerations, regional clusters, rural zones, national territories, supra-national economic blocs, and so forth—that are characterized by divergent socioeconomic conditions, developmental capacities, and institutional arrangements. Thus, within a capitalist political-economic system, inequalities are not only expressed socially, in the form of class and income stratification, but also spatially, through the polarization of development among different territories, regions, places, and scales. While these patterns of core–periphery polarization are always articulated in contextually specific forms, they generally entail the systematic concentration of advanced socioeconomic assets and developmental capacities within certain core zones and, concomitantly, the chronic marginalization or peripheralization of other, less developed places and territories (S. Amin 1979; Storper and Walker 1989).

The study of uneven development has long been one of the foundational concerns of critical geographical political economy.[6] As Smith (1990) argues in his seminal work on the topic, patterns of uneven geographical development under capitalism are not merely the accidental, contingent by-products of precapitalist geographical differences or of individual-, household-, or firm-level locational decisions. Rather, they represent systemic expressions of the endemic tension under capitalism between the drive to equalize capital investment across space and the pressure to differentiate such investment in order to exploit place-, territory-, and scale-specific conditions for accumulation.

- On the one hand, the coercive forces of intercapitalist competition pressure individual capitals to replicate one another's profit-making strategies in dispersed geographical locations, and thus tend to *equalize* the conditions for capital accumulation across space.
- On the other hand, the forces of intercapitalist competition engender an equally powerful process of geographical *differentiation* in which individual capitals continually seek out place-specific locational assets and territorially specific conditions of production that may enable them to enhance their competitive advantages.

Consequently, each phase of capitalism is grounded upon historically specific patterns of uneven geographical development in and through which the contradictory interplay of equalization and differentiation is articulated. These patterns of sociospatial polarization crystallize horizontally, among different types of places and territories, and also vertically, among divergent geographical scales stretching from the local, regional, and national to the continental and global (Smith 1990). The contours of this uneven geography are not inscribed permanently onto the institutional landscapes of capitalism, but are reworked continually through capital's restless developmental dynamic

---

[6] Key contributions include Harvey 1982; Massey 1985; Smith 1990; Soja 1989; and Storper and Walker 1989.

and through successive political strategies to subject it to some measure of state regulatory control.

Each historical pattern of uneven geographical development is also intertwined with certain basic regulatory dilemmas: for the uneven development of capital serves not only as a *basis* for the accumulation process but may also, under certain conditions, become a significant *barrier* to the latter (Harvey 1982). Uneven development, in other words, is not merely an aggregate geographical effect of differential patterns of capital investment, but generates a variety of fundamental regulatory problems, both within and beyond the circuit of capital, that may severely destabilize the accumulation process as a whole (Peck and Tickell 1995). For instance, the polarization of territorial development between dynamic urban cores and peripheralized regions may enable certain individual capitals to reap the benefits of scale economies and other externalities, but it may also generate dysfunctional political-economic effects that destabilize the space-economy as a whole. An erosion of national industrial capacities may ensue as declining industrial cities and peripheralized regional economies are constrained to adopt defensive, cost-based strategies of adjustment, leading to a premature downgrading of local infrastructures and to worsening life conditions for many local inhabitants (Leborgne and Lipietz 1991). Moreover, even within the most powerful, dynamic urban agglomerations, the problem of uneven development may also 'come home to roost' (Harvey 1989*b*: 144) as social polarization, overproduction, the threat of capital flight, and various negative externalities (such as infrastructural stress, housing shortages, traffic congestion, and environmental degradation) unsettle established patterns of industrial development. And finally, if patterns of sociospatial inequality are not maintained within politically acceptable limits, disruptive sociopolitical conflicts—between classes, class fractions, growth coalitions, social movements, and other place-based alliances—may arise within a (national or local) territory, leading in turn to severe legitimation crises (Hudson 2001). Uneven geographical development is thus associated not only with new profit-making opportunities for capital, but also with potentially destabilizing, disruptive effects that can erode the socio-territorial preconditions for sustainable capital accumulation.

While most studies of uneven geographical development have focused upon the interplay between capital investment patterns and the evolution of territorial inequalities, this book explores the major role of state institutions, at various scales, in mediating and regulating that interplay. Such an inquiry is of considerable importance because, since the consolidation of organized capitalism during the early twentieth century, national states have deployed a variety of spatial policies designed to influence the geographies of capital investment and, thereby, to manage the process of uneven development within their territorial boundaries (Hudson 2001; Lefebvre 2003*a*; Massey 1985). For instance, national states may mobilize strategies of territorial redistribution and other compensatory regional policies to promote the *dispersion* of industry across their territories, and thus alleviate intra-national territorial inequalities. However, national states may also mobilize diametrically opposed spatial policies to facilitate the *concentration* of growth capacities, socioeconomic assets, and infrastructural investments within the most economically dynamic urban regions. As Hudson (2001: 273) explains, the endemic political tension between redistributive, cohesion-oriented and developmentalist, growth-oriented forms of state spatial policy is derived from the underlying contradiction within capitalist social formations 'between [the treatment of] a location as a socially produced place to which its inhabitants are attached and [its treatment] as part of a socially produced space in which capital can make profits'.[7] During the course of twentieth-century capitalist development, state spatial policies have combined the priorities of cohesion and growth in distinctive, historically specific, and often deeply contradictory ways. In the western European context, most national states introduced nationally redistributive, cohesion-oriented regulatory strategies during the 1930s. Such strategies reached their historical highpoint during the mid-1970s, as the Fordist regime of accumulation was being destabilized (Clout 1981*a*). Subsequently, since the late 1970s, city-centric, growth-oriented approaches to spatial policy have increasingly superseded previously dominant forms of territorial redistribution (Martin and Sunley 1997). While these opposed approaches to state spatial policy have often failed to achieve their declared goals, and have frequently generated any number of unintended, dysfunctional effects, they must both be acknowledged as essential mediating influences upon the process of uneven geographical development at all spatial scales.

While I shall devote considerable attention to the consolidation of redistributive, cohesion-oriented regulatory strategies during the postwar, Fordist-Keynesian period (Ch. 4), I am equally concerned with the post-Keynesian, growth-oriented, and competitiveness-driven approaches to state spatial policy that have been deployed since the late 1970s (Chs. 5 and 6). Initially, with the ascendancy of neoliberalism and the imposition of new forms of fiscal austerity by national governments during the second half of the 1970s, inherited programs of intra-national territorial redistribution were scaled back, thereby exposing local and regional economies more directly to the pressures of Europe-wide and even global economic competition. Such policy initiatives were aimed primarily at reducing public expenditures and at undermining traditional forms of *dirigiste*, centralized economic management. Subsequently, during the course of the 1980s, a variety of entrepreneurial, competitiveness-oriented regulatory experiments were mobilized by national, regional, and local state institutions in order to promote economic rejuvenation within strategic subnational spaces (Harvey 1989*a*; Leitner and Sheppard

---

[7] This formulation parallels Logan and Molotch's (1987) emphasis on the dual role of places as use-values and exchange-values under capitalism.

1998). Thus, rather than continuing to serve as a localized relay station within national systems of territorial redistribution, urban policy has been transformed during the post-1970s period into a field of state intervention whose overarching goal is to promote localized territorial competitiveness within a European and global context. The German term *Standortpolitik*—which translates roughly as 'locational policy'—provides an appropriate characterization of this rescaled approach to urban policy, for its central aim is to promote the competitiveness of particular territorial locations within broader spaces of competition at European and global scales (Brenner 2000*b*). Such urban locational policies have not only attempted to 'turn localities [or regions] into self-promoting islands of entrepreneurship' (Amin and Malmberg 1994: 243); they have also entailed a fundamental redefinition of the national state's role as an institutional mediator of uneven geographical development.

This latter transformation is central to this book's argument. During the Fordist-Keynesian period, the problem of uneven geographical development was generally construed as a matter of redressing 'insufficient' or 'imbalanced' industrialization on a national scale. The task of state spatial intervention, under these conditions, was to mold the geography of capital investment into a more balanced, cohesive, and integrated locational pattern throughout the national territory. By contrast, with the rescaling of state space and the proliferation of urban locational policies during the post-1970s period, this project of national territorial equalization has been fundamentally inverted: *it is no longer capital that is to be molded into the (territorially integrated) geography of state space, but state space that is to be molded into the (territorially differentiated) geography of capital.* In other words, through the deployment of urban locational policies, state space is now being redifferentiated and rescaled so as to correspond more directly to the (actual or projected) imprint of transnational capital's locational preferences within each national territory. The relatively uniform, nationalized administrative geographies of postwar capitalism are thus being superseded by what might be described as a 'splintered' (Graham and Marvin 2001) institutional configuration composed of customized, place-specific regulatory arrangements designed to position particular subnational jurisdictions strategically within global and European circuits of capital. In this manner, within the polarized economic geographies of post-Keynesian western Europe, a 'parallel mosaic of differentiated spaces of regulation' is being established through ongoing processes of state rescaling and urban policy reform (Goodwin and Painter 1996: 646). The goal of national, regional, and local state spatial policies is no longer to alleviate uneven geographical development, but actively to *intensify* it through the deployment of urban locational policies designed to strengthen the place-specific socioeconomic assets of strategic, globally linked city-regions.

As we shall see, however, the systemic failure of this rescaled, post-Keynesian urban policy regime to confront the polarizing, disruptive, and politically volatile effects of uneven geographical development at any spatial scale represents one of its major internal contradictions. For, as indicated above, while unfettered uneven development may, under certain conditions, provide a temporary basis for short-term bursts of capital accumulation, it may also generate severe negative externalities, coordination problems, and legitimation deficits that threaten the medium- and long-term reproduction of capital. Accordingly, as I argue in Ch. 6, the disruptive, dysfunctional political-economic consequences of urban locational policies have become increasingly evident during the last decade, leading the European Commission and diverse national, regional, and municipal state institutions to mobilize a range of spatially selective crisis-management strategies that have involved a further extension and intensification of state rescaling processes. In particular, recent projects to promote neighborhood-based anti-exclusion programs, enhanced intra-metropolitan cooperation, and new forms of interurban networking have addressed at least some of the disruptive effects of unfettered uneven spatial development—albeit still within the parameters of an explicitly growth-driven, competitiveness-oriented model of state spatial regulation. As such, these alternative projects of state rescaling have entailed important institutional and scalar shifts within the architecture of European statehood, and thus deserve close analytical scrutiny. Accordingly, I shall analyze the evolution of state rescaling processes during the last three decades not only with reference to the proliferation of urban locational polices. In addition, I shall consider the deployment of new, highly scale-sensitive forms of crisis-management which have attempted—albeit unsuccessfully—to alleviate some of the regulatory failures of such policies.

Between generality and diversity: levels of abstraction and empirical focus

In contemporary debates on globalization, international political economy, and urban/regional restructuring, the specter of 'convergence' has generated considerable scholarly controversy. In each of these fields, a number of scholars have forecast the eventual convergence of social, political, and economic structures towards a uniform, encompassing organizational pattern. Others have vigorously rejected such predictions, emphasizing instead the continued diversity of national, regional, and local models of capitalism.[8] While this book is not intended directly to contribute to such debates, it may be useful to situate my argument in relation to them.

The following analysis suggests that a number of broadly analogous tendencies of state rescaling and urban governance restructuring have been

---

[8] For useful overviews of these debates in various research fields see, for instance, Berger and Dore 1996; Boyer 1996; Guillén 2001; Harding 1997; Le Galès 2001; Scholte 2000; and Scott 2001.

crystallizing across western Europe during the last three decades. However, my emphasis on these shared pathways of institutional and spatial reorganization among western European states should *not* be construed as an endorsement of the view that a single, generic model of territorial governance has emerged. On the contrary, I believe that individualizing and variation-finding comparisons (Tilly 1990)—which generally emphasize contextual specificity, institutional diversity, path dependency, and the divergence of evolutionary pathways—are as salient as ever under contemporary geoeconomic conditions (Brenner 2001*b*). A number of urbanists have recently directed attention to the latter issues through detailed comparative studies of economic restructuring, urban regime formation, and patterns of sociospatial polarization in western European and North American cities.[9] While I am highly sympathetic to such approaches, the analysis presented in this book has a different purpose than to demonstrate the variety of local or national responses to geoeconomic restructuring. Instead, my aim is to explore the major elements of what I view as a *systemic* reorganization of state spatiality across western Europe during the last three decades. It is highly questionable, in my view, whether a coherent, stabilized, and reproducible 'post-Fordist' framework of territorial development has crystallized through these variegated, contested, and profoundly uneven transformations (Peck and Tickell 1994). It is also evident that these shifts have unfolded at divergent speeds and in diverse politico-institutional forms within each national context, leading to highly variegated sociospatial outcomes at national, regional, and local scales. I shall argue, nonetheless, that regulatory responses to the crisis of North Atlantic Fordism have reconfigured the landscapes of western European statehood in a number of quite fundamental ways that can be analyzed in general terms, across multiple national contexts (see also Jessop 2002). Evidence for such an underlying structural transformation of state spatiality has become apparent across western Europe since the crisis of North Atlantic Fordism, even in the midst of otherwise persistently diverse institutional frameworks and regulatory geographies. One of the central tasks of this study is to present such evidence in a synthetic, yet appropriately detailed, form and to explicate its ramifications for the interpretation of contemporary statehood.

The methodological approach deployed here can be further clarified by distinguishing three levels of abstraction, each of which is central to my argument (Fig. 1.1).

1. *Abstract level.* Consideration of the abstract level enables scholars to examine the general, systemic features of a given historical social system. Depending on the degree to which such 'concrete abstractions' underpin social life within a particular historical-geographical context, this level may

---

[9] See e.g. Marcuse and van Kempen 2001; Savitch and Kantor 2002; Sellers 2002; Harding 1997; and DiGaetano and Klemanski 1999. For an early foray into such research, see Logan and Swanstrom 1990.

ABSTRACT LEVEL emphasizes theoretical generality; focuses on *longue durée* temporalities	• General features of capitalism as a mode of production and social system • General features of capitalist urbanization and capitalist sociospatial configurations • General features of modern statehood and modern state spatial organization		
MESO-LEVEL emphasizes historically specific dimensions of general processes and generalized aspects of concrete, empirical developments; focuses on secular trends within medium-term time scales	**1960s–early 1970s: high Fordism** Fordist regime of accumulation Fordist patterns of urbanization and regional development Consolidation of Keynesian welfare national states (KWNS) and nationalized spatial planning systems	**1970s: period of systemic shock and initial transition** Crisis of Fordist mass production systems, emergence of flexible/lean production systems Industrial decline, urban-regional restructuring, and crystallization of new territorial inequalities at various spatial scales Crisis of traditional Keynesian macroeconomic instruments and compensatory spatial policies	**Early 1980s–present: post–Keynesian regulatory experimentation** Accelerated geoeconomic and European integration coupled with an enhanced dependence of transnational capital upon localized agglomeration economies Intensification of interlocality competition and sociospatial polarization at global, European, and national scales Consolidation of post-Keynesian competition state regimes, rescaling of state sapce, the proliferation of subnational locational policies (*Standortpolitik*)
CONCRETE LEVEL emphasizes empirical diversity; focuses on relatively short-term time scales, conjunctures, and events	—————— 1960–2000 —————— • Nationally, regionally, and locally specific pathways of industrial restructuring and urban-regional change; production of new geographies of uneven geographical development • Nationally, regionally, and locally specific pathways of state spatial restructuring and regulatory experimentation; production of new state spatial configurations and regulatory landscapes • Empirical foundations: case study material on state spatial restructuring, institutional change, and regulatory experimentation in western European cities and states		

Fig. 1.1. Levels of abstraction considered in this book

be more or less useful to sociological inquiry. Under modern capitalism, in which abstract social forms play a critical role in mediating social interaction and historical change, the abstract level is an essential analytical lens (Postone 1993). In capitalist contexts, the abstract level provides a basis for examining, in general terms, a number of systemic processes that underpin all capitalist social formations—for instance, the commodification of labor power, the accumulation of capital, class struggle, the tendency towards large-scale urbanization, the separation of the economic and the political, and so forth (Harvey 1982). Within modern capitalist social formations, empirical studies of industrial production, urban restructuring, and state regulation usually presuppose that certain general, underlying properties define their core objects of analysis, even though the latter are often taken for granted rather than explicitly interrogated. Insofar as the abstract level denotes certain deep structures of social life that persist even through tumultuous gales of sociohistorical change, it is generally associated with *longue durée* time scales.

2. *Meso level.* The meso level refers to the relatively durable institutional arrangements, regulatory frameworks, and territorial configurations that underpin distinct periods of historical development. In a capitalist context, the meso level differs from the abstract level because it illuminates the historically specific, regularized forms in which the system's underlying social processes—such as commodification, capital accumulation, urbanization, and state regulation—are articulated. It is on this level, therefore, that periodizations of capitalist development are most commonly developed. For instance, the French regulationist categories of regime of accumulation and mode of regulation are articulated on the meso-level insofar as they attempt to identify certain historically specific institutional forms and regulatory practices that temporarily displace the endemic contradictions of capitalism.[10] While considerable institutional diversity and geographical unevenness may obtain among distinct national, regional, or local contexts within such encompassing modes of development, the meso level reveals the underlying regularities that tie together these variegated contexts within a shared historical-geographical configuration. The meso level has recently become a focal point for major scholarly controversies, particularly among globalization theorists, state theorists, macrohistorical sociologists, and comparative political economists, for it is on this level that fundamental questions regarding the character of contemporary large-scale social, political, and economic transformations can be posed. Insofar as the meso level refers to certain entrenched but potentially malleable institutional arrangements, regulatory practices and developmental tendencies, it involves the analysis of secular trends over a medium-term time scale, generally a period of several decades.

3. *Concrete level.* The concrete level refers to the contextually specific political-economic frameworks and territorial configurations through which

---

[10] For detailed overviews of the regulation approach, see Boyer 1990; Boyer and Saillard 2002; Jessop 1997, 1995, 1990b; MacLeod 1997.

everyday social reproduction unfolds. It is on this level that the differences among distinct national, regional, and local models of capitalism can be observed most coherently, for it is here that the particular properties of production systems, state institutional hierarchies, regulatory practices, and sociospatial arrangements are most readily apparent. For instance, even while acknowledging the impacts of recent meso-level transformations—such as the crisis of North Atlantic Fordism, the retrenchment of the Keynesian welfare national state, and the process of geoeconomic integration—research on the varieties of capitalism has been conducted primarily on a concrete level. On this basis, this literature has fruitfully explored a number of key empirical issues regarding the restructuring of national systems of technological innovation, industrial relations, corporate governance, finance, and macroeconomic policy.[11] The most sophisticated concrete research on the geopolitical economy of capitalism is characterized by an explicit effort to relate contextually specific institutional dynamics and outcomes to broader, meso-level transformations. This has arguably been one of the key accomplishments of recent work in regulation theory (Boyer and Saillard 2001; Lipietz 2001), neo-Marxist state theory (Radice 1999, 2000; Panitch and Gindin 2003), the new industrial geography (Storper and Salais 1997; Scott and Storper 1986), and comparative urban studies (Abu-Lughod 1999; Marcuse and van Kempen 2001), to name just a few representative strands of contemporary research on capitalist restructuring. Insofar as the concrete level entails a focus on the contextually specific features of national, regional, or local political economies, it is usually concerned with relatively short-term time scales, such as conjunctures and events.

The abstract level, the meso level, and the concrete level are not to be conceived as ontologically separate spheres of social life. Rather, they represent three analytically distinct, if dialectically intertwined, epistemological vantage points for social theory and research. In a capitalist context, consideration of each of these levels can generate useful insights about social, political, and economic relations that could not be gleaned through an exclusive focus upon either of the others. A key intellectual task, therefore, is to combine these levels of analysis effectively in order to pursue particular research questions.

In this book, my overarching analytical concern is with the *meso level*—for it is on this level that the possibility of a systemic reorganization of state spatial structures and scalar hierarchies across multiple cities, regions, and states can be most coherently investigated. In light of the foregoing discussion, however, it is clear that such an analysis must build upon the abstract and concrete levels as well. Accordingly, I consider the abstract level in order to explicate certain basic features of the capital relation, capitalist sociospatial configurations, and the modern state form (Chs. 2 and 3). Likewise, I consider the concrete level at considerable length in order to specify the major patterns of state rescaling, urban policy change, and regulatory experimentation that

---

[11] See, for instance, Berger and Dore 1996; Hall and Soskice 2001; Hollingsworth and Boyer 1997; Kitschelt et al. 1999.

have crystallized in different western European cities, regions, and states during the last four decades (Chs. 4, 5, and 6). The bulk of the book's empirical material refers to realignments, during the 1960–2000 period, in Britain, Denmark, France, Germany, Italy, and the Netherlands.

My focus on the meso level should therefore not be construed as a denial of the institutional diversity that can be readily observed on the concrete level, through the investigation of nationally, regionally, and locally specific trajectories of state rescaling and urban governance restructuring. On the contrary, the meso-level analysis elaborated in this book is grounded upon extensive empirical case studies of such trajectories, both in my own research and in the vast scholarly literatures on, among other topics, state spatial policy, intergovernmental relations, urban infrastructural systems, urban governance, and urban policy. However, in drawing upon such concrete research, my concern is not to explain the nuances of particular cases, or to engage in a systematic comparative analysis of different national, regional, or local outcomes. Instead, I deploy such research as an empirical foundation on which to articulate broader, meso-level generalizations regarding the new state spaces that have been crystallizing across western Europe. Experts on specific states, regions, and cities may find that my account neglects important contextual details regarding many of the institutional changes and policy realignments under discussion. I would hope, nonetheless, that they will find my meso-level claims to be broadly consistent with the basic facts of contemporary trends in the states, regions, and cities with which they are most familiar. My aim, in proceeding in this manner, is to situate the extensive case-study based literature on urban governance restructuring in a broader geohistorical and theoretical context, thereby revealing locally, regionally, and nationally specific trends to be expressions and catalysts of a systemic, Europe-wide transformation of statehood.[12]

Although major transformations of state spatiality and urban governance are currently occurring throughout the world economy, this book focuses upon western European developments. This empirical focus enables me to contain the investigation within a single macrogeographical region, the European Union (EU), whose member states have become increasingly interdependent during the period examined here, and whose institutional apex, the EU Commission, has in turn mobilized a variety of spatial policies throughout the European territory. The EU constitutes a key institutional arena, agent, and product of the rescaling processes examined in this book. It represents a major scale on which new competitive pressures have been exerted upon cities and regions, particularly since the consolidation of the Single European Market in

---

[12] Much of the current debate on convergence is focused largely upon the concrete level. In this view, convergence is expressed in the form of an increasing empirical identity among policies or institutions in different national, regional, or local contexts. As the preceding discussion suggests, however, the demarcation of meso-level commonalities among distinct political-economic contexts is entirely consistent with an insistence upon continued empirical diversity and politico-institutional variation among those contexts.

1993; it also represents an increasingly important level of supranational policy formation (see Chs. 5 and 6). It would be of considerable interest to explore the degree to which analogous trajectories of state rescaling and urban governance reform have crystallized in other major capitalist super-regions, such as North America and East Asia. While I shall not attempt to investigate such matters here, I believe that many of the core theoretical categories and research strategies introduced in the chapters that follow could provide an initial methodological basis for confronting such questions.

Towards a postdisciplinary approach to the study of new state spaces

This study does not fit neatly into established disciplinary approaches to social science. My goal, on the contrary, is to contribute to the advancement of what Sayer (1999) has aptly described as 'postdisciplinary' modes of social inquiry. Within such approaches, conceptual tools and methodological strategies are adopted with reference to the challenges of making sense of particular social phenomena rather than on the basis of traditional disciplinary divisions of labor. As Sayer (1999: 3) explains:

Postdisciplinary studies emerge when scholars forget about disciplines and whether ideas can be identified with any particular one; they identify with learning rather than with disciplines. They follow ideas and connections wherever they lead instead of following them only as far as the border of the discipline. It doesn't mean dilettantism or eclecticism, ending up doing a lot of things badly. It differs from those things precisely because it requires us to follow connections. One can still study a coherent group of phenomena, in fact since once is not dividing it up and selecting out elements appropriate to a particular discipline, it can be more coherent than disciplinary studies.

Such heterodox, postdisciplinary approaches to social analysis have become increasingly relevant in an era in which established divisions between social, economic, political, and cultural processes are being undermined (Jessop and Sum 2001; Wallerstein 1991). The contemporary round of global sociospatial restructuring has also unsettled the state-centric geographical assumptions that have long underpinned traditional, disciplinary approaches to social science, in which social, economic, and political processes have been presumed to be geographically congruent within national state boundaries (see Ch. 2 below). Under these conditions, at the margins of the traditional disciplinary division of labor, new heterodox modes of analysis are being developed that (*a*) explore the mutually constitutive relationships among social, political, economic, and cultural processes and (*b*) introduce alternative mappings of political-economic life that do not naturalize nationalized forms of sociospatial organization.

Over thirty years ago, Lefebvre (1996 [1968]) lambasted mainstream social science for its fragmentation of urban life in the name of scientific objectivity, arguing instead for a more synthetic, multiperspectival approach to the study of urban sociospatial dynamics. During the last three decades, Lefebvre's critique of mainstream urban studies has been taken to heart by a variety of critical urbanists, who have led the way in linking geographical, sociological, and political-economic modes of analysis and in developing new understandings of the production and transformation of urban space. Although traditional disciplinary approaches to urban processes persist within mainstream sociology and political science, the field of critical urban studies has become an extraordinarily lively terrain for postdisciplinary theoretical debate, methodological innovation, and empirical research (for a recent overview, see Soja 2000).

It is only more recently that postdisciplinary approaches to state theory have been developed (Jessop 2001). With the major exception of Marxist approaches, which never embraced traditional disciplinary boundaries, most work on the nature of statehood has been oriented towards the specific methodological and thematic concerns of particular disciplinary or subdisciplinary communities. Nonetheless, during the last decade, this situation has changed through a number of key developments. First, with the proliferation of institutional, neo-Polanyian approaches to economic sociology (Block 1994), the growing interest in the cultural constitution of state forms (Steinmetz 1999), and the development of anthropological approaches to political life (Coronil 1998), many scholars have begun to acknowledge the multifaceted character of statehood and, by implication, the limitations of disciplinary ontologies. Second, in part through a critical engagement with traditional Marxist models, new theoretical approaches to state theory have been introduced that have likewise broadened the parameters of the field to explore a variety of key themes in an interdisciplinary, if not postdisciplinary, manner. These new theoretical paradigms include Foucauldian approaches, feminist state theory, and discourse analysis (Jessop 2001). Third, many state theorists have begun more explicitly to question nation state-centric models of political space and to develop new mappings of state spatiality (Agnew and Corbridge 1994; Goswami 2004; Gupta and Ferguson 2002). Although this line of research was pioneered by geographers, spatially attuned approaches to statehood are now being pursued by scholars from across the social sciences, particularly in the context of debates on globalization and the future of statehood (Brenner et al. 2003*a*, *b*). This has opened up the possibility for approaches to state theory that transcend the traditional focus on self-enclosed national state territories.

This book is situated within, and intended to contribute to, these emergent, crosscutting currents of postdisciplinary scholarship within urban studies and state theory. Like other postdisciplinary approaches to geographical political economy, my analysis of state restructuring is premised upon the assumption that economic and political processes are not situated in ontologically distinct spheres, but mutually constitute one another at all spatial scales (Jessop 1990*a*; Poulantzas 1978; Lefebvre 1978). Additionally, one of my key concerns is to transcend the geographical assumptions associated with mainstream, disciplinary approaches to the study of modern statehood. These assumptions will be specified and criticized at length in the chapters that follow, with the aim of developing a postdisciplinary perspective on the new state spaces that are currently being forged in western European city-regions and beyond.

Structure of the book

The rest of the book is organized as follows. Chapter 2 critically examines some of the major geographical assumptions that are implicit within recent interdisciplinary work on globalization and, on this basis, develops an alternative, scale-sensitive conceptualization of contemporary political-economic transformations. While readers who are more directly interested in questions of state theory and urban governance than in the globalization debates may want to skip over this chapter, it introduces some of the key theoretical and methodological foundations for my subsequent analysis. Chapter 2 concludes by outlining various core methodological challenges for spatialized research on global capitalist restructuring. Chapter 3 addresses one of these challenges by developing a new theoretical approach to the changing geographies of statehood under modern capitalism. I argue that an explicitly spatialized, scale-sensitive approach to state theory is needed in order to decipher the reterritorialized, rescaled forms of statehood that are currently emerging. I develop such an approach through a systematic spatialization of Jessop's (1990*a*) strategic-relational state theory. This approach is then mobilized in order to characterize the broad patterns of state spatial regulation, state spatial restructuring, and state rescaling that have crystallized across western Europe during the last four decades.

Building upon these theoretical foundations, the remainder of the book explores, on meso and concrete levels, the role of urban policy as an animateur, mediator, and product of state rescaling processes during the last four decades in western Europe. Chapter 4 examines the consolidation and subsequent demise of spatial Keynesianism, the nationalizing, territorially redistributive approach to state spatial policy and urban governance that prevailed throughout most of western Europe from the early 1960s until the late 1970s. Chapter 5 investigates the rescaled, growth-oriented, and competitiveness-driven forms of state spatial policy and urban governance that began to crystallize as of the late 1970s, in conjunction with widespread concerns about urban industrial decline, intensified interspatial competition, welfare state retrenchment, European integration, and economic globalization. During the 1980s and 1990s, I argue, these new urban locational policies served as key catalysts and expressions of broader processes of state rescaling; they also contributed to an enhanced geographical differentiation of state regulatory arrangements and to an intensification of uneven spatial development across western Europe.

Finally, Chapter 6 develops a general interpretation of the deeply unstable, crisis-prone formation of state spatiality that has been consolidated through the institutionalization of urban locational policies in post-1980s western Europe. I refer to this new configuration of statehood as a Rescaled Competition State Regime (RCSR), and I argue that it contains a number of chronic regulatory deficits and crisis-tendencies. I then consider three alternative forms of state rescaling that have emerged, during the 1990s and early 2000s, in response to these problems—neighborhood-based anti-exclusion initiatives; metropolitan reform initiatives; and interurban networking initiatives. While these rescaled strategies of crisis-management have contributed to the further institutional and scalar differentiation of RCSRs, I suggest that they have deepened rather than alleviated the political-economic dislocations, regulatory failures, and territorial inequalities that were generated through previous rounds of urban locational policy. In the absence of a broader challenge to global and European neoliberalism, I argue, the establishment of an alternative, territorially redistributive framework of state spatial regulation at any geographical scale is likely to be an extremely difficult task.

TWO

The Globalization Debates: Opening Up to New Spaces?

> An argument can be made that social science has been *too* geographical and not sufficiently historical, in the sense that geographical assumptions have trapped consideration of social and political-economic processes in geographical structures and containers that defy historical change.
>
> John Agnew (1995: 379)

> the preeminence of the 'global' in much of the literature and political rhetoric obfuscates, marginalises and silences an intense and ongoing sociospatial struggle in which the reconfiguration of spatial scales of governance takes a central position...
>
> Erik Swyngedouw (2000a: 64)

Introduction: rethinking the geographies of 'globalization'

Since the early 1970s, debates have raged throughout the social sciences concerning the process of 'globalization'—an essentially contested term whose meaning is as much a source of controversy today as it was nearly three decades ago, when systematic research first began on the topic. Contemporary research on globalization encompasses an immensely broad range of themes, from the new international division of labor, transnational corporations, technological change, forms of industrial organization, the financialization of capital, the consolidation of neoliberalism and urban-regional restructuring to transformations of state power, civil society, citizenship, democracy, public spheres, war, nationalism, politico-cultural identities, ideologies, consumption patterns, environmental problems, localities, and architectural forms.[1] Yet, despite this proliferation of research on the topic,

---

[1] The social-scientific literatures on globalization have grown immensely during the last two decades. For general overviews and extensive bibliographical guides, see, among other works,

little academic consensus has been established regarding the interpretation of even the most rudimentary elements of the globalization process—its appropriate conceptualization, its historical periodization, its underlying causal determinants, or its sociopolitical implications.

Nevertheless, within this whirlwind of opposing perspectives on globalization, numerous studies have devoted detailed attention to the question of how the *geographies* of social, political, and economic life are being transformed under contemporary conditions. Major strands of contemporary globalization research are permeated with explicitly geographical concepts—such as 'space-time compression', 'space-time distanciation', 'space of flows', 'space of places', 'deterritorialization', 'glocalization', the 'global–local nexus', the 'global–local interplay', 'supraterritoriality', 'diasporas', 'translocalities', and 'scapes', among many other terms. Meanwhile, contributors to the literatures on globalization commonly deploy a variety of geographical prefixes—such as 'sub-', 'supra-', and 'trans-'—in order to describe a range of social processes that appear to be operating either below, above, or beyond entrenched geopolitical boundaries. Globalization is, in short, an intrinsically geographical concept: the recognition that social relations are becoming increasingly interconnected on a global scale necessarily problematizes the spatial parameters of those relations, and therefore, the geographical context in which they occur. Under these circumstances, space cannot be conceived as a static, pregiven platform of social relations, but must be recognized as one of their constitutive, historically produced dimensions. As Harvey (1995: 5) has suggested, the recent explosion of research on globalization provides an occasion for a broader inquiry into the socially produced character of spatial forms under modern capitalism:

One of the things that the adoption of the term 'globalization' now signals [...] is a profound geographical reorganization of capitalism, making many of the presumptions about the 'natural' geographical units within which capitalism's trajectory develops less and less meaningful (if they ever were). We are therefore faced with an historical opportunity to seize the nettle of capitalism's geography, to see the production of space as a constitutive moment within (as opposed to something derivatively constructed by) the dynamics of capital accumulation and class struggle.

In my view, the key methodological link between these major reorientations in the contemporary social sciences—the explosion of interest in globalization studies; and the recent 'reassertion of space in critical social theory'[2]—has been the pervasive questioning of the territorial nation-state as a preconstituted geographical unit of analysis for social research. As various authors have

Agnew and Corbridge 1994; Beck 2000; Guillén 2001; Held et al. 1999; Mittleman 1997; Scholte 2000; and Waters 1995. The recent special issues of *Economic Geography* (78/3, 2002), *International Sociology* (15/2, 2000), *International Social Science Journal* (June 1999), *International Journal of Urban and Regional Research* (24/2, 2000) and *Review of International Political Economy* (4/3, 1997) also provide a useful sampling of major analytical and empirical perspectives.

[2] This phrase is the subtitle of Soja's (1989) *Postmodern Geographies*.

recently argued, significant strands of twentieth-century social science have been locked into a state-centric epistemological framework in which national states are viewed as relatively fixed, self-enclosed geographical containers of social, economic, political, and cultural relations (Agnew 1994; Taylor 1996). However, to the extent that the current round of global restructuring has significantly reconfigured, and at least partially undermined, the container-like qualities of national states, this inherited model of territorially self-enclosed, nationally organized societies, economies, or cultures has become deeply problematic. Thus arises the need for new modes of analysis that do not naturalize national state territoriality and its associated, Cartesian image of space as a static block, platform, or container. Particularly since the early 1980s, globalization researchers have constructed a variety of heterodox, interdisciplinary, and even postdisciplinary methodologies that have begun to challenge the 'iron grip of the nation-state on the social imagination' (Taylor 1996: 1923). This wide-ranging effort to transcend state-centric episte-mologies arguably represents one of the unifying theoretical agendas under-lying contemporary research on globalization.

Against the background of the apparent spatial turn in contemporary global-ization studies, this chapter examines critically the efforts of globalization researchers to transcend state-centric modes of social analysis. This goal is, in practice, considerably more difficult to accomplish than is usually recognized, for it entails much more than an acknowledgement that transnational or global processes are gaining significance. On the contrary, as I suggest below, the overcoming of state-centrism requires a comprehensive reconceptualization of entrenched understandings of space as a fixed, pregiven container or plat-form for social relations. Despite the persistent efforts of critical human geog-raphers in recent decades to unsettle such assumptions, the conception of space as a realm of stasis, fixity, and stability—which contains but is not substantively modified by social action—is still surprisingly pervasive throughout the social sciences (Massey 1994).[3] Even within contemporary globalization studies, in which debates on the problematic of social spatiality have proliferated in recent decades, many analyses are still grounded upon atemporal geographical as-sumptions that are derived from an increasingly obsolete, nation state-centric configuration of capitalist development. Thus, one of the central intellectual barriers to a more adequate understanding of contemporary global transform-ations is that we currently lack appropriately *historical* and *dynamic* conceptual-izations of social space that are attuned to the possibility of systemic transformations within established political-economic geographies.

The challenges of transcending state-centric modes of analysis do not end here. Even when static, territorialist models of social spatiality are effectively overcome, the question of how more adequately to conceptualize the spatial-

---

[3] Henri Lefebvre's *The Production of Space* (1991) represents one of the most trenchant critiques of this 'timeless' conception of space.

ities of globalization remains thoroughly contentious. Those globalization researchers who have successfully transcended such state-centric geographical assumptions have generally done so by asserting that national state territoriality and even geography itself are currently shrinking, contracting, or dissolving due to alleged processes of 'deterritorialization'. A break with state-centrism is thus secured through the conceptual negation of the national state and, more generally, of the territorial dimensions of social life. I shall argue, however, that this methodological strategy sidesteps the crucially important task of analyzing the ongoing reterritorialization and rescaling of political-economic relations under contemporary capitalism. Consequently, within most standard accounts of deterritorialization, the goal of overcoming state-centrism is accomplished on the basis of a seriously one-sided depiction of currently emergent sociospatial forms.

In contrast to these positions, this chapter provides an initial sketch of the alternative conceptualization of contemporary sociospatial restructuring that will be developed at length in this book. At the heart of this argument is the contention that capitalism is currently experiencing (*a*) the transcendence of the nationalized sociospatial arrangements that prevailed throughout much of the twentieth century; and, concomitantly, (*b*) the production of new, rescaled sociospatial configurations that cannot effectively be described on the basis of purely territorialist, nationally scaled models. An essential, if apparently paradoxical, corollary of this thesis is the claim that state-centric mappings of social spatiality severely limit our understanding of the national state's own major role as a site, medium, and agent of contemporary global restructuring. Therefore, the effort to transcend state-centric modes of analysis does not entail a denial of the national state's continued relevance as a major locus of political-economic regulation. What such a project requires, rather, is a reconceptualization of how the geographies of state space are being transformed at various geographical scales under contemporary geoeconomic conditions. Such a reconceptualization is one of the key goals to be pursued in subsequent chapters of this book.

In the next section, I summarize the conceptualization of sociospatial restructuring under capitalism that grounds my analysis of the globalization debates. On this basis, I develop an interpretation of the epistemology of state-centrism, and I indicate various ways in which the contemporary round of global restructuring has undermined state-centric modes of analysis. Then, through a critical analysis of two major strands of globalization research—labeled, respectively, 'global territorialist' approaches and 'deterritorialization' approaches—I sketch an alternative interpretation of contemporary global restructuring as a contradictory process of reterritorialization and rescaling in which state institutions play crucial mediating and facilitating roles. A concluding section outlines various key methodological challenges for contemporary studies of global restructuring that will be explored in the remainder of this book.

Capitalist development and the creative destruction of sociospatial configurations

'Globalization' is a thoroughly contested term. Some researchers focus upon shifts in the world economy such as the dissolution of the Bretton Woods monetary regime in the early 1970s, the enhanced importance of trans- national corporations, the deregulation of finance capital, the liberalization of trade and investment flows, the massive expansion of foreign direct invest- ment, the intensified deployment of information technologies, and the reduc- tion in the cost and time of long-distance transport. For some scholars, globalization is associated with a variety of threats to, or transformations of, established forms of national state power. Others emphasize newly emergent forms of collective identity, political mobilization, and diaspora, often medi- ated through new information technologies, that appear to have unsettled the principle of nationality as a locus of everyday social relations. And finally, some authors have suggested that globalization has entailed the consolidation of worldwide forms of popular consciousness and political authority that open up new possibilities for human emancipation.[4]

Clearly, the relative merits of these and other approaches to globalization hinge upon their relative usefulness as tools of analysis with reference to particular research questions and political concerns. Yet, regardless of which specific social, political, economic, or cultural processes are foregrounded, it is crucial to avoid the widespread tendency to treat globalization as a single, all- encompassing mega-trend, causal force, or end-state (Dicken, Tickell, and Peck 1997). The notion of globalization is first and foremost a descriptive category denoting, at the most general level, the spatial extension of social interde- pendencies on a worldwide scale (Rosenberg 2000: 2).[5] To the extent that worldwide social interdependencies are being enhanced, this development must be interpreted as the aggregate consequence of a variety of interrelated tendencies rather than being viewed as the expression of a single, internally coherent causal mechanism. From this perspective, an adequate analysis of globalization must differentiate the multifaceted causal *processes* that have underpinned this worldwide extension of social relations, while simultan- eously attempting to trace the variegated, uneven *effects* of such processes in different political-economic contexts (Yeung 2002). In other words, 'Global- isation as an outcome cannot be explained simply by invoking globalisation as

---

[4] On the economic dimensions of globalization see, for instance, K. Cox 1997; Knox and Agnew 1995; Boyer and Drache 1996; Daniels and Lever 1996; Dicken 1998; Ruigrok and van Tulder 1995; and Wade 1996. On the political dimensions of globalization, see Cerny 1995; R. Cox 1987; Jessop 2002; Mann 1997; McMichael 1996; and Strange 1996. On globalization and the transformation of cultural forms and collective identities, see Appadurai 1996; Featherstone 1990; Magnusson 1996; Marden 1997; and Scholte 1996. On the emergence of worldwide forms of popular consciousness, see Robertson 1992; Shaw 2000; and Albrow 1996.

[5] Versions of this definition are developed by Giddens 1990; Held 1995; and McGrew 1992.

a process tending towards that outcome' (Rosenberg 2000: 2).[6] Considerable methodological reflexivity is therefore required in order to circumvent some of the many 'chaotic' presuppositions and explanations that underpin main-stream accounts of contemporary globalization (Jessop 1999c).[7]

For present purposes, my concern is to explore the implications of the current round of global restructuring for the changing geographical organization of capitalism. Thus, before examining more closely the geographical contours of the contemporary globalization debate, it is necessary first to explicate some of the key theoretical assumptions upon which my own understanding of social spatiality and sociospatial restructuring is grounded. The starting point for this analysis is a *processual* conceptualization of sociospatial forms under modern capitalism (Lefebvre 1991). In this view, space is not opposed to time and historicity, but must be viewed as a co-constitutive, dialectically inseparable moment of the latter. Thus, while concepts such as space, territory, geography, place, and scale are generally used to connote fixed objects, pregiven platforms or static things, I shall use them throughout this book as shorthand labels for more precise, if also more stylistically cumbersome, terminological formula-tions—such as spatialization processes, territorialization processes, geography-making, place-making, and scaling. In other words, all aspects of social space under modern capitalism must be understood as presuppositions, arenas and outcomes of dynamic processes of continual social contestation and transform-ation. Such a conceptualization entails the replacement of traditional Cartesian notions of 'space-as-thing' or 'space-as-platform' with a dialectical, social-con-structionist notion of 'space-as-process'. For the sake of stylistic convenience, I shall continue to use standard terms such as space, territory, place, and scale—but it must be emphasized that these labels connote ongoing *processes* of spa-tialization, territorialization, place-making, and scaling rather than fixed, pre-given, or static entities. Over two decades ago, Soja (1980) summarized this essential methodological point with the memorable phrase, 'the sociospatial dialectic'. A directly analogous idea is also at the heart of Lefebvre's (1991) now well-known concept of the 'production of space'.

---

[6] In addition to the danger of conflating causes and effects in studies of globalization, it is equally important to recognize the politically contested character of popular and academic discourse on this theme. Notions of globalization have been deployed strategically by diverse actors and organiza-tions—including transnational corporations, state institutions, nongovernmental organizations (NGOs), and oppositional social movements—in order to pursue specific political and ideological agendas. This discursive, political, and strategic aspect of globalization has played a hugely powerful role in influencing popular understandings of contemporary capitalism, whether as a means to naturalize neoliberal policy prescriptions, to promote state institutional restructuring, to reorient corporate strategies, to reinterpret social identities, or to rally anticapitalist resistance (Kelly 1999; Kipfer and Keil 1995; Bourdieu 1996).

[7] In an effort to circumvent such confusions, the remainder of this chapter adopts the terminology of 'global restructuring' rather than referring simply to 'globalization'. In contrast to the notion of globalization, which implies the existence of a singular, unified mega-trend, the notion of restruc-turing implies an uneven, multifaceted, polymorphic, and open-ended process of change (Soja 1989). However, when discussing the work of authors who deploy the notion of globalization, I shall continue to use this generic term.

A foundational question for any study of the production of space under capitalism is how such processes of spatialization, territorialization, place-making, scaling, and so forth mold and continually reshape the geographical landscape.[8] In the present context, I shall build upon Harvey's (1985, 1982) conceptualization of the production of spatial configuration under capitalism as a basis for examining the distinctively geographical parameters of contemporary forms of global restructuring.

According to Harvey (1985), capitalism is under the impulsion to eliminate all geographical barriers to the accumulation process by seeking out cheaper raw materials, fresh sources of labor-power, new markets for its products, and new investment opportunities. This deterritorializing, expansionary tendency within capitalism was clearly recognized by Marx, who famously described capital's globalizing dynamic as a drive to 'annihilate space by time' and analyzed the world market as its historical product and its geographical expression (Marx 1973 [1857]: 539). In Marx's (1973: 408) famous formulation in the *Grundrisse*, 'the tendency to create the world market is inherent to the concept of capital itself. Every limit appears as a barrier to be overcome.' Thus, for Harvey, as for Marx, capital is oriented simultaneously towards temporal acceleration (the continual acceleration of turnover times) and spatial expansion (the overcoming of geographical barriers to the process of accumulation). More recently, Harvey (1989c) has referred to these spatio-temporal tendencies within the capital relation as a process of 'time-space compression'. Insofar as they eliminate historically specific territorial barriers to accumulation, these tendencies may be said to embody capital's moment of *deterritorialization*.

At the same time, Harvey insists that the impulsion to reduce the socially necessary turnover time of capital and to expand its spatial orbit necessarily hinges upon the production of relatively fixed and immobile sociospatial configurations. Indeed, according to Harvey, it is only through the production of historically specific socio-geographical infrastructures—composed, for instance, of urban built environments, industrial agglomerations, regional production complexes, systems of collective consumption, large-scale transportation networks, long-distance communications grids, and state regulatory institutions—that processes of time-space compression can unfold. In this sense, each moment of deterritorialization hinges upon an equally essential moment of *reterritorialization* in which relatively fixed and immobile spatial arrangements are established or modified as a basis for extending and accelerating capital's orbit. As Harvey (1985: 149) explains, 'the ability to overcome space is predicated on the production of space'. From this perspective, the historical evolution of capitalism has entailed the increasing replacement of inherited precapitalist landscapes with specifically capitalist sociospatial

---

[8] This question has long preoccupied critical sociospatial theorists, particularly in the fields of urban and regional studies and geographical political economy. Detailed overviews of, and contributions to, these discussions include Benko and Strohmayer 1991; Gottdiener 1985; Hudson 2001; Katznelson 1992; Soja 2000, 1989; and Storper and Walker 1989.

configurations—a 'second nature' of socially produced geographical infrastructures that are suited to the operations of capital under particular conditions (Harvey 1989*b*: 191). In a capitalist context, these socially produced
geographical landscapes—to which I shall refer generically as 'capitalist sociospatial configurations'—represent an essential force of production: while they
serve as presuppositions, arenas, and outcomes of particular types of social
activities, they also play essential roles in providing the logistical foundations
for the process of capital circulation as a whole (Swyngedouw 1992*b*). Each
framework of capitalist sociospatial organization is closely intertwined with
historically specific patterns of uneven development insofar as it entails the
systemic privileging of some locations, places, territories, and scales and the
marginalization or exclusion of others.

Harvey refers to these historically specific sociospatial configurations, and
their associated forms of uneven development, as capital's 'spatial fix'—a 'tendency towards [. . .] a structured coherence to production and consumption
within a given space' (Harvey 1985: 146). By providing a relatively fixed and
immobile basis upon which capital's circulation process can be accelerated,
extended, and intensified, each spatial fix entails 'the conversion of temporal
into spatial restraints to accumulation' (Harvey 1982: 416). However, Harvey
also insists that no spatial fix can ever permanently resolve the endemic crisis-
tendencies that pervade capitalism. Consequently, each sociospatial configuration is merely temporary, a chronically unstable 'dynamic equilibrium'
(Harvey 1985: 136) within a broader, chaotic see-saw of perpetual sociospatial
change. On this basis, Harvey (1985: 150) interprets the historical geography of
capitalism as a process of continual restructuring in which sociospatial configurations are incessantly created, destroyed, and reconstituted anew:

Capitalist development must negotiate a knife-edge between preserving the values of
past commitments made at a particular place and time, or devaluing them to open up
fresh room for accumulation. Capitalism perpetually strives, therefore, to create a social
and physical landscape in its own image and requisite to its own needs at a particular
point in time, only just as certainly to undermine, disrupt and even destroy that
landscape at a later point in time. The inner contradictions of capitalism are expressed
through the restless formation and re-formation of geographical landscapes. This is the
tune to which the historical geography of capitalism must dance without cease.

For Harvey, then, the endemic tension between fixity and motion—'between
the rising power to overcome space and the immobile spatial structures required
for such a purpose' (Harvey 1985: 150)—provides the analytical key to the
investigation of processes of sociospatial restructuring under capitalism. Capitalist sociospatial configurations are produced as historically specific geographical preconditions for capital's globalizing dynamism, only to be eventually torn
down, reconfigured, and reterritorialized during recurrent waves of systemic
crisis, disinvestment, and institutional reorganization. Through this tumultuous process of creative destruction, inherited geographical landscapes, institu-

tional arrangements, and forms of uneven development are reshaped quite dramatically, as major factions of capital strive to amortize the full value of existing spatial configurations, to 'wash away the dead weight of past investments' and to wrest open new possibilities for accumulation (Harvey 1989*b*: 192–4).

Harvey's approach to the creative destruction of sociospatial configurations under capitalism has proven highly influential during the last two decades in the fields of geographical political economy, urban and regional studies, and sociospatial theory. My goal here is to underscore its implications for interpreting the diverse restructuring processes that are generally subsumed under the rubric of 'globalization'. As indicated, globalization is a multifaceted concept that refers, at core, to the extension of spatial interdependencies on a worldwide scale. While it would clearly be problematic to reduce this tendency to any single causal mechanism, Harvey's conceptualization of capitalist sociospatial configurations provides a useful analytical basis on which to interpret some of its core spatio-temporal dynamics. From this perspective, the contemporary round of global restructuring can be interpreted as the most recent historical expression of the *longue durée* dynamic of deterritorialization, reterritorialization, and uneven geographical development that has underpinned the production of capitalist spatiality throughout the modern era (Harvey 1995). As in previous rounds of crisis-induced sociospatial restructuring, contemporary global shifts have entailed a multifaceted, dialectical process through which: (*a*) the movement of commodities, capital, and people through geographical space has been expanded and accelerated; (*b*) relatively fixed and immobile socio-territorial infrastructures have been produced or transformed in order to enable such expanded, accelerated movement; and (*c*) inherited patterns of uneven geographical development have been systematically reworked at various spatial scales. Therefore, much like earlier periods of creative destruction under capitalism, the contemporary round of global restructuring has been grounded upon a multiscalar, dialectical interplay between deterritorializing and reterritorializing tendencies.

I shall develop this conceptualization of contemporary global restructuring in more detail below, through a critical analysis of major strands of the globalization literature. At this juncture, six initial implications of the theorization outlined above deserve special emphasis.

1. Contemporary forms of global restructuring represent conflictual, uneven, and dialectical processes of sociospatial change rather than a static end-state or a terminal condition.

2. Contemporary processes of global restructuring are both spatial (based upon the reconfiguration of inherited sociospatial configurations) and temporal (based upon the acceleration of capital's socially average turnover time).

3. Contemporary processes of global restructuring are unfolding simultaneously upon multiple, intertwined geographical scales—not only within

global space, but also through the production and reconfiguration of diverse subglobal spaces such as supranational blocs, national states, regions, cities, localities, and neighborhoods.

4. These multiscalar shifts have not entailed a total obliteration of inherited sociospatial configurations but rather their functional, institutional, and geographical redefinition: they are thus premised upon a complex mix of continuity and change.

5. Contemporary processes of deterritorialization and reterritorialization stem from a diverse range of political-economic causes—including, among others, the reorganization of corporate accumulation strategies, the consolidation of neoliberalism, financial deregulation, accelerated technological change, new population movements, geopolitical shifts, and transformations of the global labor force—rather than from a single mega-trend (Harvey 1995; Jessop 1999c). Their consequences are equally variegated in different political-economic contexts.

6. Finally, and most crucially, national territorial states must be viewed as essential geographical arenas and agents of contemporary forms of global restructuring rather than as the passive or helpless victims of these processes.

The latter point is particularly essential to my argument here. While numerous authors have usefully underscored the activist role of national states in facilitating the contemporary round of geoeconomic integration,[9] I am concerned in this book to explore the *territorializing* operations of state institutions in relation to capital at both national and subnational spatial scales. For, much like urban-regional agglomerations, national states have long operated as relatively fixed and immobile forms of (re)territorialization for successive rounds of time-space compression, particularly since the second industrial revolution of the late nineteenth century (Lefebvre 1978; Brenner 1998a). With the consolidation of national-developmentalist political regimes during that period, national states became ever more central to the promotion, regulation, and financing of capitalist expansion—above all through their role in the construction of large-scale geographical infrastructures for industrial production, collective consumption and long-distance market exchange, transportation, and communication (see Ch. 3). From this perspective, late nineteenth- and early twentieth-century forms of geoeconomic integration entailed the consolidation of the national state's role as a territorialized scaffolding for accelerated capital circulation and as an institutional interface between subnational and supranational scales. Throughout this period, processes of globalization and (national) territorialization proceeded in tandem, mutually reinforcing one another in powerful ways (Goswami 2004).

---

[9] See e.g. Helleiner 1994; Panitch 1994; Radice 1999; Sassen 1996; Scholte 1997; Sites 2003; and Weiss 1998.

I shall argue below that, under contemporary geoeconomic conditions, national states continue to operate as key forms of territorialization for the social relations of capitalism, but that the *scalar* geographies of this state-organized territorialization process have been fundamentally reconfigured. This development has systematically undermined inherited, state-centric conceptions of political-economic space. But what sorts of geographical assumptions do such state-centric visions entail? It is to this question that I now turn.

Hidden geographies and the epistemology of state-centrism

As a youthful philatelist in the mid-twentieth century, I sorted my stamps by political jurisdiction. I directed attention to the national forms—technical and symbolic—through which both intranational and international communication took place [...] Much social science sorted social relations in the same way, simply assuming the coincidence of social boundaries with state boundaries and that social action occurred primarily within, and secondarily across, these divisions. Social relations were represented by the national societies that were assumed to frame them. Just as I collected the various ephemera of national postal systems, social scientists collected distinctive national social forms.

Martin Shaw (2000: 68)

Embedded statism contains the remarkable geographical assumption that all the important human social activities share exactly the same spaces. This spatial congruence can be stated simply: the 'society' which sociologists study, the 'economy' which economists study, and the 'polity' which political scientists study all share a common geographical boundary, that of the state. However abstract the social theory, it is national societies which are described; however quantitative the economic models, it is national economies which are depicted; and however behavioral the political science, it is national governance at issue.

Peter Taylor (2000: 8)

Agnew (1995) has questioned whether recent discussions of space, territory, and place in the social sciences amount to a fully-fledged 'sociospatial turn'. Insofar as social science has always been permeated by historically specific geographical assumptions, Agnew argues, the notion of a 'resurgence' or 'reassertion' of spatial influences makes little sense.[10] Although I believe that

[10] The main target of Agnew's critique is apparently Soja's *Postmodern Geographies* (1989), which argues for a domination of 'historicism' over spatial considerations in much of postwar social science. Soja's more recent work (1996) preserves his emphasis on the 'reassertion of space in social theory' while recognizing the existence of geographical assumptions even in historicist modes of analysis.

contemporary studies of globalization have indeed confronted the problematic of social spatiality with a renewed intensity, this section provides support
for Agnew's argument. As the above-quoted statements by Shaw and Taylor
indicate, state-centric approaches do not exclude geographical considerations
to constitute a despatialized social science; on the contrary, a distinctively
ahistorical spatial ontology lies at their very heart.

In my view, state-centrism can be defined most precisely in terms of its three
most essential, if usually implicit, geographical assumptions: (*a*) the conception of space as a static platform of social action that is not itself constituted or
modified socially; (*b*) the assumption that all social relations are organized
within territorially self-enclosed spatial containers; and (*c*) the assumption
that all social relations are organized at a national scale or are undergoing a
process of nationalization.[11] The first assumption results in a *spatial fetishism*
in which space is seen as being timeless, and therefore immune to historical
change. The second assumption results in a *methodological territorialism* in
which territoriality—the principle of spatial enclosure—is treated as the necessary spatial form for social relations. The third assumption generates a *methodological nationalism* in which the national scale is treated as the ontologically
primary locus of social relations. Taken together, these assumptions generate
an internalist model of societal development in which national territoriality
is presumed to operate as a static, fixed, and timeless container of historicity
(Fig. 2.1). While all three of these assumptions have pervaded mainstream
social science, any given mode of analysis may be said to be state-centric, in
the terms proposed here, when the assumption of spatial fetishism is linked
either to methodological territorialism or methodological nationalism.

Defined in this manner, a state-centric epistemology has pervaded the
modern social sciences since their inception during the late nineteenth

Spatial fetishism	Conception of social space as timeless and static, and thus as immune to the possibility of historical change
Methodological territorialism	Assumption that all social relations are organized within self-enclosed, discretely bounded territorial containers
Methodological nationalism	Assumption that all social relations are organized at a national scale or are becoming nationalized

Fig. 2.1. The epistemology of state-centrism: three key geographical assumptions

[11] The term 'state-centric' has a different meaning in the literature on 'bringing the state back in',
in which state-centered approaches are contrasted to society-centered approaches. In these discussions, state-centered theories emphasize the autonomous institutional power of the state over and
against societal or class-based forces. For a useful critical overview of this literature, see Jessop (1990*a*:
278–306). In contrast to this literature, the notion of state-centrism developed here refers to a more
generalized sociospatial ontology that has been implicit within a wide range of research paradigms
throughout the social sciences.

century. Not surprisingly, political science has been the most explicitly state-centric among the social sciences. States have been viewed as politically sovereign and economically self-propelled entities, with national state territoriality understood as the basic reference point in terms of which all subnational and supranational political-economic processes are to be classified. On this basis, the (national) state has been viewed as the container of (national) society, while the interstate system has been mapped in terms of a distinction between 'domestic' politics and 'foreign' relations in which national state boundaries are said to separate 'inside' from 'outside' (Agnew 1994; R. B. J. Walker 1993). Crucially, however, the above definition extends the problematic of state-centrism well beyond those fields of inquiry that are focused directly upon state operations and political life to various modes of anthropological, sociological, and economic analysis in which the concept of the state may not even be explicitly deployed. Indeed, as defined above, a state-centric epistemology has arguably underpinned significant strands of sociology (due to its focus on nationally configured societies and communities), anthropology (due to its focus on bounded, territorialized cultures), and macro-economics (due its focus on purportedly self-contained, self-propelled national economies).

First, as it has traditionally been deployed, the concept of society has implied that the boundaries of social relations are spatially congruent with those of the national state (Giddens 1984; Urry 2000). Even when the notion of society has not been defined explicitly in terms of the state's national boundaries, it has still been widely understood as a territorially self-enclosed entity, essentially as a subnational replication of the state-defined society, its geographical analog on a smaller spatial scale (Agnew 1993; Häkli 2001; Pletsch 1981). Although anthropology avoided this explicit form of state-centrism prior to the advent of area studies during the postwar era, throughout its history most of the discipline has still presupposed a territorialized concept of culture as a localized, spatially fixed community (Gupta and Ferguson 1997; Malkki 1992). Finally, from Smith and Ricardo to List, Keynes, and the contemporary monetarists, macro-economic theory has long conceived the territorialized national economy as its most elemental unit of analysis, the preconstituted container of production, exchange, and consumption that is likewise said to be spatially coextensive with the state's territorial boundaries (Radice 1984). While trade theory has always contained an explicitly international dimension, this too has remained markedly state-centric insofar as national states have been viewed as the primary geographical blocks between which the factors of production are moved and in terms of which comparative advantage is measured (Taylor 1996: 1925).[12]

---

[12] As Taylor (1996: 1922–3) notes, until relatively recently even the discipline of human geography has replicated this territorialized, state-centric conceptual orientation, either with reference to the urban scale (urban ecology and the study of urban systems), the national scale (political geography), or the transnational scale (geopolitics). Due to its anarchist, anti-statist roots in the work of theorists such as Elisée Reclus and Peter Kropotkin, classical regional geography provides an

This unhistorical conception of spatiality can be usefully characterized as a *state*-centric epistemology because its widespread intellectual plausibility has been premised upon a naturalization of the modern state's specifically national/territorial form. Among the most rudimentary features of territoriality in social life is its role as a strategy grounded upon the parcelization and enclosure of space (Sack 1986). However, in the modern interstate system, territoriality has assumed a historically specific geographical significance. With the dissolution of feudal hierarchies in late medieval Europe, political space came to be organized in terms of exclusive state control over self-enclosed territorial domains (Spruyt 1994). This development was institutionalized in the Treaty of Westphalia of 1648, which recognized the existence of an interstate system composed of contiguous, bounded territories ruled by sovereign national states committed to the principle of noninterference in each other's internal affairs. The consequence of this transformation has been the long-term enclosure of political, economic, and military power within a global grid of mutually exclusive yet geographically contiguous national state territories. This bundling of territoriality to state sovereignty is arguably the essential characteristic of the modern interstate system (Gottmann 1983; Ruggie 1993; R. B. J. Walker 1993). In this system, political authority is grounded upon: (*a*) the *territorialization* of state power, in which each state attempts to exercise exclusive sovereignty over a delineated, self-enclosed national space; and (*b*) the *globalization* of the territorial state form, in which the entire globe is progressively subdivided among contiguous, nonoverlapping national state territories.

Clearly, the notion of territoriality is a polysemic category and not all its meanings refer to this statist global and national geography. However, since the late nineteenth century, the social sciences have come to presuppose a territorialist, nationalized image of social space derived from the form of territory-sovereignty nexus that has been produced and continually reinscribed at a national scale within the modern interstate system. By the mid-twentieth century, each of the conceptual building blocks of the modern social sciences—in particular, the notions of state, society, economy, culture, and community—had come to presuppose this simultaneous territorialization and nationalization of social relations within a parcelized, fixed, and essentially timeless geographical space. The resultant state-centric epistemology entailed the transposition of the historically unique territorial and scalar configuration of the modern interstate system into a generalized model of sociospatial organization, whether with reference to political, societal, economic, or cultural processes. Within this framework, sociohistorical change is said to occur

exception to this tendency insofar as regions were viewed as ecologically delimited, contextually specific environments rather than as territorial subunits of the state. Likewise, in major strands of the discipline of history, an idiographic notion of space-as-context provided an important alternative to the conception of space-as-container that dominated the other, more nomothetically oriented social sciences.

within the fixed territorial boundaries of a national state, society, culture, or economy rather than through the transformation of those boundaries, their scalar contours and the political-economic practices they putatively enclose. State-centric modes of analysis acquired a doxic, taken-for-granted character during the course of the twentieth century, as their 'spatial premises enter[ed] into the realm of "common sense" where interrogation is deemed both unnecessary and quite uncalled for' (Taylor 2000: 6).[13]

Particularly from an early twenty-first century vantage point, it is crucial to recognize that the epistemology of state-centrism was not merely a fantasy or an ideological projection. Indeed, its widespread intellectual plausibility was derived from the late nineteenth- and early twentieth-century historical-geographical context in which the social sciences first emerged, during which the territorial state's role in 'encaging' socioeconomic and politico-cultural relations within its boundaries dramatically intensified (Mann 1993; Maier 2000). Although the lineages of this statist developmental configuration can be traced to the late eighteenth century, when England's territorial economy superseded the city-centered economy of Amsterdam, it was above all during the twentieth century that the interstate system came to operate like 'a vortex sucking in social relations to mould them through its territoriality' (Taylor 1994: 152; see also Braudel 1984). Britain's attempt to institutionalize a self-regulating world market during the nineteenth century by combining imperialist expansion with trade liberalization eventually resulted in a countervailing 'great transformation' in which increasingly autarkic, protectionist regulatory frameworks were constructed throughout western Europe and North America (Polanyi 1957). Under these conditions, as McMichael (1987: 223) notes, the 'world market was internalized within the nation-state, which [...] became the locus of reproduction of capital' (quoted in Radice 1998: 267). The nationally organized forms of state regulation that were subsequently consolidated served as the institutional basis for 'organized capitalism', the

---

[13] This is not the place to analyze the complex institutional histories through which this state-centric epistemology gradually became hegemonic as a mode of social-scientific inquiry, particularly in the postwar USA but also in Europe, the Soviet Union, and much of the Third World. My concern here is less to examine the institutional consolidation of state-centrism than to characterize analytically its main geographical presuppositions. For accounts of the institutional histories of state-centrism, see Pletsch 1981; Palat 1996; and Wallerstein 1996.

In this context, it is also crucial to note that these state-centric tendencies in the classical social sciences coexisted uneasily with an opposing, if largely subterranean, 'globalist' strand of theory and research. This globalist mode of analysis was elaborated during the 19th and early 20th centuries above all in Marx's theory of capital accumulation and in the theories of imperialism developed by Lenin, Luxemburg, and Bukharin. Although major strands of Marxian social theory were also eventually infused with state-centric assumptions (such as the notion that the national scale was the main strategic locus of class struggle), this intellectual tradition was arguably the most important alternative to state-centrism within classical sociological discourse. Following World War II, various non-Marxist alternatives to state-centrism also emerged, including the *Annales* school of historiography and the figurational sociology of Norbert Elias. In addition to these strands of research, Taylor (1996: 1918–19) detects various late 19th-century contextualist alternatives to state-centric conceptions of space, such as idiographic approaches to historiography and Marshallian-inspired economic analyses focused on the problem of urban-regional agglomeration.

global regime of accumulation that prevailed from the early twentieth century until the early 1970s (Lash and Urry 1987). During the post-World War II period, under the rubric of US global hegemony, Cold War geopolitical divisions, the Bretton Woods global monetary regime, and the Non-Aligned Movement of newly decolonized states, national-developmentalist practices and ideologies were further consolidated throughout the world system, grounded upon the notion that each national state would guide its own national society and economy through a linear, internally defined, and self-propelled process of modernization (McMichael 1996). Within this nationalized but worldwide political geography, 'The organizing world principle of nation-states allowed the soothingly comprehensible vision of polities as bound up together by economic fate, all in the same large boat called the national economy, competing with other national economies in a worldwide regatta' (Reich 1991: 4–5; quoted in Larner and Walters 2002: 401).

This intensified territorialization of social relations at a national scale suggests that 'the state-centric nature of social science faithfully reflected the power containers that dominated the social world it was studying' (Taylor 1996: 1920). However, the theorization of capitalist sociospatial configuration outlined previously points toward a somewhat different interpretation: from this perspective, the epistemology of state-centrism is to be viewed less as a faithful reflection of its historical-geographical context than as a politically mediated misrecognition of that context. The epistemology of state-centrism was tightly enmeshed within the national-developmentalist round of deterritorialization and reterritorialization that unfolded during the late nineteenth and early twentieth centuries. On the one hand, processes of space-time compression intensified dramatically in conjunction with the second industrial revolution, the globalizing expansion of the world economy, and the imperialist forays of the major capitalist national states. On the other hand, this dramatic spatial extension and temporal acceleration of capitalism was premised upon the construction of qualitatively new forms of capitalist sociospatial configuration—including, most crucially, the production, distribution, and consumption infrastructures of major industrial city-regions; newly consolidated, nationalized networks of market exchange, transportation, and communication; and the highly bureaucratized institutional-regulatory systems of national states. The essence of state-centric modes of analysis, I would argue, is to focus one-sidedly upon a single term within this dialectic of deterritorialization and reterritorialization, that of territorial fixity, as embodied in the national state's bounded, territorialized form.

Lefebvre's (1991: 280) analysis of the modern state as a form of 'violence directed towards a space' helps illuminate this territorialist misrecognition. In Lefebvre's view, modern national states are grounded upon a relentless drive to rationalize, unify, and homogenize social relations within their territorial boundaries: 'Each state claims to produce a space wherein something is accomplished, a space, even, where something is brought to perfection: namely, a unified and hence homogenous society' (Lefebvre 1991: 281). But, as he (1991: 308) is quick to add: 'The space that homogenizes . . . has nothing homogenous about it.' One of the basic epistemological features of state-centric modes of analysis is to conflate the historical *tendency* towards the territorialization of social relations on a national scale—which has undoubtedly intensified during much of the twentieth century—with its full historical *realization*. Processes of territorialization and nationalization are thus represented as pregiven, natural conditions of social life rather than being seen as the products of historically specific strategies of parcelization, centralization, enclosure, and encaging at a national scale. Accordingly, as Lefebvre (1991: 287, italics in original) elaborates with reference to the 'abstract space' of modern capitalism:

Abstract space *is not* homogenous; it simply *has* homogeneity as its goal, its orientation, its 'lens'. And, indeed, it renders homogenous. But in itself it is multiform [. . .] Thus to look upon abstract space as homogeneous is to embrace a representation that takes the effect for the cause, and the goal for the reason why the goal was pursued. A representation which passes itself off as a *concept*, when it is merely an image, a mirror and a mirage; and which instead of challenging, instead of refusing, merely *reflects*. And what does such a specular representation reflect? It reflects the result sought.

Only in this specific sense, then, did the epistemology of state-centrism 'reflect' its historical-geographical context—not through an operation of mimesis, but rather through a form of reification in which the 'result sought', the 'fetishization of space in the service of the state', is treated as an actualized reality rather than as an unstable tendency within an ongoing dialectic (Lefebvre 1991: 21).

The crucial point, therefore, is that territorialization, on any spatial scale, must be viewed as a historically specific, incomplete, and conflictual *process* rather than as a pregiven, natural, or permanent condition. To the extent that the national scale (or any other geographical scale) acquires tendential primacy as an organizational arena for social, political, and economic relations, this must be viewed as a historically contingent outcome of scale-specific projects and strategies rather than being conceived as the expression of an ontological necessity. By contrast, state-centric epistemologies freeze the image of national state territoriality into a generalized feature of social life, and thereby neglect to consider the ways in which the latter has been produced and continually transformed during the history of capitalist development.

Rescaling territoriality: from globalization to the relativization of scales

As noted at the outset of this chapter, the geographies of capitalism have been profoundly transformed since the early 1970s, leading many commentators to acknowledge the socially produced, and therefore malleable, character of inherited formations of political-economic space. Smith (1996: 50–1) has aptly described this state of affairs as follows:

The solidity of the geography of twentieth century capitalism at various scales has melted; habitual spatial assumptions about the world have evaporated [. . .] It is as if the world map as jig-saw puzzle had been tossed in the air these last two decades, leaving us to reconstruct a viable map of everything from bodily and local change to global identity. Under these circumstances, the taken-for-grantedness of space is impossible to sustain. Space is increasingly revealed as a richly political and social product, and putting the jig-saw puzzle back together—in practice as well as in theory—is a highly contested affair.

Smith's formulation puts into stark relief what is arguably one of the central methodological challenges of contemporary globalization research—namely, to map the geographies of contemporary capitalism in ways that transcend the 'habitual spatial assumptions' of state-centric epistemologies. As the geographical foundations of twentieth-century capitalism are unsettled and reworked, an urgent need arises for analytical frameworks that do not imprison the sociological imagination within timeless, territorialist, and unhistorical representations of social space.

To date, however, most globalization researchers have confronted this methodological challenge in one of two deeply problematic ways—either (*a*) through an analysis of the global scale in implicitly state-centric terms, as a globally stretched territorial grid; or (*b*) through an emphasis on processes of deterritorialization that purportedly trigger the erosion of national state territoriality as such. The former approach transposes state-centric mappings of space onto the global scale, and thus remains trapped within a narrowly territorialist understanding of contemporary capitalism. The latter approach transcends the territorialist epistemology of state-centrism on the basis of two equally problematic assumptions: (*a*) the notion that globalization is an essentially non-territorial, borderless, supraterritorial, or territorially disembedded process; and (*b*) the notion that globalization entails the contraction or erosion of national state power. In the remainder of this chapter, I argue that neither of these methodological strategies can provide an adequate mapping of contemporary sociospatial transformations. In the course of this discussion, I also begin to sketch the general interpretation of contemporary rescaling processes that will be developed at length in the rest of this book.

The crux of my argument is the proposition that the contemporary round of global restructuring has radically reconfigured the scalar organization of territorialization processes under capitalism, relativizing the primacy of the national scale while simultaneously enhancing the role of subnational and supranational scales in such processes. The contemporary round of globalization arguably represents a major new wave of deterritorialization and reterritorialization in which global socioeconomic interdependencies are being significantly extended in close conjunction with the establishment, or restructuring, of relatively fixed forms of capitalist sociospatial organization at diverse, subglobal geographical scales. Crucially, however, the political-economic geographies of this dynamic of deterritorialization and reterritorialization are today being fundamentally rescaled relative to the nationally configured patterns in which it has unfolded since the late nineteenth century. Whereas previous rounds of deterritorialization and reterritorialization occurred largely within the geographical framework of national state territoriality, the current round of sociospatial restructuring has significantly decentered the role of the national scale as the primary institutional arena for the territorialization of capital.

Collinge (1996) has characterized these multifaceted shifts as a 'relativization of scales' in which, in marked contrast to earlier configurations of capitalist sociospatial organization, no single level of political-economic interaction currently predominates over any others (see also Jessop 2002). As this process of scale-relativization has proceeded apace, a range of subnational and supranational sociospatial configurations—from global city-regions, industrial districts, and regional state institutions to multinational economic blocks, supranational regulatory institutions, and regimes of global governance— have acquired major roles as geographical infrastructures for the reproduction of global capitalism. Swyngedouw (1992a: 40) describes contemporary scalar transformations in closely analogous terms:

> Over the last decade or so the relative dominance of the nation state as a scale level has changed to give way to new configurations in which both the local/regional and the transnational/global have risen to prominence. Global corporations, global financial movements and global politics play deciding roles in the structuring of daily life, while simultaneously more attention is paid to local and regional responses and restructuring processes. There is, in other words, a double movement of globalisation on the one hand and devolution, decentralisation or localisation on the other [...] [T]he local/global interplay of contemporary restructuring processes should be thought of as a single, combined process with two inherently related, albeit contradictory movements and as a process which involves a *de facto* recomposition of the articulation of the geographical scales of economic and of social life.

For Swyngedouw, these rescaling processes represent a conflictual dynamic of 'glocalization' in which global sociospatial integration is proceeding in tandem with a pervasive triadization, regionalization, and localization of social relations.[14] In this sense, 'globalization is not just about one scale becoming more important than the rest; it is also about changes in the very nature of the relationships between scales' (Dicken, Tickell, and Peck 1997:

---

[14] See also Swyngedouw 1997, 2000a. According to Robertson (1994: 36), the term 'glocalization' originated in Japanese business discourse, where it was used in the 1980s as a marketing buzzword to describe the adaptation of global corporate strategies to locally specific conditions. This term is not unproblematic, however, not least because of its apparent implication that *two* geographical scales, the global and the local, dominate contemporary rescaling processes. Like Swyngedouw, I reject this limited view of contemporary spatial transformations and insist upon their fundamentally multiscalar character. For, in addition to the global and the local, a variety of other scales—including the body, the urban, the regional, the national, and the supranational—are likewise key arenas and targets of currently unfolding rescaling processes. Moreover, the political, institutional, and cultural

159–60). The key notions of the relativization of scales and glocalization are summarized in Fig. 2.2.

The relativization of scales (Collinge 1996; Jessop 2002)	The entrenched primacy of the national scale of political-economic organization is being undermined
	New sociospatial configurations and geographies of socio-political struggle are proliferating at both supranational and subnational scales
	No single scale of political-economic organization or sociopolitical struggle predominates over others
Glocalization (Swyngedouw 1997, 1992*a*)	The process of global integration is proceeding in tandem with a reconfiguration of sociospatial configurations at various subglobal scales—including the supranational, the national, the regional, and the urban
	The scalar organization of political-economic life is being fundamentally recast; entrenched scalar hierarchies are being rearticulated; and intense struggles are proliferating regarding the appropriate configuration of scales in social, economic, and political life

Fig. 2.2. Globalization as a process of rescaling: two key concepts

The central consequence of these processes of rescaling has been to thrust the apparently ossified, entrenched fixity of national state territoriality abruptly and dramatically into historical motion, radically redefining its geographical significance, its organizational configuration, and its linkages to both subnational and supranational scales. Processes of territorialization remain endemic to capitalism, but today they are jumping at once above, below, and around the national scale upon which they tendentially converged during much of the last century. Consequently, state territoriality currently operates less as an isomorphic, self-enclosed block of absolute space than as a polymorphic, multiscalar institutional mosaic composed of multiple, partially overlapping institutional forms and regulatory configurations that are neither congruent, contiguous, nor coextensive with one another (Anderson 1996). I view this rescaling of national territoriality as the *differentia specifica* of the currently unfolding round of global sociospatial restructuring. Even though

expressions of each of these scales are being significantly redefined under contemporary conditions, thereby undermining any conceptual grammar that treats scales as if they were stable, fixed entities or platforms. Despite these analytical dangers, the notion of glocalization is useful because, like the concept of the relativization of scales, it underscores the ways in which inherited scalar hierarchies are being shaken up and rejigged under contemporary capitalism. For discussions of glocalization by other authors, see, for instance, Courchene 1995; Galland 1996; Bauman 1998; and Kraidy 1999.

contemporary forms of deterritorialization have partially eroded the container-like qualities of national borders, I shall argue that national states continue to operate as essential political and institutional sites for, and mediators of, the territorialization of social, political, and economic relations. The key point is that the political-economic geographies of this territorialization process are no longer focused predominantly upon any single, self-enclosed geographical scale.

In the next two sections, the notion of a rescaling of national territoriality is further developed through a critical analysis of the two major strands of globalization research mentioned above. Because so much of globalization research remains grounded upon state-centric or otherwise deeply problematic geographical assumptions, I consider this type of epistemological critique to be a crucial prerequisite for the project of developing a more geographically reflexive and scale-sensitive approach to the investigation of contemporary sociospatial transformations.

Global territorialism: state-centrism on a world scale

> It is truly astonishing that the concept of territoriality has been so little studied by students of international politics: its neglect is akin to never looking at the ground one is walking on.
>
> John Ruggie (1993: 174)

All accounts of globalization entail some version of the claim that the global scale has become increasingly important as an organizing locus of social relations. However, this emphasis on the global scale among globalization researchers has been intertwined with extraordinarily diverse conceptualizations of global social space. This section considers approaches to globalization studies that conceive global space in essentially state-centric terms, as a pregiven territorial container or as a form of territoriality stretched onto the global scale.

The deployment of this type of methodology—to which I shall refer as 'global territorialism'—is frequently quite explicit, as in Albrow's (1990: 9) definition of globalization as 'those processes by which the peoples of the world are incorporated into a single world society, a global society'. The concept of 'world society' has played a defining role within a major strand of mainstream research on globalization, according to which globalization entails not only the growing interconnectedness of distinct parts of the globe, but—in Waters's (1995: 3) characteristic formulation—the construction of 'a *single* society and culture occupying the planet'.[15] Other globalization

---

[15] Italics added. For other typical uses of the concept of 'world society' among globalization researchers see, for instance, Spybey 1996; Hondrich 1992; Meyer 1999; Meyer, et al. 1997; Shaw 1992; and Waters 1995. For critical discussions of this approach see Marden 1997; McGrew 1992; and Altvater and Mahnkopf 1995.

researchers have elaborated closely analogous accounts of 'global culture' and 'transnational civil society'.[16]

In each case, the modifier 'global' is positioned before a traditionally state-centric, territorialist concept—society, civil society, or culture—in order to demarcate a realm of social interaction that transcends the borders of any single state territory. Whether this sphere of interaction is understood in normative terms (for instance, as a site of universalistic values such as human rights, equality, peace, and democracy), institutionally (for instance, as a framework of globally standardized economic, political, educational, and scientific practices), or experientially (for instance, as a worldwide diffusion of American, European, or Western cultural influences), world society approaches share an underlying conception of global space as a structural analog to state territoriality. Insofar as the interpretation of global space is derived directly from an understanding of the territorially configured spaces of national societies and national cultures, the question of the qualitative socio-spatial organization of world-scale processes is essentially foreclosed through a choice of conceptual grammar. The difference between global and national configurations of social space is thereby reduced to a matter of geographical size. Meanwhile, because globalization is understood primarily as a world-scale process, the role of national and subnational territorial transformations in contemporary processes of global restructuring cannot be explicitly analyzed. In this sense, even as their unit of analysis is extended beyond national territorial boundaries, world society approaches remain embedded within a state-centric epistemology that conceives space—on both global and national scales—as a timeless, territorial container of social relations. The preconstituted geographical space of the globe is presumed simply to be filled by the social practices associated with the process of globalization rather than being produced, reconfigured, or transformed through the latter.

Robertson's neo-Parsonsian cultural sociology of globalization, as articulated in his book *Globalization: Social Theory and Global Culture* (1992), exemplifies a somewhat less explicit but still widely influential version of a global territorialist approach.[17] Here, global space is not characterized through directly state-centric terms such as society or culture, but rather through the more geographically ambiguous categories of place and field. For Robertson, globalization is a multifaceted process that has led to the formation of what he terms a situation of 'global unicity'—the development of the world 'as a single place' or 'the concrete structuration of the world as a whole' (6, 53, *passim*). Robertson's analysis of globalization consists of a synchronic aspect (a 'dimensional model' of the 'global field') and a diachronic aspect (a 'sequential phase model of globalization'). According to Robertson, the global field is an underlying structural matrix upon which sociocultural conceptions of the world are organized; its components are the 'quintessential features of the terms in

[16] See e.g. Lipschutz 1992; Peterson 1992; Spybey 1996; and Wapner 1995.
[17] All parenthetic citations in the following two paragraphs refer to this work.

which it is possible to conceive of the world' (32). Robertson classifies the latter according to four basic dimensions, 'societies, individuals, the system of societies and mankind', which are together said to constitute the 'global-human condition' (26, 77–8). Globalization is then defined as a heightened 'self-consciousness' of the relations among these dimensions that in turn leads to an increasing 'differentiation of the main spheres of globality' (26–9, 50–1). Robertson elaborates a five-stage periodization to describe this world-historical trend towards intensified 'global unicity': the 'germinal' phase (15th–18th centuries); the 'incipient' phase (mid-18th century to 1870s); the 'take-off' phase (1870s–1920s); the 'struggle-for-hegemony' phase (1920s–1960s); and the 'uncertainty' phase (1960s–present) (58–60).

Despite Robertson's concern to analyze world-scale processes, his analysis reproduces a state-centric conceptualization of global space as a timeless, territorial framework that contains historicity without itself evolving historically. First, Robertson conceives the global scale as a self-enclosed territorial container within which the structural differentiation of individuals, societies, inter-societal relations, and humanity occurs: 'globality' is viewed essentially as a macrogeographical formation of (national) territoriality. Thus conceived, as in the world society approaches discussed above, globalization entails an intermeshing of preconstituted *Gesellschaft* and *Gemeinschaft* structures on the scale of the 'world-as-a-whole' rather than a qualitative restructuring, reterritorialization, or rescaling of these inherited, statist forms of territorial organization. Second, Robertson's conception of global space is essentially unhistorical. Robertson analyzes the changing interdependencies between individuals, states, societies, and the 'global-human condition' in orthodox Parsonsian terms, as a unilinear, evolutionary process of structural differentiation among preconstituted spatial scales (Parsons 1971). This differentiation is said to occur within the pregiven space of globality; yet this global space is not said to be constituted, modified, or transformed historically. Instead, the global field is viewed as an invariant, systemic hierarchy, stretching from the individual and society to the interstate system and the global human condition. In Robertson's theorization, the globalization process passes through each of these components without qualitatively transforming them or the scalar hierarchy in which they are embedded. Consequently, by subsuming currently unfolding global transformations within a universal, historically invariant process of structural differentiation, Robertson's analysis excludes a priori the possibility of a fundamental rearticulation of entrenched scalar hierarchies or of other qualitative sociospatial transformations at any geographical scale. Robertson's cultural sociology of globalization therefore entails the transposition of state-centric modes of analysis onto a world scale rather than their transcendence.

A radically different, but equally problematic, form of global territorialism can be found within Wallerstein's approach to world-system analysis, which is otherwise among the most sustained critiques of explicitly state-centric frameworks yet to be developed in the social sciences. By demonstrating the *longue durée* and macrogeographical parameters of capitalism, Wallerstein's pioneering studies have also served as a useful corrective to excessively pre-sentist interpretations of the post-1970s wave of globalization that exaggerate its discontinuity with earlier historical configurations of capitalist develop-ment.[18] Despite these substantial achievements, I believe that Wallerstein's theoretical framework replicates on a global scale the methodological terri-torialism of the very state-centric epistemologies he has otherwise criticized so effectively. To elaborate this claim, the intersection of global space and na-tional state territoriality in Wallerstein's approach to world-system analysis must be examined more closely.

Wallerstein conceptualizes capitalism as a geographically integrated histor-ical system grounded upon a single division of labor. Global space is conceived neither as a society, a culture, or a place, but rather in terms of the more geographically and historically specific notion of the 'modern world-system'. Although Wallerstein defines the capitalist world-system on multiple levels— for instance, in terms of the drive towards ceaseless accumulation; the com-modification of production, distribution, and investment processes; and the antagonistic class relation between capitalists and wage-laborers—he argues repeatedly that its unique *scalar* form is one of its constitutive features.[19] In contradistinction to previous historical systems ('world-empires'), in which the division of labor, state power, and cultural forms overlapped more or less congruently within the same territorial domains, capitalism is composed of 'a *single* division of labor but *multiple* polities and cultures'.[20] It is through this abstract contrast between two geometrical images—world-empires in which the division of labor is spatially congruent with structures of politico-cultural organization; and world-economies in which a single division of labor encom-passes multiple states and multiple cultural formations—that Wallerstein delineates the geographical foundations of modern capitalism. In essence, Wallerstein grasps the specificity of capitalist spatiality in terms of the terri-torial non-congruence of economic structures ('singular') with politico-institutional and cultural forms ('multiple'). According to Wallerstein, the long-run reproduction of capitalism has hinged crucially upon the durability of this scalar arrangement, which has provided capital with 'a freedom of maneuver that is structurally based [and has thereby] made possible the con-stant economic expansion of the world-system' (Wallerstein 1974: 348). On this basis, Wallerstein outlines the long-run history of world capitalism with reference to three intersecting spatio-temporal processes—first, the Kondra-tieff cycles, secular trends, and systemic crises of the world-scale accumulation process; second, the cycles of hegemonic ascension and decline among the

---

[18] See Wallerstein 1974, 1980, 1989, 2000. On the specific problematic of space in world-system analysis see Wallerstein 1988.

[19] For various definitions of capitalism in Wallerstein's work see, for instance, Wallerstein 1983: 13–19; 1979: 7–19; 1974: 37–8, 348.

[20] Wallerstein 1979: 6; italics added. See also Wallerstein 1974: 67, 348–9.

core states; and third, the geographical incorporation of external areas until, by the late nineteenth century, the international division of labor had become coextensive with most of the planet's physical-geographical surface.[21]

However, considering Wallerstein's avowed concern to transcend state-centric models of capitalist modernity, national state territories occupy a surprisingly pivotal theoretical position within his conceptual framework. Although the division of labor in the capitalist world-economy is said to be stratified into three supra-state zones (core, semi-periphery, and periphery), Wallerstein argues that its most elemental geographical units are nevertheless national states, or more precisely, the bounded territories over which national states attempt to exercise sovereignty. To be sure, Wallerstein maintains that the division of labor within the world-system transcends the territorial boundaries of each national state; yet he consistently describes the historical dynamics of the world economy in terms of the differential positions of national states within its stratified core–periphery structure, rather than, for instance, with reference to firms, industries, circuits of capital, urban systems, or spatial divisions of labor. For Wallerstein, then, the economic division of labor is intrinsically composed of states; capitalist enterprises are in turn said to be 'domiciled' within their associated national state territories.[22] Wallerstein's conception of global space is thus most precisely described as an *inter-state* division of labor: national state territoriality serves as the basic geographical unit of the world economy; meanwhile global space is parcelized among three zonal patterns (core, semi-periphery, periphery) that are in turn said to be composed of nationally scaled territorial economies. National state territoriality and global space are thereby fused together into a seamless national-global scalar topography in which the interstate system and the world economy operate as a single, integrated system.[23]

In this sense, Wallerstein's concern to analyze the global scale as a distinctive unit of analysis does not lead to any qualitative modification in the way in which this space is conceptualized. In Wallerstein's framework, the primary geographical units of global space are defined by the territorial boundaries of national states, which in turn constitute a single, encompassing macro-territoriality, the world interstate system. The national scale is thereby blended into the global scale while the global scale is essentially flattened into its national components. As in the tale of the traveler Gulliver who encounters identical micro- and macro-scopic replications of human society, a society of midgets and a society of giants, the global and the national scales are viewed as structural analogs of a single spatial form—territoriality.[24] Thus conceived, the global scale simply multiplies national territoriality throughout a global

[21] In addition to the three volumes of *The Modern World-System*, see also the essays included in Wallerstein 1979, 1984.

[22] See e.g. Wallerstein 1984: 39, 27–36; 1983.

[23] It is not accurate, therefore, to reproach Wallerstein for reducing state power to economic structure (Skocpol 1977), because in his framework the latter are fundamentally identical.

[24] On this 'Gulliver fallacy', see R. B. J. Walker 1993: 133–40.

patchwork without modifying its essential geographical attributes. I would argue, therefore, that Wallerstein's approach to world-system analysis entails the replication of a territorialist model of space not only on the national scale of the territorial state but on the global scale of the entire world system.

Wallerstein's methodological fusion of the global and the national scales also leads to an interpretation of contemporary globalization primarily as a physical-geographical expansion of the capitalist system rather than as a rearticulation or transformation of the social, political, and economic spaces upon which it is based. To be sure, Wallerstein conceives global space as a complex historical product of capitalist expansion, but he acknowledges its historicity only in a limited sense, in contrast to previous historical systems such as world-empires. For, within the capitalist historical system, space appears to be frozen into a single geometric crystallization—'one economy, multiple states'—that cannot change qualitatively without dissolving capitalism's identity as a distinctive type of historical system. In Wallerstein's framework, each long wave of capitalist expansion is said to reproduce the structurally invariant geographical pattern upon which capitalism is grounded, a grid of nationally organized state territories linked through a core–periphery structure to a global division of labor. Paradoxically, then, Wallerstein's definition of the modern world-system as a global amalgamation of national spaces generates a fundamentally state-centric methodological consequence—namely, the assumption that a specifically capitalist form of globalization can unfold only among *nationally scaled* forms of political-economic organization. The possibility that the process of capitalist development might unhinge itself from this entrenched national-global scalar couplet to privilege other subnational or supranational sociospatial configurations is thereby excluded by definitional fiat.[25]

Two general methodological conclusions may be derived from this critical analysis of global territorialist approaches.

1. An emphasis on the global spatial scale does not necessarily lead to an overcoming of state-centric epistemologies. Global territorialist approaches represent global space in a state-centric manner, as a pregiven territorial container within which the process of globalization unfolds, rather than analyzing its historical production, reconfiguration, and transformation. As noted, one of the major deficiencies of state-centric modes of analysis is to conceive territorialization as a static condition rather than as an ongoing, dialectical process. Global territorialist approaches are premised upon the transposition of this state-centric misrecognition from the national to the global scale. The current round of global restructuring does indeed appear to be intensifying globally scaled forms of interaction and interdependence. However, global territorialist

---

[25] It should be emphasized, however, that these problems with Wallerstein's theory are not intrinsic to world-system analysis. For attempts to develop more historically specific analyses of capitalist spatiality within the broad parameters of a world-system methodology see e.g. Arrighi 1994; Taylor 1994, 1995.

approaches reify this emergent, contradictory tendency into an actualized, globally scaled territorial system and thus circumvent the key methodological task of analyzing global space as an historically constituted, polymorphic arena composed of multiple, superimposed spatial forms.

2. State-centric conceptions of global space mask the national state's own crucial role as a site and agent of global restructuring processes. The global territorialist approaches discussed above treat national state territoriality as a static institutional framework over and above which globalization occurs, and thereby bracket the profound transformations of state territorial and scalar organization that have played a crucial enabling role in the contemporary round of global restructuring. The persistence of state-centric epistemologies in globalization studies thus represents a major intellectual barrier to a more adequate understanding of currently emergent forms of national state territoriality and state scalar organization.

These arguments are summarized schematically in Fig. 2.3.

Main features	Two of the three key components of state-centric modes of analysis—spatial fetishism and methodological territorialism—are transposed from the national to the global scale
	Consequently: the global scale is analyzed (*a*) as a pregiven, unchanging arena for social relations; and/or (*b*) as a grid of national territorialities stretched onto the global scale
Prominent examples	• 'World society' approaches (Meyer 1999; Spybey 1996; Wapner 1995; Waters 1995)
	• Robertson's (1992) cultural sociology of globalization
	• Wallerstein's approach to world-system analysis (Wallerstein 1974, 1980, 1984, 1989)
Problems and limitations	Neglects to examine systematically (*a*) the historical constitution and continual transformation of the global scale as an arena of diverse social, economic, and political processes, or (*b*) the complex, continually changing interdependencies between global and subglobal relations
	Territoriality is conceived as the natural form in which sociospatial processes are organized; consequently, the polymorphic geographies of the global scale are described in a narrowly territorialist conceptual grammar
	Neglects to examine (*a*) the key role of national states in contemporary processes of global restructuring; and (*b*) the ways in which national states are in turn being reshaped through their role in animating and mediating these processes

Fig. 2.3. The epistemology of global territorialism: schematic overview

As suggested above, the contemporary round of global restructuring can be fruitfully conceived as a conflictual rearticulation of political-economic space on multiple, superimposed geographical scales. I shall now consider these sociospatial transformations more closely through a critical discussion of 'deterritorialization' approaches to globalization studies.

Jumping scales: between deterritorialization and reterritorialization

The question that remains open is whether territory loses its institutional role in general or whether we are just in one of the eras of rescaling of territorial resources, as in the transition from Habsburg to French power, or Dutch to British commercial strategies in the late seventeenth century, or from the province and the land to the national state and the metropolis after 1860.

Charles Maier (2000: 824–5)

As globalization intensifies it generates pressures towards a reterritorialization of socio-economic activity in the form of subnational, regional and supranational economic zones, mechanisms of governance and cultural complexes. It may also reinforce the 'localization' and 'nationalization' of societies. Accordingly, globalization involves a complex deterritorialization and reterritorialization of political and economic power.

David Held et al. (1999: 28)

In contrast to global territorialist approaches, analyses of deterritorialization confront explicitly the task of analyzing social spatiality in a historically specific manner. From this perspective, territoriality is viewed as a historically specific form of sociospatial organization that is being systematically decentered under contemporary conditions. New supraterritorial geographies of networks and flows are said to be supplanting the inherited geography of state territories that has long preoccupied the social-scientific imagination. Deterritorialization researchers have analyzed these emergent, purportedly post-territorial geographies as the outcomes of diverse causal processes, including the deployment of new informational, military, and transportation technologies; the internationalization of capital, monetary, and financial markets; the virtualization of economic activity through electronically mediated monetary transactions; the global crisis of territorialized definitions of state regulation and citizenship; the expanded activities of transnational organizations, including multinational corporations and NGOs; the intensified role of electronic media in organizing sociocultural identities; the proliferation of worldwide ecological problems; and the increasing density and velocity of transnational diasporic population movements (for an overview, see Scholte 2000).

In most research on deterritorialization, the spaces of globalization (based upon circulation, flows, and geographical mobility) and the spaces of territorialization (based upon enclosure, borders, and geographical fixity) are represented as mutually opposed systems of social interaction. Thus, for O'Brien (1992: 1–2), global financial integration has generated a situation in which 'geographical location no longer matters, or matters less than hitherto [...] Money ... will largely succeed in escaping the confines of the existing geography.' Likewise, in their widely discussed book, *Empire*, Hardt and Negri (2001: 336) speak of a 'general equalization or smoothing of social space' in which capital supersedes entrenched territorial borders and the power of national states is effectively dissolved. More generally, for Scholte (1996: 1968):

Global space is placeless, distanceless and borderless—and in this sense 'supraterritorial'. In global relations, people are connected with one another pretty much irrespective of their territorial position. To that extent they effectively do not have a territorial location, apart from the broad sense of being situated on the planet earth. Global relations thus form a non-, extra-, post-, supra-territorial aspect of the world system. In the global domain, territorial boundaries present no particular impediment and distance is covered in effectively no time.

This image of global space as a 'placeless, distanceless and borderless' realm is the geographical essence of deterritorialization approaches. From Castells' (1996) account of the 'space of flows', Jameson's (1992) theorization of 'postmodern hyperspace', Ruggie's (1993) interpretation of the EU as the world's 'first postmodern political form', and Appadurai's (1996) concept of 'ethnoscapes' to Scholte's (2000) conceptualization of globality as 'supraterritoriality', Ohmae's (1995) notion of a 'borderless world', O'Brien's (1992) thesis of an 'end of geography', and Hardt and Negri's (2001) notion of 'Empire', analyses of deterritorialization have generally been premised upon this basic conceptual opposition between the purportedly supraterritorial or deterritorialized spaces in which globalization occurs and diverse subglobal territories, localities, and places.[26]

The logical corollary of this conceptualization is the contention that globalization entails the decline, erosion, or disempowerment of the national state. Whereas global territorialist approaches map global space essentially as a territorial state writ large, studies of deterritorialization invert this territorialist epistemology to emphasize the increasing permeability or even total negation of national state territoriality. The decline of national state power is viewed at once as the medium and the result of contemporary processes of deterritorialization. On the one hand, the erosion of nationally scaled forms of territorial enclosure is said to open up a space for increasingly non-territorial forms of interaction and

---

[26] For still more extreme versions of the 'end of geography' thesis, see Der Derian 1990; Virilio 1984.

interdependence on a global scale. On the other hand, these globally scaled processes of deterritorialization are in turn said to accelerate the state's loss of control over its national borders and thus further to undermine its territorial self-enclosure. In this sense, the state decline thesis and the notion of deterritorialization entail cumulative, mutually reinforcing rather than merely additive, externally related conceptions of global sociospatial transformation. Global space can be viewed as non-territorial in form precisely because it is defined through the trope of an eroding or disappearing national scale. Meanwhile, the thesis of state decline is elaborated not through an account of the national scale per se, but rather with reference to the role of various globally scaled, purportedly supraterritorial and deterritorializing socioeconomic processes.

By emphasizing the historicity and potential malleability of territoriality, deterritorialization approaches have begun to articulate an important challenge to the epistemology of state-centrism. This methodological denaturalization of territoriality has also enabled deterritorialization researchers to construct alternative geographical categories for describing currently emergent sociospatial forms that do not presuppose their enclosure within territorially bounded spaces. Nevertheless, when examined through the lens of the conception of capitalist sociospatial configuration outlined above, deterritorialization approaches contain three serious deficiencies.

1. The historicity of territoriality is reduced to an either/or choice between two options, its presence or its absence. Consequently, the possibility that territoriality is being reconfigured and rescaled rather than eroded cannot be adequately explored.

2. The relation between global space and national territoriality is viewed as a zero-sum game in which the growing importance of the former is presumed necessarily to entail the decline of the latter. By conceiving geographical scales as mutually exclusive rather than as co-constitutive, relationally intertwined levels of social interaction, this dualistic conceptualization cannot adequately theorize the essential role of subglobal transformations—whether of supranational political-economic blocs, national state territories, regions, cities, localities, or places—in contemporary processes of global restructuring.

3. Most crucially for the argument of this book, deterritorialization approaches bracket the various forms of spatial fixity, spatial embedding, rescaling, and reterritorialization upon which global flows are premised. From this perspective, processes of deterritorialization are not delinked from territoriality; indeed, their very existence presupposes the production and continual reproduction of fixed socio-territorial infrastructures—including, in particular, urban-regional agglomerations and state regulatory institutions—within, upon, and through which global flows can circulate. Thus the apparent deterritorialization of social relations on a global scale hinges intrinsically upon their reterritorialization within relatively fixed and immobile sociospatial configurations at a variety of interlocking subglobal scales.

A major agenda of this book is to advance an interpretation of contemporary global restructuring as a rescaling of the nationally organized sociospatial configurations that have long served as the underlying geographical scaffolding for capitalist development. In the context of this ongoing scalar shift, processes of deterritorialization can be reinterpreted as concerted yet uncoordinated strategies to decenter the national scale of political-economic organization. If territoriality operates as a strategy grounded upon the enclosure of social relations within a bounded geographical space (Sack 1986), deterritorialization may be understood most coherently as a countervailing strategy to 'jump scales', that is, to circumvent or dismantle historically entrenched scalar hierarchies (Smith 1995). From this point of view, one of the most significant geographical consequences of contemporary processes of deterritorialization has been to unsettle and rearticulate the entrenched, nationally scaled configurations of political-economic organization upon which capitalist industrial growth has been grounded since at least the late nineteenth century. This denationalizing, scale-jumping strategy has also been closely intertwined with various conflictual forms of reterritorialization through which new subnational and supranational sociospatial configurations are being constructed. Crucially, however, the national territorial state—albeit now significantly rescaled and reterritorialized—has continued to serve as a crucial geographical infrastructure for this multiscalar dialectic of deterritorialization and reterritorialization. These arguments may be specified further through a critical reinterpretation of two commonly invoked forms of deterritorialization—the deterritorialization of capital; and the deterritorialization of the national state.

The rescaling of capital

The concept of deterritorialization was first developed in the early 1970s to describe the apparently footloose activities of transnational corporations in coordinating globally dispersed production networks (Agnew and Corbridge 1994). Since this period, the notion of deterritorialization has acquired a broader meaning to encompass as well the role of new information and communications technologies in linking geographically dispersed parts of the globe to create a temporally integrated world economy. The massive expansion in the role of transnational finance capital since the demise of the Bretton Woods currency controls in the early 1970s presents a further indication of capital's increasing velocity and geographical mobility in the world economy. Under these circumstances, the worldwide circulation of capital can no longer be analyzed adequately with reference to self-enclosed, discrete national economies or, more generally, on the basis of strictly territorial representations of space (Agnew 1994).

Nonetheless, no matter how rapidly turnover times are accelerated, the moment of territorialization still remains endemic to capital, a basic structural feature of its circulation process. Capital remains as dependent as ever upon relatively fixed, localized and territorially embedded technological-institutional ensembles in which technology, the means of production, forms of industrial organization and labor-power are productively combined to extract surplus value. For, as Yeung (1998: 291) succinctly remarks, capital is 'place-sticky'. The processes of deterritorialization associated with the current round of geoeconomic integration are best conceived as one moment within a broader dynamic of sociospatial transformation in which the reindustrialization of strategic subnational economic spaces—such as global cities, industrial districts, technopoles, offshore financial centers, and other flexible production complexes—has played a constitutive role.[27] These shifts have been closely intertwined with a marked rescaling of corporate accumulation strategies as key factions of industrial, financial, and service capital attempt to secure competitive advantages within global production chains through the exploitation of locally and regionally specific conditions of production (Swyngedouw 1992a). Although the growth of these urban and regional territorial production complexes has been crucially conditioned by national political-economic frameworks, a number of scholars have suggested that, due to these new forms of global localization, urbanized regions are today increasingly superseding national economies as the most rudimentary geographical units of world capitalism.[28] This pervasive rescaling of capital is illustrated schematically in Fig. 2.4.

The essential point here is that capital's drive to diminish its place-dependency does not, in practice, entail the construction of a quasi-autonomous, placeless, or distanceless space of flows, as writers such as Castells, Ohmae, Hardt and Negri, and many others have implied. We are witnessing, rather, a profoundly uneven rescaling and reterritorialization of the historically entrenched, state-centric geographical infrastructures that underpinned the last century of capitalist industrialization. From this point of view, scholarly representations of contemporary global capitalism as a 'smooth world' (Hardt and Negri 2001) or as a borderless 'space of flows' (Castells 1996) are grounded upon an uncritical appropriation of a neoliberal ideological myth. Such arguments, as Radice (1998: 274) remarks, amount to 'ideological cover for the policy preferences of big business'. In a forceful critique of Castells' recent writings, Smith (1996: 72) further elaborates this point:

Capital [...] may entertain the fantasy of spacelessness and act accordingly, but in practice, every strategy to avoid and supersede 'historically established mechanisms' [i.e. places] and territories of social control involves not the extinction of place per se but *the reinvention of place at a different scale*—a capital-centered jumping of scale. Indeed, the perpetuation of control by these organizations (and classes) depends precisely on this reinvention of discrete places where power over and through the space of flows is rooted.

---

[27] The literature on these 'post-Fordist' forms of urban and regional restructuring has expanded massively in recent decades. For useful recent overviews see e.g. A. Amin 1994; Lipietz 1993; and Storper 1996.

[28] See e.g. Benko and Lipietz 2002; Scott 1998; Scott and Storper 1992; and S. Krätke 1995.

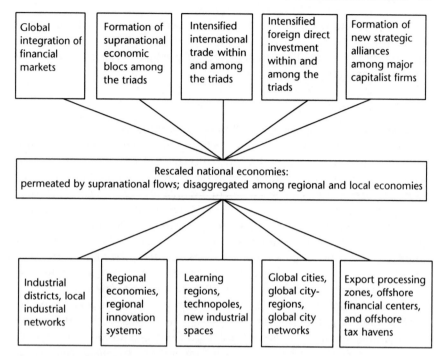

Fig. 2.4. Rescaling the geographies of capital
Source: derived from Swyngedouw 2000*b*: 548.

Deterritorialization must therefore be viewed as a distinctively geographical accumulation strategy, as a mechanism of global localization through which major capitalist firms are attempting to circumvent or restructure the nationally organized systems of social, monetary, and labor regulation that prevailed under the Fordist-Keynesian regime of accumulation (Swyngedouw 1992*a*).

To be sure, capitalist strategies of deterritorialization may well succeed in partially circumventing the constraints imposed by national territorial boundaries. But, even when successful, such strategies do not translate into a situation of pure capital hypermobility or placelessness. As capital strives to jump scale, it is forced to reconstitute or create anew viable sociospatial infrastructures for its circulation process at other scales—whether through the reorganization of existent scales or through the construction of qualitatively new ones. In this sense, capital's apparent transcendence of nationally scaled regulatory systems in recent decades has been inextricably bound up with the production of new subnational and supranational spaces of accumulation and state regulation that provide the place- and territory-specific conditions for accumulation (K. Cox 1997). Thus, rather than releasing capital from its endemic dependence upon places, cities, regions, and territories, the current round of geoeconomic integration has hinged upon 'a change in the scale at which spatial divisions of labor are organized' (K. Cox 1992: 428). The drive towards deterritorialization incessantly reinscribes the role of capitalist sociospatial configurations while, at the same time, reconfiguring their scalar architecture in pursuit of locationally specific productive capacities and competitive advantages.

Rescaling the state

As noted, accounts of deterritorialization conceptualize the emergence of global space through the trope of a declining or eroding state territoriality. The current round of geoeconomic integration has indeed rendered states more permeable to transnational flows of capital, money, commodities, labor, and information. However, this development has not entailed the demise, erosion, or weakening of the state as such. Instead, there has been a significant functional, institutional, and geographical reorganization of statehood at a range of spatial scales. While these trends have unsettled the nationalized formations of statehood that have long preoccupied social scientists, they have not undermined the centrality of state institutions—albeit now significantly reterritorialized and rescaled—to processes of political-economic regulation.

During the global economic crises of the 1970s, traditional Keynesian macroeconomic policy instruments proved increasingly ineffectual across much of the older industrialized world. Under these conditions, the national states of the OECD zone began to restructure or dismantle major elements of the postwar Fordist-Keynesian regulatory order, such as national social welfare regimes, nationally organized collective bargaining arrangements, and national monetary frameworks (Jessop 1993). Among other major policy realignments, a range of supply-side regulatory strategies were deployed in order to facilitate industrial restructuring and to encourage flexibility and technological innovation within each state's territorial economy.[29] At this time, as Yeung (1998: 296–9) indicates, national states began actively to facilitate the process of geoeconomic integration through a variety of policy strategies—by constructing and enforcing the (global and national) legal regimes within which global capital operates; by providing key domestic conditions for the global operations of transnational corporations; by acquiring large shares or full ownership of major home-country based transnational corporations; by establishing territory-specific regulatory conditions for global capital investment; by establishing new supranational or global forms of economic governance; and by controlling key conditions for the reproduction of labor-power within their territorial borders. Consequently, the widely prevalent 'myth of the powerless state' (Weiss 1998) represents a misleading basis for the understanding of contemporary political dynamics: the state is not a helpless victim of globalization but one of its major politico-institutional catalysts. As Panitch (1994: 64) explains:

[29] On these policy reorientations and their longer-term institutional consequences, see, among other works, Jessop 1993; Helleiner 1994; Panitch 1994; Radice 1999; Sassen 1996; and Weiss 2003.

capitalist globalisation is a process which also takes place in, through and under the aegis of states; it is encoded by them and in important respects even authored by them; and it involves a shift in power relations within states that often means the centralisation and concentration of state powers as the necessary condition of and accompaniment to global market discipline.

Since the 1980s, throughout the OECD zone, global economic criteria have acquired an enhanced significance in the formulation and implementation of national state policies. This transformation has been famously described by R. Cox (1987: 260) as an 'internationalization of the state' in which 'adjustment to global competitiveness [has become] the new categorical imperative'. In a similar vein, Cerny (1995) has examined the consolidation of post-Keynesian 'competition states' whose central priority is to create a favorable investment climate for transnational capital within their boundaries. According to Cerny (1995: 620), as the mobilization of territorial competitiveness policies becomes an increasingly important priority for dominant actors and alliances across the political spectrum, 'the state itself becomes an agent for the commodification of the collective, situated in a wider, market-dominated playing field'. These realignments of state power in turn generate a 'whipsaw effect' in which each level of the state must react to a wide range of competitive forces, political pressures, and institutional constraints operating both within and beyond its boundaries (Cerny 1995: 618). A central geographical consequence of this development, Cerny (1995: 620–1) proposes, has been the establishment of new 'plurilateral' forms of state power that do not converge upon any single, optimal scale or coalesce together within an internally cohesive, nationally scaled bureaucratic hierarchy.

As we shall explore at length in subsequent chapters, the consolidation of post-Keynesian competition states in contemporary western Europe has indeed been closely intertwined with fundamental, if often rather haphazard, transformations of state spatial and scalar organization. These ongoing reterritorializations and rescalings of state space cannot be understood merely as defensive responses to intensified global economic competition, but represent expressions of concerted political strategies through which state institutions are attempting, at various spatial scales, to facilitate, manage, mediate, and redirect processes of geoeconomic restructuring. On a continental scale, states have promoted geoeconomic integration by forming supranational economic blocs such as the EU, NAFTA, ASEAN, and the like, which are intended at once to enhance structural competitiveness, to facilitate capital mobility within new continental zones of accumulation, and to provide protective barriers against the pressures of global economic competition (Larner and Walters 2002; Mittelman 2000). Supranational agencies such as the IMF, the WTO, and the World Bank have likewise acquired key roles in enforcing neoliberal, market-led strategies of political-economic restructuring throughout the world system (Gill 1998a; Peet 2003). At the same time, even as national states attempt to fracture or dismantle the institutional compromises of postwar Fordist-Keynesian capitalism in order to reduce domestic production costs, they have also devolved substantial regulatory responsibilities to regional and local institutions, which are seen to be better positioned to promote industrial (re)development within major urban and regional economies. This downscaling of regulatory tasks should not be viewed as a contraction or abdication of national state power, however, for it has frequently served as a centrally orchestrated strategy to promote transnational capital investment within major urban regions, whether through the public funding of large-scale infrastructural projects, the mobilization of localized economic development policies, the establishment of new forms of public–private partnership or other public initiatives intended to enhance urban territorial competitiveness (see Ch. 5). Figure 2.5 provides an initial, schematic representation of the rescaled landscape of statehood that has been forged through these transformations.

In subsequent chapters, I shall interpret the current wave of state rescaling within western European urban regions as an expression, medium, and outcome of diverse political strategies designed to enhance the place- and territory-specific competitive advantages of particular subnational political jurisdictions.

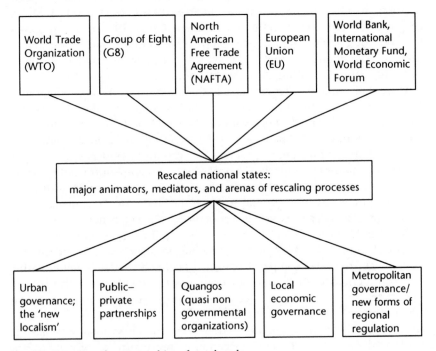

Fig. 2.5. Rescaling the geographies of statehood

Source: derived from Swyngedouw 2000*b*: 548.

In the present context, the key point is that these ongoing transformations of state institutional and spatial organization do not herald the end of territoriality as such, as deterritorialization theorists contend. We are witnessing, rather, the consolidation of increasingly polymorphic, reterritorialized political geographies in which territoriality is redifferentiated among multiple institutional levels that are no longer clustered around a single predominant center of gravity. Whereas the traditional Westphalian image of political space as a self-enclosed geographical container does today appear to have become increasingly obsolete, territoriality nevertheless remains a fundamental characteristic of statehood and an essential institutional scaffolding for the process of political-economic regulation at all spatial scales (Nevins 2002; D. Newman and Paasi 1998). As Fig. 2.5 illustrates, territoriality is no longer organized predominantly or exclusively on the national scale, for subnational and supranational levels of sociospatial organization have today come to play essential roles in processes of political-economic regulation. Under these circumstances, as Anderson (1996: 151) argues, new geographical metaphors are needed in order to grasp the structural features and dynamics of emergent, post-Westphalian political geographies:

There may sometimes be a linear chain of command between institutions—or parts of institutions—at different levels, but in general such a linear model (like a Russian dolls metaphor of nested hierarchies) does not fit the complex reality. The contemporary world is not a ladder up or down which processes move from one rung to the next in an orderly fashion, the central state mediating all links between the external or higher levels and the internal or lower ones. That was never the case, but it is even less true today. Not only are there now more rungs but qualitatively they are more heterogeneous; and direct movements between high and low levels, missing out or bypassing 'intermediate' rungs, are now a defining characteristic of contemporary life. A complex set of climbing frames, slides, swings, ropes and rope ladders, complete with weak or broken parts [. . .] might be nearer the mark. The metaphor of adventure playgrounds, with their mixture of constructions, multiple levels and encouragement of movement— up, down, sideways, diagonally, directly from high to low, or low to high—captures the contemporary mixture of forms and processes much better than the ladder metaphor.

In subsequent chapters, I shall devote detailed attention to the many challenges of theorizing and analyzing such post-Westphalian political spaces, above all at subnational scales. As we shall see, large-scale urban regions represent crucial geographical, institutional, and political arenas in which the rescaled geographies of statehood under contemporary capitalism are being forged and contested.

By indicating the ways in which a historically entrenched form of national state territoriality is being superseded, deterritorialization researchers have made an important contribution to the project of theorizing social space in an explicitly historical manner. However, because they recognize the historicity of territoriality primarily in terms of its disappearance, obsolescence, or demise, deterritorialization approaches cannot analyze the types of qualitative reconfigurations and rescalings of territoriality that have been briefly outlined above. Even if the role of the national scale as an autocentric territorial container has been unsettled, national states continue to play a key role in producing the geographical infrastructures upon which the process of capital circulation depends and in regulating political-economic life at all spatial scales. The reterritorialization and rescaling of inherited, nationally organized institutional forms and policy relays represents an important political strategy through which national states are attempting to adjust to, and to (re)assert control over, a rapidly changing geoeconomic context. Figure 2.6 provides a schematic summary of the preceding critique of deterritorialization approaches to globalization studies.

Conclusion: rethinking the geographies of globalization

Like the forms of state-centrism that have dominated the social sciences for much of the last century, the methodological opposition between global territorialist and deterritorialization approaches to globalization studies can be viewed as a real abstraction of contemporary social practices. Throughout this discussion, I have argued that each of these approaches grasps real dimensions of contemporary social reality, albeit in a truncated, one-sided manner. As noted, capital has long presupposed a moment of territorial fixity or place-boundedness as a basic prerequisite for its ever-expanding circulation process. Whereas state-centric epistemologies fetishize this territorialist moment of capitalism, deterritorialization approaches embrace an inverse position, in which territoriality is said to erode or disappear as globalization intensifies. The bifurcation of contemporary globalization studies into these opposed methodological approaches reflects these contradictory aspects of contemporary sociospatial transformations without critically explaining them.

The alternative theorization of global restructuring introduced in this chapter suggests that deterritorialization and reterritorialization are mutually constitutive, if highly conflictual, moments of an ongoing dialectic through which political-economic space is continually produced, reconfigured, and transformed under capitalism. Thus conceived, the contemporary round of global restructuring has entailed neither the absolute territorialization of societies, economies, or cultures onto a global scale, nor their complete deterritorialization into a supraterritorial, distanceless, placeless, or borderless space of flows. What is occurring, rather, is a multiscalar restructuring of capitalist sociospatial configurations, coupled with a reshuffling of entrenched hierarchies of scalar organization, leading in turn to qualitatively new geographies of capital accumulation, state regulation, and uneven development. In my view, a crucial challenge for future research on the geographies of global capitalism is

Main features	Territoriality is said to be declining, eroding, or disappearing as placeless, distanceless, and supraterritorial geographies of networks and flows proliferate throughout the world system
	Consequently: the capacity of national states to regulate their territorial jurisdictions is said to be weakening or eroding
Prominent examples	• Appadurai's (1996) theory of global cultural flows
	• Castells's (1996) theory of the 'space of flows'
	• Hardt and Negri's (2001) concept of 'Empire'
	• Jameson (1992) on 'postmodern hyperspace'
	• Ohmae's (1990, 1995) notion of the 'borderless world'
	• O'Brien's (1991) conception of the 'end of geography'
	• Ruggie's (1993) analysis of the EU as a 'nonterritorial region'
	• Scholte's (2000) theory of 'supraterritoriality' (but he explicitly rejects the thesis of state decline)
Major accomplishments	In contrast to methodologically territorialist approaches, the historicity and potential malleability of territoriality are emphasized
	Introduces alternative geographical categories for describing currently emergent spatial forms that do not presuppose their enclosure within territorially bounded geographical spaces
Problems and limitations	The historicity of territoriality is reduced to an either/or choice between two options, its presence or its absence; thus the possibility that territoriality is being reconfigured, reterritorialized, and rescaled rather than being eroded cannot be adequately explored
	The relation between global space and national territoriality is viewed as a zero-sum game in which the growing importance of the former necessarily entails the decline of the latter; consequently, the role of subglobal transformations (for instance, of national states, regions, and cities) in processes of global restructuring cannot be examined
	Brackets the various forms of spatial fixity, embedding, and (re)territorialization—particularly at national, regional, and local scales—upon which global flows are necessarily premised

Fig 2.6. The epistemology of deterritorialization approaches: schematic overview

to develop an epistemology of social space that can critically grasp these processes of deterritorialization and reterritorialization as intrinsically related dimensions of contemporary sociospatial transformations, as well as their variegated, path-dependent consequences in specific political-economic contexts. This chapter has attempted to outline some methodological foundations for confronting this task.

At the most general level, I have suggested that the contemporary round of global capitalist restructuring has destabilized the entrenched, nation state-centric geographical assumptions that have underpinned the social sciences throughout most of the twentieth century. It is for this reason, I believe, that contemporary debates on globalization have induced many scholars to develop more reflexive, dynamic, and historically specific understandings of social spatiality. The preceding discussion of these debates underscores four particularly crucial methodological challenges for contemporary studies of global sociospatial restructuring.

1. *The historicity of social space.* The contemporary round of global restructuring has put into relief the distinctive, historically specific character of national state territoriality as a form of sociospatial organization. As the primacy of national state territoriality has been decentered and relativized, the historical, and therefore malleable, character of inherited formations of political-economic space has become dramatically evident both in sociological analysis and in everyday life. The overarching methodological challenge that flows from this circumstance is to analyze social spatiality, at all scales, as an ongoing historical *process* in which the geographies of social relations are continually molded, reconfigured, and transformed (Lefebvre 1991).

2. *Polymorphic geographies.* National state territoriality is today being intertwined with, and superimposed upon, an immense variety of emergent sociospatial forms—from the supranational institutional structures of the EU to global financial flows, new forms of transnational corporate organization, post-Fordist patterns of industrial agglomeration, global interurban networks, and transnational diasporic communities—that cannot be described adequately as contiguous, mutually exclusive, and self-enclosed blocks of territorial space. Under these circumstances, the image of political-economic space as a complex, tangled mosaic of superimposed and interpenetrating nodes, levels, scales, and morphologies has become more appropriate than the traditional Cartesian model of homogenous, self-enclosed and contiguous blocks of territory that has long been used to describe the modern interstate system (Lefebvre 1991: 87–8). New representations of sociospatial form are urgently needed in order to analyze these newly emergent polymorphic, polycentric, and multiscalar geographies of global social change.[30] A crucial methodological challenge for contemporary sociospatial research is therefore to analyze newly emergent geographies in ways that transcend the conventional imperative to choose between purely territorialist and deterritorialized mappings of political-economic space.

---

[30] For important recent inroads into this task, see A. Amin 2002; Dicken et al. 2001; Graham 1997; Graham and Marvin 2001; Larner and Walters 2002; Leitner 2004; and Sheppard 2002.

3. *The new political economy of scale.* The current round of global restructuring has significantly decentered the national scale of political-economic life and intensified the importance of both subnational and supranational scales of sociospatial organization. These transformations undermine inherited conceptions of geographical scale as a static, fixed, and nested hierarchy and reveal its socially produced, historically variegated, and politically contested character. From this perspective, geographical scales must be viewed not only as the products of political-economic processes, but also as their presupposition and their medium (Smith 1995). Scalar arrangements are thus never fixed in stone but evolve continuously in conjunction with the dynamics of capital accumulation, state regulation, social reproduction, and sociopolitical struggle. Under these conditions, a key methodological challenge is to conceptualize geographical scales at once as an institutional scaffolding within which the dialectic of deterritorialization and reterritorialization unfolds and as an incessantly changing medium and outcome of that dialectic (Brenner 1998a).

4. *The remaking of state space.* Finally, this discussion has emphasized the key role of national states in promoting and mediating contemporary sociospatial transformations, and concomitantly, the ways in which national states have in turn been reorganized—functionally, institutionally, and geographically—in conjunction with this role. Contemporary state institutions are being significantly rescaled at once upwards, downwards, and outwards to create qualitatively new, polymorphic, plurilateral institutional geographies that no longer overlap evenly with one another, converge upon a single, dominant geographical scale or constitute a single, nested organizational hierarchy. These developments undermine traditional, Westphalian models of statehood as an unchanging, self-enclosed national-territorial container and suggest that more complex, polymorphic, and multiscalar regulatory geographies are emerging than previously existed. Under these conditions, an important methodological challenge is to develop a spatially attuned and scale-sensitive approach to state theory that can grasp not only the variegated regulatory geographies associated with inherited, nationalized formations of political space, but also the profoundly uneven reterritorializations and rescalings of statehood that are currently unfolding throughout the world system.

Subsequent chapters of this book confront the aforementioned methodological challenges in the context of a postdisciplinary investigation of political-economic, institutional, and sociospatial change in contemporary western Europe. These challenges are complementary insofar as addressing any one of them also opens up new methodological and empirical perspectives through which to confront the others. However, given my overarching concern in this book with transformations of state space, it is the fourth methodological challenge that occupies center stage in subsequent chapters. I shall thus grapple with each of the first three methodological challenges through a more direct confrontation with the task of deciphering contemporary processes of state spatial restructuring. Accordingly, building upon the approach to sociospatial theory introduced above, the next chapter elaborates the theoretical foundations for a spatialized, scale-sensitive approach to state theory.

THREE

The State Spatial Process under Capitalism: A Framework for Analysis

There is never a point when *the* state is finally built within a given territory and thereafter operates, so to speak, on automatic pilot according to its own definite, fixed and inevitable laws [...] Whether, how and to what extent one can talk in definite terms about the state actually depends on the contingent and provisional outcome of struggles to realize more or less specific 'state projects'.

Bob Jessop (1990*a*: 9)

Curiously, space is a stranger to customary political reflection [...] Space belongs to the geographers in the academic division of labor. Then it reintroduces itself subversively through the effects of the peripheries, the margins, the regions, the villages and local communities long abandoned, neglected, abased through state concentration [...] In the conception proposed here, the [social] *relations have social space for support*...This entails a *spatialization* of political theory, including a critique of deterritorialized abstractions which, at the same time, takes into account localities and regions [...] This entails as well a reconsideration of the economy in terms of space, of the flux of stocks, of mobile elements and stable elements, in short, of the production and reproduction of space.

Henri Lefebvre (1978: 164–5; emphasis in original)

State theory beyond the territorial trap?

State theorists and political geographers have long emphasized the specifically territorial character of political power in the modern world. Within the Westphalian geopolitical order, states are said to be composed of self-enclosed, contiguous, and mutually exclusive territorial spaces that separate an 'inside' (the realm of political order and citizenship) from an 'outside' (a realm of inter-state violence and anarchy) (R. B. J. Walker 1993). For the most part, however, even while being acknowledged as an underlying feature of modern geopolitical organization, territoriality has been treated within mainstream social science as a relatively fixed, unproblematic, and inconsequential property of statehood. Just as a fish is unlikely to discover water, most postwar social scientists viewed national state territories as pregiven natural environments for sociopolitical life (Taylor 1994: 157). Indeed, most scholars of modern politics and society have long embraced each of the state-centric geographical assumptions that were critically discussed in the previous chapter—spatial fetishism; methodological territorialism; and methodological nationalism. Consequently, in Agnew's (1994) memorable phrase, a 'territorial trap' has underpinned mainstream approaches to social science insofar as they have conceived state territoriality as a static background structure for regulatory processes and sociopolitical struggles rather than as one of their constitutive dimensions.

Such assumptions had some measure of epistemological plausibility during the Fordist-Keynesian period, in which a historically unprecedented territorial enclosure of political-economic space was attempted (Lipietz 1994). Today, however, they have become major intellectual barriers to a more adequate conceptualization of ongoing sociospatial transformations. For, in the context of contemporary debates on globalization, state-centric geographical assumptions have underpinned the unhelpful polarization of positions between proponents of the view that national states remain fully sovereign territorial power-containers and those who contend that state regulatory capacities are being eroded (see Ch. 2 above). Whereas the first position is generally grounded upon a static understanding of state territoriality as a fixed, unchanging grid of national borders, the second position can envision state restructuring only as a process of contraction or disappearance in which territoriality is being rendered obsolete. This debate narrows the conceptualization of state territoriality to two equally limiting possibilities—its presence or its absence—and thus precludes a more contextually sensitive investigation of *processes* of state spatial restructuring.

During the last decade, these entrenched methodological assumptions have been called into question, particularly by scholars working in the interstices of established disciplinary divisions of labor. As many analysts within this heterodox strand of social science have noted, the global political-economic transformations of the post-1970s period have reconfigured the Westphalian formation of state territoriality (*a*) by decentering the national scale of state regulatory activity and (*b*) by undermining the internal coherence of national economies and national civil societies. Under these conditions, the apparently ossified fixity of long-established, nationally organized formations of state territoriality has been thrust dramatically into historical motion. Contemporary scholars are thus confronted with the daunting but exciting task of developing new categories and methods through which to decipher these emergent, post-Westphalian landscapes of statehood.

Much of the new research on state spatiality can be situated within a broader body of critical social science concerned to counter neoliberal globalization narratives by emphasizing the essential role of state institutions in promoting market-based regulatory reform throughout the world economy. Thus, among the many arguments that have been advanced regarding the emergent institutional architectures of post-Keynesian states, contemporary discussions of state spatial restructuring are distinguished above all by their emphasis on the qualitatively new geographical scales and territorial contours of statecraft that have been crystallizing in recent decades. This ongoing reconceptualization of state space has been extraordinarily multifaceted, both methodologically and thematically, but it has thus far focused upon at least three intertwined axes of state spatial restructuring.

1. *State reterritorialization.* The meaning, organization, and functions of state territoriality are being reexamined in the context of debates on neomedievalism, perforated sovereignties, the internationalization of statehood, and the increased importance of dematerialized, flow-based economic transactions under globalizing capitalism. Territoriality is thus no longer viewed as a pre-given, self-enclosed platform for political relations, but is now being analyzed as a historically specific strategy of spatial enclosure and as an evolving, multi-scalar institutional configuration (Kobrin 1998; Ruggie 1993; D. Newman 1999).

2. *State rebordering.* The changing roles of state boundaries in the new geopolitical order are being systematically explored with reference to issues such as economic governance, citizenship, immigration, cross-border regions, military violence, and politico-cultural identities. Boundaries are thus no longer viewed as exclusively national demarcators of state sovereignty but are now understood as multifaceted semiotic, symbolic, and political-economic practices through which state power is articulated and contested (Newman and Paasi 1998; MacMillan and Linklater 1995; Perkmann and Sum 2002).

3. *State rescaling.* In contrast to the earlier fetishization of the national scale of political power, scholars have begun to analyze a range of rescaling processes through which new, multiscalar hierarchies of state institutional organization, political authority, and regulatory conflict are being generated. The scalar organization of state power is thus no longer understood as a permanently fixed background structure, but is now viewed as a constitutive, contested, and therefore potentially malleable dimension of political-economic processes (Swyngedouw 1997; Smith 1995; Boyer and Hollingsworth 1997).

At the present time, our understanding of the new state spaces that are currently emerging remains relatively rudimentary. Nonetheless, recent contributions to this multidisciplinary literature have clearly illuminated the historically constructed and politically contested character of state spatiality, thereby opening up a number of productive methodological and empirical starting points through which the changing geographies of contemporary statehood may be explored more systematically.[1]

Despite these accomplishments, much recent work on the production of new state spaces has proceeded without an explicit theoretical foundation. In many contributions to this literature, the geographical dimensions of state power are treated in descriptive terms, as merely one among many aspects of statehood that are currently undergoing systemic changes. Relatedly, the causal forces underlying contemporary processes of state spatial restructuring are often not explicitly specified. Yet, given the tumultuous political-geographical transformations that have been unfolding during the last three decades, there is arguably an increasingly urgent need for more systematic theoretical reflection on the nature and dynamics of state spatiality. Of particular importance, in this context, is a sustained inquiry into the conditions under which inherited geographies of state space may be transformed from relatively fixed, stabilized *settings* in which state regulatory operations occur into potentially malleable *stakes* of sociopolitical contestation. Concomitantly, there is an equally urgent need for a more explicit theoretical conceptualization of the determinate social, political, and economic processes through which transformations of state space unfold.

The present chapter confronts these tasks in a series of intertwined steps. My overarching goal is to elaborate the theoretical foundations for the analysis of state rescaling and urban governance restructuring that will be developed in subsequent chapters. The next section introduces some initial methodological premises and categories through which the geographies of state space under modern capitalism may be analyzed. On this basis, I demonstrate how the issues of spatiality, territoriality, and geographical scale may be integrated, at a foundational level, into the conceptualization of modern statehood. Building upon the strategic-relational approach to state theory developed by Jessop (1990a), I argue that state space is best conceptualized as an arena, medium, and outcome of spatially selective political strategies. I then extend this conceptualization by outlining some of the broad institutional and geographical parameters within which state space has evolved during the course of capitalist development. This line of analysis generates a multidimensional conceptual framework through which to investigate contextually specific pathways of state spatial restructuring. It also enables me to introduce a stylized model of state spatial restructuring in western Europe since the early 1960s, that serves to demarcate the theoretical and empirical terrain on which the remainder of this book is situated.

---

[1] For recent overviews of these emerging lines of research see, among other works, Brenner et al. 2003a; Blomley, Delaney, and Ford 2001; Albert, Jacobson, and Lapid 2001; Ferguson and Jones 2002; and Peck 2003, 2001a.

Methodological preliminaries: spatial process, spatial form, and spatial scale

> Is not the secret of the State, hidden because it is so obvious, to be found in space?
>
> Henri Lefebvre (2003a: 87)

Prior to the current renaissance of spatially attuned approaches to state theory, classical political geographers had already introduced a number of descriptive categories through which to map the spatial contours of state operations and political life. Some scholars addressed the issues of territoriality, borders, core/periphery structures, geopolitics, and war-making; others focused on various aspects of the state's internal spatial structure, such as federalism, administrative differentiation, gerrymandering, metropolitan jurisdictional fragmentation, and territorial politics (for overviews see Taylor 2003, 1993). By acknowledging the socially constructed and politically contested character of political jurisdictions at a variety of scales, certain strands of this literature managed at least partially to circumvent the territorial trap of state-centrism even during its historical highpoint under Fordist-Keynesian capitalism. However, classical approaches to political geography contained a number of major theoretical deficiencies, including (depending on the context) an excessively physicalist and deterministic conception of geographical influence, an excessive reliance upon biological or organic metaphors, a pervasive functionalism, a naturalization of liberal democracy as a political form, and a bracketing of the broader geoeconomic contexts of state activities (Taylor 1993).

It is only during the last thirty years, in conjunction with the intensified interest in critical social theory and radical political economy among human geographers and other spatially attuned scholars (Gregory and Urry 1985), that the geographies of state power have been analyzed in a more contextually specific manner and related explicitly to the historical dynamics of capitalist development. The key concern, from this point of view, has been to analyze 'the historical relationship between territorial states and the broader social and economic structures and geopolitical orders (or forms of spatial practice) in which these states must operate' (Agnew and Corbridge 1994: 100). Additionally, contributors to the new literature on the political geographies of statehood have investigated the role of state spatial arrangements in mediating, reproducing, and solidifying everyday power relations at a variety of geographical scales.

As argued in the previous chapter, state-centrism entails the freezing of political-economic life within reified, national-territorial structures that are presumed to defy historical change. Consequently, state-centric assumptions generate a systemic blindness to the possibility of major ruptures within inherited formations of sociospatial organization. Such assumptions are deeply problematic, not only as a basis for the investigation of contemporary sociospatial transformations, but also as a means for analyzing the changing geographies of state institutions themselves, whether in historical or contemporary contexts. Therefore, in contrast to the spatial fetishism, methodological territorialism, and methodological nationalism that continue to pervade mainstream social science, the present analysis begins from a radically different theoretical starting point. For my purposes here, state space is conceptualized (*a*) as an ongoing *process* of change rather than as a static thing, container, or platform; (*b*) as having a *polymorphic* rather than a merely territorial geographical form; and (*c*) as having a *multiscalar* rather than merely a national organizational structure (Fig. 3.1).

The goal of this section is to add some preliminary descriptive content to these opening propositions. I shall then explicate their theoretical foundations in greater detail and outline some of their substantive implications.

STATE-CENTRIC ASSUMPTION	CRITICAL ALTERNATIVE
Spatial fetishism • State space is viewed as timeless and static, and thus as immune to the possibility of systemic change	**A processual conceptualization of state space . . .** • State space is conceived as an ongoing process of political-economic regulation and institutional change
Methodological territorialism • State territoriality is viewed as an unchanging, fixed, or permanent aspect of modern statehood; • The geography of state space is reduced to its territorial dimensions	**emphasizing its polymorphic geographies . . .** • The geographies of statehood are conceived as polymorphic, multifaceted, and continually evolving; • Territoriality is viewed as one among many geographical dimensions of state space
Methodological nationalism • The national scale is viewed, in ontological terms, as the logically primary level of political power in the modern interstate system	**at a multiplicity of spatial scales** • State regulation and political struggle are said to unfold at a variety of intertwined spatial scales; • State scalar organization and scalar divisions of state regulation are said to evolve historically and, on occasion, to be significantly restructured

Fig. 3.1. Beyond state-centric approaches to the study of state space

The state spatial process: a first cut

In what sense is state spatiality a process rather than a container, a platform, or a thing? Since the seminal contributions of radical urbanists such as Lefebvre (1991 [1974]), Harvey (1973), Castells (1977 [1972]), and Soja (1980) over two decades ago, processual approaches to the production of social spatiality have been mobilized extensively in the field of critical urban and regional studies (Gottdiener 1985; Soja 2000). Surprisingly, the methodological insights of critical urban researchers and other geographically inclined social scientists have had only a minimal impact upon the fields of state theory and political sociology. I would argue, nonetheless, that the conceptualizations of socio-spatial dynamics that were developed in these pioneering analyses of urban spatiality may be fruitfully mobilized to investigate the production and transformation of state spatiality as well.[2]

Much like the term 'city', the term 'state' ostensibly connotes a fixed, thing-like entity—in this case, a closed institutional system that occupies a bordered geographical territory, as represented in the colors allotted to each country on a world map. Yet, as theorists of dialectics have argued (Ollman 1993; Harvey 1996), a reification of processes of change is entrenched within the conceptual grammar of mainstream social science, leading scholars to presume unreflexively the existence of stasis, fixity, and continuity even in the face of compelling evidence of flux, fluidity, and transformation. Along with other foundational sociological concepts such as economy, society, and culture, the notions of the city and the state are arguably among the paradigmatic exemplars of this pervasive reification of sociospatial dynamics within the modern social sciences.

Over two decades ago, radical urban scholars began to break out of these intellectual constraints by introducing more dialectical, processual concepts for describing the contemporary city—for instance, *urbanization* or, in Harvey's (1978) more precise terminology, the *urban process*. Against traditional approaches to urban locational analysis, which conceived space in Euclidian-Cartesian terms, as a flat surface upon which economic activity is extended, Harvey introduced a more dynamic, historically specific view. For Harvey, the urban must be understood simultaneously as a presupposition, a medium, and an outcome of the conflictual, continually changing social relations of capitalism. From this perspective, any historical configuration of urban spatiality represents a sedimented crystallization of earlier patterns of social interaction and an evolving grid of possibilities for, and constraints upon, future social relations.

---

[2] Henri Lefebvre is one of the few sociospatial theorists to have analyzed systematically both the production of urban space *and* the production of state space. While Lefebvre's writings on cities are now quite well known among Anglo-American urbanists (see e.g. Lefebvre 2003b, 1996), his major writings on the state have not been extensively translated and thus remain relatively obscure among English-language readers (see Lefebvre 1978, 1977, 1976a, b). Recent, abridged translations of key state-theoretical writings include Lefebvre 2003a, 2003c, 2001. For interpretations and commentaries, see Elden 2004; Brenner 2001c, 1998a, 1997a, b.

A directly analogous methodological strategy can, I propose, be developed in order to conceptualize the *state spatial process* under capitalism. Much like the geography of the city, the geography of state spatiality must be viewed as a presupposition, an arena, and an outcome of continually evolving political strategies. It is not a thing, container, or platform, but a socially produced, conflictual, and dynamically changing matrix of sociospatial interaction. The spaces of state power are not simply 'filled', as if they were pregiven territorial containers. Instead, state spatiality is actively produced and transformed through regulatory projects and sociopolitical struggles articulated in diverse institutional sites and at a range of geographical scales. Therefore, the traditional Westphalian image of states as being located within static, self-contained territorial arenas must be replaced by a dialectical, processual analysis of how historically specific configurations of state space are produced and incessantly reworked.

This proposition can be illustrated most directly with reference to the phenomenon of state territoriality, the dimension of political space which, as discussed in the preceding chapter, has been acknowledged and analyzed most explicitly in twentieth-century social science. The entrenched legacy of Euclidian/Cartesian geographical approaches to territoriality is epitomized in Weber's (1946) approach to political sociology, in which self-enclosed territorial borders were included as one of the essential definitional features of modern political organization. While Weber was highly sensitive to the historical specificity of modern state territoriality relative to premodern political geographies, he was considerably less interested in its evolution *within* the modern interstate system. Accordingly, in his major writings on political sociology, Weber reduced the issue to a point on a definitional checklist that could be presupposed relatively unproblematically in any discussion of modern bureaucratic states. This treatment of territoriality as a pregiven, fixed, unchanging, and thus relatively transparent feature of modern statehood has been reproduced unreflexively in most twentieth-century approaches to statehood, from theories of liberal democracy and realist approaches to international relations theory to major strands of development studies, mainstream analyses of social policy, and traditional Marxist debates on the relative autonomy of the state.[3]

While not empirically false, the Weberian definitional insight must be resituated within a more dialectical, historically specific conceptual framework. For, even following the historical-geographical watershed associated with the Treaty of Westphalia, in which the principle of state territorial sovereignty was first institutionalized (Spruyt 1994; Ruggie 1993), borders have never been static, pregiven features of state power. Rather, their functions within the modern geopolitical and geoeconomic system have been modified, sometimes dramatically, through historically specific regulatory strategies and sociopolitical struggles (Agnew and Corbridge 1994; Newman and Paasi 1998). Since

---

[3] For further discussion of this methodological tendency see Agnew 1993, 1994; Häkli 2001; Held 1995; and R. B. J. Walker 1993.

the long sixteenth century, the national state's role as a territorial power-container has hinged upon an expanding repertoire of regulatory activities—including (*a*) war-making and military defense; (*b*) the containment and enhancement of national economic wealth; (*c*) the promotion of nationalized politico-cultural identities; (*d*) the institutionalization of democratic forms of political legitimation; and (*e*) the provision of social welfare (Taylor 1994). Thus, from the war machines of early modern Europe and the wealth containers of the mercantile era to the national developmentalist states of the second industrial revolution and the Keynesian welfare national states of the Fordist-Keynesian period, national states have deployed a variety of regulatory strategies, and have attempted to contain a broad range of social, political, and economic activities, through the principle of territoriality. While the national state may have indeed 'acted like a vortex sucking in social relations to mould them through its territoriality' (Taylor 1994: 152) throughout much of the history of modern capitalism, this territorialization of political life has never been accomplished 'once and for all'. It must be understood, instead, as a precarious, contentious outcome of historically specific state projects of territorial enclosure (Paasi 1996). To the extent that national states have ever appeared to have captured politics through their territoriality, this situation has never represented more than a temporary moment of stabilization within ongoing struggles over their geographical architectures, regulatory operations, and political orientations. The role of territorial borders as modalities of spatial encagement is thus best understood as a medium and result of political strategies rather than as a fixed, permanent condition.

Polymorphic political geographies

Territoriality represents only one, albeit crucial, dimension within the multi-layered geographical architectures of modern state spatiality. The processual conceptualization of state territoriality sketched in the preceding paragraphs can thus be extended to illuminate a number of additional aspects of state spatiality that likewise operate as arenas, products, and stakes of ongoing regulatory strategies and sociopolitical struggles. It is useful, in this context, to distinguish two closely intertwined dimensions of state spatiality—state space in the 'narrow' sense; and state space in the 'integral' sense (Brenner et al. 2003*b*: 6).[4] This distinction provides an initial analytical basis on which to

---

[4] This distinction derives from ongoing collaborative work with Bob Jessop, Martin Jones, and Gordon MacLeod, some initial results of which were presented in Brenner et al. 2003*a*, *b*. Some of the arguments elaborated in this section represent a further development of the latter work. However, intellectual responsibility for the elaboration of these ideas in the present context lies with me alone. For purposes of this analysis, I must bracket the 'representational' aspects of state space which encompass the diverse ways in which state space is represented, interpreted, and imagined by hegemonic political-economic actors and in everyday life (for further discussion and references, see Brenner et al. 2003*b*).

conceptualize the polymorphic character of state spatiality under modern capitalism.

First, state space in the *narrow* sense refers to the state's distinctive form of spatial organization as a discrete, territorially centralized, self-contained, and internally differentiated institutional apparatus. This aspect of state space refers, above all, to the changing configuration of state territoriality and to the evolving role of borders, boundaries, and frontiers in the modern interstate system, as sketched above. Additionally, state space in the narrow sense encompasses the changing geographies of state territorial organization and administrative differentiation within national jurisdictional boundaries. With the possible exception of small-scale city-states, most state apparatuses exhibit a significant degree of internal territorial differentiation insofar as they are subdivided among multiple administrative tiers that are allotted specific regulatory tasks (Painter and Goodwin 1995). Within modern national states, this internal territorial differentiation has entailed the establishment of intergovernmental hierarchies and place- and region-specific institutional forms in which particular types of spaces—such as urban areas, metropolitan economies, rural peripheries, border zones, and so forth—are encompassed under distinctive administrative arrangements. The resultant scalar divisions of regulation may provide a relatively stabilized framework for state activities during a given period; but such scalar arrangements may also be unsettled as opposing sociopolitical forces struggle to reorganize the institutional structure, borders, or functions of subnational administrative units (K. Cox 1990).

Second, state space in the *integral* sense refers to the territory-, place- and scale-specific ways in which state institutions are mobilized to regulate social relations and to influence their locational geographies. This aspect of state space refers, most centrally, to the changing geographies of state intervention into socioeconomic processes within a given territorial jurisdiction. Each historical formation of state spatiality is associated with policy frameworks that target specific jurisdictions, places, and scales as focal points for state regulation, public investments, and financial aid (Jones 1999). Through this process of spatial targeting, state institutions attempt, for instance, to enhance territorially specific locational assets, to accelerate the circulation of capital, to reproduce the labor force, to address place-specific socioeconomic problems and to maintain territorial cohesion within and among diverse centers of economic activity and population growth.[5] Thus early industrial capitalist states channeled massive public investments into large-scale territorial infrastructures such as railroads, roads, ports, and canals. These strategies were eventually complemented by state-led initiatives to regulate urban living and working conditions and to establish large-scale public works facilities

---

[5] This list is not exhaustive. Additional examples of state spatial targeting include the delineation of 'safe areas' during times of war or in natural disasters; and the establishment of public forests, national parks, and nature preserves.

(such as hospitals, schools, energy grids, mass transportation networks, waste management systems) within major metropolitan areas. Following the second industrial revolution, the large-scale bureaucratic states of western Europe came to promote the entire national territory as an integrated geographical framework for economic growth. In this context, relatively non-industrialized rural and peripheral regions were targeted in redistributive state projects that aimed to spread urban industrial growth more evenly throughout the national territory (see Ch. 4). Most recently, following the global economic crisis of the 1970s, major urban and regional economies across western Europe have become strategically important spatial targets for a range of socioeconomic, industrial, and infrastructural policies that aim to enhance national competitive advantages (see Ch. 5).

In addition to these explicit spatial policies, state space in the integral sense also encompasses the indirect sociospatial effects that flow from apparently aspatial policies. There are two distinct aspects of this phenomenon (Jones 1999: 237–8). On the one hand, apparently aspatial policies may impact particular locations, or particular social groups within those locations, in distinctive ways. For instance, military spending in the USA is not only a form of industrial policy that subsidizes particular sectors, such as aerospace and shipbuilding, but also a form of spatial policy that generates significant employment growth in major industrial regions such as Los Angeles and Seattle. Analogously, US government-sponsored mortgage subsidies and homeowner tax breaks tend to privilege suburban areas rather than cities, in which rental housing predominates. On the other hand, many national state policies generate uneven spatial effects due to their interaction with locationally specific conditions. For example, national workfare policies may facilitate enhanced employment in buoyant local labor markets while eliciting the opposite effect within depressed local economies (Jones 1999: 238). Analogously, centrally delegated programs to create new forms of regional economic governance may generate radically divergent policy agendas in different locations due to the impacts of place-specific industrial conditions, institutional legacies, and political alliances (MacKinnon 2001). The uneven development of state regulation therefore represents an important dimension of state space in the integral sense.

The narrow and integral aspects of state space—including territoriality, territorial differentiation, spatial targeting, and indirect spatial effects— interact reciprocally to produce historically specific formations of state spatiality. Consequently, as Lefebvre (1991: 281) explains: 'each new form of state, each new form of political power, introduces its own particular way of partitioning space, its own particular administrative classification of discourses about space and about things and people in space. Each such form commands space, as it were, to serve its purposes.' The main elements of the conceptualization of state spatiality developed thus far are summarized schematically in Fig. 3.2 (overleaf).

THE STATE SPATIAL PROCESS

The spaces of state power are not simply 'filled', as if they were pregiven territorial containers. Instead, state spatiality is actively produced and transformed through sociopolitical struggles at various geographical scales. The geography of statehood must therefore be viewed as a presupposition, arena, and outcome of evolving social relations

STATE SPACE IN THE NARROW SENSE	**STATE SPACE IN THE INTEGRAL SENSE**
This refers to the state's distinctive form of spatial organization as a discrete, territorially centralized, self-contained, and internally differentiated institutional apparatus	This refers to the territory-, place-, and scale-specific ways in which state institutions are mobilized to regulate social relations and to influence their locational geographies
• **Territoriality/bordering:** the changing configuration of state territoriality and the evolving role of borders, boundaries, and frontiers in the world interstate system	• **Spatial targeting:** the mobilization of state policies, public investments, or financial subsidies to modify or transform social conditions within specific jurisdictions and at particular scales
• **Internal territorial differentiation:** the subdivision of state territories among various jurisdictional units. This occurs through the establishment of (*a*) intergovernmental hierarchies and (*b*) place- and region-specific institutional forms	• **Indirect spatial effects:** the unintended, unevenly distributed sociospatial consequences that flow from apparently aspatial state policies This occurs through (*a*) the role of hidden geographical 'selectivities' within ostensibly generic state policies and (*b*) the interaction of national state policies with locationally specific subnational conditions

Fig 3.2. The state spatial process: key dimensions

State scalar configurations

Before we can further unpack the methodological foundations for this dialectical, processual, and polymorphic conceptualization of the state spatial process under capitalism, one additional issue must be addressed—the question of the state's distinctive, historically evolving *scalar* configuration. As we have already seen, most political sociologists, political economists, and state theorists have unreflexively presupposed that 'the' state is necessarily organized as a *national* state and, by implication, that sovereignty and territoriality are permanently bundled together at a national scale. Given the pervasive nationalization of political-economic life that was pursued during the course of the twentieth century, such assumptions have, until relatively recently, had some measure of plausibility both in social theory and in everyday life. They are, however, directly at odds with the conception of the state spatial process introduced above, according to which all aspects of the state's geographical architecture, including its scalar configuration, represent expressions of on-going processes of political-economic regulation and sociopolitical contest-ation rather than permanently fixed features of statehood as such. Therefore, state scalar configurations must be conceptualized in a manner that is expli-citly attuned to the historicity, and thus the malleability, of each scale of state institutional organization, regulatory activity, and political struggle.

Shaw (2000) has recently developed a useful framework for confronting this issue. For Shaw, every historical formation of state spatiality is 'layered' among a variety of distinct but intertwined power centers and tiers of political author-ity both above and below the national scale. However, as Shaw is quick to emphasize, some scales or 'layers' of state power are subordinate to others, and thus not every level of political authority can be said to constitute, in itself, a distinct state apparatus. Shaw's explicit recognition of the layered, multiscalar character of state power opens up the fundamental question of 'why a given layer [...] of state is seen as defining a particular period' (Shaw 2000: 189). Shaw's response—which he presents as an extension of Mann's (1993) defin-ition of statehood—is of considerable relevance to the present study. According to Shaw (2000: 190; italics in original): 'to be considered a state, a particular power centre must be [...] to a significant degree *inclusive* and *constitutive* of other forms or layers of state power (i.e. of state power in general in a particular time and space).' The crucial point, therefore, is that the question of which scale of regulatory activity is primary within a given config-uration of state power is essentially an empirical-historical one, and not a matter that can be settled on an a priori basis. Consequently, even though the national scale of statehood has long encompassed and largely constituted those layers of political authority that exist at other scales, 'there is no reason to regard any particular layer of state power as *intrinsically* incapable of consti-tuting statehood' (Shaw 2000: 189; italics added). Moreover, even when a given scale of state power successfully encompasses and constitutes other scales of political authority, the latter still generally play key roles within the broader, multiscalar institutional architecture of statehood. Accordingly, Shaw points out the various ways in which both municipal state forms and inter-national organizations were subsumed within the organizational apparatuses of what he terms 'nation-state-empires' from the late nineteenth century to the mid- to late twentieth century. Concomitantly, Shaw emphasizes the ways in which municipal governments and the European Commission today remain largely subordinate to national state apparatuses (Shaw 2000: 190–1).

In the present context, Shaw's layered conceptualization of modern state-hood is particularly useful because it emphasizes (*a*) the multiscalar character of state power even under conditions in which a single scale predominates; and (*b*) the possibility that historically entrenched formations of state scalar organization may be qualitatively transformed. This conceptualization also implies that the substantive politico-institutional content of particular scales of state institutional organization and state regulatory activity likewise evolves historically. The regulatory functions, institutional expressions, and political significance of the supranational, national, regional, and local scales of state-hood are thus likely to differ qualitatively according to the broader interscalar hierarchies in which they are embedded. Building upon the processual con-ceptualization of state space introduced previously, each scale of state power may be analyzed (*a*) in a narrow sense, with reference to its internal organiza-tional form, institutional structure, and geographical boundaries; and (*b*) in an integral sense, with reference to its role as an arena for various forms of state intervention into socioeconomic life (Fig. 3.3).

	STATE SPACE IN THE NARROW SENSE	STATE SPACE IN THE INTEGRAL SENSE
SCALAR CONFIGURATION OF STATE SPACE	Organizational form, institutional structure, and geographical boundaries of supranational, national, regional, or municipal state institutions Embeddedness of a given scale of state institutional organization within a broader scalar hierarchy of state institutions	Distinctive role of supranational, national, regional, or municipal state agencies in various forms of political-economic regulation Embeddedness of a given scale of state activity within broader scalar divisions of state regulation

Fig 3.3. Decoding state scalar configurations: narrow and integral dimensions

This discussion has generated a number of initial methodological premises through which to approach the polymorphic, multiscalar, and continually changing geographies of state space under modern capitalism. These consider-ations open up two foundational questions. First, why does statehood under capitalism assume a specific spatial, territorial, and scalar form? Second, how and why has the spatial, territorial, and scalar configuration of statehood evolved during the history of capitalist development? Building towards an analysis of contemporary transformations of state space, the remainder of this chapter confronts each of these questions in turn.

State space as political strategy: a strategic-relational approach

There is an ever present tension in analyses of the capitalist state. On the one hand, it is vital to acknowledge historical-geographical specificities in the ways in which states are constituted [...] On the other hand, the universalizing effects of the capitalist mode of production mean that a theory of *the* capitalist state is both possible and necessary. There is [there-fore] an unavoidable tension between the need for a general theory of 'form' (the separation of the political and economic spheres) and for a theory of historically and territorially specific national states within the shifting limits of that form.

Ray Hudson (2001: 55)

As Hudson indicates, theorists of the capitalist state have long struggled to integrate arguments regarding the nature of the state *form* under capitalism and analyses of the *historical evolution* of specific state apparatuses within the capitalist geopolitical economy. Most traditions of state theory privilege one or the other side of this analytical divide. For instance, early Marxist state theorists and more recent contributors to the German state derivation debate focused their attention primarily on the question of how the forms and functions of state institutions (for instance, the separation of the economic and the political; and the role of state policies in promoting capital accumulation and in reproducing labor-power) are intertwined with the fundamental features of capitalism as a mode of production (such as private property relations, profit-driven production, intercapitalist competition, class domination, and the commodification of labor).[6] By contrast, other scholarly traditions—including historical sociology, institutionalist geopolitical economy, and French regulation theory—have directed attention to the diverse political and institutional arrangements upon which state power has been grounded under modern capitalist conditions.[7]

A directly analogous tension between abstract-logical and concrete-historical modes of analysis necessarily accompanies any attempt to decipher the *spatial form* of statehood under capitalism (Collinge 1996). Thus, while many theorists have emphasized the fundamental character of (national) state territoriality in the modern geopolitical order, other scholars have focused their attention upon the variegated political geographies that have crystallized in different national, regional, and local contexts and time-periods within that order.[8] While this tension is, as Hudson (2001: 55) rightly indicates, 'unavoidable', the task at hand is to confront it in a manner that can illuminate both the generic and the specific aspects of state spatiality under particular historical-geographical conditions.

I propose to grapple with this issue by integrating questions of space, territoriality, and geographical scale, at a foundational level, into the strategic-relational approach to state theory developed by Jessop (1990a). To this end,

---

[6] For an excellent overview of these debates, see Jessop 1982.

[7] The literature on state institutional evolution and comparative capitalisms is far too extensive to reference at length here. Representative contributions to this broad research field include Dyson 1982; Boyer and Hollingsworth 1997; Evans, Rueschemeyer, and Skocpol 1985; Lash and Urry 1987; Schwartz 1994; Tilly 1990; and Weiss and Hobson 1995.

[8] Taylor's (1993) excellent textbook, *Political Geography*, surveys major examples of these positions. For a more recent analysis, see K. Cox (2002).

I first mobilize Jessop's strategic-relational framework in order to provide further theoretical grounding for the general arguments regarding the processual character of state spatiality that were developed in the preceding section. On this basis, I build upon Jessop's conceptualization of 'strategic selectivity' in order to specify some of the broad parameters within which state spatial configurations have evolved under modern capitalism. Through a spatialization of Jessop's approach to statehood, it will be possible to analyze, within a single analytical framework, both the state's general spatial form under capitalism *and* the historical variation of state spatial arrangements during the course of capitalist development. Most crucially, from this point of view, neither the state's spatial form nor historically specific forms of state spatiality are ever structurally pre-given; rather, they represent arenas and outcomes of *spatially selective political strategies*. This conceptualization forms a theoretical linchpin for the analysis of state rescaling that will be developed in subsequent chapters of this book.

The strategic-relational approach to state theory: an overview

According to Jessop (1990*a*), the capitalist state must be viewed as an institutionally specific *form* of social relations. Just as the capital relation is constituted through value (in the sphere of production) and the commodity, price, and money (in the sphere of circulation), so too, Jessop maintains, is the state form constituted through its 'particularization' or institutional separation from the circuit of capital (Jessop 1990*a*: 206). However, in Jessop's view, neither the value form nor the state form necessarily engender functionally unified, operationally cohesive, or organizationally coherent institutional arrangements (see also Poulantzas 1978).

The value form is underdetermined insofar as its substance—the socially necessary labor time embodied in commodities—is contingent upon (*a*) class struggles in the sphere of production that condition capital's ability to subordinate labor power in the extraction of surplus value; (*b*) extra-economic class struggles that condition capital's ability to control labor power in the sphere of reproduction; and (*c*) the dynamics and intensity of intercapitalist competition (Jessop 1990*a*: 197–8). Consequently, Jessop (1990*a*: 198) maintains, 'within the matrix established by the value-form there is real scope for variation in the rhythm and course of capitalist development'. According to Jessop, therefore, the relatively inchoate, contradictory matrix of social relations associated with the value form can only be translated into a system of reproducible institutional arrangements through the mobilization of *accumulation strategies*. In Jessop's (1990*a*: 198) terms, an accumulation strategy emerges when a model of economic growth is linked to a framework of institutions and state policies that are capable of reproducing it (see also Jessop et al. 1988: 158).[9]

[9] Jessop mentions a number of accumulation strategies: Fordism, import-substitution and export-promotion strategies in Latin America, the fascist notion of *Grossraumwirtschaft*, the West German *Modell Deutschland*, and Thatcherism, among many others (Jessop 1990*a*: 201–2; Jessop et al. 1988).

Most crucially here, Jessop proposes a formally analogous argument regarding the *state form*, whose functional unity and organizational coherence are likewise understood to be deeply problematic. On the one hand, Jessop maintains, the establishment of a political sphere that is distinct from the spheres of production and circulation may be functional to capital insofar as states provide many of the extra-economic preconditions of successful capital accumulation. Various more concrete features of the state form may likewise contribute to this capitalist orientation, including the framework of bourgeois law, the operation of parliamentary politics, the nature of bureaucracy, the indirectness of state intervention in the economy, and the insulation of the state's economic and repressive organs from popular or legislative control (Jessop 1990a: 148). On the other hand, however, Jessop (1990a: 206) insists that the state cannot serve as an ideal collective capitalist, for its very existence 'permits a dislocation between the activities of the state and the needs of capital'. In this sense, as Jessop (1990a: 148) has frequently reiterated, 'form problematizes function': the separation of the state from the circuit of capital may seriously constrain its ability to function as an agent of capitalist interests. Among many other factors, politically induced policy oscillations, bureaucratic inefficiency, and class struggles may undermine business confidence and disrupt the state's capacity to promote capital accumulation (Jessop 1990a: 148–9).

Consequently, Jessop argues, the mere existence of the state as a distinctive form of social relations does not automatically translate into a coherent, coordinated, or reproducible framework of concrete state activities. On the contrary, the state form is an underdetermined condensation of continual strategic interactions regarding the nature of state intervention, political representation, and ideological hegemony within capitalist society. Accordingly, 'there can be no inherent substantive unity to the state *qua* institutional ensemble: its (always relative) unity must be created within the state system itself through specific operational procedures, means of coordination and guiding purposes' (Jessop 1990a: 346, 149, 161). For Jessop, therefore, the functional unity and organizational coherence of the state are never pregiven, but must be viewed as emergent, contingent, contested, and potentially unstable outcomes of on-going sociopolitical struggles between opposed social forces. Indeed, according to Jessop (1990a: 9, 346), it is only through the mobilization and consolidation of *state projects*—which attempt to integrate state activities around a set of common, coherently articulated agendas—that the image of the state as a unified organizational entity ('state effects') can be projected into civil society.[10] State projects are thus formally analogous to accumulation strategies insofar as both represent strategic initiatives to institutionalize and reproduce the contradictory social forms (i.e. the value form and the state form) of modern capitalism. The key elements of this line of argumentation are summarized schematically in Fig. 3.4.

[10] State projects are defined by Jessop (1990a: 346) not only as strategies to endow state activities with unity and coherence but also with reference (*a*) to their social bases within bourgeois society and (*b*) to their associated discourses of 'community' and 'cohesion'.

Capitalism is grounded upon two major **form-determined** social relations…	**CAPITAL RELATION** **Sphere of production** • Production is organized as a value relation in which (*a*) production is privately organized; (*b*) labor power isitself a commodity; and (*c*) producers struggle to reduce the socially necessary labor time required to produce commodities (i.e. by reducing costs and/or increasing outputs) **Sphere of circulation** • The mechanisms of price and money mediate the exchange of goods and services • Capitalists compete to reduce the market prices of commodities and to increase their own market share.	**STATE FORM** **Key element** • The state is institutionally separated or 'particularized' from the circuit of capital **Selected subsidiary elements** • The state depends upon monetary taxes to fund its activities • The state relies upon parliamentary forms of representation and rational-legal bureaucracies that presuppose the formal equality of citizens and thus mask the reality of class domination in capitalist society • The state's core economic and repressive functions are insulated from popular or legislative control
The **form** of these social relations problematizes their **functional unity** and **institutional coherence** …	• The valorization of capital depends upon capital's ability to control wage labor in and outside the production process … • Yet labor power is a 'fictitious commodity' insofar as the conditions of its commodification are a direct object of class struggle in and outside the sphere of production • Capitalists share certain general interests in the reproduction of the capital relation… • Yet capitalists also compete over the particular conditions of capitalist reproduction	• The separation of the economic and the political under capitalism enables the state to maintain various economic and extra-economic preconditions for accumulation… • At the same time, this separation enables state institutions to be mobilized in ways that are not directly beneficial, and may even be highly dysfunctional, for capital accumulation
Consequently, the functional unity and institutional coherence of these social forms are never pregiven, but can be maintained only as precarious outcomes of historically specific **strategies** and **projects**	**ACCUMULATION STRATEGIES** • 'A specific pattern, or model, of economic growth together with both its associated social framework of institutions (or 'mode of regulation') and the range of government policies conducive to its stable reproduction' (Jessop, et al. 1988: 158)	**STATE PROJECTS** • 'The state practices and projects which define the boundaries of the state and endow it with a degree of internal unity.' These include: • 'The social bases of state power, i.e. the nature of the power bloc […] whose unstable equilibrium of compromise is crystallized in the state system.' • The discourses which define the illusory community whose interests and social cohesion are to be managed by the state … (Jessop 1990a: 346)

Fig. 3.4. Strategic-relational state theory: foundations
Source: derived from Jessop 1990a.

It is on the basis of these considerations that Jessop introduces the concept of strategic selectivity, the goal of which is to develop a framework for analyzing the role of *political strategies* in forging the state's institutional structures and modes of socioeconomic intervention. Jessop concurs with Offe's (1984) well-known hypothesis that the state is endowed with selectivity—that is, with a tendency to privilege particular social forces, interests, and actors over others. According to Offe (1984: 120), 'the institutional self-interest of the state in accumulation is conditioned by the fact that the state is denied the power to control the flow of those resources which are nevertheless indispensable for the exercise of state power'. This situation, Offe contends, causes the state systematically to privilege ruling-class interests and to exclude other social forces from the process of policymaking. For Jessop, however, the ruling class selectivity of state power is best understood as an object and outcome of ongoing sociopolitical struggles rather than as a structurally preinscribed feature of the state system. Accordingly, Jessop (1990a: 260) proposes that the state operates as 'the site, generator and the product of strategies'.

• The state is the *site* of strategies insofar as 'a given state form, a given form of regime, will be more accessible to some forces than others according to the strategies they adopt to gain state power' (Jessop 1990a: 260).

• The state is the *generator* of strategies because it serves as an institutional base through which diverse societal forces mobilize accumulation strategies and hegemonic projects.

• The state is the *product* of strategies because its own organizational structures and modes of socioeconomic intervention are inherited from earlier political strategies (Jessop 1990a: 261).

In this manner, Jessop underscores the relational character of state strategic selectivity. The state's tendency to privilege certain class factions and social forces over others results from the evolving relationship between inherited state structures and emergent political strategies intended to harness state institutions towards particular socioeconomic projects.

The state strategies in question may be oriented towards a range of distinct socio-institutional targets. In particular, strategies oriented towards the state's own institutional structure may be distinguished from those strategies oriented towards the circuit of capital or the maintenance of hegemony within civil society. In Jessop's terminology, the former represent *state projects* whereas the latter represent *state strategies*. State projects aim to provide state institutions with some measure of functional unity, operational coordination, and organizational coherence. State projects are endowed with strategic selectivity insofar as particular social forces are privileged in the struggle to influence the evolving institutional structure of state power. When successful, state projects generate 'state effects' that endow the state apparatus with the appearance of unity, functional coherence, and organizational integration (Jessop 1990a: 6–9). By contrast, state strategies represent initiatives to mobilize state institutions towards particular forms of socioeconomic intervention (Jessop 1990*a*: 260–1). State strategies are endowed with strategic selectivity insofar as particular social forces are privileged in the struggle to influence the state's evolving role in regulating the circuit of capital and in the establishment of hegemony. When successful, state strategies result in the mobilization of relatively coherent accumulation strategies and hegemonic projects (Jessop 1990*a*: 196–219). While state strategies generally presuppose the existence of a relatively coherent state project, there is no guarantee that state projects will effectively translate into viable state strategies. At the same time, when state strategies are mobilized successfully, they may also significantly modify the political and institutional terrain upon which state projects are articulated. The relationship between state projects and state strategies is thus a dialectical one insofar as they mutually condition and constrain one another (Fig. 3.5).

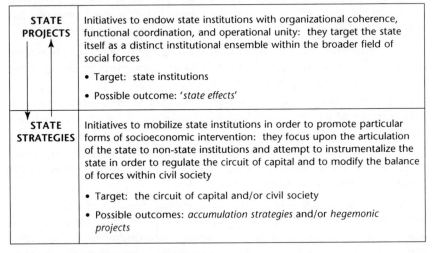

STATE PROJECTS	Initiatives to endow state institutions with organizational coherence, functional coordination, and operational unity: they target the state itself as a distinct institutional ensemble within the broader field of social forces • Target: state institutions • Possible outcome: '*state effects*'
STATE STRATEGIES	Initiatives to mobilize state institutions in order to promote particular forms of socioeconomic intervention: they focus upon the articulation of the state to non-state institutions and attempt to instrumentalize the state in order to regulate the circuit of capital and to modify the balance of forces within civil society • Target: the circuit of capital and/or civil society • Possible outcomes: *accumulation strategies* and/or *hegemonic projects*

Fig. 3.5. State projects and state strategies
Source: based on Jessop 1990*a*.

In sum, in developing the notion of strategic selectivity, Jessop is concerned to emphasize the ways in which the state serves as a 'specific political form which offers structural privileges to some but not all kinds of political strategy' (Jessop 1990*a*: 270). Rather than viewing selectivity as a pregiven structural feature of the state, Jessop contends that it results from a dialectic of strategic interaction and sociopolitical contestation within and beyond state institutions. In this view, ongoing social struggles mold (*a*) the state's evolving institutional structure and (*b*) the state's changing modes of economic intervention, accumulation strategies, and hegemonic projects. Just as crucially, the institutional ensemble in which this dialectic unfolds is viewed as an outgrowth of earlier rounds of political struggle regarding the forms and functions of state power. Accordingly, 'the state as such has no power—it is merely an institutional ensemble; it has only a set of institutional capacities and liabilities which mediate that power; the power of the state is the power of the forces acting in and through the state' (Jessop 1990*a*: 270). The conception of the state as political strategy is thus intended to illuminate the complex interplay between these evolving institutional capacities/liabilities and the ensemble of social forces acting in and through state institutions.

Spatializing strategic-relational state theory: towards state spatial selectivity

In an insightful geographical reworking of Jessop's arguments, Jones (1999, 1997) has suggested that state institutions are endowed with distinctive *spatial selectivities* as well. For Jones (1997: 851), spatial selectivity refers to the processes of 'spatial privileging and articulation' through which state policies are differentiated across territorial space in order to target particular geographical zones and scales. In developing the concept of spatial selectivity, Jones (1999) underscores the ways in which the Thatcherite program of central-local restructuring and labor market intervention targeted highly specific spaces and scales for regulatory intervention. Jones (1997: 851) also notes a number of additional instances in which a state regime has systematically privileged particular spaces or articulated a policy agenda in spatially distinctive ways. Thus Gramsci's (1971) writings on the Southern Question emphasize the Italian state's central role in the production and reinforcement of a North–South divide during Italian industrialization. Likewise, Esser and Hirsch's (1989) analysis of *Modell Deutschland* in the 1980s emphasizes the regionally specific forms of political compromise that emerged during a period of intensive economic restructuring in the Federal Republic of Germany. Consequently, as Jones (1997: 853) emphasizes, space is not only a key dimension of state institutional organization, but frequently becomes an explicit object of state strategies as they target particular geographical areas, places, and scales. Figure 3.6 (overleaf) summarizes the various dimensions of state selectivity—structural, strategic, and spatial—that have been examined so far in this discussion.

Building upon Jones's arguments, I suggest that Jessop's conceptualization of the state as political strategy can be fruitfully mobilized as a theoretical foundation for a spatialized and scale articulated conceptualization of statehood under modern capitalism. The methodological linchpin of this conceptualization is the proposition—presented schematically in the preceding section—that state spatiality is never permanently fixed but, like all other aspects of the state form, represents an emergent, strategically selective, and politically contested *process*. Jessop's strategic-relational approach provides a theoretical basis on which this proposition may be further elaborated.

As indicated, Jessop maintains that the organizational coherence, operational cohesion, and functional unity of the state are never structurally pregiven, but can be established only through the deployment of historically specific political strategies. This argument may also be fruitfully applied to the

DIMENSIONS OF STATE SELECTIVITY	
STRUCTURAL	Structural selectivity is derived from the state's dependence upon private capital for tax revenues that are essential to its own reproduction Consequently: the state engages in a 'sorting process' that systemically privileges the interests of capital in the creation and implementation of policies (Offe 1974)
STRATEGIC	Strategic selectivity results from the relational interplay between in-herited state structures and emergent strategies to transform and/or mobilize state power: the state is the site, generator, and product of strategies through which particular class factions and social forces attempt to impose organizational unity upon the state and to promote particular forms of economic intervention (Jessop 1990*a*) Consequently: 'Particular forms of state privilege some strategies over others, privilege the access by some forces over others, some interests over others, some time horizons over others, some coalition possibilities over others' (Jessop 1990*a*: 10)
SPATIAL	Spatial selectivity results from the relational interplay between the geographies of inherited state structures and emergent strategies to transform and/or instrumentalize the geographies of state power Consequently: 'the state privileges scales, places and spaces through accumulation strategies (economic policy) and hegemonic projects (ideology)' (Jones 1999: 237)

Fig. 3.6. Dimensions of state selectivity under capitalism: a schematic summary

geographies of state power. From this perspective, the territorial coherence and interscalar coordination of state institutions and policies are not permanently fixed, but can be established only through the mobilization of political strategies intended to influence the form, structure, and internal differentiation of state space. Concomitantly, extant geographies of state institutions and policies must be viewed as the products of earlier strategies to reshape state spatial configurations. Therefore, as with state institutional arrangements, the spatiality of state power may likewise be viewed as a site, generator, and product of political strategies (MacLeod and Goodwin 1999). Historically specific formations of state spatiality are forged through a dialectical relationship between inherited patternings of state spatial organization and emergent strategies to modify or transform entrenched political geographies. On this basis, by analogy to Jessop's strategic-relational theorization of the state form, state projects, and state strategies, three equally fundamental dimensions of state spatial configurations under capitalism may be distinguished—the state *spatial* form, state *spatial* projects, and state *spatial* strategies (Fig. 3.7).

STATE FORM	STATE SPATIAL FORM
The state apparatus is institutionally separated or 'particularized' from the circuit of capital	Statehood is organized in the form of territorially centralized and self-enclosed units of political authority within an interstate system defined by formally equivalent political-territorial units

STATE PROJECTS	STATE SPATIAL PROJECTS
The organizational coherence, functional coordination, and operational coherence of the state system are never pregiven but are the products of particular programs and initiatives that directly or indirectly impact state institutional structures State projects represent attempts to integrate the ensemble of state activities around a common organizational framework and shared political agendas • Target: state institutions • Possible outcome: 'state effects'	The geographical cohesion of state space is never pregiven but is the product of specific programs and initiatives that directly or indirectly impact state spatial structures and the geographies of state policy State spatial projects emerge as attempts to differentiate or integrate state institutions and policy regimes across geographical scales and among different locations within the state's territory • Target: spatially differentiated state structures • Possible outcomes: consolidation of spatial and scalar divisions of regulation; uneven development of regulation

STATE STRATEGIES	STATE SPATIAL STRATEGIES
The capacity of state institutions to promote particular forms of economic development and to maintain legitimation is never pregiven but is the product of particular programs and initiatives State strategies emerge as attempts to impose particular forms of socio-economic intervention • Target: circuit of capital and civil society • Possible outcomes: accumulation strategies and/or hegemonic projects	The capacity of state institutions to influence the geographies of accumulation and political struggle is never pregiven but is the product of particular programs and initiatives State spatial strategies emerge as attempts to mold the geographies of industrial development, infrastructure investment, and political struggle into a 'spatial fix' or 'structured coherence' (Harvey 1989*b*) • Target: the geographies of accumulation and regulation within a state's territory • Possible outcomes: spatially selective accumulation strategies and/or hegemonic projects

historically specific forms of **STRATEGIC SELECTIVITY**	**historically specific forms of** **SPATIAL SELECTIVITY**

Fig. 3.7. A strategic-relational approach to state spatiality: a conceptual hierarchy

1. *State spatial form.* Just as the state form is defined by the institutional separation of a political sphere out of the circuit of capital, state spatial form is defined with reference to the principle of territoriality. Since the consolidation of the Westphalian geopolitical system in the seventeenth century, statehood has been organized in the form of formally equivalent, nonoverlapping, and territorially self-enclosed units of political authority. Throughout the history of state development in the modern world system, the geography of statehood has been defined, at core, by this territorialization of collectively binding decision-making powers within a global interstate system (Ruggie 1993; Sack 1986). Indeed, the territorially centralized spatial form of statehood has been an essential condition of possibility for the separation of the economic and the political under capitalism, for it is territoriality that underpins the potential autonomy of state institutions from other social forces within civil society (Mann 1988; Poulantzas 1978). Even in the current era, as national state borders have become increasingly permeable to supranational flows, territoriality arguably remains the most essential attribute of state spatial form, the underlying geographical matrix within which state regulatory activities are articulated.

2. *State spatial projects.* As indicated, the organizational coherence and functional unity of the state form can be secured only through state projects that attempt to 'impart a specific strategic direction to the individual or collective activities of [the state's] different branches' (Jessop 1990a: 268). A formally analogous argument can be made with regard to state spatial form. Whereas territoriality represents the underlying geographical terrain in which state action occurs, its coherence as a framework of political regulation can be secured only through state spatial projects that differentiate state activities among different levels of territorial administration and coordinate state policies among diverse locations and scales. State spatial projects thus represent initiatives to differentiate state territoriality into a partitioned, functionally coordinated, and organizationally coherent regulatory geography. On the most basic level, state spatial projects are embodied in the state's internal scalar division among distinct tiers of administration, as defined by subnational, provincial, regional, metropolitan, and local territorial boundaries. This scalar differentiation of statehood occurs in close conjunction with intergovernmental projects to coordinate administrative practices, fiscal relations, political representation, service provision, and regulatory activities among and within each level of state power. State spatial projects may also entail programs to modify the geographical structure of intergovernmental arrangements (for instance, by altering administrative boundaries) or to reconfigure their rules of operation (for instance, through centralization or decentralization measures). In this sense, state spatial projects represent the strategic expressions of state space in the narrow sense, as described in the preceding section: they are oriented most directly towards state institutions themselves as relatively centralized, institutionally distinct, and scale articulated apparatuses of political authority within a given territory.

3. *State spatial strategies.* As we saw above, the capacity of state institutions to promote particular forms of economic intervention and to maintain societal legitimation can emerge only through the successful mobilization of state strategies. Analogous arguments can be made to characterize state strategies to influence the geographies of industrial development, infrastructure investment, and sociopolitical struggle. For, just as state institutions play a central role in the elaboration of accumulation strategies and hegemonic projects, so too do they intervene extensively to reshape the geographies of capital accumulation and political struggle. However, state capacities to engage in these forms of spatial intervention, and thus to establish a 'structured coherence' for capitalist growth within national, regional, and local economies (Harvey 1989*b*), can emerge only through the successful mobilization of state spatial strategies. State spatial strategies are articulated through a range of policy instruments, including industrial policies, economic development initiatives, infrastructure investments, spatial planning programs, labor market policies, regional policies, urban policies, and housing policies. State spatial strategies are also embodied in the territorial differentiation of policy regimes within state boundaries and in the differential place-, territory-, and scale-specific effects of those policies. State institutions do not contain a pregiven structural orientation towards any specific scale, place, or location; however, determinate forms of state spatial and scalar selectivity emerge insofar as social forces successfully mobilize state spatial strategies that privilege particular spaces over against others. Moreover, because state policies always engender divergent, contextually specific impacts upon diverse scales and locations within each national territory, there is an inherent tendency to geographical variation among state activities (Duncan, Goodwin, and Halford 1988). Whereas some state spatial strategies may explicitly promote this uneven development of regulation, this may also occur as an unintended side-effect of state operations (Jones 1997). State spatial strategies can thus be viewed as the strategic embodiment of state space in the integral sense, as defined above: they attempt to influence the geographies of social and economic relations, beyond the state apparatus proper, within a given territorial jurisdiction.

Figure 3.8 (overleaf) summarizes the structural and strategic moments of state spatiality under capitalism. This figure illustrates how the structural distinction between state space in the narrow sense and state space in the integral sense is paralleled on a strategic level by that between state spatial projects and state spatial strategies.

In sum, Jessop's strategic-relational conceptualization of capitalist states may be expanded to provide the foundations for a 'strategic-relational-spatial' framework for state theory. In this conception, the geographies of statehood under modern capitalism represent expressions of a dialectical interplay between inherited partitionings/scalings of political space and emergent state spatial projects/strategies that aim to reshape the latter. State spatiality can be

STRUCTURAL MOMENTS	State space in the narrow sense: refers to the character of state institutions as relatively delimited, spatially centralized, and scale differentiated apparatuses of political authority within a given territory	State space in the integral sense: refers to the geographies of state intervention into social and economic relations, and to the indirect effects of that intervention, within a given territory
STRATEGIC MOMENTS	State spatial projects: refers to political strategies oriented towards the reproduction, modification, or transformation of inherited patterns of state territorial and scalar organization	State spatial strategies: refers to political strategies oriented towards the reproduction, modification, or transformation of inherited frameworks of state spatial intervention at various scales

Fig. 3.8. Structural and strategic moments of state spatiality

conceived as a contested, multiscalar politico-institutional terrain on which diverse social forces attempt to influence the geographies of state territorial organization and state regulatory activity. On the one hand, through the mobilization of state spatial projects, such struggles focus upon the state's own territorial and scalar configuration. On the other hand, through the mobilization of state spatial strategies, such struggles also focus upon the geographies of state intervention into socioeconomic life. And finally, as emphasized above, the framework of state spatiality in which state spatial projects and state spatial strategies are mobilized is itself the contested institutional product of earlier rounds of regulatory experimentation and sociopolitical struggle. The spatial selectivity of specific state institutional forms may thus be understood as an expression of the continual, dialectical interaction between entrenched configurations of state spatiality and ongoing struggles to influence, modify, or transform such configurations.[11]

Extending state spatial selectivity: parameters, evolution, transformation

Equipped with this geographically reflexive and scale articulated variant of strategic-relational state theory, we can now return to the questions posed

[11] This definition of state spatial selectivity is intended to extend Jones's (1999, 1997) original formulation of the concept. Whereas Jones's definition underscores the uneven spatial *effects* of particular state forms and policies, the definition proposed here focuses upon the dialectical *interaction* between spatially selective political strategies and the state's evolving spatial structure. From this perspective, the uneven spatial effects of state policies can in turn be seen as outcomes of this dialectical interaction.

above regarding the variation, evolution, and transformation of state spatial structures and state spatial strategies during the history of capitalist development. Three issues are relevant here. First, what are the major institutional parameters within which forms of state spatial selectivity have evolved historically? Second, what types of changes occur within these parameters when inherited patterns of state spatiality are unsettled and new political geographies are forged? Third, how should the process of state spatial restructuring be conceptualized? Consideration of these issues can extend and concretize the conceptualization of state spatial selectivity introduced above. In so doing, this section will also introduce a meso-level framework through which to investigate the production of new state spaces in post-1970s western Europe.

Parameters of state spatial selectivity under modern capitalism

According to Mann (1993), modern states have been configured in a variety of politico-institutional 'crystallizations' that reflect the divergent political, economic, military, and ideological agendas that are promoted through state policies. The spatial configuration of state power under modern capitalism has likewise exhibited tremendous variation across historical and geographical contexts. I would argue, however, that the variation of state spatial selectivity cannot be explained entirely with reference to the divergent political agendas and geographical orientations of the various social forces acting in and through the state. For such agendas and orientations have in turn been circumscribed within certain determinate institutional parameters associated with (*a*) the distinctively territorial form of statehood under modern capitalism; and (*b*) the endemic problem of regulating uneven spatial development within a capitalist space-economy.

First, state spatial projects and state spatial strategies have evolved within determinate institutional parameters associated with the modern state's underlying territorial form. Because modern statehood is constituted, on a fundamental level, with reference to the territorial centralization of collectively binding decision-making powers (Mann 1988), state spatial projects and state spatial strategies necessarily target institutional arrangements or socioeconomic relations situated within the bounded space of their political jurisdictions, or some portion thereof. This targeting and molding of political-economic relations generally transpires along two core axes of variation—

• a *scalar* dimension in which state institutions and policies are differentiated hierarchically among a variety of scales within a given territory; and

• a *territorial* dimension in which state institutions and policies are differentiated areally among different types of jurisdictional units or socioeconomic zones within a given territory.

I shall refer to the former axis of variation as the *scalar articulation* of state space and to the latter axis of variation as the *territorial articulation* of state space.

As we shall see in subsequent chapters, each of these axes is the site of deep tensions and conflicts in which diverse social forces struggle over the geographical configuration of state institutions and over the form of state spatial intervention. State spatial selectivity must be viewed, simultaneously, as an inherited framework of state spatial organization/intervention within which such struggles emerge and as the very medium in which they are fought out.

Second, state spatial projects and state spatial strategies have evolved in close conjunction with the uneven geographies of capitalist development. As indicated in Ch. 1, the process of capitalist industrialization generates continually changing patterns of uneven spatial development as particular places and scales are privileged, subordinated, or marginalized during successive phases of economic growth (Smith 1990; Storper and Walker 1989). The geographies of state power do not passively reflect these patterns of uneven spatial development, but mediate and modify them in significant ways.

• State institutions provide territorially partitioned and scale articulated regulatory landscapes within which processes of capital circulation are embedded and continually reinscribed. Consequently, each formation of uneven spatial development is conditioned in key ways by the geographies of state power.

• State institutions may be harnessed in order to influence the geographies of uneven development, for they 'are invaluable in helping dominant groups organize and manage the increasingly large scale, differentiated and changing social systems of capitalism' (Duncan, Goodwin, and Halford 1988: 109). Under some conditions, state institutions may be mobilized in order to alleviate territorial inequalities, but they may also be mobilized in ways that intensify such patterns or modify the form in which they are articulated (Duncan, Goodwin, and Halford 1988). While some social forces may favor patterns of uneven spatial development that privilege specific locations or scales into which they have sunk large investments or to which they have a strong cultural attachment, the resultant forms of territorial inequality may also generate major legitimation problems to the extent that they are politicized (Hudson 2001).

Consequently, the relation of state institutions to patterns of uneven spatial development is frequently an object of intense sociopolitical contestation. While state institutions may actively contribute to the establishment of a spatial fix for capitalist growth, in which the contradictions of capitalism are temporarily displaced (Harvey 1982), such an outcome is by no means preordained. Indeed, insofar as state institutions may also be harnessed in ways that exacerbate uneven spatial development, they may seriously exacerbate, rather than displace, capital's endemic crisis-tendencies and contradictions (see Ch. 6).

Figure 3.9 synthesizes these distinctions in order to specify the determinate scalar and territorial parameters within which state spatial selectivity has

	STATE SPATIAL PROJECTS: geographies of state territorial organization and administrative differentiation within a given territory	STATE SPATIAL STRATEGIES: geographies of state intervention into socio-economic life within a given territory
SCALAR DIMENSION: the *scalar articulation* of state policies and institutions among different levels of political-economic organization within a given territory	**(1) Centralization vs. decentralization** • *Centralization* of state operations: tends to concentrate political authority at one over-arching scale of state administration (generally the national) • *Decentralization* of state operations: transfers various regulatory tasks away from the central coordinating tier of state power (generally to subnational levels)	**(3) Singularity vs. multiplicity** • Privileging of a *single* dominant scale (for instance, the national) as the overarching level for socioeconomic activities • Distribution of socio-economic activities among *multiple* spatial scales
TERRITORIAL DIMENSION: the *territorial articulation* of state policies and institutions among different types of juridical units or economic zones within a given territory	**(2) Uniformity vs. customization** • Promotion of *uniform* and *standardized* administrative coverage in which broadly equivalent levels of service provision and bureaucratic organization are extended throughout an entire territory; • Promotion of *patchy, differentiated,* or *uneven* administrative geographies in which *customized, area-specific* institutional arrangements and levels of service provision are established in specific places or geographic zones within a territory	**(4) Equalization vs. concentration** • Promotion of an *equalization* of socioeconomic activities and investments within the state's territorial borders: goal is to spread socio-economic assets and public resources as evenly as possible across a national territory and thus to alleviate territorial inequalities • Promotion of a *concentration* of socioeconomic activities and investments: goal is to promote the agglomeration of socioeconomic assets and public resources in particular locations, places, and regions within a territory

Fig. 3.9. Parameters for the evolution of state spatial selectivity (1)

evolved during the course of modern capitalist development. As the figure indicates, these parameters are defined, on the one hand, by the changing forms of state spatial organization within a given territory (state space in the narrow sense), whether with reference to the hierarchical nesting of state power among different geographical scales or to its areal articulation across different types of locations, places, and regions. On the other hand, Fig. 3.9 also specifies some of the ways in which states may attempt to influence the geographies of uneven spatial development within their territories (state space in the integral sense), whether by promoting the rearticulation of socioeconomic activities among different scales or by redistributing them across different types of locations, places, and regions. The cells of the figure illustrate (*a*) some of the core tensions around which state spatial projects and state spatial strategies have been articulated; and (*b*) the scale- and area-specific patterns of state territorial organization and state spatial intervention that may emerge through such struggles.

Cell 1: the scalar articulation of state spatial projects

An examination of the scalar dimension of state spatial projects reveals an endemic tension between the drive to *centralize* state operations at a single overarching scale (generally the national) and the impulse to *decentralize* or disperse them among multiple levels of political authority. The interplay between these competing approaches to state spatial organization has generated historically specific institutional hierarchies in which political power is more or less concentrated around a single, overarching tier. While state operations were increasingly centralized at a national scale during much of the history of capitalist development, projects of decentralization have generated significant institutional realignments and rescalings during the last thirty years, both in unitary and federal states (Bennett 1993, 1989; Sellers 2002). In the contemporary EU, the consolidation of multilevel governance systems has further advanced this simultaneous denationalization and decentralization of state scalar organization relative to the more centralized formations of state spatiality that prevailed across western Europe under Fordist-Keynesian capitalism (Bullmann 1994; Scharpf 1999).

Cell 2: the territorial articulation of state spatial projects

An examination of the territorial dimension of state spatial projects reveals an analogous, and equally endemic, tension between the agenda of promoting administrative *uniformity* across an entire territory and the goal of establishing *customized*, area-specific administrative arrangements within different types of locations, places, and regions within that territory. The French Revolution and the subsequent wave of Napoleonic administrative reforms during the early nineteenth century entailed a dismantling of the relatively patchy, uneven, and erratic political geographies associated with late feudal and early industrial states. Subsequently, more uniform frameworks of territorial administration were introduced and generalized across much of western Europe (Bennett

1993). By the second industrial revolution of the early twentieth century, large-scale bureaucratic hierarchies had been established through a variety of rationalizing state spatial projects in most western European countries (Cerny 1995). Within these relatively centralized, standardized frameworks of national territorial administration, each scale of state power was equipped with formally equivalent politico-institutional arrangements. With the consolidation of Keynesian welfare national states during the postwar period, subnational administrative tiers were charged with the task of maintaining minimum standards of public welfare and social service provision in their territorial jurisdictions (see Ch. 4). During the last three decades, however, this long-run historical trend towards administrative uniformity and standardization has been unsettled through a variety of state spatial projects oriented towards a diametrically opposed, increasingly differentiated configuration of state space. Within this countervailing model, strategic locations within a national territory—such as capital cities, major metropolitan centers, and high-technology zones—are equipped with customized, place- or scale-specific administrative arrangements that are considered to be suited to their own particular circumstances and socioeconomic assets. Across western Europe, these projects of institutional customization have significantly undermined the uniformity of national administrative arrangements and have engendered markedly divergent levels of public service provision across each territory in which they have been mobilized (see Ch. 5).

An analogous periodization of state spatial development emerges when we consider the historical evolution of state spatial strategies under modern capitalism. As with state spatial projects, state spatial strategies can be classified with reference to their scalar and territorial dimensions.

Cell 3: the scalar articulation of state spatial strategies

An examination of the scalar dimension of state spatial strategies reveals an endemic tension between the agenda of promoting a single scale as the overarching focal point for political-economic life (*scalar singularity*) and that of distributing political-economic activities in a more variegated manner, among multiple spatial scales within or beyond a given territory (*scalar multiplicity*). This tension between state strategies intended to promote scalar singularity and state strategies intended to promote scalar multiplicity is formally similar to that between administrative centralization and decentralization, as discussed above. In this case, however, the key issue is not which scale of state territorial organization is accorded primacy, but rather which scale of capital accumulation—and of socioeconomic relations more generally—is privileged through state operations. Much of the history of state formation has involved a process of nationalization in which national states have promoted the national scale as the primary focal point for socioeconomic life (Lefebvre 1978; Poulantzas 1978). However, more recent rescaling processes have engendered a rejigging of these inherited, nationalized scalar geographies as supranational and subnational layers of state power have acquired a growing strategic importance in the reproduction of capital. Under these conditions, the national state's traditional strategy of promoting scalar singularity within a relatively self-enclosed, autocentric national economy is being superseded by the problem of managing a situation of scalar multiplicity in which (*a*) supranational and subnational levels of political-economic organization are acquiring an enhanced regulatory significance; and (*b*) sociopolitical struggles are proliferating, in and outside the state apparatus, to influence the ongoing rearticulation of inherited scalar arrangements (Brenner et al. 2003*a*).

Cell 4: the territorial articulation of state spatial strategies

Finally, an examination of the territorial dimension of state spatial strategies reveals a tension between the priority of spreading socioeconomic activities evenly across a national territory (*equalization*) and that of channeling them into particular types of locations, places, and regions within that territory (*concentration*).[12] The tension between equalizing, balancing state spatial strategies, and differentiating, concentrating state spatial strategies is formally analogous to that between administrative uniformity and administrative customization, as discussed above. In this case, however, the key issue is not how the state should territorialize its own administrative and regulatory functions, but rather how it should (re)configure the geographies of capital accumulation and socioeconomic activity within its territorial borders. During the course of the nineteenth and early twentieth centuries, western European national states attempted to extend their regulatory control over all locations, places, regions, and scales within their territorial boundaries (Lefebvre 1978). It was during this period, for instance, that national states began to channel substantial resources into the construction of large-scale public or quasi-public infrastructures throughout their territories, including ports, canals, bridges, tunnels, railroads, housing facilities, public utilities systems, and communications networks (Graham and Marvin 2001: 73–81). This massive extension of state investments in the spatial infrastructure for capital circulation was also closely intertwined with new patterns of intra-national territorial inequality

---

[12] In his classic contribution to regional economic theory, *Rich Lands and Poor*, Myrdal (1957: 44) recognized this tension as follows: 'From the earliest times national states, when they came into being, almost always relied partly upon popular appeal and therefore almost always exerted a certain amount of countervailing power against the tendency to regional inequality. Every national state took some responsibility for common services and for building roads and raising the level of technology in the backward regions—though ordinarily in a poor country a disproportionate part of the meager public funds devoted to such purposes served the richer regions. In the planning of railways, considerations of short-term profitability [...] worked to the advantage of the richer regions. But from the beginning in most countries another purpose was also operative, namely, to open up underdeveloped regions [...] The same applies to the building of electrical power stations and distribution networks [...].'

and sociospatial polarization, as some places and regions were systematically privileged over others as targets for state-subsidized or state-financed capital investments. With the consolidation of Keynesian welfare national states during the second half of the twentieth century, states began to mobilize a variety of compensatory regional and social policies designed to spread industry, population, and infrastructural investment more evenly throughout their territories, and thus to alleviate inherited patterns of uneven spatial development (see Ch. 4). However, since the 1970s, in a trend paralleling that towards enhanced administrative customization, the project of promoting spatial equalization at a national scale has been largely abandoned. Instead, western European national states have attempted to rechannel major public resources and infrastructural investments into the most globally competitive cities and regions within their territories (Brenner 1999*b*, 1998*b*). The crisis of redistributive approaches to territorial regulation during the post-1970s period, and the subsequent mobilization of reterritorialized, rescaled, and place-specific forms of socioeconomic policy, is one of the key transformations of state spatiality that will be investigated in Ch. 5 below.

For analytical purposes, I have thus far distinguished the scalar and territorial dimensions of state spatial projects and state spatial strategies, treating them as if they were separate components within each formation of state spatial selectivity. I have adopted this analytical procedure in order to illustrate the conceptual distinctions introduced in Fig. 3.9. However, it is crucial to underscore that actually existing formations of state spatiality are produced through historically and contextually specific combinations of state spatial projects and state spatial strategies.

- As indicated in the previous section, state spatial projects and state spatial strategies co-evolve relationally, through a mutually transformative dialectic. Frameworks of state territorial organization generally facilitate determinate forms of state spatial intervention while excluding others. Meanwhile, the introduction of new forms of state spatial intervention generally hinges upon, and may in turn accelerate, the reworking of state territorial organization (K. Cox 1990).
- The scalar and territorial dimensions of state space do not exist in ontologically separate realms but are, in practice, tightly intermeshed. Thus, the rescaling of state spatial projects and state spatial strategies generally has immediate ramifications for the territorial articulation of state space as a whole. Concomitantly, when the areal configuration of state space is reterritorialized, state scalar configurations are also generally modified.

It should be recognized, finally, that determinate types of state spatial projects generally emerge in close conjunction with particular types of state spatial strategies. These interdependencies among particular types of state spatial projects and state spatial strategies are illustrated schematically in Fig. 3.10.

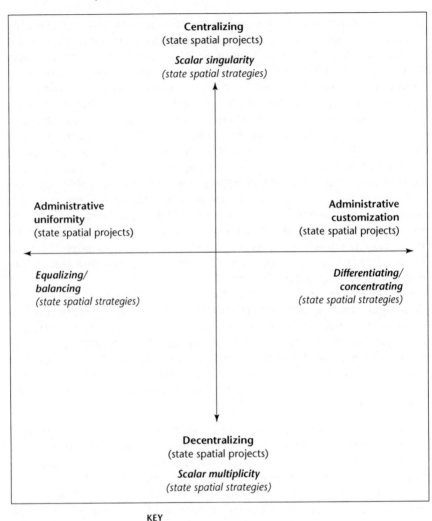

KEY

Vertical axis	scalar articulation of state institutions and policies
Horizontal axis	territorial articulation of state institutions and policies
Regular font	state spatial projects
Italicized font	state spatial strategies

Fig. 3.10. Parameters for the evolution of state spatial selectivity (2)

• State spatial projects to promote administrative centralization are generally aligned with state spatial strategies to promote scalar singularity (Fig. 3.10, top of vertical axis).

• State spatial projects to promote administrative decentralization are generally aligned with state spatial strategies to promote scalar multiplicity (bottom of vertical axis).

• State spatial projects to promote administrative uniformity are generally intertwined with state spatial strategies to promote an equalization of socioeconomic activities across a territory (left side of horizontal axis).

• State spatial projects to promote administrative differentiation are generally intertwined with state spatial strategies to concentrate socioeconomic activities at specific locations within a territory (right side of horizontal axis).

Figure 3.10 provides a schematic analytical grid through which to examine different historical forms of state spatial selectivity. The key task, in each case, is to position the state spatial projects and state spatial strategies associated with a particular historical formation of state spatiality on the scalar (vertical) and territorial (horizontal) axes represented in the figure. On this basis, the geographies of state space can be decoded as complex amalgamations—that is, as products, arenas, and catalysts—of particular types of state spatial projects and state spatial strategies that are articulated at a variety of scales and differentiated among distinct territorial locations. In principle, any formation of state spatiality could be examined through this conceptual scheme by being positioned appropriately within one of the analytical quadrants along each of the axes depicted.

Crucially, however, the purpose of this framework is not to classify formations of state spatiality in a static manner, as if the latter were composed of neatly isolated, permanently ossified institutional components. Rather, by building upon and concretizing the processual conceptualization of state spatiality introduced earlier, this model is intended as a basis for investigating the dynamic historical evolution of state spatial forms in relation to ongoing processes of capitalist restructuring. The framework presented in Fig. 3.10 may thus be deployed most fruitfully not by positioning particular state forms at isolated 'points' within the grid, but rather by specifying the determinate evolutionary *pathways* along which historically and contextually specific forms of state spatial restructuring have unfolded. This methodological strategy is represented in Fig. 3.11 (overleaf), which outlines the general parameters for state spatial change within the modern interstate system through a series of diagonal arrows stretching from the upper left quadrant to the bottom left quadrant.

The diagonal arrows are positioned so as to demarcate a variety of possible trajectories along which processes of state spatial restructuring might be expected to unfold. The bottom left and upper right corners of Fig. 3.11 have been blocked out, because they correspond to articulations among the territorial and scalar dimensions of state space that are either logically impossible

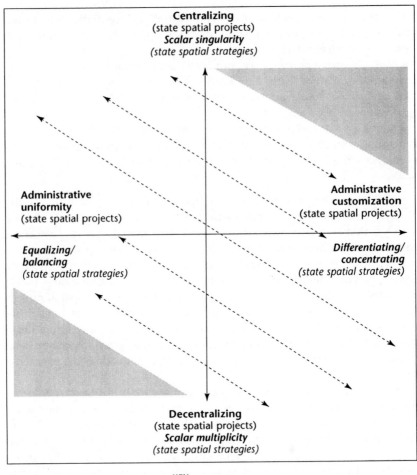

Centralizing
(state spatial projects)
Scalar singularity
(state spatial strategies)

Administrative
uniformity
(state spatial projects)

Administrative
customization
(state spatial projects)

*Equalizing/
balancing*
(state spatial strategies)

*Differentiating/
concentrating*
(state spatial strategies)

Decentralizing
(state spatial projects)
Scalar multiplicity
(state spatial strategies)

KEY

Vertical axis	scalar articulation of state institutions and policies
Horizontal axis	territorial articulation of state institutions and policies
Regular font	state spatial projects
Italicized font	state spatial strategies
Diagonal dotted arrows	hypothesized parameters for the evolution of state spatial selectivity under modern capitalism

Fig. 3.11. Parameters for the evolution of state spatial selectivity (3)

or empirically improbable. As the diagonal arrows in Fig. 3.11 indicate, pathways of state spatial restructuring may be articulated within a given quadrant, but, under conditions of systemic change or crisis, they may also traverse from one quadrant to another. This latter proposition, along with the more general notion that processes of state spatial restructuring unfold along distinctive institutional and geographical pathways, can now be developed more concretely.

Towards an investigation of state spatial restructuring: a research hypothesis

In the preceding chapter, I argued against conceptions of contemporary globalization as a process of deterritorialization by underscoring the essential role
of state institutions in mediating, shaping, and animating contemporary
geoeconomic transformations at a variety of spatial scales. In that context,
I also suggested that the active involvement of state institutions in these
transformations has been closely intertwined with major political, institutional, and geographical realignments of state power itself. One of the central
arguments of this book is that the nationally organized formation of state
spatiality that prevailed throughout western Europe during the postwar, Fordist-Keynesian period has been systematically reorganized during the last
thirty years. The expanded conceptualization of state spatial selectivity developed above provides a useful basis on which to explore more concretely the
major institutional and geographical parameters within which this rescaling
of statehood has been unfolding.

Across western Europe, the geographies of Fordist-Keynesian states were
quite multifaceted and did not correspond to a single, generic model of
political space or institutional organization. Throughout the 'golden age' of
postwar capitalism, considerable variation obtained among state spatial projects and state spatial strategies within different types of western European
states. Levels of bureaucratic centralization and administrative uniformity
differed among unitary and federal systems; the extent of economic nationalization differed among smaller, more open states and larger, more autocentric
states; and strategies to promote a spatial equalization of socioeconomic activities likewise differed according to contextually specific circumstances, territorial arrangements, and political alliances. However, even in the absence of a
complete political-geographic convergence, broadly analogous formations of
state spatial selectivity crystallized across western Europe during the Fordist-
Keynesian period. Building upon the analytical framework introduced above,
the general parameters within which the geographies of Fordist-Keynesian
states evolved during the postwar period are depicted in the inverted L-shaped
quadrant on the upper left side of Fig. 3.12 (overleaf). My argument, then, is
not that the state spaces of Fordist-Keynesian capitalism converged around a
single, generic model. I am suggesting, rather, that broadly analogous state
spatial projects and state spatial strategies were consolidated during this
period, leading in turn to distinctive institutional and geographical homolo-
gies among national states that were otherwise characterized by significant
historical, political, and cultural differences (see Ch. 4).

Figure 3.12 also points towards a closely analogous interpretation of the new
state spaces that have been emerging across western Europe since the 1970s.
Here, too, there has been considerable institutional variation across national
contexts, depending upon (*a*) the specific configuration of state spatiality that
was inherited from the Fordist-Keynesian period, and (*b*) the specific types of

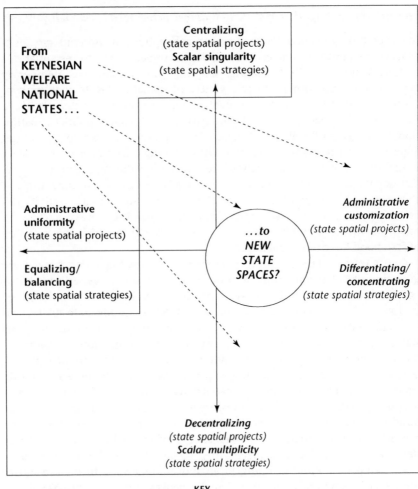

KEY

Vertical axis	scalar articulation of state institutions and policies
Horizontal axis	territorial articulation of state institutions and policies
Regular font	generic spatial features of the Keynesian welfare national state
Italicized font	hypothesized spatial features of emergent, post-1970s state forms

Fig. 3.12. The production of new state spaces? A research hypothesis

state spatial projects and state spatial strategies that were subsequently mobilized. Nonetheless, I would argue that a number of broadly parallel patterns of state spatial restructuring have been crystallizing across western Europe since the late 1970s. This development has resulted from the widespread mobilization of (*a*) state spatial projects oriented towards administrative differentiation and decentralization; and (*b*) state spatial strategies oriented towards the differentiation of socioeconomic activities within a national territory and towards the management of scalar multiplicity (see Ch. 5). Figure 3.12 depicts this profound reworking of state spatial selectivity in contemporary western Europe through the three diagonal arrows stretching from the upper left to the bottom right.

Transformations within any of the basic parameters of state spatial selectivity have not occurred simultaneously or coevally. On the contrary, they have generally occurred at markedly different rhythms, in divergent institutional patterns, and with quite variegated political-economic consequences across western European national states. This means that, even among national states that appear to be experiencing formally analogous institutional and spatial realignments, substantively different geographies of state spatial organization and state spatial intervention are frequently produced. For this reason, the newly emergent state spaces depicted in Fig. 3.12 are not enclosed within determinate borders. While these emergent forms of state space may be expected to be positioned within, or close to, the analytical zone encircled around the phrase 'new state spaces', they should be viewed as the outcomes of multiple tendencies of state spatial restructuring whose precise institutional and geographical contours remain deeply contested and thus highly unstable. Accordingly, Fig. 3.12 is intended as no more than an initial, schematic outline of the broad parameters within which new state spaces are currently emerging. It is presented here as a research hypothesis for the study of new state spaces that flows from the expanded conceptualization of state spatial selectivity introduced previously. In subsequent chapters, I elaborate and concretize this hypothesis by investigating the role of urban policy as a key mechanism of state spatial restructuring.

Path-dependency and 'layered' regulation: conceptualizing state spatial restructuring

The restructuring of state spatiality rarely entails the complete dissolution of entrenched political geographies. For, as Lipietz (1992*a*) indicates, human beings do not create new sociospatial structures under conditions of their own choosing. Rather, all social actors are circumscribed in their projects to remake territory, regions, place, and scale by sociospatial configurations inherited from the past, which serve simultaneously as constraints upon future developments and as openings for the latter. For this reason, the restructuring of state spatiality is uneven, discontinuous, and unpredictable: it is best conceived as a layering process in which newly emergent state spatial projects and state spatial strategies are superimposed upon entrenched morphologies of state spatial organization. Thus conceived, the spatiality of state power is at once a presupposition, a medium, and a product of the conflictual interplay between *inherited* geographical parcelizations of state space and *emergent* political strategies intended to instrumentalize, restructure, or transform the latter towards particular sociopolitical ends.

Massey's (1985: 119) concept of 'layers of investment' within the economic landscape provides an apt metaphor for deciphering this unpredictable interplay between inherited spatial arrangements and emergent political strategies. For Massey, the economic geography of capitalism is embodied within historically specific rounds of investment in the locational infrastructure of industrial production. The resultant spatial divisions of labor are derived from earlier rounds of investment and are modified continually as firms forge new locational geographies in response to class struggle, intercapitalist competition, and technological change. In Massey's framework, therefore, layers of investment represent, simultaneously (*a*) the ossified geographical legacy of earlier historical rounds of industrial growth, (*b*) the geographical basis for current spatial divisions of labor, and (*c*) an emergent, constantly changing locational surface on which new economic geographies are forged.

By building upon the strategic-relational-spatial approach to state theory developed above, processes of state spatial restructuring may be analyzed in closely analogous terms. In this conception, processes of state spatial restructuring may likewise be understood as a continual 'layering' of successive rounds of state regulation within a constantly evolving mosaic of state spatiality (see Peck 1998: 29).

- Just as spatial structures of production lay the basis for the geography of economic activities within a given historical conjuncture, so too do entrenched configurations of state spatiality provide a relatively partitioned, differentiated geography for the articulation of state regulatory activities. Spatial divisions of (state) regulation are thus directly analogous to spatial divisions of labor insofar as both entail determinate articulations and differentiations of particular types of social relations—whether of capitalist production or of state regulation—over an uneven territorial surface and within a chronically unstable scalar hierarchy.

- Just as new rounds of investment in the economic landscape transform the locational surface of capitalist production and thus trigger a further differentiation of spatial divisions of labor, so too do state spatial projects and state spatial strategies continually transform the political geographies of state regulation, and thus engender shifts within the state's own territorial and scalar architecture. State spatial projects and state spatial strategies may therefore be conceptualized dynamically, as the catalysts of successive 'rounds' of state spatial regulation in which multiple emergent (areal and scalar) layers of state regulatory activity are incrementally superimposed upon historically inherited geographies of state space.

This model of state spatial restructuring is depicted schematically in Fig. 3.13.

Two crucial methodological consequences follow from this conceptualization.

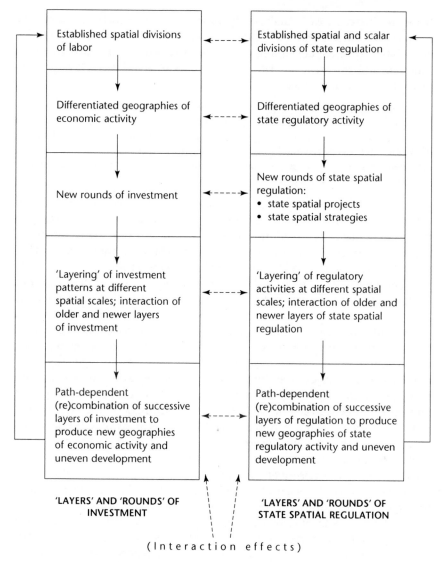

Fig. 3.13. Conceptualizing the dynamics of spatial restructuring: spatial divisions of labor and spatial divisions of state regulation

1. *The uneven development of regulation.* The transformation of state space entails neither an arbitrary juxtaposition of unconnected regulatory practices within state territories, nor the unilinear replacement of extant layers of state spatiality by entirely new, full-formed layers. For, as Massey (1995: 321) explains, layers of investment 'interact both in moulding the character the one of the other and in producing, in consequence, radical differences in any one layer

between different areas'. Analogously, processes of state spatial restructuring are likely to generate radically different outcomes in divergent institutional and spatial contexts, depending on the contextually specific ways in which inherited and emergent regulatory geographies interact. Peck (1998: 29) explains this point as follows:

The process by which new geographies of governance are formed is not a pseudo-geological one in which a new layer (or round of regulation) supersedes the old, to form a new institutional surface [...] Geographies of governance are *made* at the point of interaction between the unfolding layer of regulatory processes / apparatuses and the inherited institutional landscape. The unfolding layer ... only becomes an on-the-ground reality through this process of interaction.

From this perspective, then, each new round of state spatial regulation generates a contextually specific interaction between regulatory layers, leading in turn to new, place-, jurisdiction-, and scale-specific forms of spatial differentiation and uneven development within the regulatory architecture of statehood (see also Duncan and Goodwin 1989; MacKinnon 2001).

2. *Path-dependency and the juxtaposition of spatial structures.* All dimensions of state spatial structure do not change simultaneously or in organizationally isomorphic patterns. Indeed, much like the early settlement morphologies of major industrial cities whose underlying contours have been preserved through successive rounds of economic growth and sociospatial restructuring (Abu-Lughod 1999), certain ossified layers of state spatial regulation may remain entrenched, even as surrounding layers are reworked. For, as with many other sociohistorical processes, such as technological development and institutional restructuring (North 1990; Pierson 2000), the evolution of state spatiality is strongly path-dependent insofar as many of its fundamental characteristics may be reproduced, reinforced, and even locked in during the process of historical development. For instance, many of the constitutional, administrative, and territorial structures forged during the early nineteenth century—whether of a Napoleonic, unitary, or federal character—continue to undergird significant aspects of state space even within post-Fordist Europe (Bennett 1989). Analogously, the scalar configuration of state spatiality has likewise been characterized by a strongly path-dependent developmental trajectory. As we have seen, the national scale of statehood has served as the predominant locus of territorial administration, regulatory activity, and sociopolitical struggle, both in western Europe and elsewhere, throughout much of the geohistory of modern statehood. It is only relatively recently in the history of state spatial development that this nationalized scalar hierarchy of state power has been destabilized and reworked. The organization of state space at any historical conjuncture therefore represents a multilayered, polymorphic mosaic in which political geographies established at different moments of historical time are interwoven. Just as the spatial imprint of earlier rounds of capitalist industrialization is evident within the built environment of most

contemporary cities, the architecture of state spatiality likewise bears the unmistakable territorial markings of earlier regulatory projects, institutional compromises, and political struggles.

A key task that flows from a strategic-relational-spatial approach to statehood is to investigate the path-dependent layering processes through which successive rounds of state spatial regulation emerge within entrenched formations of state spatiality. New territorial and scalar geographies of state power are forged through a contested, open-ended interaction of historically inherited configurations of state spatial organization with newly emergent state spatial projects and state spatial strategies at various geographical scales.

Summary and conclusion

The starting point for this chapter was the challenge of escaping the 'territorial trap' (Agnew 1994) that has long underpinned mainstream approaches to state theory, political sociology, and political economy. Against this background, I have elaborated the theoretical foundations for a processual approach to the production of state spatiality. From this perspective, state institutions do not merely exist 'in' pregiven territorial containers. Rather, state institutions must be conceived as multiscalar sociospatial configurations that evolve historically, often in ways that have significant ramifications for the geographical configuration of capitalism as a whole. Concomitantly, the process of state intervention does not occur on a flat, contourless plane of social relations but is always articulated in spatially selective forms that target diverse places, territories, and scales for particular types of state operations. As Lefebvre (2003*a*: 85) once remarked, space is one of the 'privileged instruments' of state institutions as they are mobilized to regulate the social relations of capitalism. In short, within modern capitalism, statehood is configured in a geographically differentiated form; at the same time, as state institutions are harnessed to regulate the uneven geographies of political-economic life, they engage continuously in the production and transformation of places, regions, territories, and scalar hierarchies. As diverse social forces struggle to mobilize state institutions towards their own ends, state space is continuously reconfigured, whether through explicit projects to reorganize the geographies of state territorial organization and state intervention, or as indirect outcomes of ongoing regulatory experiments and sociopolitical conflicts.

I have theorized the state spatial process under capitalism through a spatialization of Jessop's strategic-relational approach to state theory. By conceiving state space, at once in its narrow and integral senses, as an arena, generator, and product of historically specific political strategies, it is possible to explore the changing geographical dimensions of state power in historical and contemporary perspective. On this basis, I have developed an expanded conception of state spatial selectivity that encompasses the role of state spatial projects and state spatial strategies in the production of historically specific formations of state space. I have suggested that state spatial restructuring under capitalism unfolds within certain determinate institutional parameters defined by the underlying territorial form of modern statehood and by the chronic problem of regulating uneven spatial development within each state territory. By distinguishing state spatial projects and state spatial strategies along scalar and territorial axes, this chapter has proposed a methodological framework through which to investigate the path-dependent historical evolution of state spatiality within those broad institutional parameters. These arguments have also provided the theoretical grounding for a number of general propositions regarding the transformation of state space in western Europe since the crisis of the Fordist-Keynesian accumulation regime in the mid-1970s. As developed here, the concepts of state spatial projects and state spatial strategies may be deployed not only to specify the form of state spatial selectivity associated with Keynesian welfare national states, but also to demarcate some of the broad tendencies of state spatial restructuring that have crystallized across western Europe during the last three decades. Finally, I have suggested that state spatial restructuring does not entail a unilinear replacement of one institutional-geographical configuration by another, fully formed framework of state space. It occurs, rather, through a conflictual, unevenly articulated, and path-dependent interaction between inherited patterns of state spatial organization and emergent projects to reconfigure the latter. The interface between in-herited and emergent state spaces therefore represents a key focal point for further research on the state spatial process under capitalism.

A number of research questions regarding the production of state space may be derived from this theoretical framework. First, one could investigate the interplay between state spatial projects and state spatial strategies under specific historical-geographical conditions, exploring the ways in which forms of state territorial organization and patterns of state spatial intervention reciprocally shape and constrain one another. Second, one could investigate the evolution of specific dimensions of state spatiality—for instance, territoriality, spatial divisions of regulation, place-specific forms of governance, or the scalar articulation of state operations—during the process of capitalist development. Third, one could investigate the evolution of the aforementioned aspects of state spatiality in relation to specific regulatory problems under capitalism—for instance, those associated with capital accumulation, social reproduction, political legitimation, and so forth. Finally, one could investigate the role of diverse social forces—including classes, class factions, political coalitions, and social movements—in shaping state spatial projects and state spatial strategies, as well as the ways in which the resultant configurations of state spatial organization in turn mold the geographies of territorial alliance formation, sociopolitical mobilization, and contention.

Each of these questions is centrally relevant for my purposes in subsequent chapters. However, my overarching aim in this book is to investigate the evolution of state spatiality in relation to the major regulatory problems generated through the process of capitalist *urbanization* since the Fordist-Keynesian period. The next chapter elaborates this agenda in three intertwined steps—first, by exploring the interface between urbanization processes and state spatial development under modern capitalism; second, by analyzing the nationalized formation of urban governance and state spatial regulation that crystallized across western Europe during the course of the postwar period; and third, by examining the systemic breakdown of the postwar configuration of state spatiality following the global economic crises of the early 1970s.

FOUR

Urban Governance and the Nationalization of State Space: Political Geographies of Spatial Keynesianism

In Italy there have been the beginnings of a Fordist fanfare: exaltation of big cities, overall planning for the Milan conurbation, etc; the affirmation that capitalism is only at its beginnings and that it is necessary to prepare for it grandiose patterns of development.

Antonio Gramsci (1971: 287)

The town, anti-nature or non-nature and yet second nature, heralds the future world, the world of the generalised urban.

Henri Lefebvre (1976c: 15)

The KWNS [Keynesian welfare national state] probably gave fullest expression to the organizational and societalizing possibilities of the national state with its retreat from formal empire and its limited commitment to integration into supranational economic blocs. This focus is not due to some teleological unfolding of this potential but to specific economic and political conditions associated with the organization of Atlantic Fordism under U.S. hegemony.

Bob Jessop (1999a: 383)

Introduction

In the western European context, contemporary forms of state spatial restructuring can be traced most immediately to the crisis of the Fordist accumulation regime and the Keynesian welfare national state during the 1970s (Jessop 2002; Swyngedouw 1997). Since this period, state rescaling has emerged as an important political strategy through which diverse governmental coalitions have attempted to manage the disruptive consequences of a deeply rooted socioeconomic crisis. This crisis-induced process of state rescaling has entailed a significant reorganization of inherited, Fordist-Keynesian forms of statehood and the establishment of qualitatively new, albeit chronically unstable, state spatial configurations. Before examining these transformations, however, it is crucial to investigate the configurations of state spatiality that prevailed during the Fordist-Keynesian period. For it is in relation to this inherited, nationalized configuration of statehood that the production of new, rescaled state spaces following the crisis of North Atlantic Fordism in the early 1970s must be understood. In the previous chapter, I argued that the process of state spatial restructuring must be conceived as a path-dependent interaction of inherited regulatory arrangements with emergent political strategies. Accordingly, in order to grasp contemporary strategies of state rescaling, it is first necessary to explore the inherited configurations of state spatiality within which such political strategies have been mobilized.

This chapter confronts this task by analyzing the political-economic geographies of spatial Keynesianism, the framework of national and local state territorial regulation that prevailed across much of western Europe during the 'golden age' of Fordist-Keynesian capitalism, roughly from the late 1950s until the late 1970s (Martin and Sunley 1997).[1] Spatial Keynesianism was a multifaceted, multiscalar, and contradictory amalgamation of state spatial projects and state spatial strategies that were constructed in response to some of the major regulatory dilemmas associated with postwar Fordist urbanization in western Europe. Its linchpin was the political agenda of alleviating entrenched patterns of uneven spatial development by spreading urban growth as evenly as possible across the entire surface of each national territory. This goal was pursued through the mobilization of:

[1] The term 'spatial Keynesianism' is used by Martin (1989) and Martin and Sunley (1997), among other scholars, to underscore the stabilizing, redistributive effects of the postwar Keynesian welfare national state upon regional and local economies. Within this framework, as Martin (1989: 28) explains, 'the problem of economically depressed areas was interpreted as being primarily due to localised structural deficiencies of demand, correctable by the regional redistribution of industry or by labour subsidies intended to reduce wage costs. Not only was regional equity itself a legitimate welfare objective, it was also justified on national economic efficiency grounds, in terms of the macro-economic gains to be derived from utilising the unemployed labour within depressed districts.' While Keynes himself devoted little attention to the regional or spatial dimensions of macroeconomic policies, a number of scholars and policymakers drew upon his economic theory in order to explore such issues and their policy implications. This work converged with a growing body of regional economic theory pioneered in the 1950s by scholars such as Perroux (1950, 1955), Hirschman (1958), and Myrdal (1957), among others, and inspired a wide range of policy agendas, to be discussed in greater detail below. See Chisholm (1990) and Holland (1976*a*) for useful overviews of the development of regional economic theory and regional policy during this period. For purposes of this chapter, the notion of spatial Keynesianism refers to the broad constellation of policy prescriptions mobilized during the postwar period in order to manage and stabilize regional and local economic development under Fordist-Keynesian capitalism. The reference to Keynesianism is therefore not intended to imply that all policy prescriptions that emerged within this framework were derived directly from the tenets of Keynesian economic theory. Rather, the point of this label is to underscore the ways in which the policies in question were embedded within the broader institutional-regulatory matrix that has subsequently come to be known as the Keynesian welfare national state (Jessop 2002, 1999*a*, *b*).

- *state spatial projects* intended to establish relatively centralized, uniform frameworks of state territorial organization; and

- *state spatial strategies* intended to channel private capital and public infrastructure investments from rapidly expanding urban cores into underdeveloped areas and rural peripheries.

Within this nationalized spatial matrix, each unit of state administration was to be equipped with relatively analogous, if not identical, institutional arrangements, and comparable infrastructural facilities, public service relays, and socioeconomic capacities were to be anchored within each local and regional economy. At the same time, the compensatory, redistributive approach to intra-national territorial inequality associated with spatial Keynesianism was seen as a means to secure a stabilized, reproducible pattern of industrial development, to promote the efficient allocation of public services and to maintain national political and geographical cohesion. Spatial Keynesianism thus represented a historically unprecedented constellation of state programs to mold the geographies of capital investment, infrastructure provision, and public services into an equalized, balanced, and relatively uniform grid of national state space.

Clearly, the far-reaching nationalization of political space that ensued under Fordist-Keynesian capitalism was shaped by, and in turn shaped, diverse aspects of state activity, policy formation, and political life during this period. Consequently, the political geographies of the Keynesian welfare national state could be investigated by examining the spatial and scalar articulations of a variety of regulatory issues—including, among others, monetary/financial regulation, industrial development, labor discipline, social reproduction, environmental relations, gender relations, and military security. My specific goal here, however, is to examine the interplay between *urbanization processes* and changing patterns of state spatial regulation during the postwar period. The point of this analytical focus is in no way to deny the importance of the aforementioned aspects of state spatial development, or any others. My purpose, rather, is to examine the ways in which regulatory responses to the Fordist form of urbanization shaped the evolution of state spatiality throughout western Europe since World War II. More generally, this chapter suggests that policies oriented towards the regulation of urban development provide an illuminating analytical window through which to examine the changing scalar geographies of state spatiality. Such policies arguably played a key role in the nationalization of state space under postwar capitalism, and as we shall see in subsequent chapters, they have also served as key mediators and catalysts of state rescaling processes during the post-1970s period. The present chapter is therefore intended to provide a historical-geographical reference point for investigating more recent processes of state rescaling.

The next section considers the relationship between urbanization patterns and forms of state spatial regulation in western Europe, focusing in particular on the intensification of national and local state initiatives to regulate various aspects of urban development since the nineteenth century. On this basis, I develop a more detailed analysis of spatial Keynesianism in postwar western Europe. I argue that spatial Keynesianism was composed of a variety of spatially selective political strategies through which western European national states attempted to manage the distinctive patterns of urbanization and uneven spatial development that crystallized across western Europe during the Fordist-Keynesian period. Finally, I analyze the destabilization of spatial Keynesianism during the course of the 1970s, a development that opened up a political and institutional space for the subsequent proliferation of state rescaling strategies across western Europe.

Industrialization, uneven urbanization, and state spatial development in western Europe

> An induced process which one could call the 'implosion-explosion' of the city is at present deepening. The urban phenomenon extends itself over a very large part of the territory of great industrial countries. It [...] crosses national boundaries: the Megalopolis of Northern Europe extends from the Ruhr to the sea and even to English cities, and from the Paris region to the Scandinavian countries. The *urban fabric* of this territory becomes increasingly tight, although not without its local differentiations and extension of the (technical and social) division of labour to the regions, agglomerations and cities.
>
> Henri Lefebvre (1996: 71)

As we saw in Ch. 2, capitalist development is premised upon the production of relatively fixed and immobile sociospatial configurations. Such configurations provide a socially produced geographical infrastructure in and through which capital can circulate: they include urban built environments, regional production systems, large-scale transportation, communication and utilities infrastructures, and state regulatory institutions. Under certain conditions, these grids of capitalist sociospatial organization may provide a stabilized basis for capitalist growth; yet they may also become a barrier to the accumulation process insofar as they tend to imprison capital within obsolete geographical landscapes that no longer generate profitable investment returns (Harvey 1982). It is for this reason that the political-economic geographies of capitalism are subjected to a process of nearly continual transformation. As Harvey (1989b: 192) notes, 'The rush of human beings across space is...matched by an accelerating pace of change in the produced landscapes across which they rush.' Historically specific sociospatial configurations are painstakingly forged in order to promote and stabilize the process of capital accumulation, only to be dismantled and reworked anew under conditions of systemic crisis (Harvey 1989b, 1982).

The process of urbanization is one of the key elements within this broader geography of capitalist sociospatial organization. For, since the large-scale industrialization of capital during the course of the nineteenth century, global capitalist expansion has been premised upon the production and continual transformation of urban spaces (Lefebvre 2003b; Harvey 1989b). This world-wide process of capitalist urbanization has been profoundly uneven: it has not entailed a linear expansion of urban centers, but rather a 'highly disequili-brated form of growth' (Storper and Walker 1989: 8) characterized by contin-ual flux in the fortunes of places, regions, and territories as industries emerge, expand, mature, and decline. While propulsive industries have generally clus-tered together within specialized local and regional economies, they have also tended to disperse away from these territorial clusters as they have matured and profit margins have been squeezed. Moreover, many new industries have emerged at a distance from established agglomeration economies, often in previously marginalized locations that provide fresh opportunities for innova-tive activities (Storper and Walker 1989: 70–99). Processes of industrial restruc-turing and technological change therefore reverberate in powerful and often destructive ways across urban and regional economies. As industries are re-structured, so too are cities, regions, and the broader spatial divisions of labor in which they are embedded. In this sense, the evolution of capitalism through successive regimes of accumulation involves not only changing industrial specializations, but also a variety of geographical transformations in which (a) the propulsive centers of industrial dynamism are periodically shifted across territories and scales; and (b) places, cities, and regions are continually restructured in relation to changing spatial divisions of labor (Storper and Walker 1989). In short, the urbanization process lies at the heart of the 'con-tinuous reshaping of geographical landscapes' (Harvey 1989b: 192) that is endemic to capitalism as an historical system.

The central issue, for our purposes, is the evolving role of state institutions in mediating the uneven geographies of capitalist urbanization at various scales within their territories. This role has significantly intensified during the course of the twentieth century, leading to a number of major modifications in the state's own spatial configuration. It is therefore imperative, in studies of terri-torial development under advanced capitalism, to investigate the ways in which state institutions shape, and are in turn shaped by, the uneven geog-raphies of urbanization at various scales within their territories.

With the advent of mercantile capitalism during the seventeenth and early eighteenth centuries, the heartlands of European urbanization shifted from northern Italy and the Mediterranean to southern England, northern France, and the Low Countries (Bairoch 1988). Following the consolidation of indus-trial capitalism from 1750, qualitatively new patterns of urban development crystallized across western Europe. Initially, protoindustrialization unfolded in the hinterlands of major towns as small manufacturing units were established in close proximity to proletarianized rural labor pools. However, this trend was reversed during the course of the nineteenth century with the intensification of industrial development and the increasing importance of large-scale fixed capital outlays in the capitalist production process. Consequently, many rural areas were deindustrialized as both capital and labor flowed into rapidly expanding cities, including older metropolitan centers such as Paris, London, and Berlin as well as newer industrial agglomerations such as Manchester, Birmingham, and the Ruhr district. During this period, Great Britain experienced explosive urbanization as medium-sized factory towns became engines of an unprecedented wave of industrial growth. By the 1880s, a new mosaic of industrial urbanism, built predominantly around the locations for capitalist production sites, coalfield regions and an extensive network of railways and inland waterways, had been established throughout much of northwestern Europe, from the Pas de Calais in northern France and Liège in eastern Belgium to Aachen and the Ruhr district in Germany. Important outlying industrial districts also emerged in Upper Silesia/northern Moravia, Lyons/Saint Étienne, Catalonia, and northern Italy (Pounds 1985).

Throughout this period of European urbanization, which corresponded roughly to the liberal-competitive phase of capitalist development (Lash and Urry 1987), the locational geography of industry was strongly conditioned by the need for easy access to coal supplies and transportation networks. Thus major industrial centers emerged in areas that contained large coalfields or were well connected to rivers, canals, and railroads (Hohenberg and Lees 1995). Under these conditions, uneven spatial development within each national territory was expressed in the form of a widening polarization between rapidly industrializing city-regions and predominantly rural, agricultural zones. From Flanders, western and central France, and parts of southern Germany to Andalucia and the Italian Mezzogiorno, internal peripheries emerged that served primarily as suppliers of raw materials and cheap labor for the core industrial regions within each national state (Soja 1989: 164–5). This internal spatial division of labor within the western European core states was replicated on a global scale through imperialist expansion and colonialism (S. Amin 1979; Arrighi 1994).

State economic intervention under liberal-competitive capitalism was in no way absent, but its impact upon urban and regional structures remained relatively indirect. Throughout much of the nineteenth century, European national governments oriented their regulatory operations primarily towards the establishment and consolidation of integrated national markets. National states attempted to remove various inherited precapitalist obstructions to market exchange; to establish the institutional preconditions for fully capitalist markets in land, commodities, and labor; to ensure sound national currencies; and to consolidate centralized bureaucratic authority within their territories (R. Cox 1987: 130–3). Nonetheless, during the course of the nineteenth century,

European national states became increasingly involved in the financing or direct provision of various types of key infrastructural facilities—such as roads, canals, railroads, and harbors—that shaped and accelerated the urbanization process at a range of spatial scales. Within cities, state institutions also became more directly involved in the production and maintenance of various public goods, such as infrastructures for water provision, energy production, communication, waste disposal, and public transportation. At this time, however, such infrastructural systems remained relatively fragmentary and disconnected; they had yet to be integrated systematically with one another or standardized across the rapidly urbanizing national territories in which they were located (Graham and Marvin 2001: 40–5). As industrial urbanism matured, major social and environmental problems proliferated, including inadequate housing, poor public health, traffic congestion, and pollution. More extensive forms of state regulation were subsequently mobilized in order to confront these increasingly evident market failures. Throughout western Europe, new techniques of urban planning were deployed to alleviate land-use conflicts and to reorganize overcrowded, polluted urban spaces. Additionally, public services such as social housing and poor relief were expanded in order to alleviate some of the most socially destructive consequences of industrial urbanism (Hohenberg and Lees 1995).

In the wake of the second industrial revolution of the late nineteenth and early twentieth centuries, capitalism evolved from a liberal-competitive configuration to a state-managed or organized form (Lash and Urry 1987). While the transition to organized capitalism unfolded in different forms and at divergent rhythms within each national territory, it was closely intertwined with qualitatively new patterns of urbanization, uneven geographical development, state power, and urban policy across western Europe. The political economy of organized capitalism entailed an increasing centralization of corporate organizational structures, the widespread application of scientific management techniques to the production process, an intensified segmentation of the labor process, and a massive expansion of internal economies of scale (Chandler 1977). Under these conditions, a new round of urban and regional expansion was spearheaded by a number of emergent heavy industries—such as steel, petrochemicals, automobiles, machinery, electrical appliances, and processed food—as well as by large retail firms oriented towards the processing, packaging, and distribution of consumer durables (Scott and Storper 1986). As these sectors expanded across western Europe, a new industrial geography crystallized in which management, financial, and control functions were concentrated within traditional city cores while manufacturing activities were increasingly decentralized into large-scale regional production clusters. This nationalized but polycentric pattern of urban and regional development was extended throughout much of western Europe during the first half of the twentieth century; and it was still further consolidated with the widespread generalization of Fordist mass production technologies following World War II.

This new industrial geography was partially superimposed upon that of the first industrial revolution of the nineteenth century; however, it also entailed an increasing marginalization of numerous older industrial regions and coal-mining districts, which had now begun to experience significant levels of deindustrialization. The geographical heartlands of western European Fordism stretched from the Industrial Triangle of northern Italy through the German Ruhr district to northern France and the English Midlands (Storper and Scott 1989).

The Fordist regime of accumulation was grounded upon nationally organized spatial divisions of labor and, therefore, upon distinctive patterns of uneven spatial development within each national territory. Large-scale metropolitan regions were transformed into 'growth poles' (Perroux 1955) in which the major, propulsive Fordist industries, their upstream suppliers, and unionized manufacturing workers were clustered. Throughout the Fordist period, these great industrial regions and their surrounding industrial satellites experienced consistent demographic growth and industrial expansion (Dunford and Perrons 1994; Rodríguez-Pose 1998). Meanwhile, during the same period, branch plants, input and service providers, and other subordinate economic functions were relegated predominantly to outlying towns and peripheral zones (Storper and Scott 1989). As the Fordist accumulation regime reached maturity in the 1960s, this decentralizing tendency intensified as large firms began more extensively to relocate branch plants from core regions into peripheral spaces (Massey 1985). Henri Lefebvre, one of the most astute observers and critics of western European Fordism, described this intra-national pattern of uneven spatial development under postwar 'neo-capitalism' thus:

Reproduction [...] is located not simply in *society as a whole* but in *space as a whole*. Space, occupied by neo-capitalism, sectioned, reduced to homogeneity yet fragmented, becomes the seat of power... space is distributed into peripheries which are hierarchised in relation to the centres; it is atomised. Colonisation [...] is made general. Around the centres there are nothing but subjected, exploited and dependent spaces: neo-colonial spaces. (Lefebvre 1976c: 83, 84–5)

The Fordist accumulation regime was propelled by the dynamism of large-scale manufacturing regions, but the latter were now, more than ever before, being embedded within the territorial economies of national states. Under these conditions, as exemplified clearly in Dickinson's (1964: 388) map of the European urban system during the high Fordist period, urban regions were generally understood as nodes within national city-systems, and thus as mere subunits of national territorial economies (Map 4.1, overleaf).

Although transnational interurban linkages were quite crucial to North Atlantic Fordism, a relatively tight fit was established during this period between urban dynamism and national economic growth (Sassen 1991). As national spatial divisions of labor and national markets were further entrenched, the geoeconomic significance of major western European city-regions could be measured most effectively with reference to the relative geopolitical power of the national state in which they were located (Taylor 1995). In western Europe, as elsewhere, the Fordist period thus represented the 'high-water mark of national capitalism' (Scott 1998: 17).

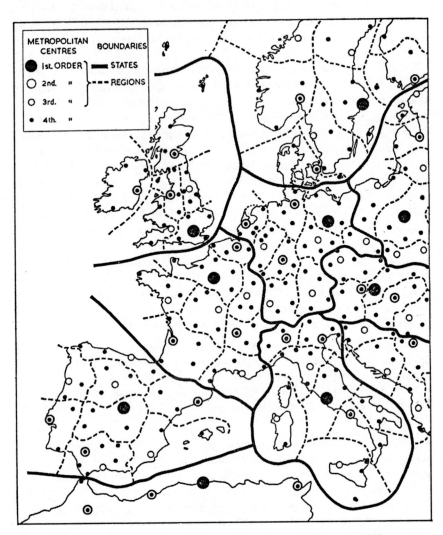

Map 4.1. The nationalization of urban hierarchies in western Europe, *c.*1950

Dickinson's (1964) map of the European urban hierarchy under high Fordism built upon Christaller's (1933) approach to central place theory. In this representation, cities and city-systems within all of the major European states are considered to be neatly enclosed within a grid of national territories. Each national urban system is said to be composed of a single metropolitan capital (*Reichsmetropole*) and a surrounding network of tributary cities and towns (for discussion, see Dickinson 1964: 388–99). *Source*: Dickinson (1964: 388); based upon Christaller (1950).

State power under organized capitalism was grounded upon centralized national economic planning, expanding state bureaucracies, large-scale investments in industrial infrastructures, and a growing reliance on corporatist bargaining arrangements to mediate labor–capital relations (Lash and Urry 1987). Within this welfare-nationalist framework, 'the state supplemented the market-sustaining functions of the liberal state with new functions intended to compensate for the negative effects of the market on significant numbers of citizens' (R. Cox 1987: 165). In this context, the major national states of western Europe also intensified their pacification, surveillance, and management of domestic social relations such that 'no point inside the state's frontiers could be left devoid of the state's control' (Maier 2000: 820). In essence, European national states began much more aggressively to 'fill' their internal territories through a range of spatially selective administrative classifications, infrastructural investments, and policy agendas. As Lefebvre (1991: 334) notes, in conjunction with this 'new political rationality' and its associated 'technostructure', 'space [was] . . . marked out, explored, discovered and rediscovered on a colossal scale'. Consequently, 'Nothing that happens within the nation's borders remains outside the scope of the state and its "services". These cover space in its entirety' (Lefebvre 1991: 378). Under these conditions, industrial development assumed a 'relatively statist' form, based upon centralized territorial planning and an intensified 'infrastructural interpenetration' of everyday life by state bureaucracies (Mann 1993: 61, 493).

Most crucially for this discussion, the extensive nationalization of political-economic space under organized capitalism was intertwined with a dramatic intensification of state intervention into processes of urban and regional development across western Europe, particularly after World War II.[2] For it was during this era that western European national states began to invest extensively in the construction of large-scale, nationalized territorial infrastructures for capital circulation and social reproduction; to engage in long-term forms of urban, regional, and territorial planning; to facilitate the devalorization and revalorization of specific localities, places, and regions within their territories; and to intervene more directly in the regulation of intranational sociospatial disparities. In many western European countries, municipal institutions were substantially reorganized in conjunction with measures to centralize intergovernmental relations and to expand the provision of public goods within major city-regions. Subsequently, as state institutions came to operate as the 'overall manager of the production and reproduction of social infrastructures' (Harvey 1982: 404) within each national territory, the politics of national economic development were interlinked ever more closely with a variety of large-scale investments in strategic urban and regional spaces. In western Europe, these state-subsidized, state-financed, or state-planned investments in urban ag-

[2] See, among other works, Castells and Godard 1974; Dunford 1988; Evers 1974; Läpple 1978; Lefebvre 1978; Lipietz 1977; Lojkine 1977; and Saunders 1979.

glomerations entailed, most importantly, the construction of large-scale transportation infrastructures such as highways, canals, ports, tunnels, bridges, railroads, airports, and public transport systems; the management of key public utilities and energy resources such as gasoline, electricity, and nuclear power as well as water, sewage, and waste disposal systems; the expansion of public housing, schools, universities, and other research facilities; the maintenance of communications networks such as postal, telephone, and telecommunications systems; and the planning and construction of *grands ensembles* and other large-scale urban development projects.

As the Fordist-Keynesian system matured, the financial resources and coordinating activities of national states enabled 'small, fragmented islands of infrastructure [to be] joined up, integrated and consolidated towards standardized regulated networks designed to deliver predictable, dependable services across... the metropolis' (Graham and Marvin 2001: 40). This increasing standardization and physical extension of infrastructural networks across regions and entire territories contributed not only to the reproduction of Fordist urban configurations; it also played a key role in catalyzing the nationalization of state space throughout the Fordist-Keynesian period. For, as Graham and Marvin (2001: 74) indicate, 'Taking control over the supply of networked infrastructure supplies to production, the territorial roll-out of networks over space, and the application of new services to modern consumption, were [...] essential components of the growth of the modern nation state itself.' Such nationally standardized, organizationally centralized, and publicly owned infrastructural networks, they argue, 'were necessary to support the integration of cities into national urban systems and markets and helped to underpin the parallel growth of Keynesian regional policies' (Graham and Marvin 1995: 173).

For Lefebvre (1978, 1977), this intensified mobilization of state institutions in managing the process of territorial development is a key aspect of a qualitatively new formation of state power, to which he refers as the 'state mode of production' (*le mode de production étatique*). In Lefebvre's conceptualization, the state mode of production (SMP) emerges as state institutions become more directly involved in constructing, maintaining, and reproducing the political-economic and territorial preconditions for the accumulation of capital during the course of the twentieth century. With this development, Lefebvre (1991: 378) argues, 'Administrative and political apparatuses are no longer content [...] merely to intervene in an abstract manner in the investment of capital [...] the state and its bureaucratic and political apparatuses intervene continually in space, and make use of space in its instrumental aspect in order to intervene at all levels and through every agency of the economic realm.' The SMP thus signals the consolidation of a system of state productivism in which 'the state takes charge of growth, whether directly or indirectly', and in which, consequently, 'economic failures are attributed to the state' (2001: 773). Following this epochal transition, Lefebvre argues, state productivism is inscribed into the modern state form, independently of fluctuations of political regime or ruling coalition. Subsequently, political struggles regarding state/economy relations came to focus increasingly upon (*a*) the appropriate regulatory strategies through which accumulation would be pursued and (*b*) the form and extent of state-led social and spatial redistribution within a given territory.[3]

In the context of the present chapter, Lefebvre's account of the SMP is relevant due to its emphasis on the interplay between state spatial configurations and the regulation of capitalist urbanization. In particular, Lefebvre examines four aspects of state spatial intervention into the urban process that have been consolidated during the course of the twentieth century:[4]

1. States operate to *mobilize space as a productive force* within major urban regions through various forms of infrastructural investment, spatial planning, industrial policy, land-use planning, urban and regional policies, and financial regulation that contribute to the productive and innovative capacities of locally embedded capitalist firms. As Lefebvre (2003*a*: 90) suggests, 'only the state is capable of taking charge of the management of space "on a grand scale" [...]—because only the state has at its disposal the appropriate resources, techniques and "conceptual" capacity'. According to Lefebvre (1977), the role of state institutions in mobilizing urban spatial organization as a productive force has substantially intensified during the course of the twentieth century through initiatives to devalorize obsolete industrial spaces and projects to create new spatial configurations for capitalist growth within their territories (see also Dunford 1988; Läpple 1978).

2. States construct and maintain the territorial conditions for *social reproduction* within major urban regions by means of various forms of housing policy, transportation policy, labor law, educational and training policy, demographic planning, welfare policy, and selected urban policies (see also Castells and Godard 1974; Castells 1976; Preteceille 1975). State actions to promote urban collective consumption may occur in a variety of forms in which the costs of social reproduction are assumed to a greater or lesser degree by public agencies.

3. States operate as the most crucial *institutional mediators of uneven geographical development* within national urban systems. Above and beyond capital's inherent tendency towards uneven development, policies that promote the

---

[3] For a more detailed discussion of Lefebvre's view of the state mode of production, see Brenner 2001*b*, 1997*a*, *b*; Elden 2004; and H. Schmidt 1985. Developed in the late 1970s, Lefebvre's notion of the state mode of production was intended to characterize state productivism not only in the advanced capitalist states of North America and western Europe, but also in the state socialist bloc of eastern Europe and the Soviet Union and in the postcolonial and developmental states of the global South (see Lefebvre 2003*a*, 2003*b*, 2001, 1978, 1977).

[4] See Lefebvre 2003*a*, 2003*b*, 2001, 1978, 1977. Each of the aspects of state spatial intervention discussed by Lefebvre may be interpreted as a distinctive state spatial strategy, as defined in the preceding chapter.

productive force of urban space may severely exacerbate inherited sociospatial disparities across a national territory, contributing to macroeconomic crisis-tendencies as well as to problems of political legitimation. Consequently, during the second half of the twentieth century, national states throughout the developed capitalist world introduced a variety of spatial policy initiatives intended to mediate, and in many cases, to alleviate, the polarizing consequences of rapid urban growth within their territories.

4. Finally, Lefebvre emphasizes the essential role of state institutions in *securing spatial fixes* for capitalist growth both within and beyond urban regions. This occurs insofar as national states attempt to embed the process of capitalist urban development within relatively stabilized territorial configurations and scalar hierarchies that provide a temporary institutional basis for sustained accumulation. As Lefebvre (1976b: 56) suggests, the national state 'transforms virtually destructive conflicts into catalysts of growth [...] It preserves the conditions of a *precarious* equilibrium.' It is ultimately through the role of state institutions in producing and reconfiguring social space, Lefebvre (1991: 378) insists, that spatial fixes for the process of accumulation—'a certain cohesiveness if not a logical coherence' of sociospatial organization—can be secured.

While the four aforementioned aspects of state spatial intervention into the urban process were initially consolidated during the early decades of the twentieth century, their politico-institutional forms have been reconfigured considerably since that period, often through intense sociopolitical contestation. The political geographies of spatial Keynesianism, which emerged across western Europe between the late 1950s and the late 1970s, represent an important institutional product and arena of such struggles over the regulation of capitalist urbanization. A more detailed examination of spatial Keynesianism can illuminate key aspects of the historically specific formation of state spatial selectivity that was associated with the postwar Keynesian welfare national state in western Europe. Accordingly, the next section examines some of the key politico-institutional pillars of spatial Keynesianism in the context of the broader formation of postwar capitalism in which it was embedded.

Mapping state spatial selectivity in postwar western Europe: geographies of spatial Keynesianism

The national economy is privileged in Keynesian theory for the purely practical reason that the nation-state system defines the geopolitical space with the necessary features convenient for the theory: a common currency, common laws, and shared institutions.

Hugo Radice (1984: 116)

the political geography of Fordism is a national geography, with international ramifications and regional qualifiers.

Frank Moulaert, Erik Swyngedouw, and Patricia Wilson (1988: 13)

Throughout the older industrialized world, the Fordist-Keynesian configuration of capitalist development was grounded upon a historically specific set
of regulatory arrangements, institutional forms, and political compromises
that provisionally stabilized the conflicts and contradictions that are inherent
to capitalism (Boyer and Saillard 2002). Although the sources of this unprecedented 'golden age' of capitalist expansion remain a matter of considerable
academic dispute (Marglin and Schor 1990; Webber and Rigby 1996), numerous scholars have emphasized the key role of the *national* scale as the pre-
eminent geographical basis for accumulation and for the regulation of political-economic life during this period (Swyngedouw 1997; Jessop 2002). To be
sure, the exact configuration of regulatory organization and political compromises varied according to the specific model of capitalism that was established in each national context. Nonetheless, Box 4.1 (overleaf) summarizes
the basic regulatory-institutional architecture that underpinned the North
Atlantic Fordist system.[5]

The North Atlantic Fordist configuration of capitalism was premised upon
a variety of regulatory arrangements that were articulated 'at the interface
of the national and the global' (Peck and Tickell 1994: 290), including US
global military hegemony, the Bretton Woods monetary regime, the General
Agreement on Tariffs and Trade (GATT), the newly consolidated institutions of
the Keynesian welfare state, and nationalized frameworks of industrial relations
and sociopolitical struggle (Agnew and Corbridge 1994; Ruggie 1982). Consequently, 'the postwar years saw the construction of an *international regulated
space*, comprised of a constellation of nation states linked one to another
through reciprocal flows of money, goods and services, complemented by a set
of international institutions which existed to manage the process of adjustment
within the international economy' (Leyshon and Thrift 1997: 71). However,
even though the Fordist-Keynesian system had determinate international (and
also subnational) dimensions, its most essential geographical building blocks
were national political-economic formations. Indeed, according to Lipietz
(1994: 29–30), 'never before ha[d] the space of capital been so closely identified
with the national framework'. Within this framework, as Jessop (1999a: 382)
explains, 'the complex field of economic relations was handled as though it was
divided into a series of relatively closed national economies'. Concomitantly, 'it
was through the national state that the national economy would be regulated as
a distinctive imagined economic space and efforts [would be] made to secure a

---

[5] On the institutional architectures of Fordist capitalism in western Europe see, among many
other works, Altvater 1992; Boyer and Saillard 2002; Herrigel 1996; Hirsch and Roth 1986; Jessop
2002, 1999a, b, 1992; Lipietz 1987.

Box 4.1. Key axes of regulation under Fordist-Keynesian capitalism
Source: based on Boyer 1996; Petit 1999; Swyngedouw 1997.

> Fordism is not a condition or stable configuration. Rather, it refers to a dynamic, contested and always precarious process of sociospatial change, during which a nested set of new or redefined scales are produced.
>
> (Swyngedouw 1997: 154)

- *Wage relation*. Collective bargaining occurs primarily at the national scale, often through corporatist accommodations between capital, labor, and the state. Wage labor is extended and standardized with the spread of mass production systems throughout national social formations. Wages are tied to productivity growth and tendentially increased in order to underwrite mass consumption.
- *Form of inter-capitalist competition*. Monopolistic forms of regulation enable corporate concentration and centralization within major national industrial sectors. Competition between large firms is mediated through strategies to rationalize mass production technologies. National states mobilize industrial and technology policies to bolster the world-market positions of their largest firms.
- *Monetary and financial regulation*. The money supply is regulated at a national scale through the US-dominated Bretton Woods system of fixed exchange rates. National central banks oversee the distribution of credit to corporations and consumers. Long-term investment decisions by capital are enabled by stabilized patterns of national macro-economic growth.
- *The state and other forms of governance*. National states engage extensively in managing aggregate demand, containing swings in the business cycle, promoting full employment, generalizing mass consumption, redistributing the social product through welfare programs, and mediating social unrest.
- *International configuration*. The world economy is parcelized among relatively auto-centric national economies and policed by the US global hegemon. As the Fordist accumulation regime matures, global interdependencies among national economic spaces intensify due to enhanced competition among transnational corporations, the expansion of trade relations, and the ascendancy of the US dollar as world currency.

---

complementary expansion of national production and consumption as the basis for a politics of prosperity' (Jessop 1999*a*: 383).

The Keynesian welfare national state was hardly a necessary teleological outgrowth of World War II. Yet, looking backwards at the history of modern state formation in western Europe, Keynesian welfare national states may be viewed as the culmination of a *longue durée* trend towards the nationalization and territorialization of political space that emerged during the mid-seventeenth century with the consolidation of the Westphalian geopolitical order and was significantly intensified during the course of the late nineteenth century (Maier 2000). After the Great Depression of the 1930s, the nationalized formations of political-economic space that had been established during the preceding wave of capitalist expansion and state development were further

entrenched. Following postwar reconstruction, Keynesian socioeconomic policies were widely deployed across western Europe in order to institutionalize
demand management, deficit spending, collective bargaining, monopoly
pricing, and counter-cyclical monetary policies, all of which presupposed the
geographical-political space of the sovereign nation-state (Radice 1984).[6]
According to Jessop's (2002) influential account, the Keynesian welfare national state was grounded upon (*a*) the primacy of national states (rather than
international or subnational levels of political authority) as the key institutional *agents* of regulatory activities; and (*b*) the primacy of national economies
and national populations as the key *targets* for state socioeconomic regulation.
Throughout the Fordist-Keynesian period, from the 1950s to the early 1970s,
the role of the national state as the primary geographical container of political-
economic life was significantly intensified across western Europe (Milward
2000). Within this nationalized politico-regulatory framework, 'public spending increased on utilities, social and physical infrastructures, and various collective goods, especially housing and nation-wide education, health care and
social benefit systems' (Martin and Sunley 1997: 280). Public sector employment increased significantly, not only through the expansion of welfare services, but due to the nationalization of key Fordist industries in a number of
European countries, including Italy, France, Britain, Belgium, the Netherlands,
and Sweden, among others (Parris, Pestieau, and Saynor 1987; Toninelli 2000).
Consequently, 'This period marks the highest stage of the national state form in
Europe as an economic, political and social power container, with its apogee
occurring at the end of the 1960s after the success of the Marshall Plan and the
development of the European Community in 1945–1968' (Jessop 2002: 60).
The scalar architecture of state regulation under Fordist-Keynesian capitalism is
summarized schematically in Fig. 4.1 (overleaf).[7]

Throughout the Fordist-Keynesian period, state intervention into processes
of urban and regional development was multifaceted: it was articulated in a
variety of politico-institutional forms in specific national contexts, and it
generated variegated effects upon patterns of urban and regional growth
across the western European space-economy. As Swyngedouw (1997: 153)
explains, 'The homogenization across national space of a series of socioeconomic aspects (wages, redistributive schemes, state intervention, socioeconomic norms, rules and procedures) was articulated with a highly uneven
and differentiated local and regional development process.' However, even
as urban and regional development patterns and governance arrangements
were differentiated extensively under Fordism, a distinctive politics of spatial
Keynesianism crystallized across much of western Europe in which national

---

[6] See P. Hall (1989) for a more detailed comparative discussion of the diffusion of Keynesian-
inspired macroeconomic policies in western Europe and the USA since the 1930s.
[7] For a more extensive discussion of the role of the Keynesian welfare national state in constructing a distinctive spatio-temporal fix for postwar capitalism, see Jessop 2002.

Spatial scale(s) of regulation	Major characteristics and institutional embodiment(s)
Global	Bretton Woods financial system and GATT underwrite global financial stability and global trade, leading to an international diffusion of Fordist institutional forms and regulatory practices
Global-national relations	National states assume independent responsibility for monetary policy in the context of continued US global hegemony
National	The Keynesian welfare national state secures the institutional conditions for mass production and mass consumption while promoting national sociopolitical and territorial cohesion
National–local relations	National governments centralize intergovernmental relations and mobilize various mechanisms of territorial redistribution intended to alleviate intra-national disparities
Local	Local welfare states serve as transmission belts for central state policies, operating primarily to plan, subsidize, and finance various aspects of social reproduction

Fig. 4.1. The scalar architecture of state regulation under Fordist-Keynesian capitalism
Source: derived from Tickell and Peck 1995: 377.

states mobilized broadly analogous strategies of territorial administration and urban-regional regulation.

On the most general level, spatial Keynesianism may be understood as a broad constellation of national state institutional forms and regulatory strategies designed to alleviate uneven geographical development within the national space-economy, and thereby, to promote stabilized national industrial growth. It was assumed, under these conditions, that 'there is a loss of output and income to the national economy from the over-development of leading regions and the under-development of others' (Holland 1976*a*: 13). The goal of state action, in this context, was less to *enhance* the productive force of capitalist sociospatial configurations than to *spread* the industrialization process as evenly as possible across the entire surface of the national territory—much like butter on a piece of bread. Insofar as significant large-scale territorial disparities were viewed as a major threat to stabilized patterns of macroeconomic growth, political strategies to alleviate intra-national sociospatial polarization came to serve as important tools of national socioeconomic and industrial policy. Writing in the mid-1970s, at the highpoint of spatial Keynesianism in western Europe, Lefebvre (1976*c*: 111–12) insightfully underscored the complex interconnections between urban regulation, the politics of economic growth and the problem of uneven spatial development under postwar capitalism:

> the period roughly between 1950 and 1970 [...] was an idyllic period for the whole of capitalism [...] The retarded or backward areas, the underdeveloped countries, could and had to be integrated into growth. To use the classic metaphor, the ship of capitalism and its leaders found itself with a motor, a rudder and a fixed course. More precisely, it now constituted for itself solid nuclei, *centres*, what François Perroux calls 'the growth poles'. Everything was subordinated to growth [...] During this euphoric period, it seemed that the problem of integrating and co-opting everything that opposed this society—ideologies, social groupings, classes—had been solved [...] An apparent truth imposed itself which has only now become paradoxical: the 'truth' of unlimited growth, the indefinite extension of the centres, nuclei and growth poles. This ruling scenario of the 1950–1970 period gave rise not only to a so-called 'logic' but also to strategies which gradually covered space as a whole [...].

As Lefebvre indicates, the attempt to integrate so-called 'lagging' or 'backward' areas into the developmental trajectory of the national space-economy as a whole was a key component within the broader postwar project of integrating oppositional forces into a national social formation oriented towards mass production and mass consumption. The productivist economic logic of postwar Fordism, with its goal of endless industrial growth, was thus inextricably intertwined with a politico-geographic logic of endless *spatial extension and homogenization*, grounded upon the continual spreading of a standardized urban grid across the entire national territory, covering 'space as a whole' (Lefebvre 1976c: 112), from suburbs and new towns to older industrial areas, rural peripheries, and outlying agricultural zones. This political project of spatial extension and homogenization—of promoting the 'Taylorization of territory' (Veltz 1996: 24)—was arguably the geographical essence of spatial Keynesianism.

Spatial Keynesianism contributed in essential, if largely unrecognized, ways to the nationalization of state space during the Fordist-Keynesian period, and it therefore provides an illuminating basis on which to investigate the distinctive form of state spatial selectivity that was produced in and through the Keynesian welfare national states of postwar western Europe.[8] Drawing upon the approach to state theory developed in the preceding chapter, spatial Keynesianism may be characterized most precisely with reference to (*a*) the mobilization of state

---

[8] A very different formation of spatial Keynesianism was consolidated in the USA during the postwar period (Friedmann and Bloch 1990). Whereas postwar European national states promoted a spatial fix under Fordism by attempting to spread industrial urbanization as evenly as possible throughout their territories, the US state promoted intense inter-urban competition among local growth machines (Logan and Molotch 1987), subsidized suburban development on a massive scale (Florida and Jonas 1991), and channeled major public resources into the military-industrial complex (Gottdiener 1989). A more systematic comparison of postwar spatial Keynesianism in western Europe and the USA has yet to be undertaken. Such a comparison would be highly illuminating, however, not only as a window into the different forms of state spatiality that underpinned the national building-blocks of North Atlantic Fordism, but also as a basis for comparing the subsequent, apparently more similar trajectories of state spatial restructuring that have crystallized in each of these contexts during the post-Fordist period.

spatial projects oriented towards the establishment of *centralized* and *uniform* frameworks of territorial administration; and (*b*) the mobilization of state spatial strategies oriented towards the *spreading* of urban development as evenly as possible across the entire *national* territory (see Fig. 4.2).

	STATE SPATIAL PROJECTS	STATE SPATIAL STRATEGIES
SCALAR DIMENSION	State administrative and regulatory capacities are *centralized* around the national scale: regions and localities are 'subordinated to the macro-economic and macro-redistributive imperatives of the [national] centre'	The *national* scale is promoted as the most essential level of political-economic life: the national economy thus becomes 'the essential geographical unit of economic organization, accumulation, and regulation over which the state is the sovereign actor'
TERRITORIAL DIMENSION	Relatively *uniform* structures of territorial administration are established throughout the national space-economy: 'consistent standards of social welfare and social infrastructure provision [are established] across regions and localities, thereby incorporating them into an increasingly *collective* or *public* space-economy'	Redistributive policies are mobilized in order to *equalize* the distribution of industry and infrastructure investment across the national space-economy: 'in most countries, postwar Keynesian interventionism was a key factor behind the steady process of regional *convergence* in per capita incomes that characterized most advanced capitalist nations until the late 1970s'

Fig. 4.2. State spatial selectivity under Fordist-Keynesian capitalism: the case of spatial Keynesianism

Source: builds on Fig. 3.9; quotations are drawn from Martin and Sunley 1997: 279, 280, 281.

In sum, under Fordist-Keynesian capitalism, national states attempted to redistribute the surplus not only socially, through institutionalized collective bargaining arrangements and national social welfare policies, but also spatially, through a variety of political strategies intended to centralize, homogenize, standardize, and equalize national political-economic space. In Peck's (2002: 338) useful terminology, such strategies entailed the establishment of various extralocal or interscalar 'rule-regimes' that served to 'constrain and channel the strategic options and tactical behavior of local actors'. Under the dominance of spatial Keynesianism, such extralocal rule-regimes operated to bring 'regions and localities within the economy under much greater central state control and dependence' by subordinating them 'to the macro-economic and macro-redistributive imperatives of the centre' (Martin and Sunley 1997:

279, 280). Within this framework, 'the local unit was seen as having no essential economic life of its own. Its job was to follow the path to growth laid down by national policies' (Sengenberger 1993: 316). At the same time, the extralocal rule-regimes associated with spatial Keynesianism established certain minimum standards of social welfare and infrastructure provision across national intergovernmental systems, 'thereby incorporating [regions and localities] into an increasingly *collective* or *public* space-economy, which in some countries extended to large-scale state ownership and management of key industries, in addition to utilities and other collective goods' (Martin and Sunley 1997: 280). Taken together, these extralocal rule-regimes directly or indirectly generated a variety of 'regional redistributive-stabilizing effects'— including the stimulation of consumer demand, the promotion of full employment, the extension of capital investments into marginalized areas, and the tendential convergence of per capita income levels—that figured crucially in the reproduction of the entire Fordist-Keynesian order (Martin and Sunley 1997: 280-1). The interplay between the rise of the Keynesian welfare national state, the diffusion of Fordist-Keynesian forms of urbanization, the mobilization of spatial Keynesianism, and the nationalization of state space is represented schematically in Fig. 4.3 (overleaf).

In the present context, I shall not attempt to provide a comprehensive investigation of the differentiated national political geographies that were generated across western Europe through the politics of spatial Keynesianism. Instead, the following analysis focuses on some of the most prevalent policy mechanisms and institutional forms through which spatial Keynesianism was articulated, across otherwise qualitatively different national, regional, and local regulatory landscapes, between the late 1950s and the mid-1970s. Boxes 4.2 (p. 135) and 4.3 (p. 136) summarize the key state spatial projects and state spatial strategies upon which spatial Keynesianism was grounded. Selected examples of the latter are then surveyed in the discussion that follows.

Compensatory regional policies

> The more effectively a national state becomes a welfare state [...], the stronger will be both the urge and the capacity to counteract the blind market forces which tend to result in regional inequalities; and this, again, will spur economic development in the country, and so on and so on, in circular causation.
>
> Gunnar Myrdal (1957: 41)

Across most of western Europe, regional policies were one of the most significant mechanisms of spatial Keynesianism, for they served explicitly to alleviate inter-place disparities, to redistribute employment within national boundaries, and thus, to induce the spatial integration of the national economy as a whole. Between the 1950s and the 1970s, a range of regional industrial

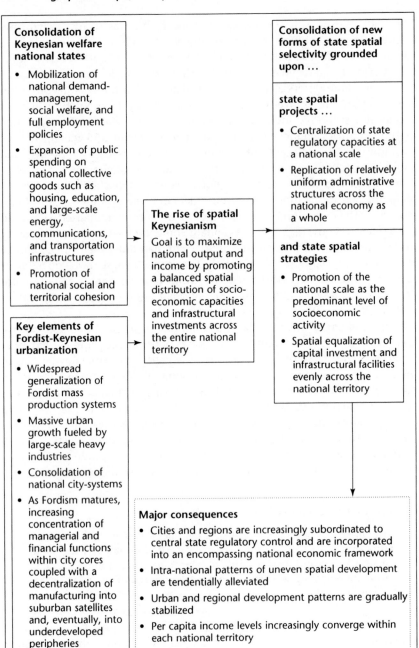

Consolidation of Keynesian welfare national states

- Mobilization of national demand-management, social welfare, and full employment policies
- Expansion of public spending on national collective goods such as housing, education, and large-scale energy, communications, and transportation infrastructures
- Promotion of national social and territorial cohesion

Key elements of Fordist-Keynesian urbanization

- Widespread generalization of Fordist mass production systems
- Massive urban growth fueled by large-scale heavy industries
- Consolidation of national city-systems
- As Fordism matures, increasing concentration of managerial and financial functions within city cores coupled with a decentralization of manufacturing into suburban satellites and, eventually, into underdeveloped peripheries

The rise of spatial Keynesianism

Goal is to maximize national output and income by promoting a balanced spatial distribution of socio-economic capacities and infrastructural investments across the entire national territory

Consolidation of new forms of state spatial selectivity grounded upon ...

state spatial projects ...

- Centralization of state regulatory capacities at a national scale
- Replication of relatively uniform administrative structures across the national economy as a whole

and state spatial strategies

- Promotion of the national scale as the predominant level of socioeconomic activity
- Spatial equalization of capital investment and infrastructural facilities evenly across the national territory

Major consequences

- Cities and regions are increasingly subordinated to central state regulatory control and are incorporated into an encompassing national economic framework
- Intra-national patterns of uneven spatial development are tendentially alleviated
- Urban and regional development patterns are gradually stabilized
- Per capita income levels increasingly converge within each national territory

Fig. 4.3. Urbanization, spatial Keynesianism, and the nationalization of state space in postwar western Europe

---

Box 4.2. Key state spatial projects promoting spatial Keynesianism

---

> This modern state promotes and imposes itself as the stable centre—defini-
> tively—of (national) societies and spaces.
>
> (Lefebvre 1991: 23)

> Having become political, social space is on the one hand centralised and
> fixed in a political centrality, and on the other hand specialised and parceled
> out. The state determines and congeals the decision-making centres. At the
> same time, space is distributed into peripheries which are hierarchised in
> relation to the centres...
>
> (Lefebvre 1976c: 84)

Spatial Keynesianism rested upon *state spatial projects* oriented towards the establishment of nationally *centralized* and *uniform* patterns of state territorial organization. These centralizing, standardizing state spatial projects included:

• *Intergovernmental centralization.* In both federal and unitary states, national governments acquired more centralized control over subnational territorial governance, enabling them to impose national socioeconomic policy priorities upon regional and local governmental units (Mény and Wright 1985; Rose 1985).

• *Local government reorganization.* As national governments attempted to standardize the provision of welfare services and to coordinate national economic policies across their territories, municipal institutions were reorganized, rationalized, and expanded in order to deliver various kinds of public services to local populations. Within this nationalized institutional configuration, local states operated primarily as transmission belts for centrally determined policies (Mayer 1991).

• *Metropolitan governmental consolidation.* Between the mid-1960s and the early 1970s, consolidated metropolitan institutions were established in major western European city-regions. These new forms of metropolitan territorial administration played important roles in distributing the public services of the Keynesian welfare national state while managing the intensive patterns of land-use and suburban expansion that crystallized within rapidly expanding Fordist city-regions (Sharpe 1995a, b).

• *Territorial reform initiatives.* In conjunction with projects to rationalize governmental bureaucracies, the number of subnational territorial units—particularly municipalities— was significantly diminished in major western European countries. Through such territorial reform initiatives, intra-national jurisdictional boundaries were simplified and many formerly contiguous units of local territorial administration were fused together.

---

and infrastructural policies were introduced to promote industrialization within each state's 'underdeveloped' peripheries (Clout 1981a; Holland 1976b). Due to their high population densities, major cities and metropolitan regions still received the bulk of large-scale public infrastructure investments and welfare services during the Fordist-Keynesian epoch. Nonetheless, a variety of compensatory policy mechanisms were introduced in order to rechannel employment and growth capacities into underdeveloped regions and rural

Box 4.3. Key state spatial strategies promoting spatial Keynesianism

> An apparent truth imposed itself which has only now become paradoxical: the 'truth' of unlimited growth, the indefinite extension of the centres, nuclei and growth poles. This ruling scenario of the 1950–1970 period gave rise not only to a so-called 'logic' but also to strategies which gradually covered space as a whole [. . .]
>
> (Lefebvre 1976c: 112)

Spatial Keynesianism was grounded upon *state spatial strategies* oriented towards the *nationalization, homogenization,* and *equalization* of political-economic life within the state's borders. These nationalizing, redistributive state spatial strategies included:

• *Compensatory regional policies.* National governments deployed various forms of financial aid, locational incentives, transfer payments, and infrastructural investments in order to promote industrial growth and economic regeneration outside the dominant city cores. Their goal was to alleviate overheating in core regions while enhancing levels of economic activity and employment in marginalized, peripheral, or underdeveloped regions (Clout 1981a).

• *Automatic stabilizers.* These entailed mechanisms of interregional resource transfer that were built-in to national fiscal and social welfare systems and activated through regionally specific economic fluctuations. They enabled low-income regions to pay lower taxes and to receive higher levels of government expenditure, with high-income regions paying higher taxes and receiving lower levels of public support (MacKay 1994).

• *National spatial planning systems.* New forms of national spatial planning were mobilized in order to guide future patterns of territorial development in a comprehensive, systematic manner. Such indicative planning initiatives were generally centralized within newly established governmental ministries—such as France's DATAR (*Délégation pour l'Aménagement du Territoire et l'Action régionale*) and the Dutch RPD (*Rijksplanologische Dienst*)—that were devoted specifically to problems of urban development, housing, population distribution, infrastructural planning, and large-scale territorial management. Like compensatory regional policies, national spatial planning systems stimulated and coordinated the channeling of investments away from overheated metropolitan cores into less developed or marginalized areas.

• *Nationalized industries.* In many western European countries, central governments assumed direct ownership of major Fordist industries—such as coal, steel, energy, shipbuilding, aerospace, and automobiles, among others. In this manner, national states enhanced employment levels and development potentials within selected localities and regions, while also adding a new layer of state-financed industrial investments within inherited spatial divisions of labor (Holland 1974; Martin and Sunley 1997).

• *New towns policies.* National governments attempted to alleviate urban congestion by establishing suburban new towns in relatively close proximity to major metropolitan agglomerations. Through indicative planning initiatives and various forms of infrastructural investment, national governments facilitated population deconcentration and guided urban and regional development across the national territory. New towns policies were particularly prominent in Britain, France, Scandinavia, and the Netherlands but were also mobilized on a smaller but significant scale in other European countries (Merlin 1971; Golany 1978).

• *Urban managerialism.* Local states and municipal governments came to serve as 'long arms' of national policies and were oriented increasingly towards managerial, social welfare functions (Harvey 1989a). They played a key role in promoting social reproduction within major city-regions through large-scale investments in the localized infrastructures of collective consumption (including transportation, housing, and education).

peripheries throughout the national territory. From the Italian Mezzogiorno and Spanish Andalusia to western and southern France, the agricultural peripheries and border zones of West Germany, the Limburg coal-mining district of northern Belgium, the Dutch northeastern peripheries, the northwestern regions and islands of Denmark, the Scandinavian North, western Ireland, and the declining industrial zones of the English North, South Wales, parts of Scotland, and much of Northern Ireland, each European national state had its so-called 'problem areas', 'lagging regions', or 'distressed areas', generally composed of economic spaces that had been marginalized during previous rounds of industrial development or that were locked into obsolete technological-industrial infrastructures (OECD 1976). Such regions 'were conceived as blank spaces on the national map of industry, to be filled by the same development strategies as such voids were to be filled in the Third World' (Sabel 1994: 126). Accordingly, throughout the postwar period until the late 1970s, a broad range of regional and spatial policies were introduced across western Europe that explicitly targeted such peripheralized spaces. As Map 4.2 (overleaf) illustrates, few of western Europe's major cities or city-regions were targeted by these classic Fordist-Keynesian regional policy initiatives, which were directed almost exclusively at underdeveloped rural peripheries, border zones, and declining coal-mining regions.

Generally justified in the name of priorities such as balanced national development and spatial equalization, these redistributive regional policies entailed the introduction of various forms of financial aid, locational incentives, and transfer payments to promote industrial growth and economic regeneration outside the dominant city cores; and they often channeled major public infrastructural investments into such locations. Some of these policies were derived from the writings of Gunnar Myrdal (1957) and Albert Hirschman (1958), both of whom suggested that various forms of public intervention were required to alleviate market-driven interregional inequalities. In the western European context, the resultant compensatory regional policies included 'rebates of interest, government guarantees, tax privileges, capital grants, construction and purchase of industrial buildings, [and] improvements of the regional infrastructure (transport facilities, roads, industrial land development, etc.)' (Albrechts and Swyngedouw 1989: 68). François

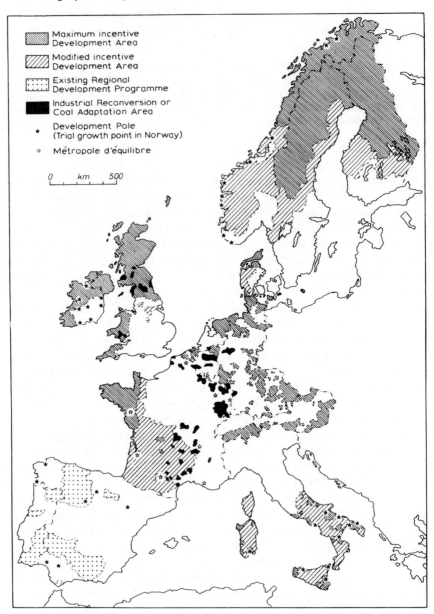

Map 4.2. Geographies of compensatory regional policy in postwar western Europe
Source: Clout (1981*a*: 27).

Perroux's (1955) growth pole theory, which emphasized the role of propulsive industries in generating investment and employment within particular areas, likewise gained considerable popularity during this period and was frequently invoked to justify a variety of industrial policies that had significant regional and local impacts (Parr 1973) (see Box 4.4). In particular, during the course of the 1960s, public policies inspired wholly or partially by growth pole theory played an important role in stimulating large-scale investments by the automobile and steel industries in a number of marginalized regions of the UK (Scotland, Merseyside), France (Brittany, Fos), and Italy (Taranto)—albeit with varying

---

Box 4.4. Intellectual foundations: regional economic theory and the logic of spatial Keynesianism
Sources: Chisholm 1990; Friedmann and Weaver 1984.

One of the conceptual foundations of postwar redistributive regional policies was the notion that intra-national territorial inequalities—as expressed through the polarization of investment, employment, and per capita income levels across the national territory—were detrimental to national economic stability. This assumption, and the various compensatory regional policies that flowed from it, were derived from a variety of major currents within postwar regional economic theory.

Gunnar Myrdal (1957) and Albert Hirschman (1958) developed theories of 'cumulative causation' that underscored the inevitability of polarized patterns of territorial development in the absence of public intervention. Both authors recommended various 'equalizing measures' (Myrdal 1957: 45) through which national states could attempt to counteract capital's chronic tendency to cluster in the most developed agglomerations. More generally, by criticizing the neoclassical assumption that spatial equilibrium—i.e. a maximally efficient geographical distribution of capital and labor—would automatically result from market forces, Myrdal and Hirschman provided an important intellectual justification for interventionist policies intended to alter the territorial distribution of the factors of production within each national territory.

François Perroux's (1955, 1950) theory of 'growth poles' was likewise an influential basis for postwar regional policies. Perroux's work focused on the role of the 'propulsive industry' as the stimulus for further industrial development within a broader matrix of inter-firm relations. Subsequently, in part through the work of Jacques Boudeville, Perroux's ageographical conception of 'poles' was applied to the analysis of 'growth centers' or agglomeration economies (Darwent 1975). From this perspective, the establishment of a large firm with a significant employment base within a given region would generate 'multiplier effects' stimulating other upstream and downstream firms to locate in close geographical proximity to the 'motor industry' and to one another. Perroux's theories thus formed the basis for a variety of growth pole policies in which governmental agencies subsidized, or fully financed, the construction of major industrial sites—generally in classic Fordist sectors such as cars, steel, and chemicals—in underdeveloped or peripheral zones (Cameron 1970). The basic assumption was that 'some of the new investment [. . .] could be steered to suitable sites to provide the initial stimulus required for establishing a growth pole, which would stimulate the economy of the laggard region. In other words, the relocation of some existing demand, combined with judicious initial expenditure on infrastructure, etc., could trigger long-term cumulative growth which would not require continuing public subsidy' (Chisholm 1990: 76). Like Myrdal and Hirschman, Perroux provided an important intellectual justification for large-scale, spatially redistributive forms of state intervention within marginalized zones of the national territory. The basic logic underlying Perroux's theory is depicted in the diagram (based on Chisholm 1990: 66).

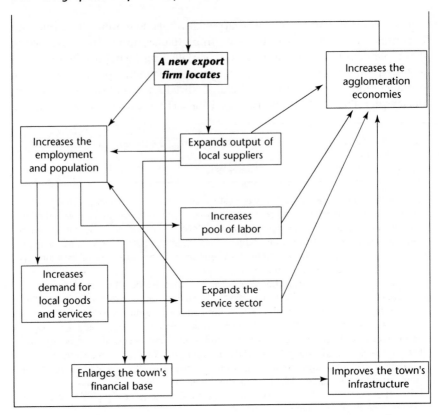

degrees of economic success over the medium and long term (Keating 1998: 48).[9]

Important examples of the types of compensatory regional policy initiatives mobilized in western Europe during the Fordist-Keynesian period include the following:

• In Britain, the Special Areas Act was approved in 1934 with the goal of promoting economic regeneration in four depressed coal-mining regions—south Wales, northeast England, west Cumberland, and central Scotland. Through the Distribution of Industry Acts, these target areas were expanded and relabeled after World War II to include a number of major towns, cities, and other areas afflicted with severe economic problems. The Industrial Development Act of 1966 established still larger target zones for regional policy,

---

[9] Writing in the late 1970s, Henri Lefebvre (2003a [1978]: 91–2) referred to the 'colossal installations' of Fordist heavy industries at Tarente and Fos-sur-Mer—as well as in Lorraine, Dunkerque, and Sagonte—as paradigmatic examples of the national state's increasing role in coordinating the interplay between fixed spaces of production and mobile flows of capital in the modern space economy.

encompassing 40 per cent of British territory and 20 per cent of the total population. The overarching goal of postwar regional policy in the UK was to redistribute employment from rapidly expanding urban cores, such as the South East and the Midlands, into the distressed areas of the north and west. Although the precise boundaries of these 'assisted areas' were modified during the course of the 1960s, they served to delineate broad zones of the UK national territory in which industrial relocation was to be encouraged through diverse regional policy measures, including development grants, employment premiums, tax concessions, and discretionary loans.[10]

• In France, postwar regional policies were developed in close conjunction with a series of five-year plans that underpinned national economic policy. Their main aim was to decentralize industrial capacities and employment out of the dominant Paris region and into major provincial cities, towns, rural areas, and border zones. Following the introduction of the Fourth National Plan in 1964, one of the cornerstones of this program was the delineation of eight 'countervailing metropoles' (*métropoles d'équilibre*)—Lyon, Marseille, Bordeaux, Lille, Strasbourg, Toulouse, Nantes, and Nancy—that were intended to serve as focal points for urban growth, population expansion, and infrastructural investment in peripheral regions dispersed outside the Parisian metropolitan area. The goal of such policies was 'to promote an urban division of labor so that each [of the *métropoles d'équilibre*] would be able to rival Paris in some way, becoming a magnet for activity in some critical area' (Ross and Cohen 1975: 746). In addition, French regional policy channeled substantial public funds into medium-sized 'regional centers' for industrial growth and rural areas while imposing tax penalties on firms committed to locating in the Paris region.[11]

• Postwar regional planning in Italy was initiated in 1950 with the establishment of the Southern Italy Development Agency (*Cassa per il Mezzogiorno*), an executive body responsible for promoting agricultural modernization, industrial growth, and territorial management throughout the Southern region. Subsequent initiatives in regional planning, in which the Cassa played a central coordinative and financial role, were oriented above all towards the alleviation of large-scale territorial disparities between the industrialized North and the predominantly agricultural South. As of the late 1950s, through tax incentives, capital grants, soft loans, and infrastructural investments, the Cassa began to mobilize a variety of fiscal incentives and grants in order to promote industrial relocation into the Mezzogiorno, where new industrial development zones, growth centers, and 'nuclei of industrialization' (*Nuclei di Industrializzazione*) were established in strategic locations. The Italian Institute for Industrial Reconstruction (IRI), a multi-sectoral state holding com-

---

[10] Brown 1972; Law 1980; Moore, Rhodes, and Tyler 1986; Thomas 1975; Yuill 1979.

[11] Allen and MacLennan 1970; Clout 1975; Dunford 1988: 231–51; Hansen 1968; Hull 1979; OECD 1976; Ross and Cohen 1975.

pany responsible for coordinating the investment activities of public enterprises, likewise played an active role in rechanneling capital into the underdeveloped Mezzogiorno during this period of so-called 'extraordinary state intervention' (*Intervento Straordinario*). From the mid-1960s, with the introduction of the first National Economic Plan, regional policies oriented towards the South were integrated more explicitly with national economic agendas.[12]

• In West Germany, postwar regional policies emerged with the approval of the Spatial Planning Law (*Raumordnungsgesetz*—ROG) in 1965 which required the promotion of 'equal life conditions' (*gleichwertige Lebensbedingungen*) across the entire national territory. The ROG distinguished urban regions, where economic growth and population expansion were expected to continue unabated, from various types of 'problem regions', including rural peripheries and marginalized zones along the eastern border. The problem regions were delineated with reference to their major cities and towns, which were labeled 'federal development areas' (*Bundesausbaugebiete*) and targeted for state aid and infrastructural investment, including capital grants, soft loans, and depreciation allowances. As of the late 1960s, the ROG was expanded to include depressed coal-mining areas in the Saarland and the Ruhr zone as important targets for state assistance. This redistributive approach to spatial planning was further extended in 1969 with the introduction of the Program for the Improvement of Regional Economic Structure (*Gemeinschaftsaufgabe 'Verbesserung der regionalen Wirtschaftsstruktur'*—GA), which was intended, above all, to enhance coordination among federal and *Land* (state) authorities in the implementation of compensatory regional policy. In general terms, then, the overarching focus of postwar regional policy in West Germany was on the spreading of developmental capacities, capital investment, and employment from the major urban regions into 'lagging' areas such as small towns, rural peripheries, and border zones.[13]

• The Netherlands represents one further variation on these broad trends within postwar regional policy. In the Dutch context, a variety of national land-management and spatial planning initiatives were mobilized during the course of the 1960s in order to disperse industry, population, and employment from the western Randstad region—composed of Amsterdam, Utrecht, Rotterdam, and the Hague—into the peripheral regions and depressed areas of the North, East, and South. The initial impetus for this project of spatial decentralization and 'concentrated deconcentration' was the Physical Planning Act of 1962 (*Wet op de ruimtelijke ordening*—WRO), which was followed in 1966 by the more comprehensive Second National Physical Planning Report (*Tweede Nota over de ruimtelijke ordening*). These national government initiatives attempted to promote a more balanced form of territorial development while simultaneously preventing unchecked suburban sprawl both within and beyond the Randstad megalopolis. They designated 'development areas' and 'development

---

[12] Allen and MacLennan 1970; Dunford 1988: 145–61; Holland 1972a; R. King 1975; OECD 1976; Ronzani 1979; Selan and Donnini 1975.
[13] Blacksell 1981; Brenner 1997a; Casper 1979; Schikora 1984; Väth 1980; Zielinski 1983.

nuclei' into which industrial capacities, infrastructural investments, and public resources were to be channeled through a variety of direct and indirect policy measures. In addition, Dutch regional policy during the postwar period addressed various contextually specific issues such as structural unemployment, land reclamation, and the development of ports and inland waterways, which were particularly crucial to the Netherlands' distribution-based national economy.[14]

Brunet's (1973) map (Map 4.3, overleaf) of the French spatial structure depicts the intended effects of these compensatory regional policies in one national economic system. The diffusion of developmental capacities, industrial investment, and employment from the Parisian metropolitan core into the country's western and southern peripheries is represented through stark, forceful arrows; and the rest of the national territory is configured into precisely defined functional zones into which metropolitan socioeconomic forces were to be diffused outwards. Throughout western Europe, closely analogous maps were disseminated by regional development agencies and national spatial planning ministries in order to represent the goals and projected consequences of compensatory regional policies within each national economy. Such maps served to glorify the modernizing power of the national state and to underscore its alleged capacity to sculpt patterns of industrial growth, population distribution, and employment according to a comprehensive, nation-wide plan.

Reflecting on the political geographies of postwar Keynesianism across western Europe, Keating (1998: 47) summarizes the logic and the impacts of these nationally specific patterns of regional policy:

a key feature of early [regional] policies was the diversion of industrial activity from one region of the state to another. From a political perspective this had the advantage of addressing several constituencies at the same time. For the problem regions, diversionary policies brought jobs and investment. For regions of full employment, they relieved pressures on infrastructures, labour markets and housing, and limited in-migration. For the national economy as a whole, the policy could be presented as a way of utilizing under-employed resources in the regions and expanding national output in a non-inflationary manner. There was also a social dimension, as territorial equity comprised part of the postwar social settlement, along with the integration of the working class. Finally, there was a political rationale, as regional policy was seen as a mechanism for consolidating the nation state in regions where dissent was likely, as well as boosting the fortunes of governing parties.

And, indeed, as many studies have subsequently indicated, such direct and indirect interregional resource transfers had a very significant impact upon the intra-national geographies of uneven development during the postwar period, contributing to an unprecedented convergence of per capita disposable income within most western European states (Ashcroft 1982; Dunford and

---

[14] Dutt and Costa 1985; Faludi and van der Valk 1994; Faludi 1991; Gay 1981; S. Hamnett 1982; Zonneveld 1989.

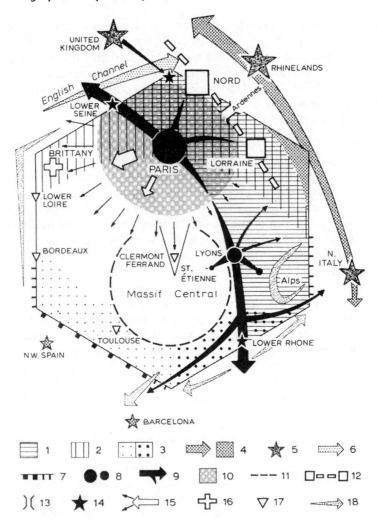

Map 4.3. Compensatory regional policy in postwar France

Key (from Clout 1981*a*: 27): 1. Industrial and urbanized areas; 2. High rates of natural increase of population; 3. 'Southern France'; 4. Rhinelands axis and its 'overspill' into France; 5. Major industrial growth centers in neighboring countries; 6. Main maritime routes; 7. Mountainous international frontiers; 8. Major industrial focus; 9. Main axes of communication; 10. Major national growth area; 11. 'Area of repulsion'; 12. Old industrial regions in need of renovation; 13. Upland core, dividing an axis of nineteenth-century industrialization; 14. Major port complex; 15. Outward expansion of economic activities from the inner Paris Basin; 16. Rural labor complex; 17. Large provincial urban centers; 18. Major areas of tourism.

Source: Brunet (1973: 251); repr. in 'France', in Clout (1981*a* 27).

Perrons 1994). This nationally oriented project of industrial decentralization, urban deconcentration, and spatial equalization must thus be viewed as one of the major state spatial strategies through which the regulatory architecture of spatial Keynesianism was articulated.

Automatic stabilizers

> A region which forms part of a political community, with a common scale of public services and a common base of taxation, automatically gets 'aid' whenever its trading relations with the rest of the country deteriorate. There is an important built-in fiscal stabilizer [...]
>
> Nicholas Kaldor (1970: 345)

In addition to explicit, locationally targeted forms of interregional resource transfer, spatial Keynesianism was also premised upon a number of so-called 'automatic stabilizers' that were activated through regionally differentiated economic fluctuations rather than through direct political intervention (MacKay 1995). In contrast to explicit regional policies, such automatic stabilizers 'transfer the economic impact of state expenditures and of differences in taxation from one area to another' (Dunford and Perrons 1994: 169). This interregional redistributive mechanism was generally 'built in' to national fiscal and social welfare systems, enabling low-income regions to pay lower taxes while receiving higher levels of government expenditure, and requiring high-income regions to pay higher taxes while receiving lower levels of public support (Kaldor 1970). The overarching purpose of automatic stabilizers was to help marginalized areas absorb the impact of economic shocks while diverting the surplus income of core regions to stabilize the national economy as a whole (MacKay 1995, 1994). The logic of automatic stabilization is summarized schematically in Fig. 4.4 (overleaf), which depicts the model of regional resource transfer among 'donor regions' and 'recipient regions' that was famously developed by the Cambridge regional economist Nicholas Kaldor (1970).

As the figure illustrates, the system of automatic stabilization was calibrated so that government expenditure would decline within each region as per capita income rose. Conversely, personal taxation levels within each region were calibrated to increase linearly with increases of per capita income. Under these circumstances, 'low-income regions enjoy fiscal gains (they pay less in taxes than they receive in services and benefits); high-income regions provide support' (MacKay 1994: 576). In sum, as one postwar commentator explained: 'the poorest region must not turn into a geographical proletariat; the growth of its *per capita* income must not be slower than the national mean' (Boudeville 1966: 56).

In the late 1970s, a detailed cross-national comparative study known as the MacDougall Report was conducted by the European Commission to examine the impact of automatic stabilizers upon regional income levels in advanced capitalist states (CEC 1977). While the study found that automatic stabilizers

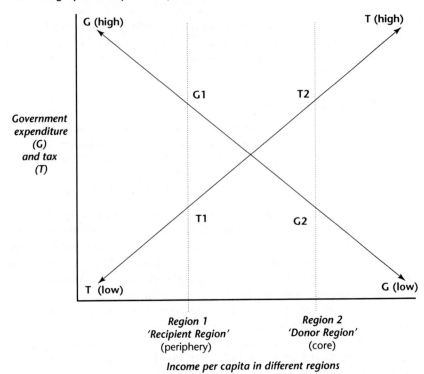

Fig. 4.4. Kaldor's model of automatic stabilizers: alleviating uneven development?
Source: based on Mackay 1994: 576

generated more explicit regional effects in federal states than in unitary states, it indicated that these mechanisms of interregional resource transfer had reduced regional income inequalities by an average of 40 per cent during the high Fordist period in the countries under investigation—five western European states (West Germany, the UK, France, Italy, and Switzerland), as well as the USA, Canada, and Australia (CEC 1977: 12). In particular, similar levels of interregional transfer (at identical income levels) were found to be occurring in the UK, West Germany, and Italy, which otherwise had quite different fiscal systems. The MacDougall Report thus concluded that 'the reality of automatic stabilization is remarkably close to the model' (MacKay 1994: 577).

Automatic stabilizers can be viewed as state spatial projects insofar as they significantly influenced the geographical distribution of governmental expenditures within each national state apparatus. Just as importantly, automatic stabilizers also served as state spatial strategies insofar as, by rechanneling state funds towards less favored or marginalized regions, they generated spatially redistributive effects across much of the national territory. For this reason, automatic stabilizers represented one of the key institutional pillars of spatial Keynesianism.

Nationalized spatial planning systems

> Economic regionalism was at first national in character. The point of this
> lies in the fact that the nation can assist the region, by embarking upon a
> complementary policy for spontaneous development as well as a rational
> policy intended to stimulate new economic activities.
>
> J.-R. Boudeville (1966: 48)

As of the late 1950s and early 1960s, a number of western European countries
introduced national systems of spatial planning designed to guide future
patterns of territorial development in a comprehensive manner. Such initiatives were generally centralized within newly established governmental ministries devoted specifically to problems of urban development, housing,
population distribution, infrastructural planning, and large-scale territorial
management. The paradigmatic exemplar of this new, comprehensive
approach to national spatial planning was the French agency, DATAR, the
Delegation for Regional Development and Territorial Planning (*Délégation
pour l'Aménagement du Territoire et l'Action Régionale*) (see Box 4.5, overleaf).

Closely analogous, if less internationally prominent, planning ministries
were established in many other western European countries, including Germany, the Netherlands, and Sweden. In other European countries, such as
Britain and Italy, comprehensive, territory-wide approaches to spatial planning were developed by national economic ministries—in the former case, by
the (short-lived) Department of Economic Affairs; and in the latter case, by the
National Commission for Economic Planning (Wannop 1995). Such programs
were viewed as an important extension of medium- and long-term macroeconomic planning.

National spatial planning generally involved efforts to forecast future
patterns of national territorial development and, on this basis, to develop
'indicative plans' that would mobilize state resources to influence those
patterns through a combination of inducements and restrictions. These new
systems of spatial planning usually entailed the comprehensive division of
each national territory into specific types of regional units, classified with
reference to basic economic indicators (per capita income, employment
levels, and so forth) that were often distinct from extant administrative
jurisdictions. These subnational economic spaces were the key geographical
reference points in terms of which future national trends were predicted
and the targets for various forms of state regulatory intervention were identified. National spatial planning initiatives also entailed strategies for incorporating local and regional interests into national policy agendas, often through
the establishment of new regional consultative bodies—for instance, the
French Regional Economic Development Commission (*Commission de Développement économique régionale*—CODER); the English Regional Economic Planning Councils (REPCs); the Italian Regional Economic Planning Committees
(CRPEs); and the Belgian Regional Economic Councils (Keating 1998: 50–1).

Box 4.5. DATAR and the rise of nationalized spatial planning in France
Sources: Allen and MacLennan 1970; Dézert 1999; Essig 1979; Ross and Cohen 1975.

Regional planning is perhaps the latest innovation in the *dirigiste* or 'neoca-
pitalist' political economy which emerged in France during the post-World
War II years. In France perhaps more than anywhere else in the advanced
capitalist world, the state has come to play a key organizing and energizing
role in economic life. Because the very rapid economic development that
flowed from these planning efforts tended to accentuate regional imbal-
ances already present in France, regional planning became a necessary
addition to the planning operation [...] French regional planning was an
attempt at injecting some geographical rationality into national economic
planning, not an attempt at giving the grass roots more say about economic
objectives. Thus it involved a *centralization* of influence, not the regionalization or decentralization of power as one might naively have expected.

(Ross and Cohen 1975: 748)

DATAR was founded under the Gaullist regime in 1963, in conjunction with the Fourth
National Plan (1961–4). Responsible to the Prime Minister, the agency was required to
advise the government on all matters of regional planning and policy. In particular, DATAR
acquired a variety of key roles in managing French national territorial development during
the period of high Fordism:

• It assumed various interministerial functions, coordinating between governmental departments involved with any aspect of regional development and spatial planning. Its remit
'was to coordinate regional development activities on a national level, on a local level, and
between levels. It was to be the general synthesizing organization for regional planning
[...] it was to serve as a general center of animation for regional planning, promoting
activity to keep the planning and execution program thriving wherever such activity was
needed' (Ross and Cohen 1975: 739).

• It supervised regional development projects in diverse policy fields, including the planning and zoning of large-scale industrial estates, water management, tourism development, and the establishment of national parks.

• It engaged in various forms of indicative planning intended to project and shape future
developmental patterns across the national territory.

• It introduced the Regional Development fund *(Fonds interministerial pour l'aménagement
du territoire en France*—FIAT) to channel state resources into strategic local public investments.

• It promoted the decentralization of industry and employment away from Paris and into
other towns and cities throughout the French territory, above all in the West, the Massif
Central, and the South. Particular attention, in this context, was devoted to the automobile, aerospace, telecommunications, and oil sectors.

• DATAR was also central to the implementation of the *métropoles d'equilibre* policies,
whose goal was likewise to disperse industrial capacities into peripheral towns and
regions.

By establishing a central institutional locus for the coordination of territorial development
policies, DATAR played a key role within the regulatory architecture of spatial Keynesianism
in France. It established new regulatory capacities for the shaping of national state space
and introduced new forms of knowledge and representation through which developmental trends could be forecast and potentially influenced through state action.

Frequently, these indicative planning initiatives were linked directly to national economic plans, which were introduced during the high Fordist period to guide macroeconomic growth. Thus, the Italian national development program or Vanoni Plan of 1954, the French National Plan of 1966, and the British National Plan of 1965 all contained specific regional policy prescriptions intended to influence future patterns of territorial development and to alleviate intra-national territorial disparities (Holland 1976*b*: 50–4).

The project of indicative planning therefore overlapped significantly with the agendas of compensatory regional policy, for both entailed the mobilization of state spatial strategies intended to divert investments away from overheated metropolitan cores into less developed or marginalized areas. However, in contrast to the relatively successful outcomes of compensatory regional policies, the project of indicative planning proved largely to be a 'white elephant' (Holland 1976*b*: 50–4). It was relatively ineffectual in practice due to, among other problems, the difficulty of translating national macroeconomic goals into viable strategies of regional development; a continued politicization of regional policy priorities; and a chronic lack of appropriate inducements to influence capitalist firms' locational decisions (Keating 1998: 48–50).

Nationalized industries: the public ownership of major Fordist firms

While public ownership of major capitalist firms predated the Fordist era, state-owned sectors expanded considerably during and after World War II in a number of western European countries (Holland 1974). Most crucially for this discussion, the nationalization of key Fordist sectors such as coal, steel, energy (oil, gas, electricity, nuclear power), shipbuilding, automobiles, and aerospace had significant spatial ramifications within many western European states. For, in financing large-scale industries, national governments were also channeling significant public resources into the places and regions where such industries were located. During the course of the Fordist period, national enterprises were increasingly instrumentalized by national governments 'in an effort to solve specific problems, as if they were agencies of the state' (Vernon 1974: 3). Crucial among these problems was that of ensuring 'the location of more investment and jobs in regions of low employment growth or actual employment decline' (Holland 1974: 31). Many of these initiatives were directly inspired by François Perroux's approach to growth poles (see Box 4.4). In such cases, the public enterprise was intended to operate as a propulsive firm or 'motor industry' whose upstream and downstream linkages to other (private) firms would enhance the spatial concentration of investment and employment within marginalized areas of the national territory. Consequently, in a number of prominent cases in France, Italy, and Sweden, among other countries, state control over public enterprise was mobilized explicitly in regional policy initiatives as a means to divert investments into marginalized areas.

The most comprehensive program to mobilize public enterprise in compensatory regional policy initiatives was embodied in the Italian Institute for Industrial Reconstruction (IRI), a state holding company that directed large-scale industrial investments into Italy's traditionally underdeveloped South (see Box 4.6).

Box 4.6. Public enterprise as a means of regional policy: the case of the Italian Institute for Industrial Reconstruction (IRI)
Sources: Allen 1972; Holland 1972a, b.

> The IRI's contribution to regional development in the South has been so large that it raises the question whether other countries with serious regional problems would be advised to create a similar institution with a similar obligation to assist the economies of their less prosperous areas.
>
> (Allen 1972: 179)

The Italian Institute for Industrial Reconstruction (*Istituto per la Ricostruzione Industriale—IRI*) was founded in 1933 as a state-owned holding company responsible for distributing credit and financial assistance to key industrial and service firms. During the subsequent decade, the IRI played a major role in financing military production; thus much of its fixed capital was damaged extensively during World War II. Following the war, the IRI reemerged and was mobilized to modernize major national industries. By the late 1950s, the IRI had been transformed into a public agency holding majority shares in key industrial and service firms. The IRI's investments were spread broadly among multiple sectors, including steel, cars, industrial machinery, electrical engineering, electronics, aircraft, shipbuilding, transport, highway construction, telecommunications, and railways.

Unlike many approaches to public enterprise that prevailed in western Europe, the 'IRI formula' attempted to integrate state control and market forces. Thus the IRI generally controlled significantly less than 100 per cent capacity in the sectors in which it operated; and it generally controlled less than a total shareholding. The IRI engaged in economic planning by attempting to steer investment into propulsive firms within multiple sectors; its goal was to generate multiplier effects that would influence private economic activity as well. In this manner, the IRI acquired a prominent role in stimulating industrial relocation into the southern Mezzogiorno region. By promoting strategic relocations within public enterprises, the IRI attempted to generate 'follow-my-leader' geographical effects in which private firms linked to those sectors would replicate their locational patterns, and thus likewise channel investment into underdeveloped zones of the national territory. In one prominent example, the IRI's decision to construct an Alfa-Romeo car plant in Naples was subsequently followed by plant construction programs in the South by the private car companies FIAT and Pirelli (Holland 1972a: 26).

These policies generated significant regional consequences. The IRI's manufacturing employment levels in the South increased by 82 per cent between 1960 and 1969; and total IRI employment (including services) increased by 63 per cent during the same period (Allen 1972: 174–5). The IRI thus represented a classic instance of a compensatory, redistributive approach to regional policy grounded simultaneously upon growth pole theory and public enterprise.

While the IRI was unique in the degree to which it explicitly promoted intra-national industrial relocation, other western European national governments likewise utilized their control over public enterprises to promote this agenda through a variety of policy mechanisms. The following examples illustrate some of the ways in which state control over public enterprise could operate as a form of regional policy:

- In 1957, the Italian national government passed a law 'requiring state-owned enterprises to locate 40 per cent of their existing investments and 60 per cent of their new investments in the Mezzogiorno' (Grassini 1981: 76). In 1968, these regulations were modified so that 100 per cent of investment in new factories and 60 per cent of total investment by public enterprises was required to be located in the South or in other marginalized areas (Holland 1974: 33). These laws regulated the activities of the IRI as well as all other state-controlled investment groups.

- The French national planning agency DATAR played a key role in influencing the locational geographies of public enterprises throughout France. For instance, in 1971, following lengthy negotiations, the French national car company Renault was forced by DATAR to build a new electrical foundry in Brittany rather than in Paris. After another protracted struggle, DATAR succeeded in influencing the French national government to require Renault to build a new assembly plant near the harbor of Nantes, along with another assembly plant in Le Havre, closer to existing production facilities in Normandy (Anastossopoulos 1981).

- The Swedish parliament followed the example of the Italian IRI by establishing a state holding company (*Statsföretag*) in 1970 to influence investments in various sectors, including mining, shipbuilding, and banking. One of its expressed goals was also to promote new employment opportunities, particularly in the defense sector, at Vasteras in the underdeveloped North (Holland 1972b: 261).

However, even in instances in which national governments did not attempt explicitly to influence the locational decisions of public enterprises, the existence of such state-financed industrial investments significantly enhanced employment levels and economic capacities within many marginalized localities and regions. In a number of western European countries, such as Britain, Germany, and Italy, state enterprises played a key role in constructing large-scale transportation infrastructures, such as railways and highways, which also generated significant consequences for regional industrial and employment growth. More generally, insofar as they established an entirely new layer of state-financed economic activity within inherited spatial divisions of labor, public enterprises formed a crucial element within the broader political and economic geographies of spatial Keynesianism (Martin and Sunley 1997: 280).

Intergovernmental centralization and urban managerialism

The postwar period witnessed an unprecedented centralization of intergovernmental relations throughout western Europe (Rose 1985; Mény and Wright
1985). This centralization of intergovernmental authority occurred in close
conjunction with the consolidation of a 'nationwide approach' to state power
in which governmental institutions were organized primarily for the 'routine
nationwide organization and delivery of services of the welfare state: health,
education, pensions and other income-maintenance programmes, public
transport, and post and telephone communications' (Rose 1985: 13–14). By
the early 1970s, nationwide public services accounted for over two-thirds of
total public expenditure among western European national governments
(Rose 1985: 17–18).

The centralization of intergovernmental relations and nationwide systems of
public service delivery during the postwar period entailed the increasing sub-
sumption of municipal and regional state institutions within nationally organized institutional hierarchies. In order to standardize the provision of welfare
services and to coordinate national economic policies, national states centralized the instruments for regulating urban development, thereby transforming
local states into transmission belts for centrally determined policies and programs. Under these conditions, '[l]ocal governments functioned as subordinate
agencies; states or regions were merely administrative units that channeled the
growth and distributed the blessings of Fordist modernization evenly all over
the nation' (Mayer 1991: 107). Within this managerial framework of urban
governance, the overarching function of state institutions at the urban scale
was the reproduction of the labor force through public investments in housing,
transportation, social services, and other public goods, all of which were
intended to replicate certain minimum standards of social welfare and infrastructure provision across the national territory (Harvey 1989a; Castells 1977).
In this manner, local states were instrumentalized in order 'to carry out a
national strategy based on a commitment to regional balance and even growth'
(Goodwin and Painter 1996: 646). Centrally financed local welfare policies also
constituted important elements of the social wage, and thus contributed significantly to the generalization of the mass consumption practices upon which
the Fordist regime of accumulation was contingent (Goodwin and Painter
1996: 641). Painter (1991: 28) summarizes the key operations of the managerial
local state under Fordism as follows:

Firstly, local government provided a range of services whose production was unprofit-
able for capital under existing technical and organizational conditions, but for which
there was a political demand. This principle of universal provision of a range of basic
services is one hallmark of the Fordist era [. . .] Secondly, local government was involved
in widespread planning and regulatory activity. This included land-use and resource
planning and environmental health regulation. Finally, the representative functions of
local government meant that the relatively consensual social democratic politics char-

acteristic of Fordism could find partial expression at the local level [...] Thus as a key component of the welfare state, local government was central to the Fordist mode of regulation [...]

This pervasive localization of the state's collective consumption functions under Fordist-Keynesian capitalism was famously theorized by Castells (1977) in his structuralist discussion of the urban question. For Castells (1977: 459), the state's role in the promotion of collective consumption was the very essence of urban politics within state monopoly capitalism:

The state apparatus intervenes in a massive, systematic, permanent and structurally necessary way in the process of consumption [...] Thus we shall witness a takeover by the state of vast sectors of the production of means essential to the reproduction of labour power: health, education, housing, collective amenities, etc. It is here that the 'urban problematic' sends down its roots [...] Since the state is taking charge of considerable, and objectively socialized, part of the process of consumption, since it intervenes in direct aid to the large economic groups that dominate that process, since consumption is becoming a central cog in the economic, political and ideological levels, whereas no centralized regulation of the process is being set up in the economic [level], the state becomes the veritable arranger of the processes of consumption as a whole: this is at the root of so-called 'urban politics'.

This conceptualization of the postwar scalar division of state regulation was further specified by Saunders (1985) in his well-known 'dual politics' thesis. Despite his otherwise deep theoretical differences with Castells, Saunders (1985: 302) likewise postulated a scalar division of state regulation in which 'consumption interventions [tend] to be focused on local, electoral levels of the state while production interventions gravitate towards higher level corporatist institutions'. While Saunders emphasized the nationally specific patterns in which this formation of state power was articulated, his analysis nonetheless underscored a broad tendency for policies oriented towards social reproduction (for instance, housing, education, and welfare services) to be locally scaled (Fig. 4.5, overleaf).

In sum, throughout the postwar period, the nationalization of state space proceeded in significant part through the instrumentalization of municipal state institutions to implement centrally determined policy agendas. Western European managerial local states thus formed a key institutional pillar within the broader regulatory architecture of spatial Keynesianism. Just as crucially, however, managerial local states also served as key institutional arenas in which the crisis and eventual breakdown of the Fordist regime of accumulation would be articulated. With the onset of economic stagnation and recession during the course of the 1970s, neoliberal, neoconservative, and monetarist pressures for state fiscal retrenchment intensified. As the institutional edifice of the Keynesian welfare national state was increasingly destabilized, the continued expansion of local government services was subjected to intense political criticism from the Right. Consequently, 'The expansion

	NATIONAL STATE	LOCAL STATE
Function	Promotion and regulation of capitalist production	Promotion of social reproduction and delivery of public services
Policy arenas	Industrial policy; labor relations; unemployment policies; regional planning policies; etc.	Public transportation; housing; health services; education; social welfare; recreational planning; etc.
Social base	Class interests	Consumption sector interests
Dominant ideology	Capitalist: private property rights	Public service: citizenship rights

Fig. 4.5. Saunders's 'dual state' thesis: mapping the scalar division of state regulation under spatial Keynesianism

Source: dervied fron Saunders 1985: 306, and *passim*; see also Saunders 1979.

of local government during the early 1970s fed into a crisis of regulation rather than contributing to a successful mode of regulation' (Goodwin and Painter 1996: 642). As we shall see in the next chapter, the managerial, welfare-oriented functions of municipal governments have been significantly reconfigured since the breakdown of North Atlantic Fordism in the early 1970s.

New towns policies and state-subsidized suburbanization

> The location, number, character and size of New Towns must be examined within the framework of national policy for the settlement system. Such a *national policy* would aim at the creation of a suitable hierarchy of settlements based on the criterion of functional integration of settlement units at different levels of economy
>
> (Galantay 1980: 25; italics in original)

Inspired in part by Ebenezer Howard's concept of garden cities, new towns were established near major British cities, above all around London, immediately following World War II (Osborne and Whittick 1977). As the Fordist pattern of urbanization matured during the course of the 1960s, a number of western European national governments likewise attempted to alleviate urban congestion, to expand housing infrastructures, and to counteract urban sprawl by establishing suburban new towns in relatively close proximity to major urban centers. While new towns were established in the Soviet Union, Eastern Europe, and Brazil as a form of compensatory regional industrial policy, in the western European context they served chiefly as a means to facilitate and coordinate the ongoing decentralization of industry and population beyond core metropolitan areas. In a number of western European cases, new towns were introduced with the explicit goal of creating new economic centers in previously underdeveloped areas. Examples of this trend included Mourenx in southwestern France; Wulfen and Marl in the northern Ruhr district of Germany; Salzgitter in the German Harz mountains; Wolfsburg in Germany's Lower Saxony region; Cwmbran in South Wales; Corby in the East Midlands, England; Newton Aycliffe, Washington, and Peterlee in northern England; Skelmersdale outside Liverpool; and Luossavaara-Kiiruna in northern Sweden, among others.[15] However, the majority of new towns policies in postwar western Europe were intended to subsidize and plan the process of suburban development, particularly around large urban centers. Thus large-scale urban planning initiatives in London, Paris, Copenhagen, Stockholm, the German Ruhr zone, and the Dutch Randstad delineated particular axes along which development was to be channeled and specific growth nodes into which population settlement was to be concentrated (Burtenshaw, Bateman, and Ashworth 1981). Major national examples of new towns policies included the following (for an overview, see Merlin 1971; Golany 1978):

• In Britain, the New Towns Act of 1946 established a national legal and administrative framework for the construction of new towns in suburban zones during much of the Fordist period. It established New Town Development Corporations to guide the growth of new towns and introduced various financial incentives and restrictions intended to influence firms to decentralize their investments outside the most congested urban cores. Other components of the framework were intended to reduce metropolitan-wide population densities by encouraging residential decentralization. To this end, new forms of public infrastructure and housing were planned and eventually constructed outside London and other major cities such as Glasgow, Edinburgh, Cardiff, Newcastle, Liverpool, Manchester, and Birmingham. In conjunction with the planning of suburban new towns, large-scale green belts were also established around many urban areas (Osborne and Whittick 1977). However, while over a half million people moved into the new towns during the two decades following World War II, these settlements absorbed only a relatively minimal proportion of total population growth within major British metropolitan regions (Merlin 1971: 59).

• The French new towns program was developed following World War II to address an increasingly serious housing crisis. Large-scale housing estates, or *grands ensembles*, were subsequently constructed with considerable state financial aid through a variety of public or quasi-public agencies. As of 1958, a number of priority development areas (*Zones d'Urbanisme en Priorité*—ZUPs) were delineated throughout the Paris region—including Aulnay-Sevran,

---

[15] Clout 1981*b*: 50; Merlin 1971: 243–4; Burtenshaw, Bateman, and Ashworth 1981: 280.

Créteil, Vitry, and Massy-Antony—in which such residential clusters were to be concentrated (Merlin 1971: 142; Scargill 1983). Smaller *grands ensembles* were subsequently established at the fringes of other major French towns as well as, in a few cases, in relatively marginal, monoindustrial zones and peripheral regions. The French new towns program was significantly expanded in 1965 following the introduction of a master plan for urban development in the Paris region (*Schéma Directeur d'Aménagement et d'Urbanisme de la Région Parisienne*—SDAURP), which demarcated a constellation of new, relatively self-contained urban centers that were to be constructed along two preferential axes running along a southeast to northwest arc roughly parallel to the Seine beyond the city's most densely developed core. Broadly analogous master plans were subsequently introduced for Lyon, Nancy, Nantes, and Rouen-Le Havre. All were intended to forecast emergent urbanization patterns and demographic trends, and on this basis, to establish a new planning framework through which appropriate infrastructures for housing and transportation could be established. The priority of constructing and regulating new towns was also reflected in national policies and integrated directly into the Sixth and Seventh National Plans of 1971–5 and 1976–80. In addition, during this period the earlier ZUPs were replaced by concerted development zones (*Zones d'Aménagement Concertée*—ZACs) in order to channel both private capital investment and governmental subsidies into the new towns (Rubenstein 1978).

• In the Netherlands, new towns policies likewise acquired considerable prominence during the postwar period (Constandse 1978). The previously mentioned project of 'concentrated deconcentration', which was introduced through the Second Report on Physical Planning of 1966, contained an explicit agenda of counteracting suburban sprawl and preserving open spaces. It attempted to achieve these goals in part through the establishment of new towns in close proximity to major urban cores, both within and beyond the western Randstad megalopolis. In addition to overspill towns or 'growth towns' in immediate proximity to Rotterdam, the Hague, and Amsterdam, major new towns such as Almere, Lelystad, Dronten, and Emmeloord were also constructed on reclaimed land in the polder zones of the Zuider Zee. The Dutch approach to new towns was thus focused above all on channeling residential investments beyond the city cores, on coordinating urban development and preserving open space within the Randstad's 'Green Heart', on expanding regional transportation infrastructures, and on managing demographic expansion throughout the national territory.

To be sure, the decentralization initiatives embodied in new towns policies were articulated at a more circumscribed scale than the types of regional policies discussed above. For the most part, they promoted a dispersion of industrial investment, infrastructural facilities, and population *within* major Fordist industrial regions rather than across the entire national territory of Fordist-Keynesian states. Nonetheless, insofar as western European new towns policies were mobilized in significant measure through national governmental initiatives, and were articulated with reference to politically delineated target areas that were dispersed widely across each national territory, they must be viewed as key spatial strategies through which the regulatory architecture of spatial Keynesianism was articulated. Moreover, as Fordist urban regions expanded beyond the inherited boundaries of traditional industrial city cores, new towns policies became crucial regulatory instruments through which state institutions—at once on national, regional, and local scales—attempted to manage the process of urban and suburban development within their territories. While new towns policies did not disappear with the crisis of North Atlantic Fordism in the early 1970s, their broad diffusion in the western European context must be understood above all in relation to the distinctive types of state spatial strategies that emerged under the Fordist-Keynesian configuration of capitalist development.

Consolidated metropolitan government

Within this nationalized system of urban governance, metropolitan political institutions acquired an important mediating role between managerial local states and centrally organized, redistributive systems of spatial planning. Between the mid-1960s and the early 1970s, diverse types of consolidated metropolitan institutions were established in a number of major western European city-regions. Among the major metropolitan institutions established during this period in western Europe were the Greater London Council (1963), the Madrid Metropolitan Area Planning and Coordinating Commission (1963), the *Rijnmond* or Greater Rotterdam Port Authority (1964), the urban communities (*communautés urbaines*) in French cities such as Bordeaux, Lille, Lyon, and Strasbourg (1966), the Stuttgart Regional Association (*Regionalverband Stuttgart*) (1972), the metropolitan counties in British cities such as Manchester, Birmingham, Liverpool, Leeds, Sheffield, and Newcastle (1974), the Barcelona Metropolitan Corporation (*Corporació Metropolitana de Barcelona*) (1974), the Greater Copenhagen Council (*Hovedstadsrådet*) (1974), the Greater Frankfurt Association (*Umlandverband Frankfurt*) (1974), and the Ruhr Municipal Agency (*Kommunalverband Ruhr*) in the Ruhr agglomeration of Germany (1975) (see Keating 1998: 55–71; Lefèvre 1998: 14–16; Sharpe 1995a).

Debates on the construction of metropolitan and regional institutions during this era focused predominantly upon the issues of administrative efficiency, local service provision, regional planning, and spatial redistribution within the nationally organized macroeconomic policy frameworks of the Keynesian welfare national state (Lefèvre 1998). Thus, newly established metropolitan institutions came to operate as key, coordinating administrative tiers within the centralized hierarchies of intergovernmental relations that prevailed under spatial Keynesianism. The establishment of larger units of urban territorial administration was viewed as a means to rationalize welfare service provision and to reduce administrative inefficiencies within rapidly expanding urban agglomerations. At the same time, metropolitan institutional forms were seen as being analogous to Fordist forms of mass production insofar as they were thought to generate economies of scale in the field of public service provision (Keating 1997: 118). Accordingly, in a 1969 report to the British government, the Redcliffe-Maud Royal Commission maintained that a population of 250,000 inhabitants was the optimal size threshold for effective, efficient local government (Lefèvre 1998: 12; Keating 1997: 119). As suburbanization and industrial decentralization proceeded apace during the course of the 1970s, metropolitan political institutions came to be justified as a means to establish a closer spatial correspondence between governmental structures and functional territories (Lefèvre 1998). Numerous consolidated metropolitan institutions were introduced in order to differentiate urban and regional spaces functionally among zones of production, housing, transportation, recreation, and so forth. Metropolitan authorities subsequently acquired important roles in guiding industrial expansion, infrastructural investment, and population settlement beyond traditional city cores into suburban fringes, primarily through the deployment of comprehensive land-use plans and other policy mechanisms to influence intra-metropolitan locational patterns. Box 4.7 summarizes the basic features of Rotterdam's *Rijnmond*, which repre-

---

Box 4.7. Rotterdam's *Rijnmond*: a typical case of metropolitan governance under spatial Keynesianism
Source: Hendriks and Toonen 1995.

The Greater Rotterdam port authority, or Rijnmond, was established by the Dutch national parliament in 1964 to coordinate urban and regional planning in the large-scale industrial region encompassing Rotterdam, its surrounding municipalities, and the extensive seaport zone. Whereas Rotterdam had previously attempted unsuccessfully to annex many suburban municipalities, the Rijnmond provided a new institutional framework through which local physical plans (*bestemmingsplannen*), land-use planning and housing construction could be coordinated. The authority was governed by the Rijnmond Council, which was directly elected by the population of the participating municipalities. The Council could not enact binding laws; its more circumscribed remit was to offer guidelines to the municipalities regarding issues of regional concern, including harbor and industrial development, industrial and commercial locations, housing, infrastructural development, transportation, and environmental matters. It thus represented 'a fully-fledged authority... with a restricted competence' (Hendriks and Toonen 1995: 152). It operated primarily on a voluntary basis, through a range of planning and policy initiatives articulated with reference to the Rotterdam region's position in the Dutch national space-economy:

• *Physical planning* programs were mobilized to coordinate the development of the port and other industrial zones and to establish an appropriate functional division of regional space. Housing zones were concentrated within the cities and towns and separated from polluted industrial areas; and open space was to be preserved as much as possible.

• In the field of *economic development*, the Rijnmond played a more limited, coordinative role. It introduced a Regional Economic Plan that contained a vision for infrastructural development in the area. It also indirectly addressed various issues related to economic development, including unemployment, transportation, and education.

• The Rijnmond played a key role in determining the distribution of *housing construction* throughout the region. Quotas for housing construction were established at a national scale but exact intra-regional locations were determined by the Rijnmond.

• Additionally, the Rijnmond assumed an important role in various forms of *recreational and environmental policy*. It coordinated the maintenance of recreational areas, monitored noise and pollution levels, and regulated various aspects of waste management.

The Rijnmond embodied the large-scale bureaucratic institutions that underpinned processes of urban and regional governance during the Fordist period. It served as an important institutional relay within the Dutch framework of spatial Keynesianism while also addressing various place-specific regulatory problems that emerged within the Rotterdam port region during the Fordist phase of urbanization.

sents a typical instance of metropolitan governance within a large-scale Fordist industrial city-region.

Metropolitan governmental institutions appear significantly to have influenced the geographies of state power and urban development during the era of high Fordism. They represented, on the one hand, state spatial projects insofar as they entailed the construction of new layers of political authority and regulatory capacity within inherited national administrative geographies. At the same time, insofar as they were generally harnessed in order to influence land-use and investment patterns within major western European city-regions, the consolidated metropolitan governments of this period also provided an important institutional platform for the mobilization of new types of state spatial strategies at urban and regional scales.

Summary

Four broad generalizations regarding the political geographies of Fordist-Keynesian capitalism in western Europe may be derived from the preceding analysis.

1. The Keynesian welfare national states that emerged throughout western Europe during the postwar period were premised upon new ways of organizing, producing, and transforming political-economic space: they entailed a variety of spatially selective institutional changes and policy initiatives that fundamentally transformed inherited patterns of state spatial organization and intervention.

2. The problem of regulating and reproducing Fordist forms of urban development figured crucially in the production of these new forms of state space under postwar capitalism. As the Fordist pattern of urbanization accelerated and expanded, a new politics of spatial Keynesianism emerged across western

Europe in response to some of its major accompanying regulatory dilemmas. These dilemmas included, above all, improving administrative efficiency in metropolitan public service delivery, subsidizing and coordinating urban collective consumption, controlling the growth of rapidly expanding urban cores, securing an appropriate spatial fix for Fordist regional production systems, and, above all, alleviating newly emergent patterns of uneven development within each national territory. National states thus played a key role in constructing, regulating, and reproducing the historically specific sociospatial configurations upon which the Fordist regime of accumulation was grounded.

3. The regulatory architecture of spatial Keynesianism was composed of diverse state spatial projects and state spatial strategies that, taken together, contributed in fundamental ways to the pervasive nationalization of political-economic space that unfolded during this period.

• State spatial projects were mobilized in order to centralize regulatory control over local development and to subsume all locational points within the national territory—from cities, industrial regions, suburbs, and new towns to outlying areas and rural zones—within relatively uniform, standardized administrative frameworks.

• State spatial strategies were mobilized in order to embed local and regional economies within an encompassing national space-economy and to equalize the distribution of industry, infrastructure, and population across the entire national territory.

To be sure, across western Europe, each national state mobilized contextually specific combinations of such state spatial projects and state spatial strategies, and their precise institutional contours and regulatory orientations frequently became major focal points for political and territorial struggles. Nonetheless, the basic elements of spatial Keynesianism, as defined in the preceding discussion, crystallized in some form within all major western European national states between the early 1960s and the mid-1970s.

4. The politics of spatial Keynesianism signaled a significant intensification of state intervention into processes of urban and regional development. During the postwar period, national states not only rationalized, homogenized, and standardized subnational administrative structures, but mobilized a variety of political strategies intended, simultaneously, to facilitate economic expansion and social reproduction within core urban regions and to disperse socioeconomic capacities and infrastructural investments outwards into suburban areas, outlying towns, and peripheralized regions. In this manner, cities, regions, and all other subnational economic spaces were increasingly enclosed within nationalized interscalar rule-regimes. Such rule-regimes served at once to subordinate cities and regions to the centralizing regulatory controls of national governments and to position them within nationally configured spatial div-

isions of labor. While these interscalar rule-regimes were constructed, in a trial-and-error manner, through the various institutional forms and policy mechanisms outlined above, they eventually came to define the basic parameters for local political-economic life under the Fordist-Keynesian system.

The politics of spatial Keynesianism thus shaped the institutional landscapes of postwar capitalism in profound, far-reaching ways. Spatial Keynesianism played a key role in producing, stabilizing, and reproducing the distinctive urban built environments, land-use patterns, regional agglomeration economies, and nationwide infrastructure networks associated with Fordist urbanization. At the same time, the mobilization of spatial Keynesianism accelerated, deepened, and intensified the nationalization of political life that was unfolding under North Atlantic Fordism, and in this manner, contributed significantly to the establishment of qualitatively new forms of state spatial selectivity. Indeed, spatial Keynesianism arguably represented the historical high-point of twentieth-century state strategies to alleviate uneven geographical development and territorial inequality within national borders. Insofar as intra-national polarization was widely viewed as a significant barrier to stabilized national macroeconomic growth, the project of alleviating spatial disparities and equalizing socioeconomic capacities across the national territory acquired an unprecedented political-economic significance throughout western Europe.

The crisis of North Atlantic Fordism and the collapse of spatial Keynesianism

> the old Fordist mechanisms were developed to regulate the interaction of
> regional economies within a single nation state rather than the interaction
> of interdependent regional and national economies in Europe.
>
> Mick Dunford and Diane Perrons (1994: 170)

During the early 1970s, a number of tumultuous political-economic shifts sent shock-waves through the North Atlantic Fordist configuration of territorial development. These included, most crucially, the breakdown of the Bretton Woods monetary order, the eruption of the 1973 oil crisis, the intensification of economic competition from newly industrializing countries, the decline of traditional Fordist mass production industries, the rise of mass unemployment, the increasing saturation of Fordist mass consumption markets, and the fiscal crisis of Keynesian welfare national states (Armstrong, Glyn, and Harrison 1991). These developments significantly destabilized the interscalar arrangements on which the Fordist-Keynesian political-economic order was organized—national regulation of the wage relation and international regulation of currency and trade (Peck and Tickell 1994). The deregulation of financial markets and the global credit system since the collapse of the Bretton

Woods system in 1973 undermined the viability of nationally organized demand management and monetary policies. Meanwhile, the intensified globalization of production, inter-capitalist competition, and financial flows diminished the capacity of Keynesian welfare national states to treat their territorial economies as if they were self-enclosed, quasi-autarchic economic spaces (Agnew and Corbridge 1994; Jessop 2002). Under these circumstances, as Dunford (1994: 102) explains:

The connection between a national model of productivity growth and national macro-economic mechanisms was weakened: in the [Fordist] past, wages paid in a particular country were also a major determinant of demand for the products of firms located in that country; with internationalization, wages appeared increasingly as nothing more than a cost to be minimized. As successive governments adopted monetarist strategies, demand stagnated. World demand is just the sum of demand in each individual nation, however, and so as countries copied one another, world demand stagnated and the recession was internationalized.

The global economic recession persisted into the 1980s, and processes of deindustrialization spread throughout the older industrialized world. Growth rates continued to plunge during this decade even as monetarist and neoliberal regulatory strategies superseded the traditional Keynesian formula of promoting full employment, institutionalizing demand management, and guaranteeing national social welfare (Fig. 4.6). Taken together, these trends heralded the dissolution of the Fordist developmental regime, the systematic

	1960–8	1968–73	1973–9	1979–89
Real GDP	4.7	4.8	2.5	2.2
Real GDP per head	3.8	4.2	2.1	1.9
Civilian employment in manufacturing	0.5	0.6	−0.9	−1.2
Civilian employment in services	1.7	1.9	1.7	2.1
Real GDP per person employed	4.6	4.3	2.4	1.6
Real value added in manufacturing per person employed	5.2	5.6	3.1	2.6
Real value added in services per person employed	3.0	3.2	1.7	0.6

Fig. 4.6. The end of the 'golden age'? Output, employment, and productivity growth in the EU, 1960–89: average annual percentage rates of growth
Source: Dunford 1994: 101, using data derived from OECD 1991.

collapse of the interscalar arrangements upon which the postwar regulatory order had been grounded, and the dramatic proliferation of rescaling processes throughout the North Atlantic zone (Fig. 4.7).[16]

For present purposes, my concern is to summarize the ways in which the political-economic and scalar transformations of the 1970s destabilized the regulatory system of spatial Keynesianism that had been established in western Europe and opened up a political space in which alternative approaches to the regulation of capitalist urbanization could be mobilized. In this context, four distinct but closely intertwined processes of political-economic restructuring are of particular relevance.

Spatial scale(s) of regulation	Regulatory tensions and contradictions underlying the crisis of North Atlantic Fordism
Global	International financial instability intensifies following the crisis of the Bretton Woods system in 1971; intensified competition from newly industrialized countries threatens US global economic hegemony and contributes to the formation of a new international division of labor
Global–national relations	The internationalization of capital accelerates, undermining the viability of Keynesian demand-management strategies and macro-economic policies. Domestic macroeconomic problems are transmitted globally
National	With the decline of Fordist mass production systems, deindustrialization deepens, leading in turn to mass unemployment. Consequently, national governments experience extensive fiscal crises under conditions of declining control over interest rates and intensifying domestic distributional conflicts
National–local relations	New forms of intra-national uneven development emerge and classical approaches to territorial redistribution become increasingly ineffectual; fiscal retrenchment shrinks local budgetary resources and intergovernmental conflicts intensify
Local	As national fiscal crises worsen, local welfarism is undermined. Urban social exclusion and sociospatial polarization intensify

Fig. 4.7. The crisis of North Atlantic Fordism and the destabilization of state scalar configurations

Source: derived from Peck and Tickell 1994: 300–2.

[16] For general overviews of these transformations and their geographical consequences, see Swyngedouw 1992*a*; Soja 1989; and Brenner and Theodore 2002*a*. The character of these ruptures, and their implications for the future trajectory of capitalist development, remain a matter of intense academic controversy. Useful overviews of the major positions in these debates can be found in Albritton et al. 2001; Boyer and Drache 1996; and A. Amin 1994. See Crouch and Streeck 1997 for an overview of different national trajectories of restructuring during the post-1970s period.

1. *The decline and restructuring of mass production industries.* The traditional mass production industries upon which the Fordist growth dynamic was grounded—such as steel, petrochemicals, machine tools, appliances, shipbuilding, and the like—contracted and declined as of the early 1970s due to a combination of intensified international competition, market saturation, and accelerated technological change (Lipietz 1987). Unemployment rates skyrocketed as a wave of plant closings, layoffs, and industrial relocations swept across the western European economic landscape (Coriat and Petit 1991). Although revitalized, neo-Fordist forms of mass production eventually crystallized within these sectors in a number of European manufacturing regions, their industrial output and their share of total employment were markedly diminished relative to the levels associated with the high Fordist period. In the wake of these shifts, many of the boom regions of European Fordism, such as the English Midlands and the German Ruhr district, experienced long-lasting crises that were manifested in mass unemployment, social upheaval, infrastructural decay, and extensive ecological degradation (Albrechts and Swyngedouw 1989). The decline of Fordist industries also had a profound impact upon more economically diversified metropolitan regions, such as London, Paris, Hamburg, and Milan, which confronted analogous problems within their traditional manufacturing sectors. Whereas Fordist systems of production have in no way disappeared from the western European economic landscape, they have been profoundly restructured during the last three decades, as the socio-institutional conditions for maintaining industrial competitiveness in the manufacturing sector have been reconstituted under a new geoeconomic configuration (Benko and Dunford 1991; Martinelli and Schoenberger 1991).

These developments presented major dilemmas for the forms of territorial redistribution that had been introduced during the Fordist-Keynesian period. Spatial Keynesianism targeted relatively underdeveloped regions as the key geographical focal points for redistributive public subsidies. Throughout the postwar period, large-scale manufacturing regions were viewed as economic spaces in which continued industrial development and social prosperity could be presupposed unproblematically. However, following the crisis of North Atlantic Fordism, this widespread equation of core city-regions with consistent economic growth, permanent full employment, and stable demographic expansion became increasingly problematic. Instead, a new configuration of territorial development began to crystallize in which (*a*) cities and regions across each national territory were restructured according to their relative positions within supranational spatial divisions of labor; and (*b*) new forms of territorial inequality were superimposed upon inherited national patterns of core–periphery polarization. Within this transformed economic landscape, in which all major local and regional economies were undergoing systematic, highly disruptive transformations, the project of alleviating intra-national uneven development through *national* state intervention was significantly complicated. For, in contrast to the Fordist territorial configuration, in which spaces of growth, spaces of decline, and lagging areas appeared to be separated neatly among distinct geographical zones within each national territory, these different types of spaces were now being superimposed and interlinked at all geographical scales (Veltz 1997: 84). During the course of the 1970s, a number of western European countries attempted to confront this situation by including declining industrial cities on the list of target areas for redistributive territorial policies. Yet, as economic stagnation persisted and national budgets were further squeezed, the viability of promoting spatial equalization at a national scale was widely called into question.

2. *The rise of flexible production systems.* As traditional manufacturing sectors declined, productivity, output, and employment began to expand significantly in newer industrial sectors grounded upon flexible or lean production systems. These flexible production systems have been characterized by (*a*) the use of non-dedicated machinery and multi-skilled labor at the firm level, (*b*) expanding social divisions of labor, dense subcontracting relationships, and short-term contracts at the inter-firm level, and (*c*) increasing product differentiation in the sphere of circulation (Storper and Scott 1989). Although flexible production methods have had a profound impact upon labor practices and industrial organization throughout the advanced industrial economies (Moody 1996), they have been particularly prevalent within three broad sectoral clusters—high-technology industry, advanced producer and financial services, and revitalized craft production (Scott and Storper 1992). Additionally, during the last three decades, flexible production methods have been introduced into traditional mass production sectors such as automobiles, as large firms have mobilized new strategies in order to enhance efficiency, to bolster market share, and to externalize risks in an increasingly turbulent geoeconomic environment. Such strategies have generally involved the construction of new spatial divisions of labor in which (*a*) command and control functions are centralized at selected headquarters locations, (*b*) low-cost production facilities are dispersed outwards through global sourcing arrangements, and (*c*) other major production functions are subcontracted or outsourced to diverse supplier networks (Nilsson and Schamp 1996). These organizational changes have been facilitated through advanced information technologies that provide 'new opportunities for increased flexibility in the production process and [. . .] new options to customize products and production' (Nilsson and Schamp 1996: 122).

The nature of the industrial divide between Fordist production systems and their putative successor(s) remains a matter of considerable dispute (A. Amin 1994; Gertler 1992; Lovering 1995). The crucial point here is that, during the last three decades, the firms and regions associated with these flexibly organized, high-technology sectors have come to account for an increasing proportion of industrial output and employment in major western European economies (Storper 1996). As in other zones of the world economy, the crystallization of flexible production systems in the western European context has been particularly evident in so-called 'neo-Marshallian industrial districts', where small- and medium-sized firms have traditionally dominated the local economic fabric and where mass production technologies were never widely adopted (Sabel 1994; Scott 1988). In addition to these new industrial spaces, flexible production systems and high-technology industrial clusters have also acquired prominence within and around major European global cities such as London, Paris, Amsterdam, Copenhagen, Frankfurt, Zürich, and Milan. Here, large transnational corporations rely extensively upon local webs of producer and financial services industries that are generally organized in flexible, decentralized forms (Amin and Thrift 1992; Sassen 1993).

The postwar project of spatial Keynesianism entailed various top-down political strategies to establish standardized socioeconomic assets, integrated policy frameworks, uniform institutional forms, and territory-encompassing infrastructural arrangements across the entire national space-economy. However, with the crystallization of flexible production systems, corporate and political elites have come to emphasize the importance of customized, specialized, and place-specific conditions of production within local and regional economies as a means to secure global competitive advantages. As Veltz (1997: 79) explains:

Economic development is increasingly 'systemic' and presumes highly specific conditions in the environment, in the production and use of techniques and in competencies. Whereas in Taylorist-Fordist mass production, territory mainly appeared as a stock of generic resources (raw materials, labour), nowadays it increasingly underpins a process of the creation of specialized resources. Competitiveness among nations, regions and cities proceeds less from static endowments as in classical comparative-advantage theories, than from their ability to produce new resources, not necessarily material ones, and to set up efficient configurations in terms of costs, quality of goods or services, velocity and innovation.

As we shall see in subsequent chapters, the increasingly widespread demand for place-specific regulatory, institutional, and infrastructural arrangements is to be interpreted less as the reflection of inexorable economic requirements than as the expression of newly emergent *political strategies* intended to position particular subnational economic spaces within supranational circuits of capital accumulation. In the present context, the key point is that the diffusion of flexible production systems across the western European space-economy has helped to create a political-economic environment in which the traditional, compensatory regulatory strategies associated with spatial Keynesianism are considered increasingly obsolete.

3. *The globalization and integration of European economic space.* The aforementioned sectoral realignments have occurred in close conjunction with an intensified globalization and supranational integration of the European space-economy. Since the early 1980s, European national economies have been fused

together through the institutions of the European Community and, subsequently, the European Union (EU). With the consolidation of the Single European Market (SEM) and the resultant abolition of tariff and non-tariff barriers to trade in 1993, international trade and foreign direct investment among the EU member states' economies were further accelerated. These developments, coupled with the deregulation of the financial sector and the process of European monetary integration, have significantly enhanced the mobility of capital within the EU states, reduced transaction costs, and intensified inter-firm competition for European market shares (Leyshon and Thrift 1995). Consequently, 'companies are increasingly restructuring themselves to serve the European market as a whole rather than a set of national markets. They eliminate national headquarters and have just a European headquarters; they have European-wide marketing strategies; and they streamline their product range and concentrate their production' (Cheshire and Gordon 1995: 109).

Meanwhile, non-European foreign direct investment has also increased throughout the European economic zone, above all in the United Kingdom, France, the Netherlands, and Germany (Dicken and Öberg 1996; Amin and Malmberg 1994). Through a combination of mergers and acquisitions, the formation of international strategic alliances, and new greenfield investments, North American and Japanese corporations, among others, have become major players in European economies, competing directly with European firms for national market shares. Dunford (1994: 106) reports that 'direct overseas investment in EU countries reached $98.4 billion [in the early 1990s] compared with $14.8 billion in the 1980s, increasing some three times faster than gross domestic fixed capital formation in most of the large EU economies'. Major European corporations have likewise internationalized their activities to become an important source of foreign direct investment in North America, Japan, and Europe itself. Cross-border mergers, acquisitions, and strategic alliances among European firms have also significantly intensified as of the 1980s (Amin and Malmberg 1994).

In short, during the last three decades, a 'tidal wave of massive organizational and geographical restructuring' (Dicken and Öberg 1996: 115) has been under way within western Europe as major European, North American, and Japanese firms compete aggressively for market positions within the European economy while struggling to adjust to rapid geoeconomic fluctuations. As a result of these developments, places throughout the EU are being embedded ever more directly in the 'hyperspace' of transnational corporate capital (Swyngedouw 1989). Even in the midst of the deepening localization and agglomeration tendencies associated with the proliferation of flexible production systems and processes of global city formation, the economic vitality of cities and regions has come to hinge still more directly upon their positions within international corporate geographies (Amin and Malmberg 1994; Amin and Thrift 1994).

The politics of spatial Keynesianism were oriented towards the patterns of core–periphery polarization that had emerged during the Fordist period within relatively autocentric national economies and extensively nationalized urban systems. Within this framework, territorial inequality was expressed, above all, in the form of a divide between expanding industrial city cores and relatively underdeveloped rural peripheries. However, post-1980s patterns of globalization and Europeanization have destabilized this pyramid-shaped model of territorial organization by (*a*) embedding national economies within European and global spatial divisions of labor; (*b*) expanding the geographic scope of transnational corporate activities; and (*c*) enhancing the significance of horizontal linkages among large metropolitan regions situated in different national territories (Veltz 1997: 83). As Veltz (1996) indicates, within this 'archipelago economy' metropolitan city cores are being delinked from their immediate hinterlands and connected instead to a transnational inter-urban network. In this new geoeconomic context, the project of generating spread effects within a single national territory, as had been envisioned by postwar regional economists such as Myrdal and Hirschman, has become increasingly problematic. As Holland (1976*a*: 39) already recognized in the 1970s, multinational corporations have little reason to cooperate with the regional development priorities of their host countries; they thus contribute very little to the spreading of industrial capacities beyond the major metropolitan centers in which their own operations are located. More generally, by undermining the territorial and functional coherence of national economies, contemporary processes of globalization and European integration have at once enhanced sociospatial polarization at a variety of spatial scales and undermined inherited national political strategies for alleviating the latter (Veltz 2000).

4. *The crisis of the Keynesian welfare national state.* The Keynesian welfare national states that had been consolidated throughout postwar western Europe underwent a major crisis during the course of the 1970s (Jessop 2002). The geoeconomic trends outlined above undermined the viability of traditional Keynesian macroeconomic objectives such as full employment, price stability, and sustained economic growth while also generating major new regulatory problems such as rising unemployment, growing public debt, decaying public infrastructures, and shrinking state budgets. Subsequently, a variety of post-Keynesian regulatory experiments were mobilized whose aggregate effect, by the late 1980s, was to erode the institutional foundations of the postwar welfare state and to establish a more fragmented, multitiered, and market-oriented regime of state regulation than previously existed (Cerny 1995). At different times and speeds in western Europe, the redistributive mandate of the welfare state was superseded by a new framework of political imperatives, such as promoting structural competitiveness, labor market flexibility, efficient public management, and permanent innovation. In this new political regime, labor is treated primarily as a cost of production in world markets rather than as a source of (domestic) consumer demand; accordingly, social policy is increasingly subordinated to the priority of maintaining labor market flexibility in a global context (Jessop 1993; Mayer 1994). Meanwhile, the demand-side polit-

ical programs that prevailed within the Keynesian welfare state, such as employment policy, fiscal policy, and monetary policy, have been subordinated to supply-side agendas intended to enhance the flexibility of markets, firms, and sectors and to construct advanced communications and transportation infrastructures for transnational corporations (Torfing 1999). In this manner, western Europe has witnessed the widespread consolidation of competition states, as outlined in general terms in Ch. 2 above.

This transformation of inherited forms of state regulation necessarily had major implications for the politics of spatial Keynesianism across western Europe. First, the crisis and retrenchment of the Keynesian welfare state occurred under conditions in which demands for state aid were significantly increased while tax revenues were shrinking. The availability of public funds for redistributive spatial policies was thus severely constrained, and traditional forms of compensatory regional policy, like other forms of social policy, were scaled back. Second, the rise of New Right and neoliberal political agendas in many western European states entailed an aggressive ideological assault upon many established forms of state redistribution, which were now widely represented as an unnecessary interference in market relations. Consequently, the postwar view of socio-territorial inequality as a barrier to stable macroeconomic growth was called into question. Intra-national spatial disparities were increasingly reinterpreted as unavoidable preconditions and consequences of market-driven growth rather than being seen as regulatory problems in their own right (Brenner and Theodore 2002*a*). The project of promoting territorial redistribution within the national territory was thus widely dismissed as an obsolete remnant of an earlier, gentler configuration of political-economic life. Third, and finally, the establishment of multiscalar regulatory arrangements within post-Keynesian competition states introduced a further complication for inherited forms of spatial Keynesianism. Within these newly emergent institutional hierarchies stretching from the EU downwards to regional and municipal governments, national states are no longer the singular, predominant scale of political-economic governance and territorial redistribution. Consequently, even in national contexts in which political support for projects of spatial equalization has persisted, there has been considerable confusion, disagreement, and debate regarding the appropriate scale at which such projects should be mobilized. The national scale is no longer taken for granted as the primary level on which the regulation of capitalist territorial development should occur (Keating 1998). Therefore, coupled with the aforementioned geoeconomic trends, processes of welfare state retrenchment during the 1980s significantly destabilized the politico-institutional foundations for spatial Keynesianism, causing its various regulatory components to be weakened, redefined, or, in some cases, dismantled.

Drawing on the stylized conceptualization of spatial Keynesianism that was presented in Fig. 4.2, Fig. 4.8 (overleaf) provides a schematic representation

	STATE SPATIAL PROJECTS	STATE SPATIAL STRATEGIES
SCALAR DIMENSION	State regulatory capacities are *centralized* around the national scale	The *national* scale is promoted as the most essential level of political-economic life
	Emergent contradictions:	*Emergent contradictions:*
	• As the crisis of Fordism deepens, state regulatory burdens expand and the tax base shrinks. This leads many central governments to streamline large-scale national bureaucracies and systems of public service delivery • Place-specific socioeconomic problems proliferate. This undermines the viability of centralized, top-down regulatory arrangements and lends increasing support to decentralization initiatives	• Global and European economic integration relativize inherited scalar hierarchies and undermine the territorial coherence of national economies. Core metropolitan economies are increasingly delinked from their hinterlands. This undermines efforts to channel spread effects into lagging areas of the national territory • The regulatory architecture of state power becomes increasingly multiscalar, stretching from the European and national levels to the regional and local levels. The lack of a privileged scale of state power seriously complicates the attempt to alleviate intra-national patterns of uneven development
TERRITORIAL DIMENSION	Relatively *uniform* structures of territorial administration are established throughout the national space-economy	Redistributive policies are mobilized in order to *equalize* the distribution of industry and infrastructure investment across the national space-economy
	Emergent contradictions:	*Emergent contradictions:*
	• With the decline of Fordist manufacturing industries, local and regional state institutions attempt to construct customized institutional forms and policies to confront their own, place-specific regulatory problems. This undermines the uniformity of national administrative structures • With the spread of flexible production systems, corporate demands intensify for customized, place-specific conditions of production. This undermines the project of establishing a generic, highly standardized grid of state institutions and public infrastructural configurations across the national territory	• As deindustrialization intensifies, new forms of territorial inequality are superimposed upon inherited patterns of core–periphery polarization. Urban cores can no longer be equated with continuous economic growth. This generates a crisis of traditional compensatory approaches to spatial policy • The fiscal crisis of the national state shrinks the public resources available for redistributive social and spatial policies • The ascendancy of the New Right undermines public support for redistributive policy measures. Uneven spatial development is increasingly reinterpreted as a necessary *basis* for macro-economic growth rather than as a potential *barrier* to the latter

Fig. 4.8. Emergent contradictions of spatial Keynesianism during the 1970s (Compare Fig. 4.2, p. 132)

of its destabilization following the crisis of North Atlantic Fordism. As the figure indicates, due to the patterns of crisis-induced restructuring reviewed above, the key state spatial projects and state spatial strategies associated with spatial Keynesianism became increasingly problematic during the course of the 1970s. These restructuring processes generated a variety of contradictions that undermined the basic political, institutional, and geographical preconditions upon which spatial Keynesianism was premised. By the end of the 1970s, therefore, it had become apparent that the project of alleviating uneven spatial development through the promotion of balanced urbanization within relatively closed national economies was as short-lived as the Fordist accumulation regime itself.

Conclusion

Spatial Keynesianism played an essential role in constructing and reproducing the nationalized forms of state spatial selectivity that were consolidated during the Fordist-Keynesian period. However, with the relativization of scales following the geoeconomic crises of the early 1970s, the primacy of the national scale of state power was significantly decentered, leading to new conflicts and struggles over the rearticulation of state scalar arrangements. Crucially, however, spatial Keynesianism was not dismantled through a single, catastrophic rupture. Rather, its constitutive elements were eroded due to a confluence of distinct processes of restructuring, leading in turn to path-dependent, politically contested regulatory realignments and institutional modifications within each national state apparatus. Despite considerable variation in the form and pace of these national responses, such shifts opened up a political and institutional space in which alternative, significantly rescaled approaches to the political regulation of capitalist urbanization could be mobilized. In the next chapter, I analyze the consolidation of these post-Keynesian approaches to urban policy and territorial regulation, and their implications for the geographies of state spatiality. Such an investigation provides an illuminating basis on which to decipher the emergence and subsequent evolution of new state spaces in contemporary western Europe.

FIVE

Interlocality Competition as a State Project: Urban Locational Policy and the Rescaling of State Space

The State's role in favour of foreign or transnational capital heightens the uneven development of capitalism within each country in which foreign capital is reproduced. It does this most notably by designating particular regions as 'development areas' to the detriment of certain others—a process which [. . .] produces fissures in the national unity underpinning the bourgeois State.

Nicos Poulantzas (1978: 213)

Rather than be constrained by an external force of globalization [. . .], the state has created conditions whereby it must make a normative differentiation between different aspects of its 'national' economy with respect to the global. The state has not retreated but reconfigured the way it applies its regulations, so that they are no longer 'national' in the sense of being universally and evenly applied throughout the territory of the state [. . .] National economic policies and institutions are increasingly being geared towards promoting internal competition between different industrial regions for investment . . .

Angus Cameron and Ronen Palan (1999: 282)

Urban governance and the political geographies of the competition state

As noted in our initial discussion of state restructuring in Ch. 2, the early 1980s witnessed the consolidation of post-Keynesian competition states throughout western Europe, as national governments struggled to adjust inherited institutional frameworks, regulatory arrangements, and modes of intervention to a radically transformed geoeconomic configuration. In contrast to the redistributive agenda associated with the Keynesian welfare national state, the competition state attempts to promote economic regeneration by enhancing the global competitive advantages of its territory—including its major firms, its labor force, its technological infrastructure, and its most important cities, regions, and industrial districts. In the western European context, this agenda has been pursued through diverse political strategies, including, most prominently, (*a*) neoliberal initiatives intended to dismantle inherited regulatory constraints upon capital accumulation and thus to reduce the costs of public administration and economic activity within particular locations; and (*b*) social democratic initiatives intended to establish the institutional, social, and technological preconditions for high road pathways of (re)industrialization in which the priorities of profitability and social equity are reconciled (V. Schmidt 2002; Scharpf and Schmidt 2000). Box 5.1 summarizes some of the

---

Box 5.1. Key perspectives on the post-Keynesian competition state

---

'Competition state' is used here to characterize a state that aims to secure economic growth within its borders and/or to secure competitive advantages for capitals based in its borders, even where they operate abroad, by promoting the economic and extra-economic conditions that are currently deemed vital for success in competition with economic actors and spaces located in other states [. . .] [T]he competition state prioritizes the pursuit of strategies intended to create, restructure or reinforce—as far as it is economically and politically feasible to do so—the competitive advantages of its territory, population, built environment, social institutions and economic agents.

(Jessop 2002: 96)

Rather than attempt to take certain economic activities *out* of the market, to 'decommodify' them as the welfare state was organized to do, the competition state has pursued *increased* marketization in order to make economic activities located within the national territory, or which otherwise contribute to national wealth, more competitive in international and transnational terms.

(Cerny 1997: 259)

the state in the contemporary global economy can be legitimately regarded as a *competition state* [. . .] In this respect, states take on some of the characteristics of firms as they strive to develop strategies to create competitive advantage [. . .] Both are, in effect, locked in competitive struggles to capture global market shares. Specifically, states compete to enhance their international trading position and to capture as large a share as possible of the gains from trade. They compete to attract productive investment to build up their national production base, which, in turn, enhances their competitive position. In particular, states strive to create, capture, and maintain the higher value-adding elements of the production chain.

(Dicken 1994: 112)

key perspectives on the competition state that have been developed by critical political economists.

Competition states should not be construed as fully consolidated, internally coherent state forms. They are generally grounded upon speculative, mutually contradictory political strategies intended simultaneously to promote economic development, to enhance national competitive advantages, to alleviate proliferating socioeconomic tensions, and to maintain political legitimation. For this reason, within each state territory, the consolidation of competition states generates new fault-lines of political conflict at various geographical scales, leading in turn to further rounds of trial-and-error regulatory experimentation, institutional evolution, and sociopolitical struggle (Cerny 1995; Panitch 1994). Competition states must thus be viewed as unstable politico-institutional matrices in which a variety of structural realignments, policy realignments, and sociopolitical struggles are unfolding.

Most importantly for our purposes, the consolidation of competition states has entailed a number of fundamental transformations of state spatial selectivity. In contrast to the comprehensive nationalization of regulatory space that was pursued under Fordist-Keynesian capitalism, the current round of global restructuring has entailed the systematic destabilization of inherited national political geographies and the construction of new scalar configurations in a number of major regulatory spheres (Box 5.2). The re-articulation of these regulatory arrangements has been intertwined with a major shaking-up and reconstitution of worldwide interscalar hierarchies. Indeed, current transformations of national state spatiality have been provoked by, and have in turn significantly accelerated, the relativization of scales and the other rescalings, reterritorializations, and rearticulations of capitalist sociospatial organization that were outlined in Ch. 2. This 'reshuffling of the hierarchy of spaces' (Lipietz 1994: 36) has not established a stable interscalar architecture for the regulation of global capitalism, either above or below the national state. On the contrary, these worldwide rescaling processes have triggered an intensely contested 'search for a new institutional fix' (Peck and Tickell 1994) characterized by the proliferation of political strategies intended to manage the disruptive supranational, national, regional, and local consequences of geoeconomic restructuring. The newly forged patterns of spatial selectivity associated with post-Keynesian competition states must be understood in relation to these broader interscalar transformations and the diverse regulatory experiments and political struggles they have provoked.

Against this background, the present chapter develops an interpretation of contemporary transformations of state spatiality in western Europe. My central argument is that urban governance has served as a major catalyst, medium, and arena of state rescaling processes. In the previous chapter, the nationalization of state space under postwar western European capitalism was interpreted as an outcome of political and institutional responses to the

---

Box 5.2. The rescaling of regulatory forms *after* Fordism
Sources: derived from Brenner and Theodore 2002*a*; Swyngedouw 1997; Petit 1999.

> What is generally referred to as 'post-Fordism' [...] is a series of highly contested, deeply contradictory and variegated processes and power struggles that often revolve around scale, control over particular scales, the content of existing scales, the construction of new scales, and the articulation between scales
>
> (Swyngedouw 1997: 156)

- *Wage relation.* Nationalized collective bargaining agreements and national regulations ensuring workers' rights are undermined. In many contexts, wage levels, working conditions, and workers' benefits are renegotiated, in downgraded forms, on a regional, local, sectoral, or plant-level basis.

- *Form of inter-capitalist competition.* National protectionist policies and national barriers to foreign direct investment are weakened or dismantled. Due to the expansion of information and communications technologies, new spheres and methods of inter-capitalist competition emerge. As Japanese and German capital threaten US firms' market shares, inter-capitalist competition intensifies on a global scale.

- *Monetary and financial regulation.* National monetary systems and financial markets are deregulated with the collapse of the Bretton Woods system. As finance capital expands its control over industrial capital, the link between savings and investment is undermined. Global financial speculation intensifies with the rise of 'stateless monies' that lie beyond national regulatory control. Offshore banking centers proliferate and the role of global regulatory bodies expands.

- *The state and other forms of governance.* Traditional Keynesian forms of national demand-management, national macroeconomic policy, and national social welfare policy are undermined. State finances are reduced under conditions of sustained fiscal crisis, and public employment is retrenched. New, supply-side and monetarist programs of state intervention are mobilized, along with programs to promote structural competitiveness, technological innovation, and internationalization in major industries. Redistributive welfare policies are widely superseded by workfare policies intended forcibly to conscript workers into low-wage, contingent labor markets. New scales of regulation emerge at global, supranational, and subnational levels.

- *International configuration.* With the growing dominance of neoliberal ideologies, geo-economic integration intensifies and deepens. Deregulatory initiatives facilitate the expansion of foreign direct investment and global financial speculation. The national scale of capital accumulation is increasingly superseded by supranational economic blocs (the 'triads') and by subnational agglomeration economies (urban growth poles, regional production systems, and industrial districts). Neoliberal political-economic forces promote the further deregulation, liberalization, and privatization of global, supranational, national, and local economic spaces.

---

regulatory dilemmas generated by Fordist-Keynesian forms of urbanization. Analogously, the present chapter interprets the rescaling of western European statehood as an expression of diverse political and institutional responses to the tumultuous, crisis-induced forms of urban restructuring that have unfolded since the 1970s.[1]

The regulation of urban restructuring in post-1970s western Europe has been pursued through a broad array of political strategies, at a variety of spatial scales, and by means of diverse institutional realignments. However, across the western European city-system, the attempt to regulate urban development during the post-1970s period has entailed significant rescalings of state spatial organization and state spatial regulation. For, in pursuing their overarching goal of enhancing the supranational competitive advantages of their territories, western European national, regional, and local states have mobilized a number of profoundly place- and scale-sensitive approaches to institutional reorganization and regulatory intervention, many of which have explicitly targeted cities and city-regions. These include:

- *state spatial projects* intended to establish customized, place-specific regulatory capacities in major cities, city-regions, and industrial districts and, more generally, to decentralize key aspects of economic regulation to subnational (regional or local) institutional levels; and

- *state spatial strategies* intended to reconcentrate socioeconomic assets and advanced infrastructural investments within the most globally competitive city-regions and, more generally, to enhance the territorial competitiveness of major local and regional economies.

This rescaling of statehood has not only eroded the nationalized formations of urban governance and the redistributive forms of state spatial policy that prevailed during the Fordist-Keynesian period. It has also entailed the consolidation of new interscalar rule-regimes (Peck 2002) that have enhanced fiscal constraints and competitive pressures upon cities and regions, impelling their regulatory institutions to privilege the goals of local economic development and territorial competitiveness over traditional welfarist, redistributive priorities. I shall refer to the diverse institutional realignments and regulatory strategies mobilized by post-Keynesian competition states as forms of *urban locational policy* insofar as they explicitly target cities and urban regions as sites for the enhancement of territorial competitiveness (Brenner 2000b). The key institutional features of such urban locational policies, their major political forms, and their relation to the contemporary rescaling of statehood, will be examined at length below.

[1] My intention here is in no way to assert that contemporary processes of state rescaling result entirely or predominantly from state projects and state strategies oriented towards the regulation of urban restructuring. Instead, following from the mode of analysis developed in the preceding chapter, urban governance is conceived here as one among many possible empirical reference points through which the contemporary rescaling of western European statehood may be investigated. Other key reference points for such an analysis include European integration, multilevel governance, welfare state retrenchment, cross-border regions, and the new regionalism. In addition, the process of state rescaling may be fruitfully investigated with reference to the geographies of specific state policies—including, for instance, industrial, labor, immigration, monetary, trade, welfare, housing, and infrastructure policies.

The new, growth-oriented forms of state intervention into urban and regional development that have crystallized in the wake of contemporary rescaling processes have been discussed by numerous urban scholars under the rubric of 'urban entrepreneurialism'.[2] While the present chapter draws upon the empirical insights generated in such studies, I shall embed them within the spatialized state-theoretical framework developed in Ch. 3. From this point of view, the pervasive reorientation of urban governance from the managerial, welfarist mode of the Fordist-Keynesian period to an entrepreneurial, growth-oriented, and competitiveness-driven framework during the post-1970s period is not to be understood merely as a realignment of local institutional forms and functions. Rather, as I indicate below, the proliferation of entrepreneurial approaches to urban governance represents a key expression and outcome of the place- and scale-specific types of state spatial projects and state spatial strategies that have been mobilized by post-Keynesian competition states. As such, entrepreneurial urban policies have been closely intertwined with contemporary processes of state rescaling.

The next section examines the rearticulation of the western European urban system during the last three decades, focusing in particular upon the crystallization of a new mosaic of uneven spatial development in conjunction with ongoing processes of industrial restructuring and European economic integration. On this basis, I consider the new approaches to urban policy that have been mobilized since the 1970s as western European national, regional, and local states have attempted to confront the multifaceted regulatory problems associated with the new configuration of urbanization. Initially, deindustrializing cities and regions mobilized endogenous development policies that attempted to address place- and scale-specific forms of economic decline while strengthening inherited social compromises and forms of territorial redistribution. However, the post-1980s period witnessed a pervasive turn towards urban locational policies—spatially selective state initiatives intended, above all, to enhance the supranational competitive advantages of strategic cities and city-regions. Like the endogenous development policies of the 1970s and early 1980s, these new urban locational policies have emphasized the need for place- and scale-specific forms of state regulatory intervention, but they have been oriented more directly towards positioning major cities strategically within broader global and European spatial divisions of labor than towards the traditional priority of facilitating intra-national or intra-regional territorial redistribution. I argue that, since the mid-1980s, urban locational policies have been an increasingly pervasive state response to the regulatory challenges of geoeconomic restructuring and European integration, and that

---

[2] The literature on urban entrepreneurialism is too extensive to review at length here. For foundational statements, see Harvey 1989*a*; Leitner 1990. For overviews of the transition to urban entrepreneurialism in western Europe, see, among other works, Hall and Hubbard 1998, 1996; Harding et al. 1994; Jensen-Butler, Shachar, and van Weesep 1997; Jewson and MacGregor 1997; Mayer 1992, 1991, 1990; Moulaert and Demazière 1995; and Stöhr 1990.

such policies have in turn triggered a number of fundamental rescalings of state space. In the remainder of the chapter, I survey the major state spatial projects and state spatial strategies through which urban locational policies have been mobilized, and I examine their cumulative impact upon the scalar configuration of western European statehood.

Urban restructuring and uneven spatial development: towards Archipelago Europe?

> The 'core islands' of Archipelago Europe already have a name: the Parisian region; London East Anglia; the new Edinburgh, Glasgow area; the Frankfurt, Stuttgart, and Munich regions; the new Berlin; Brussels 'district'; Rotterdam and Antwerp, together with the rest of the Dutch Randstad; Denmark; Stockholm, Lombardia, the new Veneto, Torino, Madrid, Barcelona. The most aggressive financial resources will be 'available' in these cities/regions, the 'best' universities, research centres and scientific institutions, the 'greatest' theatres, operas, concert houses and musea, headquarters of multinational organisations and networks of the most dynamic SMEs [small- and medium-sized enterprises]. The 'core islands' will tend to establish, maintain and strengthen tighter flows and linkages among themselves than with the rest of 'their' national, European and global peripheries [...] The linkage between the core islands of the Archipelago and the rest are growing increasingly weaker.
>
> Riccardo Petrella (2000: 70–1)

The spatial consequences of the crisis of North Atlantic Fordism have been widely noted (Benko and Dunford 1991; Scott and Storper 1992). In the western European context, this crisis entailed the tumultuous decline of many large-scale manufacturing regions that had been grounded primarily upon Fordist mass production industries. As deindustrialization accelerated and established economic specializations were reworked, formerly dynamic cities and regions were confronted with unforeseen developmental blockages, decaying industrial infrastructures, and proliferating social problems. The urbanized industrial heartlands of western Europe—including the British Midlands, northeast France, western Belgium, the Paris Basin, and the German Ruhr region—experienced devastating socioeconomic and infrastructural crises during this period. In many European countries, as manufacturing industries were downsized, unemployment rates in major cities exceeded 20 per cent, up to twice the national average (CEC 1992: 108). Even in countries in which average unemployment rates did not reach these levels, major cities experienced particularly massive job losses, above all in the manufacturing sector, during the course of the 1980s (Figs. 5.1 and 5.2).

	Total Manufacturing Employment		
	1973 (000s)	Change 1973–81 (000s)	%
Highly urbanized regions (21)	11,414	–2,044	–17.9
Urbanized regions (23)	10,188	–988	–9.7
Less urbanized regions (32)	7,318	–548	–7.5
Rural regions (29)	3,838	–57	–1.5
Total EEC9 regions (105)	32,758	–3,637	–11.1

Fig. 5.1. The decline in manufacturing employment in the European urban system
Source: Keeble 1986: 171; derived from Eurostat Labor Force Survey Data.

	1980	1984	1988
Liverpool	16	24	20
Birmingham	15*	20	15
Copenhagen	8	13	11
Paris	7	8	9
Lyon	6	7	8
Marseille	12	15	17
Brussels	6	10	16
Dortmund	6	16	17
Frankfurt	3	6	6
Hamburg	3	11	12
Amsterdam	8	17	19[†]
Rotterdam	9	17	17[†]
Milan	5*	7	5
Naples	14	15	25
Dublin	10*	14	19[†]
Barcelona	15*	17	14
Madrid	12	18	16

* corresponds to 1981 figure
† corresponds to 1987 figure

Fig. 5.2. Per cent unemployment in major European cities, 1980–8
Source: derived from CEC 1992: 110–18; percentages are rounded to the nearest whole number.

However, some older industrial cities, such as those located in key border regions or in major transportation hubs—for instance, Lille, Barcelona, or Glasgow—were able to renew their strategic importance within the changed geoeconomic configuration. Still other European city-regions—particularly major metropolitan centers such as London, Paris, Amsterdam, Copenhagen, and Milan—experienced simultaneous processes of economic decline and economic rejuvenation as different sectors within their local economies struggled to adjust to the rapidly changing competitive environment. Just as importantly, in the midst of these major sectoral and geographical realignments, new spaces of growth emerged in a number of erstwhile lagging or marginalized regions that were 'insulated from the older foci of Fordist mass production' (Storper and Scott 1989: 27). From Bristol, Cambridgeshire, Grenoble, and Montpellier to West Jutland, Baden-Württemberg, the Swiss Jura, Emilia-Romagna, and Tuscany, these new industrial spaces have been grounded upon flexible production systems and have demonstrated impressive dynamism in a variety of internationalized, high-technology sectors and revitalized craft industries (Scott 1988; Cooke and Morgan 1998). Such new industrial spaces also proliferated on the fringes of major European city-regions, in locations such as the M4 corridor (in western London), Eschborn and Darmstadt (near Frankfurt), the Cité Scientifique in Southern Île de France, the Schiphol airport zone (adjacent to Amsterdam), northern Rotterdam, and northern Copenhagen (Hall and Castells 1994; CEC 1991: 48). Thus, even though historically entrenched territorial disparities decisively conditioned the developmental pathways of cities and regions, the current period has been characterized by qualitatively new forms of uneven development and core–periphery polarization at European, national, regional, and local geographical scales (Dunford and Kafkalas 1992; Lever 1996; Moulaert 1996). These new, Europe-wide geographies of uneven spatial development may be understood as the expression of four closely related trends.

1. *Metropolitanization and the rise of the archipelago economy.* The sectoral transformations and new corporate accumulation strategies of the last three decades have intensified established spatial divisions between advanced, highly developed urban and regional cores and lagging, peripheralized zones (Amin and Tomaney 1995). Faced with enhanced geoeconomic volatility during the last three decades, the leading metropolitan areas of western Europe have been able to exploit two crucial locational advantages—their strategic positions within advanced communications and transportation networks; and their large concentrations of high-skilled workers (Dunford and Perrons 1994: 172–3). Consequently, since the early 1980s, the strategic importance of major metropolitan cities within the western European economy has been significantly enhanced. Veltz (1996) refers to this trend as a process of 'metropolitanization' in which (*a*) high value-added socioeconomic capacities, advanced infrastructures, industrial growth, inward investment, and labor flows are increasingly concentrated within major metropolitan regions, and (*b*) territorial disparities between core urban regions and peripheral towns and regions are significantly intensifying across the entire European economy. Such metropolitanization tendencies have been embodied, during the last two decades, in a number of spatial transformations within European national urban systems, including:

- the increased concentration of high-skilled, high-tech jobs and productivity growth in Paris, which now accounts for over 30 per cent of French
  GNP (Veltz 1996);
- the increasing centralization of management and control functions in
  major German cities such as Frankfurt, Stuttgart, Cologne, Hamburg,
  Munich, and Berlin (S. Krätke 1991);
- the growing dominance of Greater London in producer and financial
  services (Sassen 1991);
- the enhanced significance of the Dutch Randstad as a center for corporate
  headquarters and logistics functions (Dieleman and Musterd 1992); and
- the intensified economic dynamism of local production systems, grounded
  upon a variety of industrial specializations and institutional configurations, in many major European urban and regional economies (Crouch
  et al. 2001).

The consolidation of the Single European Market in 1993 unleashed powerful
centripetal forces that further contributed to the process of metropolitanization and the consequent intensification of territorial disparities (Cheshire
1999). In short, processes of industrial restructuring since the 1970s have
engendered a 'self-reinforcing polarization of high-level activities in well-
resourced and well-connected nodes' (Dunford and Perrons 1994: 173)
throughout the European space-economy. Within the resultant 'archipelago
economy', according to Veltz (1997: 83), 'metropolitan growth creates autonomous centres of development that benefit more from their networked horizontal relationships with other large poles than from their traditional vertical
relationships with the hinterland'.

   2. The formation of transnational urban hierarchies. The rescaling of inherited
urban hierarchies has also contributed to the establishment of new patterns of
uneven spatial development during the last three decades. During the 1950s
and 1960s, each European national economy contained an internal hierarchy
of cities, suburbs, industrial regions, and lagging areas organized according to
their specific functions within Fordist production systems and nationalized
spatial divisions of labor. By contrast, in the current period, processes of industrial restructuring, globalization, and European integration have contributed
to the formation of new transnational urban systems in which the most
globally integrated cities are linked together ever more tightly while disadvantaged places and less favored regions are further marginalized (Sassen 1993; S.
Krätke 1993). Following a massive wave of mergers and acquisitions during
the 1980s, foreign direct investment accelerated markedly across western
Europe, causing transnational corporate control over employment, output,
and trade to be extended in many local economies (Amin and Malmberg
1994). One major consequence of this development has been the formation
of a European network of global cities in which advanced management,
financial, and corporate control functions—both for global and Europe-wide

investment activities—have been centralized (Taylor and Hoyler 2000). Because such functions are heavily dependent upon a complex of specialized producer and financial services, they generate spillover effects into local economies that reinforce the metropolitanization tendencies discussed above (Sassen 1993). Major European global cities include, among others, London, Paris, Amsterdam, Frankfurt, Zürich, and Milan (Box 5.3).

These European global city economies now capture many of the administrative and managerial functions that were previously concentrated within regional centers or national capitals. Moreover, as Fig. 5.3 indicates, a large number of global and European corporate headquarters—in banking, commerce, and industry—are concentrated within a relatively small network of European metropolitan centers.

Box 5.3. Global city formation in western Europe

Urban researchers have identified various 'global cities' or 'world cities' as key spatial nodes of contemporary global capitalism. Since the initial formulation of the world city hypothesis in the early 1980s by Cohen (1981) and Friedmann and Wolff (1982), world city theory has been consolidated as a major framework for critical urban studies (Knox and Taylor 1995; Hitz et al. 1995). While various criteria have been proposed for the specification of the world urban hierarchy (Beaverstock, Smith, and Taylor 2000), most researchers concur that world cities represent key basing points for global capitalist firms due to their high concentrations of corporate decision-making, financial planning, and control capacities. In addition to their role as locations for TNC headquarters, global cities contain other propulsive industries that are linked to the activities of TNCs. The most important among these are advanced producer and financial services sectors—for instance, banking, accounting, advertising, financial management and consulting, business law, insurance, and the like—which serve the command and control requirements of transnational capital (Sassen 1991; Thrift 1987).

Friedmann's (1986a) foundational statement on world city theory included a number of European cities within the global urban hierarchy—London, Paris, Rotterdam, Frankfurt, Zürich, Brussels, Milan, Vienna, and Madrid. More recently, Friedmann (1995) has noted the role of Amsterdam, Barcelona, Lyon, Munich, and the Ruhr agglomeration as important nodes within the emergent transnational urban system. Many European global cities, such as London, Paris, and Amsterdam, have a much longer history as administrative hubs of colonial empires and as coordinating centers for global trade (King 1991). Others, such as Frankfurt and Barcelona, have only more recently acquired worldwide or continental economic significance. As the methodology of world city theory has been refined, more precise models and more detailed descriptions of the European global city system have been developed (Kunzmann 1998; Shachar 1996). Such models have underscored not only the strategic functional roles of global cities within a vertically configured urban hierarchy but also their increasingly dense, horizontally articulated interlinkages with one another (Taylor and Hoyler 2000).

Research on global cities has drawn attention to the following major realignments within the European urban system:

- The increased articulation of major European cities to the global economy through their role as global or continental headquarters locations for TNCs (Castells 1994; Feagin and Smith 1989);
- The stratification of the European global city hierarchy among 'alpha', 'beta', and 'gamma' tiers according to major cities' different levels of connectivity within the global city network (Taylor and Hoyler 2000);
- The consolidation of advanced producer and financial services complexes as major sources of economic dynamism and employment growth within European global city-regions (Sassen 1993);
- The emergence of new forms of sociospatial polarization within European cities as urban labor markets are increasingly bifurcated or 'dualized' between high-wage corporate jobs and routinized, low-wage jobs in the formal and informal economy (Fainstein, Gordon, and Harloe 1992; Fainstein 2001; C. Hamnett 1996, 1994);
- The increasing integration of strategic suburban peripheries into transnational circuits of capital as selected global city functions are decentralized beyond traditional downtown cores (Ronneberger and Keil 1995);
- The massive expansion of advanced infrastructures for communication and transport—including high-speed rail lines, airports, logistics centers, and customized telecommunications networks—ensuring high levels of connectivity among the most strategically significant European urban centers (Graham 1999).

	London	Paris	Frankfurt	Amsterdam	Brussels	Milan
Headquarters of the world's top 500 banks (by total value of transactions)	15	17	12	4	7	5
Headquarters of top 200 European banks	13	13	12	3	7	7
Headquarters of Europe's top 300 commercial companies (by turnover)	49	18	7	4	4	3
Headquarters of Europe's top 500 industrial companies	85	72	9	4	8	11

Fig. 5.3. Corporate headquarters in various European global cities as of 1990
Source: derived from CEC 1992: 52–5.

3. *The new inter-metropolitan polarization.* The new spatial divisions of labor that have been generated through the combined processes of geoeconomic restructuring and European integration have transformed inherited patterns

of urban development, even in cities and regions that lack the transnational command and control capacities associated with global cities (Läpple 1985). As processes of deindustrialization and reindustrialization have deepened, the entire European urban system has been differentiated extensively among cities and regions attempting to position themselves strategically within the Single European Market and the new international division of labor (Fig. 5.4). As in the USA, where processes of industrial restructuring during the 1980s polarized urban development patterns between the declining snowbelt cities of the northeastern manufacturing belt and the sunbelt boomtowns of the south and west (Sawers and Tabb 1984), these shifts within the western European urban system have rearticulated and intensified nationally specific patterns of inter-urban polarization. Consequently, as evidence of intensifying intra-national disparities mounted during the 1980s, debates on the 'regional problem' were renewed both in political and academic circles (Box 5.4, p. 186). As we shall see below, political responses to this situation during the post-1980s period have differed significantly from those that predominated during the Fordist-Keynesian epoch.

4. *New zones of marginalization and exclusion.* New zones of marginalization and exclusion have emerged at the fringes of Europe's vital axis as trans-national corporations have continued to decentralize routinized, low value-added economic functions and back offices into semi-peripheral and peripheral regions of Mediterranean and southern Europe and, more recently, into the border states of eastern and central Europe (Hadjimichalis and Sadler 1995; Nilsson and Schamp 1996). From Spain, Portugal, southern Italy, and Greece to Poland, the Czech Republic, and Hungary, these zones are dominated by cities and towns that lack large clusters of skilled workers and an advanced industrial, transportation, and communications infrastructure. Given the centripetal forces and large-scale sociospatial disparities that have been unleashed through the process of European integration, it has been extraordinarily difficult for cities and regions located in these marginalized zones of the European space-economy to break out of deregulatory, defensive modes of adjustment (Moulaert 1996). Figure 5.5 (p. 188) illustrates the intensifying disparities among strong and weak European regions, measured in GDP per inhabitant, during the 1980–8 period.

The new patterns of uneven geographical development that have resulted from the aforementioned four trends have been described through a number of spatial metaphors—including the 'blue banana', the 'blue star', the 'cucumber', the 'European green grape', the 'bowl of fruit', the 'boomerang', and the 'red octopus'.[3] Map 5.1 (p. 189) depicts one of the most widely disseminated spatial images of post-1970s Europe, the so-called 'blue banana', which was first elaborated by Brunet (1989) in a report for the French spatial planning agency

---

[3] For discussions of such metaphors, see Dematteis 2000; Kunzmann and Wegener 1991; Kunzmann 1998; Nijkamp 1993; Taylor and Hoyler 2000; Lever 1993; and Wegener 1995.

Urban type	Key features	Examples
Global cities	Large concentrations of financial, economic, political, and cultural headquarters; significant clusters of producer and financial services industries; restructured/modernized industrial base	London, Paris, Frankfurt, Amsterdam, Zürich, Milan
Administrative/ governmental centers	Large concentrations of governmental functions as well as international governmental organizations (IGOs) and nongovernmental organizations (NGOs)	Brussels, Geneva, the Hague, Berlin, Madrid, Rome
High-tech/ services cities	Advanced industrial base, center of innovative activities, significant concentrations of research and development facilities, and producer services	Bristol, Cambridge, Reading, Toulouse, Lyon, Montpellier, Stuttgart, Barcelona
Declining industrial cities and regions	Traditional, monostructural industrial base, obsolete industrial infrastructure, mass unemployment, population decline, extensive environmental degradation	Located throughout the British Midlands, the German Ruhr region, the Nord-Pas de Calais and Lorraine regions of France, and Belgian Wallonia
Port cities	Declining shipbuilding industries, extensive environmental degradation, structural unemployment; extensive spatial restructuring as ports attempt to modernize their infrastructures	Liverpool, Dunkirk, Rotterdam, Duisburg, Hamburg, Genoa, Marseille, Antwerp, Athens
Expanding cities without an industrial base	Large informal economy, marginalized working class, lack of physical planning and adequate public infrastructure, environmental deterioration	Palermo, Thessalonika, Naples
Company towns	Middle-sized towns in which local economy is dominated by a single corporation	Leverkusen, Eindhoven, Höchst, Ludwigshafen, Sindelfingen, Turin
New towns	Relatively self-contained towns inhabited by overspill populations from large urban centers	Milton Keynes, Runcorn, Evry, Lelystad, Almere
Monofunctional satellites	New urban growth centers, generally located in close proximity to traditional urban centers, whose local economies are specialized on a single function (technopoles, 'science cities', tourist outposts, airports)	Sophia-Antipolis, Roissy, Euro-Disneyland, Haarlemmermeer
Small towns and rural centers	Smaller cities and semi-urbanized zones in rural regions, often located near coastlines and isolated from major transportation corridors	Throughout Europe
Tourism and culture cities	Local economic base depends extensively on international tourism and European cultural events	Salzburg, Venice, Prague, Avignon, Florence
Border and gateway cities	Hinterland is crosscut by a national border; such cities often serve key administrative functions and become gateways for economic migrants and refugees	Aachen, Strasbourg, Arnhem, Basle, Frankfurt/ Oder, Trieste, Malaga, Cadiz, Palermo, Thessalonika

Fig. 5.4. The differentiation of urban economies in western Europe

Source: based on Kunzmann and Wegener 1991: 35, 36–43.

Box 5.4. The return of the 'regional problem': North/South divides in Germany, Britain, and Italy in the 1980s

whereas the development of the post-war space economy up to the early 1970s was generally convergent, for the past decade or more, and especially since the late 1970s, it has been divergent. The pattern of uneven development is now one of increasing spatial division, at a variety of spatial scales. To a large extent these 'divergent geographies' reflect the different roles of different areas and localities in the old and new regimes of accumulation, and on a wider front their position in the changing international division of labor.

(Martin 1989: 31)

The regional repercussions of this [. . .] loosening up of the landscape of capital [. . .] have been dramatic and perplexing. Relatively stable mosaics of uneven regional development have suddenly become almost kaleidoscopic. Once highly industrialized and prosperous core regions—segments of the American manufacturing belt, north-east England and Wales, northern France, Wallonia, the Ruhr—have been experiencing accelerated economic decline and deindustrialization, while many poor peripheral regions [. . .] have become new centres of industrial growth and expansion. These 'role reversals of regions' [. . .] reflect what has been the most extensive geographical decentralization and internationalization of industrial production since the origins of industrial capitalism

(Soja 1989: 172)

The geoeconomic dislocations of the 1970s intensified territorial disparities across the European space-economy (Dunford and Perrons 1994). These new territorial disparities were articulated on a variety of spatial scales, but one of their most significant expressions was the intensified polarization of spatial development *within* each national territory. Under these circumstances, traditional urban/rural divisions were increasingly superseded by differentials in employment, population, and investment levels among already urbanized local and regional economies (Läpple 1985). In the FRG, the UK, and Italy, academic and public discussions of the so-called 'North/South divide' proliferated during the 1980s in conjunction with debates on deindustrialization, mass unemployment, and urban decline.

• In the (West) German context, researchers detected evidence of a North/South regional divide during the mid-1980s, as disparities intensified between the declining, older industrial areas of the west and north (the Ruhr region, Lower Saxony, Hamburg, and Bremen) and the more diversified southern regions (such as Hesse, Bavaria, and Baden-Württemberg), where many high-technology firms had recently agglomerated (Friedrichs, Häußermann, and Siebel 1986; Läpple 1986). Analogous forms of territorial polarization were articulated within the (West) German urban system during this period. While all major cities in the Federal Republic of Germany (FRG) experienced population growth and high employment levels until the mid-1960s, by the early 1970s conditions among cities located in different zones of the national territory had come to differ significantly. Northern industrial cities such as Berlin, Hamburg, Bremen, Hannover, Düsseldorf, Bochum, and Essen became sites of disinvestment and mass unemployment. Meanwhile, southern urban centers such as Frankfurt, Stuttgart, and Munich became important centers for high-tech industries and advanced producer and financial services. The economic dynamism of these southern cities was reflected in relatively low unemployment rates throughout the 1980s (S. Krätke 1991; Esser and Hirsch 1989).

- In Britain, the North/South divide has a long historical legacy. While spatial inequalities were partially counterbalanced during the postwar period, as regional per capita incomes tendentially converged, they intensified following the onset of global recession and the consolidation of Thatcherism (Dunford 1995; Martin and Rowthorn 1986). These new territorial disparities were debated most explicitly in the UK as a resurgence of the country's recurrent 'regional problem' (Massey 1986; Martin 1989, 1988). During the 1980s, the historically entrenched North/South divide in Britain was exacerbated through a combination of (*a*) accelerated economic growth in the South East, the South West, and East Anglia; (*b*) continued industrial decline and socioeconomic crisis in the older manufacturing regions of the West Midlands, the North West of England, Scotland, and Wales; and (*c*) significantly increased North/South divergence in unemployment levels, household income, and new business registrations (Dunford 1995; Hudson and Williams 1989). The intensification of inward investment around Greater London, the process of global city formation in the City's core financial district and, more generally, the growing 'London-centeredness' of the entire UK economy, contributed further to these trends.

- Italy represents another major European national state in which an inherited North/ South divide was exacerbated during the 1980s. While it was grounded upon historically entrenched spatial divisions, the new pattern of territorial polarization was the product of three post-1970s developments. First, in the northwestern heartlands of Italian Fordism, the industrial centers of Genoa and Turin underwent significant deindustrialization and (partial) reindustrialization; meanwhile, Milan was transformed into an important second-tier European global city-region, generating important spillover effects for its surrounding regional economy. Second, the northeastern and central industrial districts of Emilia-Romagna and the Third Italy were consolidated as major sites for flexible production systems, above all in revitalized craft sectors dominated by small and medium-sized firms. Third, despite the redistributive regional policy programs that had been mobilized during the postwar period, the southern Mezzogiorno region experienced a severe economic crisis characterized by mass unemployment, capital flight, and insufficient capital investment. Thus, even though the national space-economy was often said to have been differentiated among 'three Italies' during this period, the North/South division continued to represent the predominant axis of territorial inequality (Bagnasco and Oberti 1998; Dunford 1988; Sablowski 1998).

DATAR. Such simplistic spatial models have been criticized, however, because they ossify complex networks of interdependencies and ongoing sociospatial transformations into a static territorial grid (Krätke, Heeg, and Stein 1997). Moreover, insofar as they are usually promulgated by public agencies that have a strong political interest in depicting particular localities, regions, or countries as the boom regions of the future, such models are often based 'less on empirical evidence than on creative geopolitical imaginations' (Taylor and Hoyler 2000: 179).

For present purposes, the key point is that recent processes of geoeconomic restructuring, European integration, and metropolitanization have

188   *Urban Locational Policy, State Rescaling*

	1980	1982	1984	1986	1988
Average 10 weakest regions	47	46	45	45	45
Average 10 strongest regions	145	147	149	151	151
Average 25 weakest regions	57	56	55	55	56
Average 25 strongest regions	135	136	137	138	137
Disparity*	26.1	26.8	27.2	27.9	27.5

*Weighted standard deviation

Fig. 5.5. Disparities in GDP per inhabitant among European regions, 1980–8
Source: derived from CEC 1991: 87. Data are in PPS (i.e. adjusted to reflect differences in purchasing power among EU states). EUR 12 = 100; regions refer to NUTS 2, excluding French overseas territories.

fundamentally transformed the patterns of geographical industrialization and territorial development that prevailed under Fordist-Keynesian capitalism (Storper and Walker 1989). Consequently, as Petrella (2000) indicates in the statement quoted at the outset of this section, the economic geography of the new Europe is now dominated by a broad urban arc stretching from the South East of England through the German Rhinelands southwards to the northern Italian Industrial Triangle (see also S. Krätke 1993). The heartlands of this densely urbanized 'vital axis' are located, first, in the traditional northwestern urban cores of London, Paris, Brussels, and the Dutch Randstad, and second, in the dynamic cities of southern Germany (Frankfurt, Stuttgart, Munich), Switzerland (Geneva, Zürich) and northern Italy (Milan, Turin, and Bologna), whose accelerated growth in recent years has pulled Europe's economic center of gravity southwards (Dunford and Perrons 1994: 165). This transnational urban corridor, whose components are tightly interlinked through advanced communications and transportation infrastructures, is surrounded by a number of important outlying cities, such as Barcelona, Hamburg, Copenhagen, Berlin, and Vienna, and by a number of affluent, traditionally corporatist countries, including Switzerland, Austria, Norway, Sweden, and Finland. An outer layer of relatively underdeveloped peripheries, characterized by low wage economies and strong deregulatory policy orientations, stretches from the western Atlantic coast to the southern Mediterranean economies and Greece, and now also includes eastern Germany and parts of eastern and central Europe (Dunford and Perrons 1994: 165–6). Although these emergent patterns of uneven spatial development have a longer lineage within previous rounds of capitalist industrialization (Braudel 1984; Rokkan and Urwin 1982), their current articulation is a powerful expression of the centripetal, polarizing forces that have been unleashed since the crisis of North Atlantic Fordism. Thus, as Soja (1985: 187) explained in the mid-1980s:

Paradoxical as it may initially appear, part of the change has involved an intensification of preexisting patterns of uneven regional development and a reinforcement of old core and periphery relations. Many well-established core regions have experienced sustained and even expanded relative economic and political power, while many backward peripheries have plunged deeper into relative impoverishment [...] These 'intensified

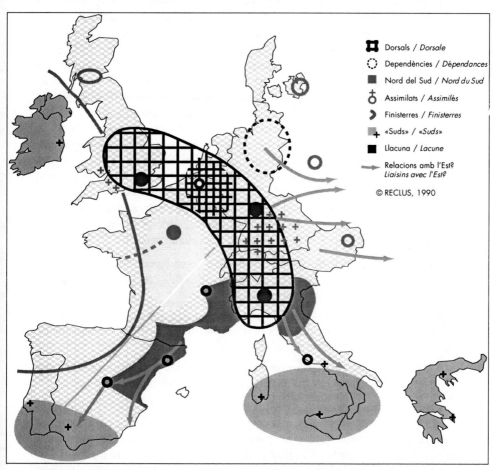

Legend:
- **Dorsals** / *Dorsale*
- **Dependències** / *Dépendances*
- **Nord del Sud** / *Nord du Sud*
- **Assimilats** / *Assimilés*
- **Finisterres** / *Finisterres*
- **«Suds»** / *«Suds»*
- **Llacuna** / *Lacune*
- **Relacions amb l'Est?** / *Liaisins avec l'Est?*

© RECLUS, 1990

Map 5.1. Mapping the new territorial disparities: the European 'blue banana'

Brunet's famous 'blue banana' represented an influential attempt to map the future impact of the Single European Market upon the urban and regional system. In contrast to the nationalized vision of urban hierarchies that prevailed during the Fordist-Keynesian period (see Map 4.1), the city system was now viewed as a transnational network of tightly interlinked and globally competitive metropolitan centers, surrounded by a variety of outlying industrial regions and peripheries. The blue banana was conceived as a zone of intense economic dynamism, accelerated technological innovation, highly skilled labor, and advanced infrastructural facilities that was ideally suited for the activities of transnational corporations.

Source: DATAR (1989: 79).

continuities', however, are not simply more of the same, for they have been occurring under a new set of sectoral, social, political, and technological conditions which have significantly modified how GUD [geographically uneven development] is produced and reproduced.

Urban economists have developed a variety of ranking systems, based on diverse data sources and conceptual schema, in order to examine the changing structural positions of European cities within this new spatial mosaic.[4] In the present context, S. Krätke's (1995, 1993) analysis of the new European urban hierarchy is particularly useful. In this model, the urban hierarchy is composed of two overlapping dimensions—first, the position of cities within global, European, and national spatial divisions of labor, as defined by their dominant forms of industrial production and economic specialization; and second, the position of cities within networks of corporate control, as defined by their role as global, European, or national headquarters locations or as management, financial, or control centers for major firms. This two-dimensional, 'hooks-and-ladders' conceptualization of the European urban hierarchy is represented in Fig. 5.6. This figure is intended to represent an unstable, evolving system of relations and interdependencies between cities rather than a fixed hierarchy of positions. As the arrows in the diagram indicate, various forms of economic restructuring may alter a city's position in the urban hierarchy.

- Cities may ascend the hierarchy as their local economies are upgraded from standardized mass production systems into flexible, decentralized, and innovation-oriented production systems.

- As new headquarters locations and command, management and steering functions are attracted to a city, it may likewise ascend within the hierarchy (S. Krätke 1995: 139–43).

- Cities may also move downwards within the hierarchy if their industrial base or command and control functions are significantly downgraded.

Figure 5.6 thus represents a multiscalar geographical forcefield in which inherited spatial infrastructures, new corporate locational strategies, and localized processes of industrial restructuring interact to produce differential pathways of urban development within a rapidly changing geoeconomic environment.

In sum, the economic geography of post-1970s western Europe is characterized by (*a*) an enhanced concentration of socioeconomic capacities, high-skilled labor, and advanced infrastructure investments into major metropolitan areas ('metropolitanization'); (*b*) a growing differentiation among local and regional economies according to their particular specializations within global and European spatial divisions of labor; (*c*) enhanced levels of connectivity and interdependence among the most dynamic, globally integrated metropolitan cores; and (*d*) an increasing functional disarticulation of major urban regions

[4] See e.g. Champion, Mønnesland, and Vandermotten 1996; Cheshire 1999; CEC 1992; Kunzmann and Wegener 1991; Lever 1999, 1993.

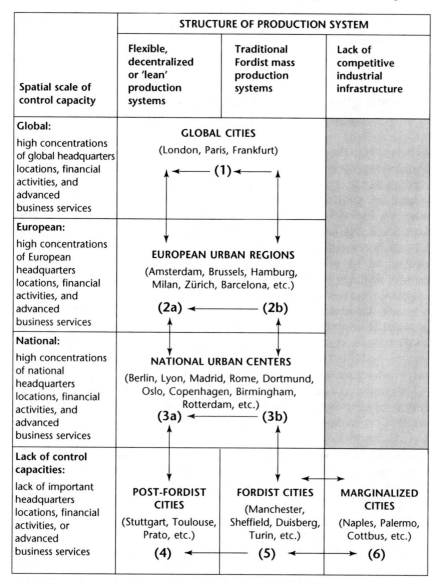

	STRUCTURE OF PRODUCTION SYSTEM		
Spatial scale of control capacity	**Flexible, decentralized or 'lean' production systems**	**Traditional Fordist mass production systems**	**Lack of competitive industrial infrastructure**
Global: high concentrations of global headquarters locations, financial activities, and advanced business services	**GLOBAL CITIES** (London, Paris, Frankfurt) ↑← (1) ←↑		
European: high concentrations of European headquarters locations, financial activities, and advanced business services	**EUROPEAN URBAN REGIONS** (Amsterdam, Brussels, Hamburg, Milan, Zürich, Barcelona, etc.) **(2a)** ← **(2b)**		
National: high concentrations of national headquarters locations, financial activities, and advanced business services	**NATIONAL URBAN CENTERS** (Berlin, Lyon, Madrid, Rome, Dortmund, Oslo, Copenhagen, Birmingham, Rotterdam, etc.) **(3a)** ← **(3b)**		
Lack of control capacities: lack of important headquarters locations, financial activities, or advanced business services	**POST-FORDIST CITIES** (Stuttgart, Toulouse, Prato, etc.) **(4)** ←	**FORDIST CITIES** (Manchester, Sheffield, Duisberg, Turin, etc.) **(5)** ←	**MARGINALIZED CITIES** (Naples, Palermo, Cottbus, etc.) → **(6)**

Fig. 5.6 The changing European urban hierarchy
Source: derived from S. Krätke 1995: 141.

from their surrounding peripheries and from other marginalized areas within the same national territory. In light of these trends, which are exacerbating territorial inequalities at all spatial scales, the notion of an 'archipelago economy' introduced by Veltz (1996) and the vision of an 'Archipelago Europe' proposed by Petrella (2000) provide vivid, if also disturbing, characterizations of the new spatial (dis)order that has emerged in western Europe during the last three decades.

Urban governance in transition: from endogenous development to locational policy

As indicated in the penultimate section of Ch. 4, the regulatory architecture of spatial Keynesianism was destabilized following the crisis of North Atlantic Fordism due to a confluence of geoeconomic realignments, industrial trans-formations, political shifts, and internal crisis-tendencies. However, even as inherited approaches to spatial policy were being undermined, urban crises were deepening, and thus the problem of regulating the process of capitalist urbanization remained as acute as ever. The new patterns of urbanization outlined above presented state institutions at all spatial scales with any number of major regulatory dilemmas—including, in particular, deindustri-alization, mass unemployment, decaying public infrastructures, declining tax revenues, labor deskilling, rising sociospatial inequalities, and intensified interspatial competition. The key question, then, is how inherited state spatial configurations were recalibrated, as the obsolescence of spatial Keynesianism became widely evident, in order to confront the rapidly proliferating regula-tory challenges associated with newly emergent urbanization patterns.

I suggested in Ch. 3 that the production of new state spaces cannot be conceived adequately as a complete destruction and transcendence of inherited political geographies. Instead, state spatial restructuring is best viewed as a layering process in which newly emergent state spatial projects and state spatial strategies interact with inherited configurations of state space. This interaction generates new, multilayered formations of state spatiality that eclectically com-bine elements of inherited state spatial arrangements with newly forged regula-tory geographies. This conceptualization provides a useful methodological basis on which to investigate the reworking of state intervention into the urban process during the post-1970s period. For, the transformation of urban governance during the last three decades has not entailed the simple replace-ment of spatial Keynesianism with a single, coherent, post-Keynesian model. It has been premised, rather, upon a series of ad hoc, trial-and-error regulatory experiments through which national, regional, and local state institutions have attempted, with divergent degrees of success, to confront the various aspects of urban restructuring discussed in the preceding section. However, despite their variegated effects upon cities and regions, these processes of regulatory experi-mentation have cumulatively engendered a number of systemic transform-ations of state spatiality at both local and supralocal scales.

As we saw in Ch. 4, spatial Keynesianism was grounded upon top-down, redistributive policies intended to spread certain generic socioeconomic assets, infrastructural arrangements, and public services as evenly as possible throughout the entire national territory. In stark contrast to this postwar project of promoting the 'Taylorization of territory' (Veltz 1996: 24), the new urban policies of the post-1970s period have been recalibrated to emphasize place- and scale-specific industrial legacies, socioeconomic conditions, institutional configurations, and developmental resources. Consequently, as Messner (1997: 31) declares, 'Traditional industrial policies, formulated far from the sites concerned by the planning staffs in capital cities, are obsolete.' I shall argue that such state initiatives to address place- and scale-specific regulatory dilemmas—in significant measure through the rescaling of state institutional structures and modes of intervention—represent an essential feature of post-Keynesian forms of urban governance.

Interscalar tensions, endogenous development strategies, and the new politics of place

Throughout the 1970s, political alliances in many European national states attempted to defend the redistributive policy relays of spatial Keynesianism. The goal of such preservationist alliances was to 'intensify still further traditional regional policy instruments, to refine their criteria and spatial orientation towards specific crisis areas and locations and [. . .] to shift to more directly effective instruments' (Stöhr 1986: 67). Initially, national governments mobilized 'fire-brigade type crash programmes' intended to address particularly drastic urban-industrial crises through direct subsidies or incentives to large firms (Stöhr 1986: 67). Subsequently, however, as crisis tendencies within the boom regions of Fordism deepened, the inherited policy framework of spatial Keynesianism was further differentiated (*a*) to include deindustrializing, distressed cities as key geographical targets for state financial assistance; and (*b*) to remove barriers to investment within major industrial centers. Thus, in contrast to classical Keynesian forms of spatial policy, which had focused almost exclusively upon underdeveloped peripheries, national *urban* policies were now introduced in major western European states in order to address the specific socioeconomic problems of large cities. Key examples of such policies in the 1970s included the West German Urban Development Assistance Act, the French Plan of Action for Employment and Industrial Reorganization, the Dutch Big Cities Bottleneck Program, and the British Inner Urban Areas Act (Fox Przeworski 1986). In this manner, many of the redistributive policy relays associated with spatial Keynesianism were significantly expanded. The national state's underlying commitment to the project of spatial equalization at a national scale was thus strongly reinforced during the course of the 1970s. Indeed, this decade may be viewed as the historical culmination of the various projects of national territorial redistribution that had been introduced during the postwar period, albeit under geoeconomic conditions that were systematically undermining the viability of the Fordist-Keynesian developmental model.

While redistribution-oriented political alliances prevailed at a national scale during the first half of the decade, the tide began to change in many European national states during the late 1970s, as industrial restructuring accelerated and inherited frameworks of interscalar relations became increasingly unstable. At this time, across much of western Europe, the national scale became an important institutional locus for diverse restructuring-oriented political alliances that aimed to dismantle many of the redistributive, compensatory policy relays that had prevailed within the Keynesian welfare national state. In particular, a range of devolutionary national policy initiatives and intergovernmental realignments were introduced in order to scale back inherited, managerial-welfarist approaches to urban governance. Following the global economic recession of the 1970s, western European national governments were increasingly pressured to rationalize public expenditures. National grants to subnational administrative levels were markedly reduced; and local government expenditure as a share of GDP likewise declined significantly (Pickvance and Preteceille 1991*b*). These newly imposed forms of fiscal austerity impelled many European local governments to become more dependent upon locally collected taxes and non-tax revenues such as charges and user fees (Mouritzen 1991). In the wake of these shifts, many municipalities attempted to adjust to the new fiscal climate by delaying capital expenditures, by drawing upon liquid assets, and by increasing their debts, but these efforts proved to be no more than temporary, stop-gap measures. Whereas the new national urban policies introduced during this period enabled many cities to capture supplementary public resources, most local governments were nonetheless confronted with unprecedented budgetary constraints due to the combined impact of national fiscal retrenchment and rapidly intensifying local socioeconomic problems. Subsequently, additional public revenues were sought in, among other sources, local economic development projects (Fox Przeworski 1986).

More generally, within the newly imposed framework of interscalar relations, there was a proliferation of so-called 'endogenous development' strategies intended to promote economic growth and technological innovation from below, without extensive reliance upon external investments or national subsidies (Box 5.5). Thus, in contrast to their earlier focus on welfarist redistribution, local governments now began to introduce a range of initiatives intended to rejuvenate local economies, beginning with anti-closure initiatives, land-assembly programs, and land-use planning schemes, and subsequently expanding to diverse firm-based, area-based, sectoral, and job-creation measures (Eisenschitz and Gough 1993). Although this new politics of urban economic development would eventually be diffused in diverse political and institutional forms throughout the western European city-system, during the 1970s it remained most prevalent within manufacturing-based cities and regions, often dominated by a single industry, in which economic restructuring had generated particularly devastating consequences (Hudson 1994;

Box 5.5. Endogenous development strategies and the new politics of place in the 1980s

---

By definition the concept of endogenous local development means that development can be initiated and organized 'from the inside'. It entails mobilizing to the maximum and optimum extent possible the resources in a given area, including capital, labour, and such institutional resources as the local infrastructure, instead of waiting for—or trying to attract—outside capital and outside firms to foster growth and employment.

(Sengenberger 1993: 310)

It would appear that monocentric reliance on traditional large-scale, market-driven, large-organization and central-government-initiated development processes has steadily weakened the capability of territorial communities to confront the challenges of worldwide economic restructuring by indigenous innovation and flexibility [...] Central [state] policies have frequently aggravated this. They may have been able to redistribute growth during growth-dominated periods but they have been unable to generate local innovative capacity and promote flexibility during periods dominated by restructuring needs.

(Stöhr 1990: 2)

The notion of endogenous development can be traced to the activities of European mercantilist states from the sixteenth to the eighteenth century and to the protectionist agenda of the German *Zollverein* during the nineteenth century (Friedmann 1986*b*; Hahne 1985). During the Fordist-Keynesian period, the politics of endogenous development were redefined in the context of the import substitution industrialization strategies pursued in the newly industrializing countries, especially in Latin America, as well as through postcolonial initiatives to promote autocentric forms of national economic growth in other zones of the world economy (S. Amin 1986). As of the 1970s, however, the notion of endogenous development was redeployed in the core national states of western Europe with reference to ongoing processes of regional industrial restructuring. Initially, the notion of self-reliant or endogenous development was introduced as a means to promote economic revitalization in the peripheralized rural regions of western Europe (Stöhr and Taylor 1981). Subsequently, endogenous growth strategies were mobilized in declining European industrial regions as well (Hahne 1985: 29–169; Bassand et al. 1986). By the early 1980s, the project of endogenous development was being embraced by a broad array of place-based, neocorporatist political alliances in crisis-stricken manufacturing regions. While their specific political agendas and policy strategies varied extensively, such alliances were generally formed in order to address place-specific processes of industrial restructuring without extensive reliance upon national government planning guidance or financial aid. Under these conditions, the slogan of endogenous growth was used to denote, simultaneously, (*a*) a *method* of state intervention into the urban process (oriented towards 'indigenous' socioeconomic capacities rather than 'exogenous' investments or redistributive transfers); and (*b*) a *vision* of autocentric territorial development (based upon internally negotiated compromises rather than externally imposed political agendas or corporate power). In this sense, such initiatives articulated a *politics of place* grounded upon 'a deeply felt, and to varying degrees collectively shared, attachment to place that was grounded in the spatially defined routine of everyday life' (Hudson and Sadler 1986: 173).

Parkinson 1991). Under these conditions, even as most western European national governments continued to promote territorial equalization at a national scale, neocorporatist alliances proliferated within monostructural, rustbelt cities and regions, from Hamburg and the German Ruhr district to Lorraine and the Nord in France, Belgian Wallonia, Rotterdam, and the English Midlands. Their central goal was to mobilize regionally and locally specific sectoral, technology, and employment policies that would reverse industrial decline and facilitate economic restoration within particular places (Stöhr and Taylor 1981). As Hudson and Sadler (1986: 173) note—borrowing a political slogan that was used in opposition to a plant closing in Longwy, France—these alliances were concerned 'to defend the right to "live, learn, and work" in particular places'. While some commentators characterized these initiatives as 'labor-oriented regional policies' (Stöhr 1986), most were, in practice, grounded upon a variety of cross-class, sectoral, and place-based alliances concerned to rejuvenate locally fixed capital investments and, thereby, to 'ward off the threat of localized, place-specific devaluation' (Harvey 1982: 420). Accordingly, throughout the 1970s and into the early 1980s, such place-based, neocorporatist alliances attempted to establish negotiated strategies of industrial restructuring in which economic regeneration and technological revitalization were to be linked directly to priorities such as intra-regional redistribution, job creation, vocational retraining, investments in collective consumption, and, more generally, class compromise (Hahne 1985; Hudson 1994).

Another important strand of endogenous development strategy during this period emphasized the role of cities and regions as strategic arenas for radical political reform and grassroots democratic renewal (Castells 1983; Mayer 1993). Such democratic-associationalist priorities were counterposed to the centralizing administrative hierarchies of the (now increasingly crisis-stricken) Keynesian welfare national state, which was criticized as a bureaucratic monolith lacking genuine democratic accountability. These local reform initiatives were elaborated from a wide range of political perspectives, including Green, feminist, eco-socialist, socialist, and social-democratic standpoints, but all viewed municipalities as privileged institutional platforms for various forms of democratic self-determination by local populations. In the West German discussion, for instance, municipalities were represented as a 'counterforce' (*Gegenmacht*) against national state policies (Bullmann and Gitschmann 1985). Likewise, in Britain, the municipal socialist movement attempted to mobilize local councils in order to counteract the neoconservative policies of the consolidating central state under Thatcher (Boddy and Fudge 1984). Throughout the early 1980s, the Greater London Council (GLC) mobilized a variety of industrial and social policies intended at once to alleviate concentrated unemployment, to enhance municipal control over capital investment, and to address other 'new urban left' concerns such as nuclear disarmament and the rights of women, gays, and ethnic minorities

(Eisenschitz and North 1986; Mackintosh and Wainwright 1987). And, similarly, in France, the late 1970s witnessed a variety of 'self-management' (*autogestion*) initiatives by dissident socialist groups and trade unionists concerned to assert workers' control over major factories and, more generally, to promote grassroots democratic control over local territorial units (Lefebvre 2001; Lourau 1974).

In essence, then, the municipality-as-counterforce, local socialism, and *autogestion* movements entailed the defense of local 'islands of reform' and radical economic democracy within an increasingly hostile, turbulent political-economic environment. Unlike many of the place-based alliances that emerged in older industrial regions during this period, which often took the form of spatially exclusionary, 'militant particularist' loyalties to particular communities and locales (Hudson and Sadler 1986), the democratic-associationalist approach to endogenous development generally coupled its local political initiatives with efforts to forge broader connections to progressive social forces located in other, equally embattled locations and territories. However, during the second half of the 1980s, as central governments continued to transpose the costs of economic restructuring onto fiscally enfeebled subnational institutions, such movements lost momentum or collapsed (Krätke and Schmoll 1987). Nonetheless, these democratic-associationalist approaches to endogenous development played an important role in animating the broader politics of place that was crystallizing during this period in many western European cities and regions.

The endogenous development initiatives of the 1970s and early 1980s were grounded upon a neo-Fordist political project intended to recalibrate the institutional infrastructures of spatial Keynesianism from the national scale to the regional or local scale. In contrast to national policies of territorial redistribution, in which local and regional economies were viewed as agglomerations of generic resources (such as labor, infrastructure, and raw materials), cities and regions were now recognized to have their own, place-specific socioeconomic assets, developmental trajectories, and structural problems. In this sense, the new projects of endogenous development laid the foundations for a customized, scale-sensitive approach to spatial policy that would be focused explicitly upon the regulation of particular places and regions rather than treating them either as subunits of the national space-economy or as localized relay stations within national administrative hierarchies. At the same time, however, the basic Fordist-Keynesian priorities of social redistribution, territorial equalization, and class compromise were maintained, albeit now within the more bounded parameters of regional and local economies rather than as a project to be extended throughout the entire national territory. Some of these neocorporatist local and regional economic initiatives would persist into the 1980s, albeit in reconfigured political forms, in a rescaled institutional framework, and in a transformed geoeconomic environment. The salient point here is that such localized strategies of endogenous growth, economic development, democratic renewal, and territorial self-management first emerged during a period in which spatially redistributive, neo-Keynesian priorities continued to predominate at a national level. Under these conditions, due to their differentiating, fragmenting impacts upon each national urban system, the subnational neocorporatisms and place-based alliances of the 1970s contributed to the ongoing destabilization of spatial Keynesianism that was gathering momentum during that decade.

The 1970s is thus best viewed as a transitional period in which state institutions at various spatial scales attempted to adjust to the destabilizing national, regional, and local effects of geoeconomic restructuring. It was characterized by interscalar struggles between political alliances concerned to preserve the nationalized institutional infrastructures of spatial Keynesianism and other, newly formed political coalitions concerned (*a*) to scale back the redistributive interscalar relays associated with postwar welfarism and (*b*) to introduce more place-sensitive frameworks of economic governance. Although the new regulatory spaces sought by such modernizing coalitions remained relatively inchoate at both national and local scales, they were generally grounded upon a rejection of nationally encompassing models of territorial development and oriented towards the goal of promoting endogenous local and regional growth within particular places. The diffusion of endogenous development strategies during this period and into the early 1980s thus appears to have engendered significant institutional fractures within the inherited political geographies of spatial Keynesianism. Paradoxically, then, the first major cracks in the edifice of spatial Keynesianism appeared during a decade that was otherwise the historical highpoint for state projects of national territorial redistribution.

Yet, given the geographically localized, politically unstable, and institutionally inchoate character of endogenous development strategies, it would be problematic to claim that they contributed to the establishment of a new territorial basis for urban development within any European national state. Rather, such regulatory experiments are best understood as localized and regionalized forms of crisis-management, grounded upon an attachment to specific places and regions, through which a new spatial layer of subnational regulatory arrangements was superimposed upon the nationalized political geographies that had prevailed under Fordist-Keynesian capitalism. It was through the conflictual interaction of this newly emergent, subnational layer of state spatial regulation and the inherited (if increasingly unstable) national geographies of spatial Keynesianism that the broad contours of a new, rescaled landscape of state spatiality began to emerge as of the late 1970s. Insofar as the endogenous development strategies of the 1970s were largely uncoupled from the nationally equalizing, redistributive agendas of spatial Keynesianism, they established a significant political opening for the more radical rescalings of urban governance and state spatiality that would subsequently unfold.

*Neoliberalism, the new interspatial competition, and the rise of urban
locational policy*

During the course of the 1980s, the process of geoeconomic restructuring
intensified and accelerated, leading to a new phase of urban policy reform
and state spatial transformation across western Europe. The strategies of national and local crisis-management of the 1970s had neither restored the
conditions for a new national regime of accumulation nor successfully resolved
the deepening problems of economic stagnation, rising unemployment, infrastructural obsolescence, and industrial decline within western European cities
and regions. Consequently, during the course of the 1980s, most European
national governments abandoned traditional Keynesian macroeconomic policies in favor of monetarism: a competitive balance of payments replaced full
employment as the overarching goal of monetary and fiscal policy (Scharpf
1999). Meanwhile, the process of European political and economic integration
regained momentum as preparations were made under the Delors Commission
for the completion of the Single European Market (SEM) and, subsequently,
Economic and Monetary Union (EMU) (Ross 1998).

By the late 1980s, neoliberal political agendas such as welfare state retrenchment, fiscal discipline, trade liberalization, privatization, and deregulation
had been adopted not only in the United Kingdom under Thatcher and in
West Germany under Kohl, but also in many traditionally social democratic,
statist, or social/christian-democratic countries, including the Netherlands,
Belgium, France, Italy, Spain, Denmark, and Sweden.[5] While such agendas
did not, in most instances, generate Thatcher-style ideological and institutional transformations, they nonetheless entailed what might be termed a
'subversive' neoliberalization of key arenas of socioeconomic policy, as
growth-first, anti-welfarist, market-driven logics were increasingly naturalized
as the necessary technical parameters within which public policy must be
articulated (Rhodes 1995; Peck and Tickell 2002). Accordingly, Müller and
Wright (1994: 2) contend that a major 'paradigm shift' occurred throughout
western Europe during the 1980s as the character of state intervention shifted
'from Keynesianism to monetarism and neo-liberalism, from *dirigisme* (explicit
or gently disguised) to market-driven solutions, from fiscal expansionism to
restraint, from mercantilism to free trade'. During the same period, a variety of
international institutions, including the International Monetary Fund (IMF),
the World Bank, the Bank for International Settlements, the Organization for
Economic Cooperation and Development (OECD), and the General Agreement on Tariffs and Trade (GATT), became important agents of the so-called
'Washington Consensus', which attempted to diffuse neoliberal policy
agendas such as fiscal discipline, regulatory downgrading, trade liberalization,

[5] For useful overviews of these trends, see Rhodes, Heywood, and Wright 1997; Majone 1994;
Müller and Wright 1994; Rhodes 1995; Overbeek 1991; and Wright 1994. This neoliberalization of
western European political systems is also examined in special issues of *West European Politics* (17/3,
1994) and *Tijdschrift voor Economische en Sociale Geografie* (91/3, 2000).

labor market flexibility, the privatization of public services, and unrestrained foreign direct investment on a global scale (Gill 1995; Tickell and Peck 2003). In the European context, such market-building, liberalizing, and deregulatory policy agendas were further reinforced and generalized through a series of EU-level directives, including, above all, the Single European Act of 1987, which massively intensified Europe-wide market integration, foreign direct investment, and corporate mergers and acquisitions, while also contributing to the weakening and eventual marginalization of the Social Charter within the 1991 Maastricht Treaty (Pollack 1998; Röttger 1997).

The mobilization of neoliberal critiques of Fordist-Keynesian forms of public policy did not entail a simple 'rolling back' of the state as self-regulating markets, now supposedly liberated from political constraints, were unleashed. On the contrary, neoliberalism must be viewed as a concerted political strategy through which qualitatively new *forms* of state–economy relations have been constructed, at various spatial scales, in order 'to subject the majority of the population to the power of market forces whilst preserving social protection for the strong' (Gill 1995: 407). From this point of view, the mobilization of neo-liberal forms of political-economic restructuring during the last two decades has entailed moments of institutional destruction *and* institutional creation—the former, insofar as neoliberal restructuring strategies strive to dismantle the regulatory infrastructure and social compromises of Fordist-Keynesian capitalism; and the latter, insofar as such strategies seek to establish new forms of statecraft and institutional 'hardware' through which to enforce market discipline, to extend market-oriented regulatory arrangements, and to enhance the discretionary power of capital at all spatial scales (Brenner and Theodore 2002*a*; Peck and Tickell 2002). The processes of institutional creative destruction unleashed through these neoliberalization strategies have in turn contributed to the consolidation of post-Keynesian competition states, both in western Europe and beyond (Hirsch 1995; Jessop 2002; Röttger 1997).

During the 1980s, the consolidation of neoliberal state practices at the EU level and their diffusion among western European national states imposed additional fiscal constraints upon most municipal and metropolitan governments, whose revenues had already been reduced significantly during the preceding decade. Under these conditions, political support for large-scale strategic planning projects waned; welfare state bureaucracies were downsized, not least at metropolitan and municipal levels; and traditional, redistributive approaches to spatial policy were significantly retrenched. The localized relays of the Keynesian welfare national state were attacked as being excessively bureaucratic, expensive, and inefficient; subsequently, new forms of municipal governance, based upon neoliberal principles such as fiscal discipline, lean administration, privatized service provision, and the new public management, were introduced (Pickvance and Preteceille 1991*a*; Wright 1994). Meanwhile, during the mid-1980s, inherited metropolitan institutions such as the Greater London Council, the English metropolitan counties, the Metropolitan Barcelona authority, the Greater Copenhagen Council, and the *Rijnmond* in Rotterdam were abolished. In other western European city regions, metropolitan institutions were formally preserved but weakened in practice due to centrally imposed budgetary pressures and enhanced competition between city cores and suburban peripheries for capital investment and state subsidies (Barlow 1991). The intensified fiscal squeeze upon public expenditure in cities and regions and the weakening or dissolution of inherited metropolitan institutions were thus among the major localized expressions of the processes of national welfare state retrenchment that began to unfold during the 1980s. As of this decade, the national preconditions for municipal Keynesianism were systematically eroded as local and metropolitan governments were increasingly forced to 'fend for themselves' in securing a fiscal base for their regulatory activities (Mayer 1994; Rödenstein 1987).

The acceleration of European integration during the second half of the 1980s—itself an expression and product of neoliberal statecraft—also generated new challenges for cities and regions throughout the continent. For, among all EU member states, the consolidation of the Single European Market (SEM) in 1993 was widely viewed as a dramatic ratcheting-up of interspatial competition among urban regions on a European scale. With the removal of national barriers to trade and investment, European cities were now seen to compete far more directly with one another than had previously been the case. The much-discussed Cecchini Report, published in 1988, famously articulated this view within a neoclassical framework and interpreted the SEM as a means to increase the efficiency of the European economy as a whole (CEC 1991). By contrast, critics of the Cecchini Report argued that the SEM would reinforce centripetal tendencies within the European economy by strengthening the dominant role of large corporations and major urban regions while further marginalizing peripheral cities and regions (Amin and Malmberg 1994; Dunford and Kafkalas 1992). While various forms of interspatial competition on a European scale were recognized prior to the 1990s, both defenders and critics of the Cecchini Report concurred that the SEM (and, subsequently, EMU) would significantly intensify that competition by undermining the ability of national governments to insulate their cities and regions from transnational market forces by means of monetary and fiscal policies. Consequently, since the consolidation of the SEM, economic competition within the EU has been widely understood as inter-urban and interregional competition rather than as a competition among national economies. Box 5.6 (overleaf) presents some typical expressions of this viewpoint that were articulated by European, national, and local policymakers following the introduction of the SEM.

During the 1980s and 1990s, as cities and regions throughout the EU attempted to adjust to the neoliberalization of key fields of state policy, and simultaneously, to prepare themselves for the new competitive pressures associated with the Single European Market, qualitatively new forms of state intervention into the urban process were mobilized. Drawing upon the notion

---

Box 5.6. The Single European Market and the new interspatial competition

---

With the disappearance of national borders within Europe [...] urban regions (cities and suburbs) are competing internationally with other urban regions. This expanding scale [of competition] occurs in conjunction with a concentration and specialization of economic activities in various realms. In this context, it is of considerable importance to the Dutch economy that the Dutch urban regions maintain a strong position

(from a law on metropolitan institutional reform in
the Netherlands approved in 1994; MBZ 1994: 10)

The political developments associated with the creation of open borders within Europe and the reunification of Germany have led to a situation in which competition with other metropolises, such as London, Paris, Amsterdam or Zürich, has become much more direct, with Berlin emerging as well as a new source of competition within our own country

(from a planning report commissioned by the municipal
government of Frankfurt am Main; Speer 2000: 1–2)

The internationalization of the European economy has intensified the competition between the cities of Europe. The single market in the European Community will provide new opportunities for the cities and towns in Denmark. But no city will get anything for free in future transnational competition. An active effort is required to obtain the potential benefits

(from a 1992 national spatial planning document in
Denmark; MoE 1992: 11)

The completion of the internal market and the abolition of internal frontiers within the Community is the latest stage in the process of internationalization [...] [T]he single market will trigger further adjustments in the roles and functions of cities, as national boundaries and interests will be less important than before. Increased inter-urban competition for development will be an important driving force [...] Changes in national urban hierarchies will occur as some cities emerge onto a wider European stage, in addition to their national or regional one

(from a report on urban trends published by the
European Commission; CEC 1992: 44)

---

of *Standortpolitik*, which has become a keyword of German neoliberal political discourse since the late 1980s, I propose to interpret the new approaches to urban governance of the post-1980s period as forms of *locational policy*.[6] As

---

[6] While this term is derived from contemporary German policy debates on *Standort Deutschland* (Germany as an investment location), it is used here in a more specific, social-scientific sense. For more detailed discussions of the ideology and practice of locational policy in the contemporary German context, see Brenner 2000*b*; M. Krätke 1999.

conceived here, the essential feature of locational policies is their overarching goal of enhancing the economic competitiveness of particular places, territories, or scales in relation to broader, supranational circuits of capital accumulation. Locational policies may involve direct subsidies and other public schemes to lure the investments of specific firms, but they are best understood as being oriented towards the *general* conditions for capital accumulation within particular territorial jurisdictions. While locational policies have a long history under modern capitalism, they have most frequently been mobilized at a national scale, in conjunction with national-developmentalist strategies of industrialization and nationalized approaches to territorial development (McMichael 1996; Lefebvre 2003*a*). It is only since the 1980s that western European states have deployed locational policies extensively at an urban scale, in the field of urban governance. Since this period, urban locational policies have been mobilized aggressively by national, regional, and local state institutions throughout western Europe in order to promote the territorialized competitive advantages of strategic cities and regions in relation to supranational (European or global) spaces of economic competition (Cheshire and Gordon 1996). In this transformed political-economic context, cities are no longer seen as containers of declining industries and intensifying socioeconomic problems, but are increasingly viewed as dynamic growth engines through which national territorial competitiveness may be promoted. In short, as Lipietz (1994: 37) notes, the locality is increasingly construed as a 'breeding ground for new productive forces', which state institutions at various spatial scales (European, national, and local) are now actively attempting to cultivate.[7]

The urban locational policies of the 1980s and early 1990s built, in significant ways, upon the legacies of previous strategies of endogenous development. For, like the endogenous growth policies that had prevailed during the preceding decade, the new urban locational policies emphasized place- and scale-specific regulatory problems and mobilized place- and scale-specific forms of state intervention in order to confront them. Insofar as urban locational policies broke decisively from top-down, standardized, and nationally encompassing approaches to the regulation of urban development, they sig-

---

[7] A variety of strands of contemporary urban political economy have amassed extensive evidence for the proliferation of urban locational policies during the last two decades. For instance, the vast literatures on urban entrepreneurialism have underscored the enhanced mobilization of local state institutions to promote economic development and to attract external capital investment (Eisenschitz and Gough 1993; Hall and Hubbard 1998; Harding 1997; Mayer 1992). Concomitantly, albeit from a different methodological and political angle, many studies of local production milieux, industrial districts, and regional innovation systems have explored the role of place-specific regulatory systems—which state institutions, at various spatial scales, help constitute—in producing and maintaining territorially embedded competitive advantages (Cooke and Morgan 1998; Garofoli 2002; Le Galès and Voelzkow 2001; Storper and Salais 1997). More recently, a number of studies of territorial competition in the EU have likewise documented the proliferation of urban locational policies during the last two decades (see e.g. Begg 1999; Gordon 1999; Cheshire and Gordon 1998, 1996, 1995).

nificantly deepened the fragmentation and erosion of spatial Keynesianism that had been initiated during the previous wave of urban policy reform.

However, the endogenous development strategies of the 1970s emerged in a political-economic context in which western European national governments remained firmly committed to the priority of national spatial equalization. By contrast, the urban locational policies of the 1980s and early 1990s were articulated under conditions in which newly consolidated, post-Keynesian competition states were scrambling to enhance their competitive advantages within a rapidly integrating global and European space-economy. Under these circumstances, the project of promoting territorial redistribution at any spatial scale was increasingly viewed as 'a luxury belonging to an earlier period of economic growth' (Läpple 1985: 52). Consequently, 'national commitments to geographically "balanced" growth in the name of equity have increasingly given way to concern with the way in which the characteristics of particular localities can enhance the growth prospects of firms and support national economic competitiveness' (Harding 1997: 307). In at least four key respects, then, the urban locational policies of the post-1980s period have entailed a significant break from the endogenous development strategies of the preceding decade.

1. Whereas endogenous development strategies attempted to combine the agendas of economic rejuvenation and territorial redistribution within particular subnational spaces, urban locational policies have privileged the goals of securing territorial competitiveness and promoting economic growth. Redistributive concerns have not disappeared from the field of urban governance, but they have been subordinated to, or recast in terms of, developmentalist, entrepreneurial priorities (Mayer 1994).

2. Whereas endogenous development strategies attempted to promote 'self-reliant', locally controlled forms of economic renewal within relatively bounded, autocentric places, urban locational policies have been aggressively extrospective, oriented towards the goal of positioning major cities and city-regions strategically within supranational scales of capital circulation. The issues of popular control and local democratic accountability have continued to arise within urban political struggles, but they have been largely dissociated from the field of urban economic policy (Keil 1998*b*).

3. Whereas endogenous development strategies were mobilized above all within crisis-stricken manufacturing cities and regions, urban locational policies have been generalized throughout the European urban system. Anecdotal evidence suggests that urban locational policies were pioneered during the early 1980s in a number of vanguard cities and regions—such as Hamburg, Bologna, Lyon, Lille, Rotterdam, Birmingham, and Glasgow—in which national, regional, or local political-economic coalitions embarked upon proactive programs of place-marketing, advanced infrastructure investment, and growth-promotion (Cheshire and Gordon 1996). However, as these initial,

ad hoc experiments in urban locational policy were diffused, the costs and risks associated with a failure to mobilize such policies intensified. This situation, coupled with the widespread embrace of an 'alarmist vocabulary of globalization' (Eisenschitz and Gough 1998: 762) after the introduction of the SEM, led national, regional, and local governments throughout western Europe to adopt closely analogous initiatives within their own cities and city-regions (Harding 1997; Leitner and Sheppard 1998). National governments now came to view their most globally integrated cities and city-regions as key motors for national economic growth, and thus targeted them with particular intensity for various types of urban locational policies.

4. Whereas endogenous development strategies were grounded primarily upon bottom-up initiatives, in which local or regional institutions steered the process of regulatory experimentation, urban locational policies have emerged through the interaction of multiple scales of political authority, from the European and the national to the regional and the urban. While some urban locational policies have indeed been initiated through the activities of local growth coalitions, the latter are now embedded within a significantly transformed intergovernmental context in which both European political institutions and national states have imposed new competitive pressures and fiscal constraints upon cities (Le Galès 2002). These new, market-driven, and competition-oriented interscalar rule-regimes have been derived, in significant measure, from the neoliberalization processes outlined above (Peck and Tickell 2002), and as we shall see, they have played a major role in the generalization of urban locational policies across western Europe.

Figure 5.7 (overleaf) provides a schematic comparison among spatial Keynesianism, endogenous development strategies, and urban locational policies as distinct but partially overlapping approaches to the regulation of capitalist urbanization. Figure 5.7 is also intended to underscore the incremental and path-dependent, rather than linear, character of urban governance restructuring since the early 1970s. During the initial round of crisis-induced regulatory restructuring of the 1970s, endogenous development strategies destabilized the institutional foundations of spatial Keynesianism while preserving, at subnational scales, a political commitment to the project of territorial equalization. During the 1980s, in a subsequent round of crisis-induced regulatory experimentation, urban locational policies built upon the subnational policy repertoires and institutional scaffolding that had been forged through the endogenous development strategies of the preceding decade. Indeed, it was on the basis of this recently established layer of place- and scale-specific forms of state intervention that urban locational policies could be articulated, entrenched, and eventually generalized across the western European urban system. However, even as they drew upon certain regulatory instruments of endogenous growth strategies, the urban locational policies of the post-1980s period also systematically suppressed their spatially redistributive agendas.

	Predominant scale of operation	Predominant mode of implementation	Major regulatory goal	'Projected' geography of economic development
Spatial Keynesianism: 1960s–early 1970s	National	Mobilizes generic spatial policies evenly across the entire national territory	Promotes balanced development and territorial redistribution at a particular scale	Autocentric: promotes a particular scale as a relatively self-contained, self-propelled unit of economic development
Endogenous Development Strategy: 1970s–early 1980s	Regional and urban	Grounded upon customized, place- and scale-specific forms of spatial policy	Promotes balanced development and territorial redistribution at a particular scale	Autocentric: promotes a particular scale as a relatively self-contained, self-propelled unit of economic development
Urban Locational Policy: early 1980s–present	Regional and urban	Grounded upon customized, place-and scale-specific forms of spatial policy	Promotes economic growth, external capital investment, and territorial competitiveness at a particular scale	Multiscalar: promotes economic development by positioning a particular scale strategically within broader, transnational interscalar hierarchies and networks

Key

| Cells shaded gray | *unique* features of a given approach |
| Cells enclosed within bold lines | features *shared* with another approach |

Fig. 5.7. Three approaches to urban governance: spatial Keynesianism, endogenous development strategy, and locational policy

Place- and scale-specific approaches to urban governance were thus transformed from a basis for promoting economic rejuvenation and territorial redistribution within crisis-stricken industrial urban regions (1970s–early 1980s) into a means for positioning major cities and regions strategically within global and European spatial divisions of labor (post-1980s period).

Urban locational policies and the question of territorial competitiveness

At any spatial scale, locational policies hinge upon the assumption that territorial units, like capitalist firms, compete against one another in order to maximize profits and economic growth. In this viewpoint, the competitiveness of a given territory is said to flow from its capacity to achieve these goals effectively and durably—whether by attracting inward investment flows, by lowering investment costs, by increasing productivity levels, by providing a suitably skilled labor force, by creating an innovative environment or by means of other strategies intended to enhance the value of economic activities located within its boundaries (Begg 1999). The goal of locational policy, therefore, is to promote territorial competitiveness by maintaining and continually expanding the capacities for profit-making and economic growth that are embedded within specific political jurisdictions.

Some economists, notably Paul Krugman (1994), have criticized attempts to apply the notion of competitiveness to territorial units. For Krugman, the notion of competitiveness is an attribute of capitalist firms, not of territorial units such as cities, regions, or countries. When applied to such entities, Krugman (1994: 31) argues, the notion of competitiveness represents a 'dangerous obsession' because they 'have no well-defined bottom line'. Krugman's critique of competitiveness discourse among economists and policymakers has been addressed in the urban studies literature as well, in which a number of scholars have debated the intellectual plausibility of divergent conceptions of urban locational competitiveness.[8] However, even the most subtle deconstructions and critiques cannot occlude the mounting evidence that territorial competitiveness has become a pervasive concern among policymakers at all scales of political authority, from the OECD and the European Commission to national governments, regional administrations, and entrepreneurial municipalities. Consequently, the 'dangerous obsession' of territorial competitiveness cannot be dismissed as a mere conceptual fallacy or ideological illusion. As Dicken (1998: 88) explains: 'Whether Krugman is right or wrong in his analysis, there seems little likelihood of policy-makers actually heeding his warnings and refraining from both the rhetoric and the reality of competitive policy measures. As long as the concept of national competitiveness remains in currency then no single state is likely to opt out.'

For our purposes, then, it is not necessary to embrace a particular definition of competitiveness, either for firms or for territories. The key point here is that, since the early 1980s, national, regional, and urban policymakers across western Europe have become concerned to enhance various attributes of cities that are considered to contribute to their 'competitiveness' relative to other global and European investment locations (Gordon 1999; Lever 1999). Given the earlier, Fordist-Keynesian understanding of cities as localized subunits of national economies, this new emphasis on urban territorial competitiveness in

---

[8] See e.g. Budd 1998; Begg 1999; Camagni 2002; and Lovering 1999.

relation to supranational circuits of capital represents a striking political, ideological, and scalar realignment (Lovering 1999; Veltz 2000). The proliferation of urban locational policies during the last two decades is at once an expression and an outcome of this changing conception of how cities contribute to economic life.

Urban locational policies have been articulated in divergent political forms, both within and among national intergovernmental systems. While such policies are frequently justified with reference to the widely disseminated writings of business school gurus such as Michael Porter (1990) and Kenichi Ohmae (1990), among others, they have been grounded, in practice, upon a diverse range of assumptions regarding the sources of competitive advantage within local economies and the role of state institutions, at various spatial scales, in promoting the latter (Begg 1999; Cheshire and Gordon 1996). More generally, as Lovering (1999: 389) notes: 'The choice invoked by the concept of competitiveness is not simply between favouring different industries and firms, but is also about deciding between different groups of workers, different social structures and different national economic geographies. It is no less than a choice between different visions of the collective economic and cultural future.'

I shall not attempt, in the present context, to compare systematically the nationally, regionally, and locally specific types of urban locational policies that have crystallized in western European city-regions during the last two decades. Instead I proceed on a meso level in order to specify three key axes on which basis such policies may be decoded.

1. *Forms of territorial competition.* According to Storper and Walker (1989), inter-firm competition under capitalism occurs in weak and strong forms. Whereas weak competition is oriented towards the reduction of costs and the redistribution of resources within a given spatial division of labor (static comparative advantages), strong competition is oriented towards the transformation of the conditions of production in order to introduce new technological capacities and a new spatial division of labor (dynamic competitive advantages). Urban locational policies may likewise be oriented towards weak or strong forms of inter-firm competition, depending on the balance of cost-cutting, deregulatory state initiatives, and those that attempt to enhance firm productivity and innovative milieux within the jurisdiction in question (Leborgne and Lipietz 1991). Neoliberal or defensive approaches to urban locational policy attempt to capitalize upon weak forms of inter-firm competition; they are based upon the assumption that lowering the costs of investment within a given territory will attract mobile capital investment and thus enhance its competitiveness. By contrast, social democratic or offensive approaches to urban locational policy attempt to capitalize upon strong forms of inter-firm competition; they are based upon the assumption that territorial competitiveness hinges upon the provision of non-substitutable socioeconomic assets such

as innovative capacities, collaborative inter-firm networks, advanced infra-structural facilities, and skilled labor power (Eisenschitz and Gough 1996). Within any national or local context, the precise balance among neoliberal/defensive and social democratic/offensive approaches to locational policy is an object and outcome of intense sociopolitical struggles over the form of state intervention into the urban process (Eisenschitz and Gough 1993).

2. *Fields of territorial competition.* Building upon Harvey's (1989*a*) study of urban entrepreneurialism, four distinct fields of urban locational policy may be delineated according to the particular circuits of capital they target. First, urban locational policies may attempt to enhance a city's advantages within spatial divisions of labor, generally by establishing or strengthening place-specific conditions for the production of particular types of goods and services. Second, urban locational policies may attempt to enhance a city's advantages within spatial divisions of consumption, generally by creating or strengthen-ing a localized infrastructure for tourism, leisure, or retirement functions. Third, urban locational policies may attempt to enhance a city's command and control capacities in the spheres of finance, information processing, and government. Finally, urban locational policies may attempt to enhance a city's economic capacities by procuring governmental resources, whether from the European Commission or from national state agencies. While these fields of territorial competition may be distinguished analytically, most urban loca-tional policies attempt, in practice, to enhance a city's position simultaneously within multiple fields.

3. *Geographies of territorial competition.* Finally, urban locational policies entail the delineation of determinate geographical parameters within which the process of economic development is to unfold. These parameters may be defined with reference to three key elements. First, urban locational policies generally entail the demarcation of determinate spaces of competitiveness within which place-specific economic capacities are to be mobilized—for in-stance, central business districts, inner-city enterprise zones, revitalized manu-facturing and port areas, new media enclaves, high-technology suburbs, and so forth. Second, urban locational policies entail the targeting of broader spaces of competition, including the Single European Market and the world economy as a whole, within which cities (or some component thereof) are to be positioned as attractive investment locations. Third, a variety of spatially selective political strategies may be mobilized in order to position urban spaces of competitiveness within supranational spaces of competition (Healey 1998; Jessop 2002: 190–2). For instance, some urban locational policies attempt to transform an urban economy into a key articulation point within a nested hierarchy of regional, national, and supranational economic spaces. Other urban locational policies may attempt to delink an urban economy from surrounding regional and national economic spaces by expanding its command and control capacities or its supranational transportation and communications links. Still other urban locational policies may attempt to

reorganize inherited urban hierarchies—whether vertically, through the promotion of new forms of cooperation among different tiers of state power (for instance, within metropolitan regions); or horizontally, through the promotion of transversal alliances among geographically dispersed cities occupying complementary positions in the European or global division of labor (see Ch. 6 below). Therefore, even though all urban locational policies strive, in some manner, to position cities and regions favorably within supranational circuits of capital, this goal may be pursued through diverse political-geographical strategies (Jessop 1998).

Urban locational policies have an inherently speculative character due to 'the inability [of political alliances] to predict exactly which package [of local investments] will succeed and which will not, in a world of considerable economic instability and volatility' (Harvey 1989a: 10–11). Moreover, urban locational policies are often grounded upon untenable assumptions and unrealistic predictions regarding the possible future trajectories of local economic development (see Ch. 6). Despite these endemic problems, the proliferation of urban locational policies during the last two decades has engendered a fundamental transformation in the character of state intervention into the urban process throughout the EU. Most crucially for our purposes, urban locational policies have not only entailed an intensified mobilization of state institutions to promote territorial competitiveness within strategic local economies; they have also contributed to a fundamental rescaling of state institutions themselves.

Mapping state spatial selectivity in post-1980s western Europe: urban locational policies and the rescaling of state space

If the Keynesian state was concerned to integrate its constituent regional and local economies and to cushion them from economic instability, the approach of its successor [...] has been to *dismantle* and *fragment* those systems of support in deference to the restructuring forces of global competition, destabilizing its regions in the process.

Ron Martin and Peter Sunley (1997: 282; italics in original)

What we are witnessing with the demise of Fordism is the emergence of much greater geographical unevenness in the system of regulation. The abandonment of national redistributive strategies and the emerging global mosaic of regional economies have led to the development of a parallel mosaic of differentiated spaces of regulation.

Mark Goodwin and Joe Painter (1996: 646)

Insofar as urban locational policies were first mobilized within formations of state spatiality that had been inherited from the Fordist-Keynesian era, their institutional and geographical consequences were highly uneven, varying considerably within each national, regional, and local context according to (*a*) the resilience of preservationist political alliances concerned to defend the institutionalized social compromises and territorial arrangements of the Fordist-Keynesian order; and (*b*) the distinctive strategies of restructuring and rescaling adopted by modernizing political-economic forces (Lipietz 1994). Consequently, the diffusion of urban locational policies in western European national states did not simply erase earlier geographies of state regulation, but generated contextually specific, politically contested rearticulations of inherited state spatial configurations at a range of geographical scales. In general terms, the rescaled geographies of state spatiality that crystallized during the post-1980s period must be conceived as expressions of a conflictual, path-dependent interaction between (*a*) the standardized, nationally configured regulatory geographies that were inherited, albeit in a destabilized form, from the transitional period of the 1970s; (*b*) the endogenous development strategies of the late 1970s and early 1980s, with their goal of mobilizing negotiated, place-specific restructuring strategies to address localized socioeconomic crises; and (*c*) subsequent forms of urban locational policy, with their goal of mobilizing place- and scale-specific forms of state intervention to enhance urban territorial competitiveness.

However, despite the incremental, path-dependent character of state spatial restructuring following the initial crisis of North Atlantic Fordism, it was evident, by the late 1980s, that rescaled configurations of urban governance and state spatiality were being superimposed upon inherited national regulatory geographies. Whereas early forms of urban locational policy were articulated while the institutional framework of spatial Keynesianism was still being provisionally defended at a national scale, the consolidation and subsequent diffusion of such policies during the post-1980s period entailed a more sustained attack upon that framework. As urban locational policies acquired increasingly prominent regulatory roles within post-Keynesian competition states, the nationalized, centralized, standardized, and redistributive policy relays associated with spatial Keynesianism came to be viewed as major institutional impediments to the new priority of enhancing the territorial competitiveness of cities and city-regions. Under these circumstances, a radically transformed interscalar framework for the regulation of capitalist urbanization was seen to be required in order to maximize the place-specific locational advantages of major cities and city-regions.

The process of envisioning and establishing such an interscalar framework was geographically uneven, institutionally diffuse, and politically contested. It involved a variety of Europe-wide, nationally specific, and place-based debates regarding the appropriate institutional form and strategic orientation of (national, regional, and local) state intervention into the urban process.

Accordingly, much like the endogenous development strategies of the preced-ing decade, post-Keynesian initiatives to reconstitute the national, regional, and local geographies of urban governance were initially grounded upon ad hoc, trial-and-error intergovernmental realignments, policy adjustments, and regu-latory experiments. Eventually, however, with the entrenchment of neoliberal policy agendas at a European scale and the progressive consolidation of post-Keynesian competition state regimes at a national scale, these reform initiatives gained significant political momentum and acquired an enhanced institutional solidity.[9] Consequently, across western Europe, the nationally standardized political geographies of spatial Keynesianism were eroded; inherited relays of national territorial redistribution were ruptured; centralized systems of inter-governmental relations were recalibrated; and qualitatively new, competition-oriented frameworks of interscalar regulation were introduced.

These newly constituted, state-organized interscalar rule-regimes were explicitly designed to facilitate urban locational policies by channeling 'the strategic options and tactical behavior of local actors' (Peck 2002: 338) towards developmentalist, competitiveness-driven agendas. More generally, such interscalar rule-regimes attempted to institutionalize entrepreneurial, com-petitiveness-oriented, and 'growth first' approaches to urban governance (*a*) by exposing cities and regions more directly to geoeconomic pressures and (*b*) by subjecting them to competitive regimes of intergovernmental resource allocation based upon market position, performance, and efficiency rather than social need (Peck and Tickell 2002: 47–8). From this point of view, the new interlocality competition of the post-1980s period cannot be under-stood simply as the aggregate expression of localized policy responses to global and European market integration. On the contrary, the grim, neoliberal requirement for cities to 'compete or die' (Eisenschitz and Gough 1998: 762)—which aptly encapsulates the aggressively competitive spatial logic underlying urban locational policy—must be interpreted as a *politically*

---

[9] Such initiatives were further reinforced through the activities of diverse supranational organiza-tions—including the European Commission, the OECD, the World Bank, the United Nations, and URBAN 21—which likewise began to advocate a variety of national intergovernmental reforms during this period in the name of priorities such as territorial competitiveness, administrative efficiency, market responsiveness, and fiscal responsibility. Various aspects of national administrative reform and territorial governance were thematized in diverse EU, World Bank, OECD, and United Nations documents as of the late 1980s, resulting in a range of 'expert' policy recommendations regarding the need to reorganize the public sector. URBAN 21 is a more recent 'expert commission', funded by the governments of Germany, Brazil, South Africa, and Singapore, and assigned to evaluate the challenges of contemporary urban policy around the world (see Hall and Pfeiffer 2000). The role of these and other supposedly neutral supranational bodies in providing political support and ideological legitimation for the remaking of national state spaces during the last two decades has yet to be investigated empirically. Wright (1994) provides a highly suggestive, but largely anecdotal, foray into such an analysis with reference to the diffusion of 'new public management' approaches across western Europe. While the issue of cross-national policy transfer has been exam-ined in detail with reference to welfare-to-work initiatives and other 'Third Way' reform agendas (Peck 2001*a*, *b*; Peck and Theodore 2001), this process remains to be investigated in other insti-tutional spheres. Such an analysis would arguably form a key element within any systematic account of the political geographies of neoliberalism (see also Wacquant 1999; Peck and Tickell 2002).

constructed imperative that was imposed upon local and regional economies in significant measure through the rescaling of national state spaces. Concomitantly, national states should not be conceived as static territorial containers within which urban locational policies have been mobilized. Rather, national state institutions actively promoted such policies by recalibrating their internal intergovernmental hierarchies, modes of intervention, and policy repertoires in order to facilitate the strategic positioning of their major local and regional economies within Europe-wide and global circuits of capital.

Building upon the theoretical framework introduced in Ch. 3, and replicating the analytical strategy deployed in Ch. 4 to analyze the political geographies of spatial Keynesianism, the key elements of this transformation of urban governance and state spatiality during the post-1980s period are depicted in Fig. 5.8 (overleaf). First, urban locational policies were grounded upon qualitatively new state spatial projects intended to enhance state capacities for mobilizing place-specific forms of intervention within strategic cities and city-regions. To this end, state regulatory configurations were *decentralized* towards subnational tiers and *customized* according to place- and jurisdiction-specific conditions. Second, urban locational policies were grounded upon qualitatively new state spatial strategies intended to enhance the competitiveness of major cities and city-regions. To this end, state institutions at various spatial scales promoted the *localization* of major socioeconomic assets within strategic urban and regional economies and the increasing *differentiation* of urban and regional developmental pathways across the national territory. Thus, in contrast to the centralized, standardized, and nationalized geographies of state space that prevailed under the Fordist regime of accumulation, the establishment of this new, competitiveness-oriented institutional infrastructure for urban governance during the post-1980s period entailed an increasing geographical splintering, fragmentation, and differentiation of state space at various spatial scales.

This rescaling of state space was closely intertwined with a fundamental inversion of inherited postwar approaches to the political regulation of uneven spatial development. Whereas postwar strategies of spatial Keynesianism were oriented explicitly towards the *alleviation* of territorial inequalities, the mobilization of urban locational policies during the post-1980s period actively *intensified* uneven spatial development in a variety of ways—(*a*) by promoting a systematic reconcentration of socioeconomic capacities within each national territory's most globally competitive locations, (*b*) by encouraging divergent, place-specific forms of economic governance, public service provision, and territorial administration within different subnational political jurisdictions, and (*c*) by institutionalizing competitive relations, whether for public subsidies or for private investments, among major subnational administrative units. In his recent study of the transatlantic circulation of neoliberal workfare policies, Peck (2002) has underscored the ways in which, rather than treating intra-national spatial polarization as a regulatory problem requiring political intervention, national, regional, and local state institutions are today

	STATE SPATIAL PROJECTS	STATE SPATIAL STRATEGIES
SCALAR DIMENSION	Tendential *decentralization* of state administrative arrangements towards subnational tiers of political authority Regional and local state institutions acquire new responsibilities in the development, financing, and implementation of economic development policies	Increasing *localization* of socioeconomic assets as national, regional, and local state institutions attempt to enhance territorial competitiveness within strategic urbanized spaces Cities and city-regions are viewed as key geographical engines of economic development within increasingly volatile global and European interscalar hierarchies
TERRITORIAL DIMENSION	Increasing *customization* of state administrative arrangements according to place- and jurisdiction-specific conditions and priorities This generates an increased differentiation of local and regional institutional forms and an enhanced divergence of local and regional policy regimes across each national territory	Increasing *differentiation* of national political-economic space as state institutions attempt to channel major socioeconomic assets and advanced infrastructure investments into the most globally competitive urban and regional spaces This generates an increasing divergence of social welfare standards and an enhanced differentiation of developmental pathways among local economies within each national territory

Fig. 5.8. Urban locational policies and the transformation of state spatial selectivity (builds on Fig. 3.9, p. 97, compare Fig. 4.2, p. 132)

explicitly promoting geographical differentiation, interlocality competition, and spatial unevenness within their territories. Peck's (2002: 356) description of neoliberal workfare policies therefore provides a strikingly appropriate characterization of urban locational policies in post-1980s western Europe:

Uneven geographic development is being established as an intentional, rather than merely incidental, feature of the delivery of workfare programs, while local experimentation and emulation are becoming seemingly permanent features of the policy-making process. Under workfarism, spatial variability, the churning of persistently reformed programs, rapid interlocal policy transfers, and the ceaseless search for local success stories that are ripe for replication are all effectively normalized. In stark contrast to the aspirations to fair and equal treatment under welfare regimes, when spatial unevenness, local discretion and instances of atypical [. . .] treatment were often constituted as policy problems in their own right [. . .] workfare makes a virtue of geographic differentiation, subnational competition, and [. . .] circumstance-specific interventions.

The multifaceted interplay between the consolidation of post-Keynesian competition state regimes, the restructuring of European urban economies, the rise of urban locational policy, and the rescaling of state space is summarized schematically in Fig. 5.9 (p. 217). Boxes 5.7 and 5.8 (pp. 218–19) summarize the major state spatial projects and state spatial strategies through which urban locational policies have been mobilized during the post-1980s period. These diverse pathways of politico-geographical and institutional transformation have engendered a 'new scalar gestalt of governance' characterized by the dominance of a 'boosterist, entrepreneurial development vision' within strategic urban locations and, frequently, by the contraction of inherited lines of democratic accountability at multiple scales of state power (Swyngedouw, Moulaert, and Rodriguez 2003: 22). I shall not attempt here to provide a comprehensive, comparative account of each of the spheres of policy reform, regulatory experimentation, and institutional restructuring summarized in Boxes 5.7 and 5.8, or to trace systematically their variegated sociospatial consequences in different European cities, regions, and national states. Instead, drawing on evidence from across the western European city-system, the remainder of this chapter examines three specific realms of political-institutional restructuring that clearly illuminate the links between urban locational policy and the rescaling of state space: (1) the decentralization of intergovernmental relations; (2) the metropolitanization of national spatial planning systems; and (3) the splintering of large-scale urban infrastructural configurations.

Box 5.7. Key state spatial projects promoting urban locational policy

---

Since the [national] state cannot seek to assure everywhere the same form of macroeconomic regulation [. . .] the issue is to equip the regional armatures with more powerful instruments of economic and social regulation and to reserve for the nation-state the administration of the external relation (support to industries, administration of foreign exchange). In comparison to Fordism, which is above all and by definition 'national', this new division of capacities between the national and the regional means a contraction of the national legislation and collective agreements and a larger variability for the regional armatures in their choice of the social protection level.

(Lipietz 1994: 38)

Urban locational policy has been grounded upon *state spatial projects* oriented towards an enhanced *decentralization* of state regulatory capacities and an extensive *customization* of state administrative arrangements according to place- and jurisdiction-specific conditions within each national territory. These decentralizing, customizing state spatial projects have included:

- *Intergovernmental devolution.* In both federal and unitary states, national governments have devolved various regulatory responsibilities to subnational administrative units. Such projects of intergovernmental rescaling have been viewed as a means to promote fiscal retrenchment within state bureaucracies while impelling subnational institutions to seek new sources of revenue through proactive economic development programs. At the same time, such rescaling initiatives have enabled regional and local state institutions to introduce customized regulatory arrangements and policy strategies oriented towards place- and scale-specific problems of economic governance (Fox Przeworski 1986; Keating 1998).

- *Local government reorganization.* As national governments have promoted fiscal retrenchment, the managerial, public service functions of local governments have been streamlined or privatized. Local states have introduced new, market-driven approaches to public management and have established new forms of public–private partnership to promote economic rejuvenation. The new priorities of maximizing administrative efficiency and enhancing consumer responsiveness have thus superseded the traditional goal of facilitating local social welfare. Local economic regulation is increasingly grounded upon flexible governance networks that involve not only entrepreneurial local state institutions but also various private actors and 'third sector', community-based organizations (Mayer 1994; Clark 1997).

- *Metropolitan institutional reform.* In many European city-regions, particularly from the early 1990s, new forms of metropolitan economic coordination have been introduced (see Ch. 6). These reconstituted or newly established metropolitan institutional forms are intended to bundle together region-wide socioeconomic assets, to market major city-regions as unified locations for external capital investment, and to minimize destructive, zero-sum forms of intra-regional competition (Brenner 2003*a*; Lefèvre 1998).

- *The construction of place- and scale-specific institutional forms.* National, regional, and local governments have attempted to channel urban (re)development into particular locations by introducing new, jurisdiction- and area-specific institutional forms. Prominent examples of this trend have included enterprise zones, urban development corporations, airport development agencies, training and enterprise councils, inward investment agencies, and development planning boards, all of which have been designed, in some manner, to intensify and accelerate economic growth within strategic, clearly delineated urban zones. Such institutions are often autonomous from local state control and dominated by unaccountable political and economic elites. They have also frequently entailed the suspension of existing planning regulations in favor of 'exceptional' (but increasingly normalized) policy tools and modes of intervention within strategic areas or infrastructural configurations (Swyngedouw, Moulaert, and Rodriguez 2002).

Rise of post-Keynesian competition states

- Traditional Keynesian welfarist, demand management policies are undermined
- Priorities of promoting territorial competitiveness, fiscal responsibility, labor market flexibility, and technological innovation gain significance

The rise of urban locational policy (*Standortpolitik*)

proliferation of place- and scale-specific state initiatives designed to enhance territorially embedded competitive advantages in global and European circuits of capital; major cities and city-regions are increasingly targeted for such policies

State spatial selectivity is transformed by means of new ...

state spatial projects ...

- Decentralization of key state regulatory capacities towards subnational scales
- Customization of state administrative arrangements according to place- and jurisdiction-specific conditions

and state spatial strategies

- Promotion of cities and city-regions rather than the entire national economy as key scales of economic competitiveness
- Concentration of major socioeconomic assets and advanced infrastructure investments into the most economically dynamic and globally competitive cities and city-regions

Key elements of post-1970s urban restructuring

- Industrial restructuring reworks postwar patterns of urban and regional development
- The spread of flexible production systems enhances the importance of localized, place-specific socio-economic assets and innovative capacities
- Accelerated geoeconomic and European integration generates new forms of economic uncertainty for cities and regions
- Interlocality competition intensifies as cities and regions attempt to attract investment from mobile capital

The rise of endogenous development strategies

place- and scale-specific state initatives designed to promote negotiated forms of economic rejuvenation and territorial redistribution within crisis-stricken industrial cities and regions

Major consequences

- Cities and regions are increasingly forced to 'fend for themselves' to secure local revenues and external capital investment
- Predatory, zero-sum bidding wars erupt among localities competing to attract mobile capital investment
- The geographies of state regulation are increasingly splintered and differentiated, thus undermining the relatively uniform administrative structures that had prevailed under Fordist-Keynesian capitalism
- New forms of uneven spatial development and territorial inequality proliferate at all scales

Fig. 5.9. Urbanization, locational policy, and the rescaling of state space in post-1970s western Europe (compare Fig. 4.3, p. 134) .

Box 5.8. Key state spatial strategies promoting urban locational policy

---

> many countries are ... concentrating their public expenditures on their most dynamic, globally-linked agglomerations at the expense of basic equity issues both within these agglomerations and between them and other areas of the national territory.
>
> (Scott and Storper 2003: 588)

> Cities [...] are seen as the motors for national competitive success [...] national governments across western Europe have increasingly come to stress the potential contribution of cities, particularly large cities, to national economic competitiveness and performance
>
> (Leitner and Sheppard 1998: 294)

> Urban policy no longer aspires to guide or regulate the direction of economic growth so much as to fit itself to the grooves already established by the market in search of the highest returns
>
> (Smith 2002: 94)

Urban locational policy has been grounded upon a variety of *state spatial strategies* oriented towards the *localization* of major socioeconomic assets and the *concentration* of advanced infrastructural investments within the most globally competitive cities and city-regions. These localizing, metropolitan-centered state spatial strategies have included:

- *Rescaled, 'metropolitanized' spatial planning policies.* In contrast to earlier, compensatory approaches to spatial planning, national governments have demarcated the most competitive urban regions within their territories as key geographical focal points for state-sponsored economic development initiatives and strategic planning programs. These rescaled, city-centric approaches to national spatial planning have explicitly targeted metropolitan regions for external capital investment and for major public infrastructural projects. Whereas spatial planning previously served as a mechanism of territorial redistribution, these new 'metropolitanized' approaches have been oriented above all towards the goal of enhancing the place-specific competitive advantages of major local and regional economies within global and European markets.

- *Local economic initiatives.* Through 'partnerships' with private and community-based organizations, municipal governments have mobilized a range of entrepreneurial policies intended to promote local economic (re)development. These policies have included labor market programs, industrial policies, infrastructural investments, place-marketing initiatives, and property redevelopment campaigns (Eisenschitz and Gough 1993; Mayer 1992). At the same time, local states have sought actively to acquire additional public subsidies through national or European industrial and sectoral programs. In contrast to earlier forms of urban managerialism, which emphasized public welfare and collective consumption initiatives, the priorities of maintaining a good business environment, attracting external capital investment, and promoting local economic growth now predominate (Hall and Hubbard 1998; Leitner and Sheppard 1998).

- *State-financed mega-projects and advanced infrastructural investments.* National, regional, and local state institutions have channeled public resources into large-scale development projects within strategic urban infrastructural configurations. Such urban development projects have included airports, bridges, waterfronts, convention centers, office complexes, business parks, high-technology enclaves, logistics centers, advanced telecommunications networks, and tourist/recreational facilities. Under conditions of intensifying interlocality competition, such state-led urban development initiatives have been intended to provide the customized, place-specific infrastructural foundations for high value-added capital investment and dynamic economic activity within and among strategic urban nodal points. These urban mega-projects and high-performance infra-structural investments have also served as an institutional mechanism through which national, regional, and local states channel public funds into strategically located, market-oriented development initiatives (Swyngedouw, Moulaert, and Rodriguez 2002; Moulaert, Rodriguez, and Swyngedouw 2003).

• *Decentralized approaches to industrial policy.* European, national, and regional state institutions have mobilized various policy initiatives in order to create decentralized inter-firm networks, particularly among small- and medium-sized firms (Ansell 2000). While such policies have not always been oriented explicitly towards specific geograph-ical areas, they have usually generated significant spatial consequences insofar as the targeted firms and sectors are agglomerated within major urban and regional econ-omies. These new, decentralized approaches to regional industrial policy have been mobilized not only through extant governmental institutions, but also through newly established urban and regional development agencies designed to facilitate inter-firm networking and enhance innovative milieux in strategic subnational territorial areas (Cooke and Morgan 1998).

Decentralization tendencies and the recalibration of intergovernmental relations

> The growing significance of spatial-structural factors for the competitive-ness of firms points unequivocally to the need for decentralization policies and a redefinition of the competencies of national, regional and local policy-making authorities [. . .] What is . . . gaining rapidly in significance is the expansion of the competence and the financial scopes of regional and local administrations. The objective is to build institutional structures that make it possible to shape the structures in local and regional industrial locations . . .
>
> Dirk Messner (1997: 31)

As of the early 1980s, national governments throughout western Europe began to transfer diverse public policy responsibilities to subnational (regional and local) administrative tiers. While these institutional realignments were most dramatically evident within historically centralized states, such as France and Spain, far-reaching programs of decentralization were undertaken in many other western European states as well, leading to profound, lasting transform-ations within inherited intergovernmental landscapes (Crouch and Marquand 1989; Pickvance and Preteceille 1991*a*). According to Sellers's (2002: 91) evalu-ation, this new emphasis on 'governing from below' entailed nothing less than a 'sea change in prevailing ideas about how policy making should be done'. In contrast to the highly centralized, hierarchical, and vertically integrated national administrative frameworks that prevailed during the Fordist-Keynesian period, the post-1980s wave of decentralization established new subnational layers of state institutional organization and regulatory activity through which major local and regional political-economic actors—and, in some cases, local and regional populations—could more directly influence subnational policy outcomes (Ansell 2000). Thus, as Sellers (2002: 90) concludes, 'The more that national, intermediate and transnational governments have tried to shape urban political economies, the more that governing from above has depended on governing from below.'

The decentralization initiatives of the 1980s and 1990s were motivated by a variety of political agendas, including neoliberal critiques of welfarism, social democratic and associationalist demands for enhanced local democracy, and ideologically hybrid arguments regarding the superior efficiency of decentralized models of public service provision (Keating 1998; Wright 1998). In addition to these positions, however, decentralization programs were also animated by developmentalist claims that 'local and regional tiers [of the state system] are better placed to forge durable and interactive relations with firms' (Cooke and Morgan 1998: 23). In this sense, decentralization initiatives can be viewed as an essential institutional mechanism for the mobilization of urban locational policies, for such intergovernmental realignments were intended simultaneously to 'limit the considerable welfare demands of urban areas and to encourage lower-level authorities to assume responsibility for growth policies that might reduce welfare burdens' (Harding 1994: 370). Insofar as programs of fiscal decentralization often reduced central grants to subnational governmental tiers and enhanced municipalities' dependency upon locally collected taxes, they impelled local alliances, regardless of their political orientation, to become 'more receptive to strategies to increase local investments' (Salet, Thornley, and Kreukels 2003a: 12). In many instances, decentralization programs also established qualitatively new regulatory instruments through which regional and local state institutions could promote industrial regeneration, economic growth, and external capital investment within major city-regions. In short, even though decentralization cannot be reduced to the agenda of enhancing urban territorial competitiveness, this priority figured crucially in the formulation and implementation of such programs across western Europe during the post-1980s period:

• One of the most comprehensive programs of intergovernmental decentralization was initiated by the Socialist government in France as of the early 1980s. The 1982 *Loi Defferre*, named after a former mayor of Marseille who served in the national government during the reform process, established local governments that were formally independent of direct central control and, more generally, gave 'more power, more autonomy of decision and control of resources, more responsibilities and competencies to the non-central tiers of government—municipalities, départements and regions' (Preteceille 1991: 127). This decentralization program served as a 'major spur to local economic development'; for it 'incorporated a mandate to all levels of local government to promote economic development, business expansion, and innovation' and impelled 'all local elected officials, whether mayors, departmental presidents, or regional presidents, on the right or the left [...] to see one of their major roles as that of fostering the "enterprise spirit" and of encouraging the growth of business in their constituencies' (V. Schmidt 1988: 54, 63). In practice, considerable responsibility for mobilizing these new economic development programs was transferred to regional councils, which came to play a key role in coordinating relations between the DATAR and local authorities; they were subsequently transformed into 'the equivalent of local industrial development brokers' (V. Schmidt 1988: 63). While local economic initiatives had been mobilized by French municipalities as of the mid-1970s, the decentralization programs of the 1980s institutionalized this priority and provided new regulatory mechanisms through which it could be pursued, thus triggering 'an unprecedented amount of local economic activism' (V. Schmidt 1988: 67; Biarez 1994).

- The institutional structure of German federalism was redefined during the post-1970s period (Jeffery 1998; Benz 1998). Following a wave of centralizing crisis-management measures during the 1970s, a countervailing process of intergovernmental decentralization was initiated during the 1980s under the Kohl government. During this period of heightened fiscal austerity, the *Länder* and the municipalities acquired new regulatory tasks and financial burdens, and many *Länder* began more actively to mobilize regionally and locally specific industrial, technology, labor market, and planning policies (Bade 1998; Esser 1989). Meanwhile, as both the federal government and the *Länder* reduced their grants to local governments, municipal budgets were severely constrained (Häußermann 1991). As of the mid-1980s, various significant sources of local revenue, including the wage tax (*Lohnsummensteuer*) and the tax on working capital (*Gewerbekapitalsteuer*), were cut back through federal legislation. Consequently, municipalities were 'confronted with a scissors movement of growing tasks and burdens on the one hand and structurally limited financial resources for local policies on the other hand' (Hanesch 1997: 32). Local governments were subsequently impelled to engage more actively in the mobilization of local economic development programs, which were viewed as a means simultaneously to secure additional public revenues and to address deepening socioeconomic problems (Esser and Hirsch 1989; Mayer 1992). In the German federal system, then, the intergovernmental shifts of the 1980s served primarily to shift expenditures downwards to the *Länder* and the municipalities while consolidating revenues within the central government (Hesse 1991, 1987). The mobilization of urban locational policies by municipalities was not directly mandated by the German federal government or the *Länder*, but this trend was facilitated, in fundamental ways, by the new centrally and regionally imposed fiscal constraints of this period (Rödenstein 1987).

• Intergovernmental decentralization programs were initiated in Italy during the 1970–7 period in conjunction with a retrenchment of postwar, redistributive approaches to regional policy; they subsequently evolved through a variety of power-sharing, co-management arrangements between the central government and regional authorities (Gualini 2001). Italian national economic policies had long contributed significantly to the consolidation of decentralized production systems based upon small- and medium-sized firms (Weiss 1989). However, the decentralization initiatives of the post-1970s period deepened this 'territorially differentiated development strategy' by facilitating the mobilization of regionally based, place-specific economic policies (Weiss 1989: 116). The latter were designed (*a*) 'to encourage entrepreneurship, investment and innovation' and (*b*) 'to expand the marketing opportunities of individual firms and regionally typical products and services' within Italy's major industrial districts (Weiss 1989: 117). In the wake of these shifts, particularly but not exclusively in the Third Italy, regional governments became the 'planners and pace-setters of industrial policy, devising innovative growth strategies and delivering a rich array of services to the local economy' (Weiss 1989: 109).

• In the Netherlands, intergovernmental decentralization proceeded during the 1980s in close conjunction with national fiscal austerity measures and a retrenchment of municipal finance. Under the Lubbers coalition cabinets, a number of decentralizing reforms were accompanied by budgetary cuts, privatization initiatives, and downsizing measures that significantly reduced municipal revenues (Kickert 1996; Kreukels and Spit 1989). Nonetheless, the basic institutional elements of the Dutch system of co-governance (*medebewind*) were maintained during this period, impelling national and local state agencies to continue to coordinate decision-making authority on major policy, planning, and budgetary issues (Toonen 1993, 1991). Due to the extreme fiscal centralization of the Dutch state, which enabled municipalities to continue to derive the bulk of their revenue from central grants, these intergovernmental realignments only minimally facilitated the mobilization of local entrepreneurial policies. However, by the end of the decade, a more radical program of national and local administrative reform was mobilized that explicitly embraced the priority of enhancing territorial competitiveness within major Dutch cities and city-regions. The 1989 report of the Montijn Committee, a commission of prominent corporate executives and government officials that had been appointed by the Secretary of the Interior, advocated the creation of four 'agglomeration municipalities' (*agglomeratiegemeenten*) in the major Randstad cities (Amsterdam, Rotterdam, Utrecht, and the Hague) as well as the establishment of new informal mechanisms of coordination and cooperation for the Randstad as a whole in the form of a Randstad Administrative Council (*Bestuurlijk Platform Randstad*). According to the Montijn Report, and a series of subsequent governmental policy studies, such administrative reforms were essential in order to bolster the place-specific competitive advantages of major Dutch cities relative to their European competitors and, more generally, to ensure the long-term dynamism of the Dutch national economy as a whole (MBZ 1989; WRR 1990). While the Montijn Committee's specific proposals were not successfully implemented, they initiated an intensive nationwide debate on administrative reform and territorial competitiveness in Dutch city-regions that persisted into the 1990s (Box 5.9).

Box 5.9. Intergovernmental reform in the Netherlands: the quest for *bestuur op niveau*

The administrative organization of the Netherlands has become an increasingly heavy handicap (of its own making!) as the acute [...] competition between European urban regions becomes ever more important for the economic welfare of the participating countries [...] The time is ripe for change which, in any case, must be accomplished swiftly.

(MBZ 1989: 43)

The existing organization of tasks and responsibilities has created difficulties for the large cities as they attempt [...] to secure a strong position for themselves within the single European market.

(MBZ 1990: 13)

The problem of the 'regional gap' between the provinces and the municipalities has generated recurrent debates on intergovernmental reform in the Netherlands since the late 1950s (Toonen 1993, 1987). During the postwar period up through the mid-1970s, such debates focused predominantly upon issues of bureaucratic efficiency and public service provision. By contrast, during the late 1980s and early 1990s, the question of intergovernmental reform re-emerged under a new rubric—the need to enhance the territorial competitive advantages of major Dutch cities under conditions of intensifying European interspatial competition. In this context, a series of widely discussed policy studies commissioned by the national government argued that inherited administrative structures were undermining the economic competitiveness of Dutch cities relative to other European metropolitan centers. A variety of alternative intergovernmental frameworks were proposed, all of which entailed the creation of new urban and metropolitan institutional arrangements designed to facilitate local economic development. For example:

• The Montijn Committee and the Advisory Council on Internal Administration (*Raad voor het binnenlands bestuur*) advocated the introduction of new administrative units—either small-scale provinces or large-scale municipalities—in the major Randstad cities (MBZ 1990, 1989).

• The Dutch Scientific Council for Government Policy (*Wetenschappelijke Raad voor het Regeringsbeleid*) advocated an intensive fiscal decentralization of the Dutch state in order to facilitate local entrepreneurialism. This council also advocated the creation of various special-purpose administrative districts, which were seen as a means to address place-specific economic problems and regulatory challenges in urban regions (WRR 1990).

Building upon these proposals, the Dutch national cabinet subsequently embraced an administrative reform policy oriented towards 'tailor-made solutions, regional variation, plurality in administrative forms, the rejection of uniformity and administrative blueprints imposed "from above", and the call for administrative reform proposals "from below"' (Toonen 1990: 85–6). To this end, the cabinet proposed the creation of new metropolitan authorities (*stedelijke gebiedsauthoriteiten*) in seven major Dutch city-regions—including the four large Randstad cities as well as Arnhem-Nijmegen, Eindhoven-Helmond, and Enschedé-Hengelo.

The Dutch national cabinet's plan for administrative reform in these urban regions was elaborated during the early 1990s in a trilogy of policy documents entitled *Bestuur op Niveau* (BON), which roughly means 'Administration at the Right Scale'. On a national level, the BON proposals were further concretized in 1992 through the introduction of a Framework Law on Administrative Restructuring (*Kaderwet bestuur in verandering*). The Framework Law provided a temporary but legally binding basis for institutional restructuring in the seven urban regions that had been selected by the central government as sites for administrative reform; it sought to create seven metropolitan regions by 2001 that would encompass 171 municipalities and roughly 40 per cent of the entire Dutch population. The Framework Law was officially approved in the national parliament in July 1994 by a 'purple coalition' composed of Social Democrats, Liberals (VVD), and Liberal Democrats (D66).

By this time, various projects of administrative reform had gained significant momentum on the local level, above all in Rotterdam and Amsterdam. Whereas intergovernmental restructuring had become a central political project of the Dutch national government as of the early 1990s, its implementation hinged upon political negotiations and struggles within each of the metropolitan regions that were targeted for reform. However, the national government's proposal to establish 'city-provinces' (*stadsprovincies*) in Amsterdam and Rotterdam was rejected by the local populations within each of these cities in the late 1990s, and the broader intergovernmental reform agenda embodied in the Framework Law was subsequently put on hold. Nonetheless, the debates on intergovernmental reform that had been initiated during the late 1980s contributed to a major reorientation of urban governance in major Dutch cities during the subsequent decade. As a result of these national and local debates concerning 'administration at the right scale', a number of significant formal and informal changes were enacted within the Dutch intergovernmental system. While these intergovernmental realignments were multifaceted and assumed place-specific forms in different provincial and municipal jurisdictions, one of their encompassing goals was to establish new state capacities for economic coordination, infrastructure investment, industrial policy, and place-marketing within the major Randstad cities (Terhorst and van de Ven 1995; Toonen 1993; Brenner 1999c).

As the preceding discussion illustrates, intergovernmental decentralization frequently impelled subnational state institutions to engage more actively in the promotion of urban economic development—whether through explicit programs to transfer responsibilities for such tasks downwards within state administrative hierarchies; through new, centrally imposed fiscal pressures; through the creation of qualitatively new institutional tiers within established intergovernmental hierarchies; or through some combination of the latter methods. However, as the case of Thatcherite Britain demonstrates, decentralization was not the only form of intergovernmental rescaling through which urban locational policies were promoted during this period. For, in the British case, a wave of concerted intergovernmental centralization was initiated during the course of the 1980s that likewise fundamentally transformed the institutional fabric of urban governance and contributed to a marked proliferation of urban locational policies (Box 5.10).

Box 5.10. Towards central government localism? Intergovernmental reform and urban locational policy in Thatcherite Britain

Sources: Harding 1989; Pickvance 1991, 1990; Duncan and Goodwin 1989.

Central government has used its legislative supremacy [since the 1980s] to constrain independent local authority initiatives and to limit local control over the development process. Legislative and administrative power has also been used significantly to extend the role of central departments, centrally appointed agencies and the private sector in the formulation and implementation of urban economic development policy.

(Harding 1989: 35)

Urban policy was arguably the arena in which the full character of the neoliberal response to the crisis of British Fordism first became evident.

(Wilks-Heeg 1996: 1266)

In the UK under Thatcher, intergovernmental relations were transformed in conjunction with a neoliberal program of political-economic and spatial restructuring. Indeed, throughout the 1980s, the reconfiguration of central–local relations played a key role in a centrally guided accumulation strategy designed to promote London as a global and European financial center while suppressing the territorialized opposition of both industrial capital and manufacturing workers, including that within London itself. The basic elements of these intergovernmental realignments can be summarized as follows:

- Key elected metropolitan institutions, such as the Metropolitan County Councils (MCC) and the Greater London Council (GLC) were abolished as the central state attempted to create alternative, non-elected regional and local state agencies that it could directly control. This regional state solution entailed 'the removal of sub-national state functions to non-electoral local states, while electoral local governments are left formally in position but with much reduced powers' (Duncan and Goodwin 1989: 249).

- Major urban public services, such as council housing and public transportation systems, were streamlined, contracted out, or privatized.

- The central state imposed new fiscal constraints upon local governments through a combination of spending control measures and rate-capping policies. These fiscal austerity measures were manipulated so as to affect Labour councils most significantly.

- The central state attempted to integrate private-sector interests more directly into extant and newly established local political institutions.

- The central state established new, market-oriented local institutions, such as Enterprise Zones, Freeports, and Urban Development Corporations. Such institutional innovations were intended to deregulate restrictions on local economic development and to provide financial incentives to private firms for investing within certain centrally designated urban areas.

In short, through intergovernmental restructuring, the Thatcherite central state attempted to impose a neoliberal approach to urban locational policy upon municipal councils that generally remained committed to local welfarism and to negotiated projects of endogenous economic development. The centralization of intergovernmental relations enabled the British national government to circumvent recalcitrant local authorities and to establish a new, market-oriented infrastructure for urban governance in UK cities.

The rescaled state spaces that were produced through intergovernmental restructuring during this period did not result from a unilinear transfer of regulatory capacities downwards to subnational institutional tiers. Rather, the realignments described above were premised upon centrally coordinated recalibrations of intergovernmental relations that redefined the forms, functions, and scalar configuration of state institutions at both subnational *and* national scales. As Messner (1997: 31) explains:

Just as in modern corporations greater autonomy for profit centers does not in the least imply any sort of abolition of the top corporate levels, and indeed instead presupposes an expansion of controlling capacities and modified tasks for central management (networking and development of strategic visions for the overall enterprise instead of central management of all corporate divisions), any effective decentralization [of state power] is reliant on complementary changes at the central level.

The centralization of intergovernmental relations in the UK under Thatcher, though apparently 'out of step' (Crouch and Marquand 1989) with western European trends, clearly illustrates this point. In this instance, an intensified geographical differentiation of subnational regulatory arrangements was imposed by central government fiat, rather than through the negotiated, decentralizing approaches to intergovernmental restructuring that prevailed within other western European states. But, as elsewhere in western Europe, the consolidation of 'central government localism' (Duncan and Goodwin 1989) in Britain likewise entailed the establishment of a new, differentiated layer of subnational regulatory institutions oriented towards, among other priorities, local economic development. Moreover, the rescaling of intergovernmental relations in the UK entailed a profound reconfiguration of state institutions at both local *and* national scales—for it was only as of the 1980s that the British central government adopted an aggressively activist orientation towards the issue of local economic governance. During the late 1980s and early 1990s, these intergovernmental realignments were at once intensified and accelerated throughout western Europe due to the increasing role of regional or 'meso' institutions within the multilevel intergovernmental hierarchies and policy relays of the EU.[10]

The 1980s was thus a decade in which the inherited intergovernmental hierarchies of the Fordist-Keynesian period were significantly recalibrated. While the political mechanisms, institutional pathways, and policy outcomes of intergovernmental rescaling varied considerably by national context, a

---

[10] See Jones and Keating 1995; Keating 1998; Le Galès and Lequesne 1998; Sharpe 1993.

general trend towards decentralization became evident in most western European countries during this period. Along with the increasing Europeanization of intergovernmental hierarchies, these intra-national decentralization tendencies differentiated the relatively standardized, uniform political geographies that had prevailed during the Fordist-Keynesian period and created rescaled national institutional landscapes in which divergent, place-specific administrative arrangements and regulatory regimes could be established. More generally, insofar as the intergovernmental rescaling processes of this period opened up a political space in which territorially customized, place-specific regulatory arrangements could be constructed, they served as important institutional catalysts for the activation of urban locational policies in western European cities.

The metropolitanization of national spatial planning systems

In the 1950s, 1960s and even 1970s, national governments used to support backward regions, but in the new, post-1980s competitive context they feel the need to place their bet on the strongest regional horses [...] For electoral reasons, some [national governments] are obliged to continue to give some support to backward regions, but their real concern remains the improvement of the strong regions.

Willem Salet, Andy Thornley, and Anton Kreukels (2003a: 12)

A number of major trends are visible in the 12 Member States, even though they tend to be stronger and more advanced in those with a long history of spatial planning [...] There is [...] a wider recognition of the need to *take account of market forces* within the spatial planning process. A growing sophistication in the means of attracting inward investment and a freer choice as regards location for many companies has strengthened the need for spatial plans to respond more fully to market circumstances and requirements. Increased competition in the Single Market is a major factor underlying this trend.

Commission of the European Communities
(CEC 1994: 142; italics in original)

As we saw in Ch. 4, national spatial planning systems contributed in key ways to the establishment and reproduction of nationalized state spaces during the Fordist-Keynesian period. More recently, however, spatial planning has become a major institutional arena in which the rescaling of state space has been promoted, in significant measure as a means to facilitate the mobilization of locational policies within major urban regions. Indeed, spatial planning is arguably one of the politico-institutional arenas in western Europe in which the interplay between state rescaling and urban locational policy has been most dramatically evident. We have already seen above how the compensatory, territorially redistributive role of spatial planning policies was eroded during the course of the 1970s. As of the mid-1980s and early 1990s, a qualitatively transformed approach to national spatial planning was forged in major western European states. As Fig. 5.10 indicates, this new, rescaled approach to spatial planning has been characterized by a number of key features, including:

- an emphasis on strategic, globally competitive cities and city-regions rather than lagging, outlying towns and rural peripheries as the most urgently important targets for state spatial intervention;
- an emphasis on unleashing urban growth potentials and enhancing urban territorial competitiveness rather than redistributing resources from over-heated urban cores into underdeveloped or non-industrialized zones;
- an emphasis on the perceived constraints associated with intensified global and European economic competition rather than the project of integrating local spaces into a cohesive national space-economy;
- an emphasis on regulatory coordination among state institutions at multiple spatial scales rather than unilaterally centralized, top-down control;
- an emphasis on the European institutional context in which local, regional, and national spatial planning initiatives are embedded.

Since the mid-1980s, this rescaling of national spatial planning frameworks has been promoted along two main pathways.

1. *Comprehensive national reforms.* National spatial planning systems have been comprehensively reorganized so as to replace traditional, redistributive policy relays with new, developmentalist policies oriented towards major metropolitan regions. These comprehensive reform projects generally encompass the entire national territory, but entail the demarcation of qualitatively new geographical targets—such as strategic city-regions, major international transportation corridors, and cross-border regions—as the privileged focal points for state spatial intervention.

2. *Area-based, territorially customized reforms.* Often in direct conjunction with the former tendency, national, regional, and local governments have also mobilized area-based, territorially customized spatial planning reforms within strategic urban regions and development zones. Such place-specific approaches to spatial planning are viewed as a means to unleash growth capacities and attract inward capital investment within major cities and city-regions that are considered to be essential to national economic competitiveness.

While both of these rescaling projects have been initiated and managed at a national scale, generally by central government planning agencies, they have also entailed new forms of regulatory coordination among local, regional, national, and, increasingly, EU-level state institutions (Atkinson 2001).

	Nationalized spatial planning systems (1960s–1970s)	'Metropolitanized'/rescaled spatial planning systems (1980s–present)
Perceived regulatory problems	Overheating of urban cores due to rapid economic growth and physical expansion Intra-national territorial disparities undermine macroeconomic stability	Accelerated economic restructuring coupled with intensified global and European interspatial competition Maintaining territorial competitiveness, promoting economic growth, and attracting mobile capital
Predominant regulatory response(s)	Redistributive regional policies: goal is to channel employment, private capital investment, and public infrastructure into outlying towns, underdeveloped areas, and rural peripheries Spatial planning serves as a key political mechanism of intra-national territorial redistribution	New, 'metropolitanized'/rescaled forms of state spatial planning: goal is to reconcentrate socioeconomic assets, developmental capacities, and advanced infrastructural investments within strategic, globally competitive cities and city-regions Spatial planning serves as a key political mechanism of urban (and, in some cases, regional) locational policies
Major geographical targets	National economy as a whole Outlying towns, underdeveloped areas, and lagging regions	Strategic urban regions, particularly those that are already tightly embedded within, or connected to, European and global circuits of capital and transportation networks
Predominant mode of implementation	Top-down, centralized: the national state imposes its standardized spatial planning agenda upon subordinate regional and local state institutions within a relatively inflexible administrative hierarchy	Multilevel, decentralized: spatial planning is increasingly grounded upon the flexible coordination of regulatory activities among diverse scales of state institutional organization, from the European and the national to the regional and the local
Implications for forms of state spatial selectivity	Spatial planning serves as a key political mechanism in the nationalization of state space during the postwar period	Spatial planning serves as a key political mechanism in the rescaling, differentiation, and splintering of state space during the post-1980s period

Fig. 5.10. Reworking spatial planning in post-1980s western Europe: from nationalization to metropolitanization?

Among major western European national states, comprehensive reforms of spatial planning systems have been most prominent during the post-1980s period in Germany, the Netherlands, and Denmark. In each of these contexts, national governments have introduced explicitly metropolitanized, developmentalist approaches to spatial planning, often in close conjunction with new, growth-oriented forms of national urban policy. And in each instance, the rescaling of spatial planning regimes has been justified as a necessary political response to the pressures imposed by intensified European and global interspatial competition.

 • As of the mid-1990s, the German Spatial Planning Law (*Raumordnungsgesetz*—ROG) was radically redefined and a new approach to national spatial planning was introduced through the Framework for Spatial Planning Policy Orientation (*Raumordnungspolitischer Orientierungsrahmen*—ORA) and the Framework for Spatial Planning Policy Implementation (*Raumordnungspolitischer Handlungsrahmen*—HRA). The ROG, the ORA, and the HRA emphasized urban regions rather than the entire national economy as the most crucial geographical target for spatial planning policies. In explicit contrast to the earlier focus on the equalization of industrial growth and the overcoming of spatial disparities within the national territory, these policy initiatives privileged the question of urban territorial competitiveness as the central focus of national spatial planning. According to the ORA, a regionalization of spatial planning is required because 'The major urban regions [...] are the regional growth engines for the spatial development of the national territory as a whole' (BMBau 1993a: 6). A strengthening of 'endogenous regional capacities' was thus viewed as the appropriate means to enhance the competitiveness of 'Germany and its regions as investment locations' (BMBau 1993a: 13). The HRA reinforced this regional focus with reference to the same constellation of economic priorities and delineated six 'European metropolitan regions'—Berlin-Brandenburg, Hamburg, Munich, Rhine-Main, Rhine-Ruhr, and Stuttgart—as the 'engines of societal, economic, social and cultural development' (BMBau 1995: 27–9). This new political emphasis on 'agglomerations of international or inter-regional standing' is illustrated in Map 5.2, which depicts the major urban targets for spatial planning initiatives within thick hexagonal enclosures.

Crucially, these new approaches to spatial planning were mobilized not only in the largest metropolitan regions, but also in less densely urbanized regions as well. To this end, the HRA introduced a project to create 'city networks' (*Städtenetze*) that would bundle the socioeconomic assets of small- and medium-sized German cities and towns and thus establish larger, more internationally significant regional clusters for economic planning and industrial development (Map 5.3, p. 232).

While the problematic of socio-territorial 'equalization' (*Ausgleich*) remained central to this rescaled approach to national spatial planning, the issue

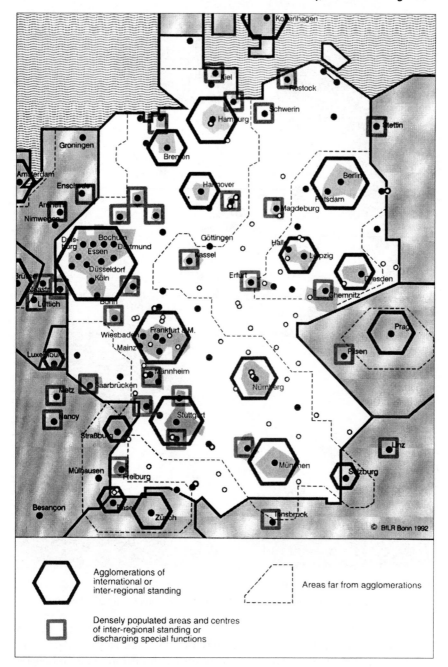

Agglomerations of
international or
inter-regional standing

Areas far from agglomerations

Densely populated areas and centres
of inter-regional standing or
discharging special functions

Map 5.2. Targeting city-regions: the metropolitanization of national spatial planning in the FRG

Source: Federal Ministry for Regional Planning, Building and Urban Development (1993: 5).

Map 5.3. German 'city networks' as forms of urban locational policy
Source: BMBau, Bundesministerium für Raumordnung, Bauwesen und Städtebau (1996: 19).

was fundamentally redefined in terms of the federal government's new priority of enhancing the territorial competitiveness of major urban regions (Box 5.11).

Taken together, these policy realignments entailed the most comprehensive reconfiguration of national spatial planning in the FRG since its introduction during the mid-1960s. Within this new framework, intra-national uneven spatial development is understood as a necessary expression of local and

---

Box 5.11. Reworking the politics of uneven geographical development: the case of spatial planning in post-unification Germany

---

> How shall we organize the spatial structures of our country so that they [. . .] secure economic competitiveness for this location (*Standort*) relative to other locations (*Standorten*) in Europe and the world? This is the *central question*, and it will be posed more explicitly as the process of globalization continues
>
> Klaus Töpfer, Federal Minister of Spatial Planning
(1998: 19; italics added)

The redistributive agenda of German spatial planning has traditionally been justified as an effort to execute Article 72 of the German federal constitution (*Grundgesetz*), which requires the 'uniformity of living conditions' (*Einheitlichkeit der Lebenverhältnisse*) through-out the national territory (Väth 1980: 152–9). However, the post-reunification redefinition of national spatial planning has generated qualitatively new understandings of what this requirement entails. Although the priority of socio-territorial equalization (*Ausgleich*) is still formally embraced within the official discourse of national spatial planning, its substantive political and geographical content has been, in practice, fundamentally inverted. During the postwar period, the equalization of living conditions was thought to entail the replication of certain minimum infrastructural conditions and levels of service provision across the entire national territory. By contrast, during the post-unification period, the project of equalizing life conditions has been equated increasingly with intensified intra-national geographical differentiation and local economic specialization. This fundamental policy reversal was made most explicit in the 1993 Framework for Spatial Planning Policy Orientation (ORA), which argued that 'the alleviation of spatial inequalities can only be realized in the long-term through the concerted promotion of self-reliant regional trajec-tories' (BMBau 1993*a*: 21). Analogously, the Spatial Planning Report of 1993 redefined the notion of 'spatial equalization' through a distinction between the 'equivalence' (*Gleich-wertigkeit*) and 'similarity' (*Gleichartigkeit*) of regional conditions:

> The equivalence (*Gleichwertigkeit*) of living conditions should not be con-fused with their similarity (*Gleichartigkeit*). Enough room for maneuver (*Spielraum*) must be maintained to enable different trajectories as well as initiatives from below (*Eigeninitiativen*) [. . .] The state cannot guarantee an equalization in all areas, but can merely provide assistance for investments and initiatives—particularly in the realm of infrastructure—that favor self-reliant regional development.   (DB 1994: 2)

The classical Fordist problem of spreading growth from core industrial regions into the 'lagging' peripheries has thus been superseded, in post-unification Germany, by various political initiatives designed to differentiate national economic space among specialized urban regions—each with its own unique, place-specific locational advantages, develop-mental trajectory, and position in the international spatial division of labor.

---

regional economic specialization—and thus as the appropriate geographical basis for national competitiveness—rather than as a hindrance to sustainable macroeconomic growth. In post-unification Germany, then, national spatial planning has been redefined from a political mechanism for alleviating intra-national territorial inequalities into a form of urban locational policy designed to enhance the competitive positions of major German urban regions within global and European circuits of capital.

• Analogously, in the Netherlands, the postwar framework of spatial planning, which was oriented towards the spatial diffusion of urbanization beyond the western agglomeration of the Randstad, has been radically reversed since the late 1980s. These realignments were initiated through two major national spatial planning initiatives, the Fourth Report on Spatial Planning of 1988 and the Fourth Report Extra of 1990 (known by its Dutch acronym, VINEX). These new frameworks for national spatial planning specified the Randstad megalopolis as the regional engine of national economic growth and, on this basis, advocated the systematic reconcentration of socioeconomic assets, advanced infrastructures, and capital investment into that region (Faludi and van der Valk 1994; Tömmel 1992). Their goal was to develop 'an internationally competitive climate for inward investment in a limited number of [Randstad] cities' while encouraging major regional economies throughout the Netherlands to 'make full use of their own particular assets' (Galle and Modderman 1997: 15–16). Under these circumstances, spatial planning was transformed into an 'economic policy of location factors' in which 'regions, city regions and locations were primarily assessed—and classified—in terms of their "potential" as a locational environment for pre-selected "target groups" of companies, services and households' (Vermeijden 2001: 223). Accordingly, in addition to delineating nine specialized 'urban nodal points' (*stedelijke knooppunten*) as the primary spatial units of economic growth, the Fourth Report introduced the conception of 'regions on the strength of their own assets' (*regio's op eigen kracht*) as a crucial part of its strategy to promote internationally competitive investments within each of the county's major regional economies, particularly within the Randstad and the 'Central Netherlands Urban Ring' (*Stedenring Centraal-Nederland*) (see Map 5.4).

The VINEX was introduced in 1990 and significantly extended the major policy agendas of the Fourth Report (Faludi and van der Valk 1994; MVROM 1988, 1991). Extensive investments in the 'mainports' (the Rotterdam harbor and Amsterdam's Schiphol airport) and other 'key locations' (*toplocaties*) were presented as a key precondition for 'stimulating a metropolitan business climate that is internationally competitive [and] drawing new business to the Randstad' (Staalduine and Drexhage 1995: 192). Meanwhile, nine urban 'spearheads' were delineated as the major growth clusters of the Dutch national economy. The VINEX definitively abandoned the earlier policy of promoting deconcentrated growth on a national scale, in favor of a new 'compact cities' approach oriented towards the intensive concentration of urban growth in close proximity to existing settlements and transportation corridors. The

STEDELIJKE KNOOPPUNTEN

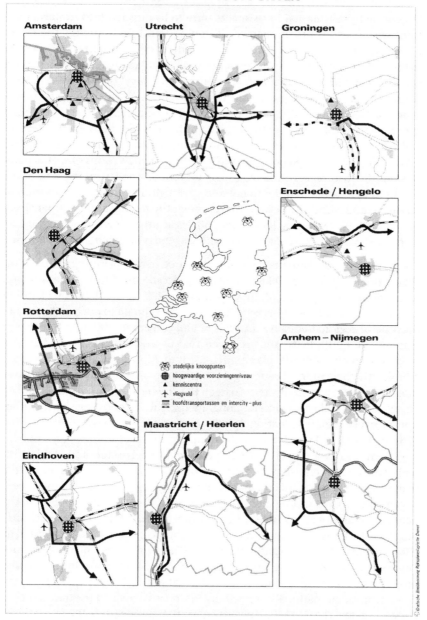

Map 5.4. Rescaling national spatial planning in the Netherlands: 'urban nodal points' as targets for locational policies

Source: Tweede Kamer der Staten-Generaal (1987–8: 96).

VINEX also outlined various 'key projects' (*sleutelprojecten*) through which large-scale infrastructural investments were to be directed into strategic locations within major urban regions—including, most prominently, the IJ-embankment and the eastern port zone in Amsterdam, the Central Station zone in the Hague, and the Kop van Zuid project in Rotterdam. In addition, ten 'areas subject to combined spatial and environmental policy' (*ROM-Gebieden*) were delineated in order to regulate territorial development in strategic socioeconomic sites such as Schiphol airport, the Rotterdam seaport, the Green Heart (central agricultural area) of the Randstad, the IJsel lake between Amsterdam and Almere, and various additional environmentally sensitive locations. And finally, like the Fourth Report, the VINEX promoted new forms of spatial planning, infrastructural investment, and socioeconomic policy on the scale of the Randstad as a whole in order to enhance the region's competitive position in European and world markets. In this manner, the mobilization of intensively customized, place-specific locational policies at urban, metropolitan, and regional scales became one of the overarching agendas of Dutch spatial planning.

• An equally fundamental transformation of spatial planning unfolded in Denmark as of the late 1980s. Following a decade of industrial decline and intensifying unemployment in Copenhagen, the 1989 National Planning Report stated that conditions were no longer appropriate to pursue 'the former doctrine of regional equality' (Andersen and Jørgensen 2004: 4); the goal of 'appropriate multiplicity' thus replaced that of 'equality' as the overarching priority for national spatial planning (Jørgensen, Kjœrsdam, and Nielsen 1997: 47). Shortly thereafter, all central government regional subsidy and incentives programs were summarily terminated; the '*raison d'être*' of regional policy changed from addressing interregional inequalities to boosting the contribution of every region to national economic competitiveness' (Halkier 2001: 328). In 1990, the Danish national parliament initiated a debate on Cophenhagen's future as a global and European economic center, and the Danish national government subsequently introduced a new approach to spatial planning oriented towards the promotion of city-regions, particularly Copenhagen and its surrounding metropolitan fringes, as the growth engines of the national economy as a whole. In this context, Prime Minister Poul Schlüter proposed to transform Copenhagen into 'the power centre of Scandinavia' (Hansen, Andersen, and Clark 2001: 858). The 1992 spatial planning report, *Denmark in the Year 2018*, initiated a variety of large-scale infrastructural projects and planning schemes intended to enhance urban territorial competitiveness and supranational connectivity in Copenhagen and the transnational Ørestad region (MoE 1992). In particular, the conservative-liberal national government established a new, business-oriented Metropolitan Development Board (*Hovedstadens Udviklingsråd*) and an Ørestad Development Corporation responsible for promoting urban growth within a large plot of land between the central city and the airport. In addition, the national government channeled public resources into the redevelopment of Copenhagen's docklands, a new subway line, and the construction of the Sound Link, a combined tunnel and bridge linking Copenhagen to Malmö, Sweden (Andersen and Jørgensen 1995: 19–20). These new institutional forms and infrastructural configurations signaled a significant break from the earlier, redistributive remit of Danish spatial planning and the consolidation of a new approach to urban development 'as a strategic tool in order to achieve a better competitive position *vis-à-vis* other European city regions for investments' (J. Andersen 2003: 98). As a result of this fundamental policy reorientation, Copenhagen was transformed from 'an urban problem to a national asset within less than five years' time' (Andersen and Jørgensen 2004: 4–5). This new, Copenhagen-centric vision of Danish national spatial planning is illustrated in Map 5.5 (overleaf).

In contrast to the cases of Germany, the Netherlands, and Denmark, changes in the Italian, French, and British national spatial planning systems were induced less through comprehensive, nation-wide realignments than through the interaction of national regulatory reforms and diverse, place- and scale-specific policy initiatives. While the consequences of this interaction varied by national and local context, it generally entailed an increased differentiation of subnational institutional forms, regulatory arrangements, and planning techniques within each of these national territories. Moreover, many of the territorially customized, place- and area-specific spatial planning and urban policy initiatives that were mobilized in Italy, France, and Britain during this period were justified explicitly as a means to enhance the international competitive advantages of major urban areas. Such locally and regionally specific planning reforms 'punctured' inherited systems of national spatial planning by channeling socioeconomic assets, major infrastructural investments, and public resources into designated urban nodal points that were in turn to be positioned strategically within European and global economic networks. The post-1980s evolution of spatial planning into a form of urban locational policy in three major European global city-regions—Milan, Paris, and London—clearly illustrates these trends.

• The institutional landscape of Italian spatial planning was significantly reorganized as of the early 1990s, with the passage of a series of national laws oriented towards local government reorganization, metropolitan institutional reform, and urban economic growth. During the preceding decade, the period of 'extraordinary intervention' (*Intervento Straordinario*) in the Mezzogiorno had been terminated; and many state-owned enterprises were privatized. In 1991, the *Cassa per il Mezzogiorno* was abolished and replaced by locally elected administrations in the South. Although redistributive regional policies were not entirely abandoned, qualitatively new, developmentalist spatial policies and area-based initiatives were subsequently mobilized in order to enhance the international competitive positions of major Italian local and regional economies (Gualini 2001). In particular, since the early 1990s, 'territorial pacts'

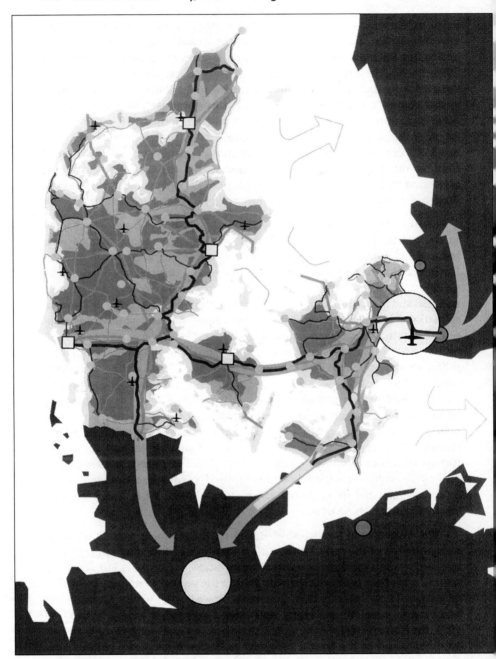

Map 5.5. City-centric spatial planning in Denmark: promoting Copenhagen/Øresund as node in transnational networks

Source: Ministry of the Environment (1992); cited in Commission of the European Communities (1997: 169).

(*patti territoriali*) have been introduced in order to promote public–private cooperation, inter-sectoral networking, and territorial identification in strategic local economies (Gualini 2001: 760). Consequently, a 'leopard skin' model of specialized cities and regions replaced the traditional North/South economic geography that had traditionally animated Italian regional policy (Bozzi 1995).

In conjunction with these national reforms, a number of explicitly entrepreneurial local planning initiatives were introduced during the 1980s in Milan that were based upon ad hoc, project-oriented modes of state intervention rather than a comprehensive statutory plan. This fundamental reorientation of local spatial planning precipitated what Gualini (2003: 272, 273) terms an ' "extraordinary" format for policy-making' that situated Milan 'in an exceptional, "unorthodox" position in the Italian planning landscape'. First, a number of local territorial agencies introduced a 'proactive and flexible approach to urban modernisation' oriented towards major development and infrastructural projects—including the Malpensa airport, the Garibaldi-Repubblica financial district, the Portello-Fiera fair district, the regional rail system, the Milan Stock Exchange, the Bicocca technopole, and various older industrial sites—that were intended to upgrade 'Milan's central functions in the European urban hierarchy' (Gualini 2003: 273–4). Second, new Regional Laws were introduced in Lombardy that 'moved away from the objective of achieving territorial balance' and aimed 'at enhancing and internationalizing' the region's economic development capacities (Bozzi 1995: 278). Third, the Province of Milan—whose regulatory capacities were enhanced through a 1990 national law—introduced a Provincial Socio-Economic Plan (PSEP) intended to coordinate economic development policy, inter-firm relations, and vocational training within the extended metropolitan region. More generally, the post-1980s period witnessed the end of the model of a 'public, equitable city protected against private speculative interests' in favor of a new form of spatial planning oriented towards 'the encouragement of all opportunities for cooperation and partnership with private developers and the business world in general, seen as the only way to beat public sector inefficiency and to compete against other cities internationally' (Balducci 2001: 160).

• Following the publication of the Guichard Report in 1986, the French national spatial planning agency, DATAR, became increasingly engaged in the promotion of urban and regional territorial competitiveness (Biarez 1994). Different French regions were now analyzed with reference to their structural position in the European economy and their relative capacities to compete against other major European regions. The national government introduced a new mechanism of spatial planning and urban policy, the *Chartes d'Objectif*, through which local and regional officials were encouraged to formulate economic development projects designed to position major French cities strategically in the European space-economy (Newman and Thornley 1996; Biarez

1994). Due to its emphasis on local economic competitiveness in a European context and its relatively decentralized mode of implementation, this new spatial planning initiative undermined the centralized, redistributive agenda associated with the postwar *métropoles d'équilibre* program. The national government abandoned the long-entrenched assumption that Paris 'grew at the cost of other French metropolitan areas' and began more directly to acknowledge 'the specific needs of the Paris area as a world-class city in competition with London, Tokyo and New York' (Lefèvre 2003: 292). Indeed, Paris was now increasingly considered to be 'the locomotive of the whole national economy' (Biarez 1994: 200).

Against this background, the regional plan in the Paris region (known as the *Schéma Directeur Régional*, SDR) was renewed through a combination of national and local government consultations in the late 1980s. In the wake of Brunet's (1989) influential DATAR report on the European 'blue banana', French political-economic elites came to accept the view that further economic growth and spatial expansion would be required in the Île-de-France region in order to 'bypass London in the competition for the title of "the" megalopolis of Europe' (Lipietz 1995: 147). Thus the initial SDR proposal of 1990, the *Livre Blanc Île-de-France*, promoted an aggressive concentration of high-speed transportation infrastructures, high-technology industries, and transnational firms in the Paris region. Following extensive national and local debates, and the national electoral defeat of the socialists, a compromise solution known as the Grand Bassin Strategy was proposed and subsequently adopted (Burgel 1997). The resultant 'Grand Bassin Charter', which was approved by the national government in 1994, was designed to combine continued growth in the urban core of Île-de-France with the channeling of overspill development into a historical ring of medium-sized cities—'a supernova beyond the administrative limits of the central region' (Lipietz 1995: 151)—including Chartres, Dreux, Évreux, Beauvais, Creil, and Compiegne (Map 5.6). The new national commitment to promoting concentrated economic growth in the Paris region was further solidified in 2000, with the abandonment of the authorization procedure that had long required firms seeking to locate in the Paris region to acquire central government permission (Lefèvre 2003).

• During the post-1980s period, the inherited British system of regional and spatial planning has been increasingly overlain by diverse policy initiatives oriented towards place- and scale-specific conditions and the general priority of local economic development (Wannop 1995). During the course of the 1980s, the Thatcherite central government introduced a number of deregulatory, market-oriented urban planning programs and aggressively promoted London as a global and European financial center. Urban Development Corporations (UDCs), Enterprise Zones (EZs), and Simplified Planning Zones (SPZs) were established in a variety of strategic urban locations, including parts of London,

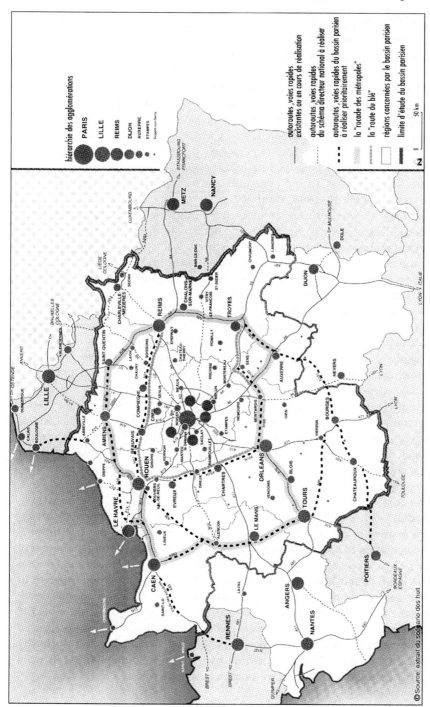

Map 5.6. The 'Grand Bassin Strategy': reconcentrating growth in the Paris Île-de-France region
Source: IAURIF (Institut d'Aménagement et d'Urbanisme de la Région d'Île-de-France) (1993: 48).

Cardiff, Sheffield, Bristol, Leeds, and Manchester. These localized regulatory experiments bypassed traditional planning rules and local relays of democratic accountability while providing property developers with significant investment inducements, such as streamlined decision-making structures, simplified planning regulations, and tax exemptions (Gaffikin and Warf 1993). As of the early 1990s, a new cluster of national urban policies—including City Challenge, City Pride, and the Single Regeneration Budget—introduced a more inclusive, socially oriented, and partnership-based approach to urban redevelopment, but nonetheless perpetuated the growth-oriented regulatory agenda of the UDCs by impelling localities to formulate economic development strategies and to bid competitively for central government funding (Davoudi and Healey 1995; Ward 1997).

In this national context of simultaneous administrative centralization, institutional fragmentation, and economic deregulation, spatial planning in the London region was significantly restructured. While the goal of regional decentralization had already been abandoned in the mid-1970s, the subsequent decade witnessed the consolidation of more concerted national *and* local political strategies designed to promote economic growth, local entrepreneurialism, and property redevelopment throughout the London metropolitan area (Gordon 1995). The centrally induced 'Big Bang' of 1986, which deregulated key financial services industries, was intended to strengthen the City's strategic position relative to other European financial centers. However, following the 1986 abolition of the Greater London Council, spatial planning in the extended London region was fragmented among various agencies, including the centrally controlled Department of the Environment (DoE), London and South East Regional Planning Conference (SERPLAN), the London Planning Advisory Committee (LPAC), and the London Docklands Development Corporation (LDDC). A report commissioned in 1991 by LPAC and other local governmental agencies, *London: World City*, outlined a variety of boosterist strategies and policy measures through which London's global and European competitive advantages could be enhanced (LPAC 1991). Subsequently, London's lack of strategic planning came to be viewed as a locational disadvantage relative to other European metropolitan regions, and the institutional fragmentation of the London region was counterbalanced during the course of the 1990s. New local promotion agencies, such as London Forum and London First, were established and, with the initiation of the City Pride program in 1992, a more comprehensive program of urban planning and economic development was elaborated whose aim 'was to ensure London's position as the only world city in Europe' (Thornley 2003: 48). This emphasis was reinforced in the early 2000s under the newly established Greater London Authority (GLA), led by Ken Livingstone, whose spatial planning program has likewise heavily emphasized the need to promote London's role as a world city.[11]

---

[11] See e.g. Gordon 1999; Newman and Thornley 1997; Thornley 2003; Syrett and Baldcock 2003.

In short, just as the nationally redistributive spatial planning policies of the postwar era actively facilitated the universalist political agendas of the Keynesian welfare national state, so too have the rescaled, metropolitanized spatial planning frameworks of the post-1980s period contributed significantly to the developmentalist, growth-oriented projects of post-Keynesian competition state regimes. For, in order to pursue their goal of enhancing national competitive advantages in European and global circuits of capital, post-Keynesian competition states across western Europe have attempted to establish new approaches to spatial planning through which to reconcentrate socioeconomic assets, advanced infrastructural configurations, and transnational capital investment within their most internationally competitive city-regions. Spatial planning has served as an essential institutional mechanism for such urban locational policies, for it has supplied state institutions at all geographical scales with place-specific and territorially customized policy instruments through which to channel developmental capacities into strategic urban locations. Galle and Modderman's (1997: 15) comment on the Dutch VINEX law of 1990 thus provides a more generally applicable summary of this transformation of national spatial planning into a form of urban locational policy during the post-1980s period: 'Spatial planning would not determine where economic activities should take place, which had proved ineffectual in the past. Rather, it would support the further development of the economically attractive areas of the country.'

Splintered infrastructural networks, urban mega-projects, and the rescaling of regulatory space

> We are starting to witness the uneven overlaying and retrofitting of new, high performance urban infrastructures onto the apparently immanent, universal and (usually) public monopoly networks laid down between the 1930s and 1960s. In a parallel process, the diverse political and regulatory regimes that supported the 'roll out' of power, transport, communications and water networks towards the rhetorical goal of standardized ubiquity are, in many cities and states, being 'unbundled' or even 'splintered', as a result of widespread movements towards privatization and liberalization [...] What this amounts to [...] is the uneven emergence of an array of [...] 'premium networked spaces': new or retrofitted transport, telecommunications, power, or water infrastructures that are customized precisely to the needs of powerful users and spaces, whilst bypassing less powerful users and spaces.
>
> Stephen Graham (2000: 185)

As discussed in the preceding chapter, national, regional, and local state institutions have long played a central role in the construction of large-scale transportation, communications, utilities, and development infrastructures both within and among major western European cities. During the course of the postwar period, such state-planned, state-financed infrastructural configurations figured crucially in the establishment of Fordist urban production systems, in the consolidation of nationalized urban hierarchies, and in the embedding of cities within the nationally standardized, centralized regulatory configurations of the Keynesian welfare national state (Graham and Marvin 1995). However, this inherited model of urban infrastructure provision was systematically unsettled following the crisis of spatial Keynesianism in the 1970s. As the urban production systems, land-use complexes, and public infrastructural configurations of the North Atlantic Fordist order were rendered increasingly obsolete, local, regional, and national governments were confronted with the problem of establishing new territorial infrastructures in and through which both transnational and local capital could circulate profitably.

The transformations of western European spatial planning systems described above were designed not only to revitalize major agglomeration economies and to channel globally competitive capital investments into strategic urban locations. Additionally, the rescaling of spatial planning was generally intertwined with concerted state spatial strategies to construct customized, high-performance technological infrastructures for telecommunications, energy provision, transportation, and economic development within major European urban regions. Such infrastructures have included, among other elements, 'globally oriented "teleports", international "hub" air and water ports, "wired" technology parks, high speed railways, as well as international supply connections in electricity, gas and water' (Graham 2000: 188). Given the importance of seamless, uninterrupted, long-distance geographical connectivity under conditions of intensified geoeconomic interdependence (Castells 1996; Sassen 1991), these advanced technological infrastructures have become highly important locational factors for all major factions of capital during the post-1980s period. In light of this, state strategies to produce what Graham (2000: 185) terms 'premium networked spaces'—namely, urban spatial infrastructures 'that are customized precisely to the needs of powerful users and spaces, whilst bypassing less powerful users and spaces'—have become increasingly ubiquitous across western Europe.

As summarized in Fig. 5.11, this intensified mobilization of national, regional, and local state institutions to produce premium networked infrastructural configurations has entailed a fundamental break from the universalist, nationalizing model of public infrastructure provision that prevailed during the Fordist-Keynesian period. Indeed, despite the neoliberal rhetoric of privatized, market-led investment that pervades mainstream discourse on these newly established, high-performance infrastructures, their construction across the western European urban system has, in practice, been premised upon a variety of quite intensive state regulatory operations. To be sure, due to the

	Standardized public infrastructural monopolies (1960s–1970s)	Premium networked infrastructural configurations (1980s–present)
Major providers	National, public corporations engaged in the provision of public goodst	Local, national, and international private firms in collaboration with state and para-state agencies at multiple spatial scales (public–private partnerships)
Predominant orientation	National economic development, supply-driven	Premium, demand-driven markets; goal is to enhance levels of Europe-wide and global connectivity among strategic urban areas
Type of regulation	Central government direction and internal management of public corporations	Facilitated through deregulation and liberalization of European and national markets; national, regional, and local state agencies continue to supply important regulatory, institutional, and spatial preconditions for the production of new, networked infrastructures
Objectives of state regulators	Provision of universal service at standard tariffs; use of standardized technologies to facilitate nation-wide coverage	Enhancement of territorial competitiveness, generally through the systematic channeling of advanced technological infrastructures into major global and European cities and high-speed inter-urban transportation networks
Production-economic dimensions	National economic development, inter-regional equalization, economies of scale	Rebalancing of tariffs, recommodification, local and regional growth promotion, cross-investment: goal is to promote particular urban locations as key nodes within global and European capital flows and transport networks
Social-consumption dimensions	Universal, nation-wide access to standard social services through domestic mass markets	Enhanced social polarization and fragmentation at European, national, regional, urban, and intra-urban scales as new forms of connectivity and disconnectivity are produced
Roles in urban development	Promotes national sociospatial cohesion and interregional redistribution	Promotes the splintering of political-economic space and the intensification of uneven geographical development at all scales throughout the European urban system

Fig. 5.11. State spatial strategies and the production of large-scale infrastructural configurations

Sources: based on Graham and Marvin 1995: 174; Graham 2000.

liberalization and deregulation of national and international markets for key public goods, private corporations have been involved more directly in the establishment and operation of large-scale, premium infrastructure networks. However, state and para-state institutions have figured crucially in the planning, financing, construction, management, and promotion of such infrastructural projects—in most cases, by assuming or sharing their major financial risks; by channeling significant public resources into their financing; and by establishing location- and project-specific regulatory arrangements to facilitate their implementation, effective operation, and profitability (Swyngedouw, Moulaert, and Rodriguez 2002). The overarching goal of such infrastructure-oriented state spatial projects and state spatial strategies has been to undercut inherited monopolistic, redistributive, and socially inclusive regulatory arrangements while mobilizing state institutions actively towards the construction of new, targeted spaces of capital accumulation through 'selective deregulation, stripping away red tape and investment "partnerships"' (Swyngedouw, Moulaert, and Rodriguez 2002: 200). Thus, in contrast to the technocratic, comprehensive, and universalizing approach to public infrastructure provision that prevailed during the Fordist-Keynesian period, an institutionally fragmented, market-oriented, locationally selective, and spatially splintered model has emerged in which 'planners and urban governance agencies [...] fight for the best possible networked infrastructures for their specialized district, in partnership with (often privatized) network operators' (Graham 2000: 191).

This qualitatively transformed role of national, regional, and local state institutions in what Lefebvre (2003a: 90) described as the 'production of space "on a grand scale"' can be summarized in general terms:

• *The primacy of urban locational policy.* The overarching goal of state infrastructural provision is no longer to provide universal, standardized public services through the geographical 'rolling out' of utilities, communications, and transport grids evenly across the entire national territory. Instead, national, regional, and local state institutions have constructed customized, high-performance, place-specific infrastructural configurations as a key mechanism of urban locational policy, that is, as a means to enhance the territorial competitiveness of selected urban zones. While such projects have frequently been justified to national, regional, and urban populations through the assertion that their benefits will eventually 'trickle down' in the form of new jobs and investments, they have been driven above all by the priority of promoting territorial competitiveness within circumscribed urban locations rather than by redistributive concerns at any spatial scale (Graham 2000; Healey et al. 1997).

• *Rescaled geographies.* The geographies of state infrastructural provision have been rescaled. As we saw in the previous chapter, Keynesian welfare national states attempted to extend public infrastructures as evenly as possible throughout their territories. By contrast, state spatial strategies to construct premium infrastructural configurations during the post-1980s period have entailed the reconcentration of major socioeconomic assets and public resources into certain targeted urban zones or inter-urban corridors, which are in turn to be positioned optimally within European and global capitalist networks (Graham and Marvin 2001, 1996). This rescaling of state spatial strategies has also generally entailed significant transformations of the urban built environment, as targeted plots of urban land are revalorized, extant buildings are dismantled or retrofitted, and entirely new building complexes are constructed in order to provide an appropriately 'delocalized' physical-technological space for the operation of advanced, high-performance infrastructural configurations.

• *The normalization of 'exceptional' spaces.* In contrast to the comprehensive, relatively standardized, and hierarchically nested land-use plans that prevailed during the Fordist-Keynesian period, premium infrastructural networks are grounded upon new, strategic planning arrangements that permit flexible, site-specific decision-making procedures, funding schemes, zoning specifications, planning guidelines, and regulatory techniques. Through such exceptional, locationally circumscribed planning mechanisms, high-performance infrastructures are 'unbundled' from their immediate geographic contexts and regulatory environments, while being positioned more directly within supranational telecommunications, transport, and commercial networks. Of course, such exception-based, project-specific planning mechanisms had been mobilized, in certain instances, even prior to the current period—for instance, in the construction of national airports or strategic military installations—but they have become increasingly normalized during the last two decades as essential tools of urban infrastructural and economic policy (Healey et al. 1997).

• *New institutional configurations.* The institutional arrangements underlying state infrastructure provision have become increasingly complex, both in organizational and geographical terms. The collective public monopolies that dominated infrastructure provision during the Fordist-Keynesian period were generally grounded upon relatively transparent, legally codified national bureaucratic hierarchies. By contrast, the construction of premium infrastructural configurations has been premised upon new forms of 'partnership' and 'collaboration' between (national, regional, and local) state institutions and private capital; upon location-specific, special-purpose, para-state agencies assigned to promote specific development projects; and upon flexible, informal governance networks whose goals, decision-making procedures, and participants may be continually renegotiated. These special-purpose development agencies have become increasingly pervasive across the western European urban landscape, not least because 'they can be tasked with equipping strategic economic spaces with high-quality infrastructure without facing onerous political challenges or the imperatives of cross-subsidies and territorial equalisation' (Graham and Marvin 2001: 310). While the spatial boundaries of these new institutional configurations are generally defined with reference to those of the infrastructural investments in question, they often involve the interaction of multiple levels of political authority, including European, national, regional, and local state institutions (Moulaert, Swyngedouw, and Rodriguez 2003; Motte 1997).

• *The contraction of democratic accountability.* In many European city-regions, the establishment of premium networked infrastructures has entailed a contraction of inherited relays of democratic control over the process of urban development. Rather than operating through formal channels of representation and public accountability, many of the state agencies and quasi-governmental bodies involved in the planning, construction, and management of high-performance infrastructural configurations are dominated by planning 'experts', business and legal advisers, boosterist corporate elites, and other national and local 'power brokers'. Accordingly, such agencies generally embrace the agendas of politically unaccountable national, regional, and local growth coalitions while excluding the concerns of the place-based constituencies that are most directly effected by their decisions (Swyngedouw, Moulaert, and Rodriguez 2003, 2002).

The interplay between the construction of premium infrastructural configurations and the rescaling of state space has been dramatically evident since the early 1980s in city-regions of all types throughout western Europe, from global cities, international financial centers, and major transportation/logistics nodes to high-technology production centers, revitalized manufacturing districts, and even declining industrial regions. In each case, the construction of new, high-performance infrastructures for communications, transportation, utilities provision, and economic development has been justified as a means to maintain, enhance, or revive the competitive advantages of a given city (or some part thereof) within supranational circuits of capital. And, in each case, new, rescaled state regulatory arrangements have been promoted as a key politico-institutional precondition for the establishment and effective operation of such infrastructural configurations. The following examples illustrate the role of rescaled state institutions as financiers, producers, regulators, and managers of premium, high-performance infrastructural networks in a number of major western European cities.

• *Euralille TGV Interchange.* Euralille is a large-scale urban development project centered around a strategic high-speed rail (*trains á grand vitesse*, TGV) interchange in the industrialized Nord Pas-de-Calais region in northwestern France. Planning for this interchange, which lies along two major northern European rail lines (including the TGV line linking France to Britain via the Channel Tunnel), was initiated in the late 1980s through the efforts of Lille's entrepreneurial Socialist mayor, Pierre Mauroy, and a local lobbying group, *TGV-Gare de Lille.* Their common goal was to 'transform Lille into a postindustrial, high-technology service city' (Levine 1994: 396). Thus, in addition to its transnational logistical functions, Euralille was also intended to ignite economic development at both urban and regional scales through a variety of *grands projects*, including an office tower, a shopping and hotel complex, and a conference center (*Lille Grand Palais*) designed under the direction of Rem Koolhaas. The construction of the Euralille infrastructure configuration was grounded upon a public–private partnership known as an *SEM* (*Société d'Economie Mixte*). The Euralille *SEM* was headed by Mauroy and composed of a combination of private stakeholders (including the French national railway company, local chambers of commerce, and various local and foreign banks) and diverse public agencies (including major local municipalities, the *Département* of Nord, and numerous regional institutions). While the various elements of Euralille have been embedded within a masterplan (*schéma directeur*) defined by state agencies, they have been implemented and managed 'outside the constraints of local government bureaucracies', through a place-specific, project-based, development-oriented, and semi-autonomous institutional formation (Newman and Thornley 1995: 243).[12]

• *Øresund Link and Ørestad, Copenhagen.* Proposals to construct a bridge and tunnel across the Øresund link, the waterway separating Copenhagen, Denmark, and Malmö, Sweden, date to the 1960s. The Øresund link proposals were rejuvenated in the late 1980s by the European Council of Industrialists and were subsequently concretized and approved by the Danish Parliament in 1991. In this context, the Øresund link was viewed as the infrastructural foundation for the creation of a new, dynamic 'cross-border learning region' based upon a cluster of advanced R&D intensive industries and fueled by a network of local universities, business schools, and research institutes (Maskell and Törnqvist 2000). At an estimated cost of 11.7 billion Danish Kronen (at 1990 prices), this combined railway/highway link is 'one of the largest cross-national infrastructure projects in the world' (Flyvbjerg, Bruzelius, and Rothengatter 2003: 13). On the Danish side of the Øresund, the construction of the bridge/tunnel connection has also been linked to a large-scale, flagship urban development project on a land grid known as the Ørestad, situated on the island of Amager, midway between the Copenhagen city core and the cross-border waterway. The Ørestad has been planned as a high-performance, knowledge-based urban nodal point in which educational institutions, technologically advanced office buildings, and light industry are to be clustered along a strategic transportation axis; its construction has also been closely intertwined with a major expansion of the Copenhagen Metro system.

As indicated in our discussion of the rescaling of Danish national spatial planning above, these newly constructed, premium infrastructural projects in the Greater Copenhagen region have been implemented through place-specific, customized institutional forms, exceptional planning arrangements,

---

[12] This account draws upon Newman and Thornley 1995; Levine 1994; Salin and Moulaert 1999*a, b*.

and public–private partnerships. Thus, the Øresund link project led to the establishment, in 1993, of a new cooperative planning organization, the Øresund Committee, which has served to facilitate regulatory partnerships among regional and local governmental agencies throughout the border region, to lobby the European Commission for financial support through the INTERREG program, and, more generally, to market the region as an attractive investment site within an integrated European economy.[13] Analogously, the Ørestad Development Corporation (ODC) was established in 1992 as an autonomous company owned by various state agencies (the city of Copenhagen and two national departments, the Ministry of Finance and the Ministry of Transport). The ODC was modeled on the British Urban Development Corporations (UDCs) and has been oriented towards a 'Schumpeterian strategic growth policy, based at the state, regional and municipal level' (J. Andersen 2003: 103). Despite relatively low levels of private investment and increasing debt levels during the second half of the 1990s, the ODC has attempted to fund the new Ørestad infrastructure through the sale of newly valorized urban land; it has created an exceptional, project-specific planning scheme within the confines of the Ørestad zone that circumvents traditional, local land-use regulations, and it has contributed to the adoption of an entrepreneurial, developmentalist approach to urban governance throughout the Greater Copenhagen region.[14]

• *London Docklands*. As mentioned above, during the early 1980s, the Thatcher government established UDCs in declining urban zones throughout Britain. The largest and most prominent was established in the London Docklands, a derelict port zone adjoining the Thames in the city's eastern periphery. Even though the 6,500 acre area was technically owned by three local boroughs (Tower Hamlets, Southwark, and Newham), discretionary control over local land use was transferred to a quango (quasi-autonomous nongovernmental organization), the London Docklands Development Corporation (LDDC), which thereby acquired primary responsibility for planning and development in the area. Insofar as the LDDC was dominated by centrally appointed developers and corporate elites, local development in the Docklands zone was effectively 'taken out of the electoral orbit of local government and placed in the hands of a non-elected body appointed centrally and responsible to the centre' (Duncan and Goodwin 1989: 133). The UK national government channeled massive financial resources into the LDDC—during the 1981–90 period it received over 59 per cent of the *total* grants-in-aid funding distributed among eleven UDCs (Deakin and Edwards 1993: 98). The Docklands project was intended to replace brownfield sites across the port zone with an advanced transport, telecommunications, and development infrastructure designed to

---

[13] See: http://www.oresundskomiteen.dk/english; and http://www.oresund.com/oresund/welcome2.htm, accessed 13 Feb. 2004.

[14] This account draws upon J. Andersen 2003; Hansen, Anderson, and Clark 2001; Maskell and Törnqvist 2000; Jørgensen and Anderson 2002; and Jørgensen, Kjærsdam, and Nielsen 1997.

reinforce the global and European competitive advantages of London. Accordingly, the LDDC installed a number of large-scale, premium infrastructural configurations, including a customized light rail line, a small airport, two teleports, dedicated energy and highway access links, a variety of superimposed fiber optic grids, and a large-scale, high-technology office development complex at Canary Wharf overseen by the Canadian developer Olympia and York (Map 5.7, overleaf). Consequently, as Graham and Marvin (2001: 323) indicate, the Docklands can be viewed as the material product of a concerted national state strategy intended to create 'new packaged landscapes for the global financial services industries'.[15]

• *Mainports, Randstad.* Since the late 1980s, the Dutch national government has devoted extensive public resources to the upgrading, expansion, and promotion of the country's two most important infrastructural sites, or 'mainports'—Schiphol airport near Amsterdam and the Rotterdam deep-sea container seaport. With the consolidation of the Single European Market, each of the Dutch mainports was perceived to be confronted with intensified competitive pressures from other major European locations—London (Heathrow and Gatwick), Paris (Orly and Charles de Gaulle), and Frankfurt, in the case of Schiphol airport; and Antwerp and Hamburg, in the case of the Rotterdam seaport. Consequently, one of the central agendas of Dutch national economic policy in the 1990s was to promote the Netherlands as a 'distribution land', specialized in the transport of goods into and out of European markets, in significant measure through the establishment of high-performance logistical infrastructures within each of the mainports. As discussed above, the development of the mainports into major global and European logistical nodes was an explicit agenda of the rescaled spatial planning initiatives that were mobilized through the Fourth Report (1988) and the VINEX (1990). These policies also promoted a number of additional, premium infrastructural projects across the Randstad region, including the Betuwe rail freight line, the High Speed Rail Line South, the Amsterdam teleport in Sloterdijk, Amsterdam's South Axis, Amsterdam's eastern seaport, the Kop van Zuid in Rotterdam, and the New Centre of the Hague.

These publicly financed infrastructural projects in the Randstad were closely intertwined with the introduction of new, place-specific forms of intergovernmental coordination and public–private partnership. The mainports were designated as 'projects of national importance' and, on this basis, customized planning policies, special-purpose development agencies, and public–

---

[15] This account draws upon Brownill 1999, 1993; Deakin and Edwards 1993; Fainstein 1994; Graham and Marvin 2001: 323–7. Despite the crash of Olympia and York in the early 1990s, property markets on the Isle of Dogs were significantly revived during the second half of the decade and private investment has subsequently been rejuvenated (Fainstein 2001). The LDDC was phased out under the Blair government in 1998 and replaced by an array of successor bodies, including local boroughs, English Partnerships, and the London Development Agency (see http://www.lddc-history.org.uk/, accessed 13 Feb. 2004.).

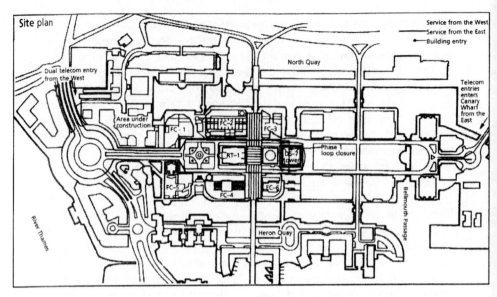

Map 5.7. Premium infrastructural networks and the differentiation of state space: the case of the London Docklands

Source: Graham and Marvin (2001: 325), adapted from D. Chevin, 'All the right connections', *Building*, 19 (July), 47.

private partnerships were introduced within their immediate environs. Concomitantly, during the course of the 1990s, the Dutch national government established a variety of place-specific consultative bodies, development agencies, and public–private partnerships in order to coordinate economic, transportation, and infrastructural policies at the scale of the entire Randstad. These have included the Randstad Administrative Commission (*Bestuurlijke Commissie Randstad*—BCR), the Randstad Consultation on Spatial Planning (RoRo), the Consultative Body on Structural Investments (*Overleg Ruimtelijke Investeringen*—ORI) and, most recently, the Randstad Public Agency (*Openbaar Lichaam Randstad*—OLR). Thus, even in the absence of the comprehensive administrative reforms associated with the city–provinces initiative (see Box 5.9, p. 223), the Dutch national government's project of establishing premium network infrastructures across the 'Delta metropolis' was closely intertwined with a significant rescaling of state institutional organization and state regulatory activity.[16]

As this discussion indicates, the production of premium infrastructural networks has been enabled by, and has in turn significantly intensified, the rescaling of state space throughout western Europe. For, in the process of

[16] This account draws on Frieling 1994; Kreukels 1992; Kreukels and Spit 1990; Premius 1997, 1994; and Premius and van der Wusten 1995.

constructing and managing premium infrastructural networks within and among their major cities, western European states have rescaled their own institutional hierarchies and modes of regulatory intervention. Such rescaled state spaces, with their customized, special-purpose, and place-specific regulatory configurations, are viewed as essential institutional preconditions for the establishment and effective operation of globally competitive, high-performance urban infrastructural grids. From this perspective, the construction of premium, high-performance infrastructures for communications, transportation, and economic development in major western European city-regions has entailed not only an 'unbundling' of the centralized, nationally standardized, and territorially integrated infrastructural configurations that prevailed within high modernist and Fordist cities (Graham and Marvin 2001). Just as crucially, the establishment of such infrastructures has been intertwined with a differentiation of inherited frameworks of state spatial organization, as a city-centric patchwork of place-specific regulatory enclaves has been stretched unevenly across the western European political landscape.

Coda: a note on urban entrepreneurialism, interscalar alliances, and state rescaling

The foregoing analysis has explored the interplay between processes of state rescaling and the proliferation of urban locational policies during the last two decades. As of the early 1980s, experimental prototypes for urban locational policies were being pioneered by entrepreneurial local growth coalitions within a relatively small vanguard of western European city-regions. However, by the mid-1990s, the processes of state rescaling examined above had contributed to the transnational generalization of such competitiveness-oriented urban policy agendas throughout much of the western European city-system. At the same time, the continued diffusion of urban locational policies across the European urban system added further momentum to political initiatives to create customized, place- and scale-specific forms of state spatial organization and state spatial intervention within major local and regional economies. These rescaling processes entailed the erosion of inherited, redistributive-welfarist forms of territorial regulation; the imposition of new, market-based forms of local fiscal management, economic policy, and place-promotion; the extension and intensification of aggressively competitive interlocality relations at European, national, and subnational scales; and the mobilization of new political strategies designed to enhance the global and European territorial competitiveness of major urban economies. Thus, even though urban locational policies were articulated in diverse political and institutional forms, both within and among western European national states, their underlying entrepreneurial, competitiveness-driven logic was institutionalized quite pervasively across western Europe. It is in this sense, I would argue, that the spread of urban locational policies and the concomitant rescaling of state space led to the consolidation of a qualitatively new interscalar rule-regime in which—to repeat Lipietz's (1994: 37) succinct formulation—cities were increasingly viewed as a 'breeding ground for new productive forces'.

This is not to suggest that the complex, multifaceted, and intensely contested field of urban governance was thereby reduced to a narrowly economistic agenda of positioning cities competitively within supranational circuits of capital. My claim, rather, is that the priority of promoting international territorial competitiveness—which is increasingly understood with reference to both economic *and* extra-economic factors (Messner 1997; Jessop 2002)—has come to define the political and institutional parameters within which other dimensions of urban policy may be articulated. Given the overarching role of redistributive, collective consumption functions at the urban scale within the postwar framework of spatial Keynesianism, the primacy of urban locational policies within the newly consolidated interscalar rule-regime of the post-1980s period represents a striking politico-institutional realignment.

The account of urban locational policies developed in this chapter suggests a distinctive vantage point from which to interpret the vast, case-study based literature on entrepreneurial urban governance in western Europe.[17] While such case studies have contributed significantly to our understanding of contemporary European cities, they have tended to conceive the transition to urban entrepreneurialism as the product of localized, often business-led, responses to newly imposed, supranational economic constraints (see e.g. Jensen-Butler, Shachar, and van Weesep 1997). By contrast, the preceding analysis has emphasized the role of rescaled state spatial projects and state spatial strategies in facilitating the mobilization, institutionalization, and generalization of urban locational policies. To be sure, the proliferation of place-specific economic crises and the intensification of foreign direct investment within urban economies provided local political-economic elites with significant, market-led incentives to form place-based, developmentalist alliances, to embrace the narrative of global and European interlocality competition, and, on this basis, to introduce local competitiveness policies (Cheshire and Gordon 1996). However, in light of the above discussion, the spread of urban growth machines and competitiveness-oriented local territorial alliances across western Europe must also be understood in relation to the rescaled national political geographies, intergovernmental configurations, and institutional landscapes that were being forged during this same period. For, as Harvey (1989a: 15) emphasized over a decade ago, the transition to urban entrepreneurialism 'required a radical reconstruction of central to local state relations and the cutting free of local state activities from the welfare state and the Keynesian compromise'. It was through the rescaling of inherited state

---

[17] See the works cited in n. 2.

spatial configurations and the recalibration of established interscalar relays that *localized spaces for regulatory experimentation* were opened up in which aggressively extrospective, yet place-specific, urban development strategies could be mobilized and generalized across western Europe.

The urban locational policies described in this chapter were introduced by political alliances rooted within, and articulated across, a variety of spatial scales. In some cases, they involved tangled interscalar articulations among European, national, regional, and local political-economic forces, which together attempted to rejig the framework of urban governance and to channel public and private resources into strategic urban locations. In other instances, urban locational policies were mobilized by national governments, often by circumventing extant municipal institutions and by establishing centrally controlled forms of local regulation. Under still other circumstances, locally embedded political-economic alliances appear to have played a formative, durable role in the mobilization of urban locational policies, often by capitalizing upon strategic opportunities generated through the process of European integration. While activist, entrepreneurial mayors frequently contributed to the formation of such 'local' development regimes—for instance, in cities such as Hamburg, Lille, Lyon, Milan, and Barcelona—the rescaling of national state spatial configurations described above was one of their essential institutional conditions of possibility (Le Galès 2002; McNeill 2001). It is crucial to recognize, finally, that many of the aforementioned patterns of interscalar and territorial alliance formation coexisted within the same national institutional landscapes. The salient point here, then, is that urban locational policies were implemented during the post-1980s period through a diverse array of interscalar and territorial alliances. Any systematic, comparative study of urban governance restructuring in post-1980s western Europe would need to examine the contextually specific political, institutional, and geographical bases of urban economic development strategies within each national territory (for an important recent contribution to such an investigation, see Savitch and Kantor 2002).

I have argued in this chapter that urban locational policies represent experimental, ad hoc political responses to the proliferation of place-specific economic crises, regulatory problems, and sociopolitical conflicts following the crisis of North Atlantic Fordism. Such policies were articulated through a broad range of state spatial projects and state spatial strategies designed (*a*) to promote urban regions rather than national economies as the most essential geographical targets for economic development initiatives, and (*b*) to customize the institutional infrastructure of urban governance according to place-specific political-economic conditions. More generally, the regulatory realignments induced through urban locational policies were premised upon the assumption that a rescaling of state institutional organization and state regulatory activity could resolve the regulatory failures of spatial Keynesianism and unleash new economic growth capacities within major urban regions.

However, while the post-Keynesian state spatial projects and state spatial strategies surveyed in this chapter shared an underlying commitment to the creation of place-specific institutional configurations, to the mobilization of localized, area-based economic development strategies, and to the concentration of advanced socioeconomic assets within strategic city-regions, they diverged considerably in the visions of political-economic transformation they aspired to realize. For, as we have seen, urban locational policies were promoted by a variety of opposed class forces and political alliances within each national, regional, and local context—including neoliberal coalitions concerned to grant new discretionary powers and public subsidies to transnational capital; neocorporatist coalitions concerned to promote cross-class cooperation and to forge 'high-road' developmental pathways; and neo-statist coalitions concerned to enhance the capacity of state institutions to override class-based coalitions (Gough 2002; Eisenschitz and Gough 1996). Yet, despite these profound differences in ideology, political agenda, and socioeconomic base, all forms of urban locational policy entailed a fundamental break from the nationalizing, spatially equalizing regulatory project associated with spatial Keynesianism. In this sense, urban locational policies contributed markedly to the erosion of the nationalized forms of class compromise, territorial redistribution, and urban managerialism that had prevailed during the 1960s and early 1970s, and they likewise played a central role in facilitating a significant geographical differentiation of political-economic space throughout western Europe during the post-1980s period. This splintering of state space represents the most widespread political expression and institutional outcome of urban locational policies.

SIX

Alternative Rescaling Strategies and the Future of New State Spaces

Rather than resolving the contradictions of space, state action makes them worse.

Henri Lefebvre (2003a: 91)

Reprise: state space and the new geopolitics of uneven development

Before proceeding to the final stage of this inquiry, I shall recapitulate, in broad strokes, the theoretical and empirical terrain we have traversed in the foregoing chapters. Throughout this study, I have returned repeatedly to the endemic problem of uneven spatial development under capitalism. On a theoretical level, I have confronted this problem through three distinct but intertwined arguments.

1. This analysis has been framed around the contention that the current round of global restructuring represents an intensification and reworking of inherited patterns of uneven spatial development. I have interpreted this transformation as the latest expression of the tension between deterritorialization and reterritorialization that has long underpinned the production of capitalist sociospatial configurations.

2. This analysis has underscored the role of state institutions, at various spatial scales, in mediating and transforming patterns of uneven development. I have argued that state institutions may seek to influence the geographies of uneven spatial development through diverse political strategies, including redistributive policies intended to alleviate sociospatial inequalities and competitiveness-driven, growth-oriented policies that intensify the polarization of territorial development.

3. Through an investigation of the interplay between state spatial projects, state spatial strategies, and uneven development, this analysis has attempted to mobilize a processual conceptualization of state spatiality, and on this basis,

258 The Future of New State Spaces

to decipher the changing geographies of statehood under modern capitalism. I have proposed, on the one hand, that state spatial projects generate more or less centralized, more or less uniform, matrices of state spatial organization. Concomitantly, I have argued that, within each inherited framework of state spatial organization, state spatial strategies generate more or less nationalized, more or less equalized, geographies of political-economic life. Taken together, state spatial projects and state spatial strategies produce historically specific configurations of state spatial selectivity in which (a) inherited patterns of uneven development are provisionally regulated; (b) new forms of regulatory experimentation are articulated; and (c) new geographies of political-economic life are forged.

While the above propositions were elaborated on an abstract level in Chs. 2 and 3, Chs. 4 and 5 explored their ramifications on meso and concrete levels, through an investigation of uneven development, urban policy restructuring, and the remaking of state spatiality in western Europe during the last four decades. In particular, three meso-level arguments—corresponding to each of the three abstract propositions summarized above—have emerged:

1. In post-1980s western Europe, the current round of worldwide deterritorialization and reterritorialization has entailed a deepening and rearticulation of inherited patterns of uneven spatial development. European economic space has been simultaneously homogenized and redifferentiated through EU-level and national political strategies designed to dismantle inherited barriers to Europe-wide economic competition and to establish integrated commodity, capital, and labor markets at a European scale. This has facilitated the development of transnational corporate accumulation strategies oriented towards Europe-wide spatial divisions of labor. At the same time, this wave of supranational market integration has provoked various national, regional, and local political strategies intended to enhance the territory-, place-, and scale-specific features of particular investment locations. In this sense, the tendential integration of European political-economic space (the moment of deterritorialization) has been tied to processes of sociospatial differentiation and rescaling, as diverse political coalitions have maneuvered to position their respective territories strategically within a rapidly changing geoeconomic order (the moment of reterritorialization). These contradictory tendencies of integration, differentiation, and rescaling have produced a new European sociospatial mosaic characterized by intense economic dynamism within a select group of powerful, globally interlinked cities, regions, and industrial districts and by enhanced stagnation, marginalization, and exclusion within many of Europe's older industrial cores and underdeveloped, peripheral zones.

2. Across western Europe, the last four decades have witnessed an inversion in state approaches to the regulation of uneven development. During the

Fordist-Keynesian period, state institutions sought to alleviate intra-national territorial inequalities, which were viewed as an impediment to balanced, stabilized macroeconomic growth. Following a transitional period of crisis-induced restructuring and regulatory experimentation in the 1970s, the redistributive policy relays of spatial Keynesianism were undermined. As of the 1980s, a new, growth-oriented and competitiveness-driven approach to urban governance was consolidated. With the proliferation of urban locational policies during this decade and thereafter, state institutions at various spatial scales began actively to intensify uneven development by promoting the most strategic cities and city-regions within each national territory as privileged sites for transnational capital investment. Under these conditions, uneven spatial development is increasingly viewed as an unavoidable precondition for profitable capital accumulation rather than as a potentially destabilizing barrier to the latter.

3. In conjunction with the aforementioned realignments, patterns of state spatial selectivity have been fundamentally transformed. During the Fordist-Keynesian period, a nationalized, territorially uniform configuration of state space was established through the historically specific constellation of state spatial projects and state spatial strategies associated with spatial Keynesianism. Within this nationalized interscalar rule-regime, state administrative arrangements were centralized and standardized; urban policies were subordinated to national regulatory imperatives; urban economies were subsumed within national spatial divisions of labor; and inherited territorial inequalities were alleviated through nationally redistributive spatial policies. Following the crisis of North Atlantic Fordism, however, this formation of state spatiality was thoroughly destabilized. By the 1980s, a significantly rescaled configuration of state spatial selectivity was forged as urban locational policies proliferated across western Europe. Such policies were premised upon new state spatial projects and state spatial strategies designed to enhance the supranational territorial competitiveness of major cities and city-regions. Within this transformed interscalar rule-regime, state regulatory capacities have been decentralized and customized according to place-, scale-, and jurisdiction-specific conditions; major socioeconomic assets and advanced infrastructural investments have been reconcentrated within strategic urban and regional economies; and urban policy has been reoriented from redistributive-managerial priorities towards the goal of positioning major cities and city-regions (or strategic locations therein) advantageously within global and European circuits of capital. In short, the proliferation of urban locational policies during the last two decades has facilitated the consolidation of a rescaled, territorially differentiated configuration of state space in which interlocality competition, divergent local developmental pathways, and the intensification of intra-national sociospatial polarization are actively promoted through state institutions and policies.

The transformed configuration of state spatiality that has crystallized through these transformations may be provisionally characterized as a Rescaled Competition State Regime (RCSR)—*rescaled*, because it rests upon scale-sensitive political strategies intended to position key subnational spaces (localities, cities, regions, industrial districts) optimally within supranational (European or global) circuits of capital accumulation; a *competition state*, because it privileges the goal of economic competitiveness over traditional welfarist priorities such as equity and redistribution; and a *regime*, because it represents an unstable, evolving institutional-geographical mosaic rather than a fully consolidated framework of statehood.[1] Within this rescaled configuration of state spatiality, national governments have not simply down-scaled or upscaled regulatory power, but have attempted to institutionalize competitive relations between subnational administrative units as a means to position local and regional economies strategically within supranational (European and global) circuits of capital. In this sense, even in the midst of the wide-ranging rescaling processes that have unsettled traditional, nationally focused regulatory arrangements, national states have attempted to retain control over major subnational political-economic spaces by situating them within rescaled, but still nationally coordinated, accumulation strategies. The transformation of western European Keynesian welfare national states into RCSRs has been mediated through diverse political agendas and has been pursued along divergent pathways of institutional and scalar restructuring in different national contexts. Despite this, however, I have argued that a systemic transformation of western European statehood has become evident during the last three decades. The notion of an RCSR is intended to summarize the main institutional and scalar contours of this transformation, as initially outlined in Fig. 3.12 (p. 106).

---

[1] This formulation partially parallels Jessop's (2002: 252) characterization of Schumpeterian workfare postnational regimes. One key difference is that the notion of 'regime', in Jessop's conceptualization, refers to the enhanced role of self-organizing governance networks, rather than hierarchical-governmental apparatuses, in compensating for market and state failures. By contrast, as used here, the term 'regime' is intended to underscore the institutionally and geographically unstable character of currently emergent state forms.

In a number of essays that were written prior to the completion of this book, I described currently emergent state forms as 'Glocalizing Competition State Regimes' (GCSRs) (Brenner 2004*a*, *b*) or, more simply, as 'glocal states' (Brenner 1999*b*, 1998*b*). Elsewhere (Brenner 2003*a*, *b*), I have referred to contemporary processes of state rescaling as an expression, medium, and outcome of 'glocalization strategies'. For further discussion of the genealogy of this terminology, and its associated disadvantages and advantages, see Ch. 2 n. 14. For present purposes, I have replaced the semantic couplet of glocalizing/glocalized with that of rescaling/rescaled, which I now consider to be more appropriate labels for contemporary processes of state rescaling. The former terms can be easily misconstrued as substantive characterizations of a newly fixed architecture of state scalar organization. By contrast, the notions of rescaling/rescaled are more generic, dynamic, and open-ended: they usefully underscore the continually evolving scalar configuration of state institutions and policies. I believe that this situation of 'scalar flux' is an endemic feature of post-Keynesian statehood in western Europe—it is the predominant political expression of the relativization of scales, as described in Ch. 2. It is essential, therefore, to deploy concepts that underscore the fluidity of contemporary scalar configurations and interscalar relations.

In this concluding chapter, my goal is to extend this 'first-cut' conceptual-ization of RCSRs by exploring their continued institutional and scalar evolu-tion during the 1990s and early 2000s. To elaborate such a 'second-cut' analysis, I argue, first, that the splintered institutional landscapes of RCSRs are permeated by chronic regulatory deficits and crisis-tendencies. For, despite their goal of unleashing new economic development capacities, urban loca-tional policies have contributed to a variety of disruptive, dysfunctional trends that have destabilized the accumulation process and undermined the territor-ial coherence of political-economic life. On this basis, I examine three alterna-tive strategies of rescaling that have been mobilized in response to this situation: (*a*) neighborhood-based anti-exclusion initiatives; (*b*) metropolitan reform initiatives; and (*c*) interurban networking initiatives. This latest round of state rescaling has partially counteracted some of the most polarizing, contradictory effects of urban locational policies, and has contributed to a further institutional evolution and scalar differentiation of RCSRs. It has also opened up some new spaces of regulatory experimentation in which diverse political alliances are attempting to return issues of territorial cohesion back to the center of debates on the urban question. I argue, however, that these highly scale-sensitive approaches to crisis-management have done little to subvert the competition-driven, growth-first logic upon which urban loca-tional policies are grounded; they thus represent evolutionary modifications *within* RCSRs rather than a transcendence of the latter.

This second-cut interpretation suggests that RCSRs have been locked into a vicious cycle in which ineffectual regulatory experiments engender equally dysfunctional institutional innovations, causing the economic, social, and political dislocations of post-Keynesian urban governance to be further exacer-bated. I conclude by considering the prospects for a more optimistic, 'third-cut' transformation of RCSRs, in which the regulatory deficits and crisis-tendencies of urban locational policies would be counterbalanced through the establish-ment of a Europe-wide, territorially equalizing interscalar rule-regime.[2] I argue that such a scenario will be difficult, if not impossible, to accomplish unless the forces of transnational neoliberalism, and the socially regressive regulatory geographies they promote, are challenged.

---

[2] My references to the first, second, and third cuts into the interpretation of RCSRs are derived in part from Harvey's (1982) terminology in his classic account of crisis theory in *Limits to Capital*. My adoption of this terminology has also been inspired by the innovative recent work of Jones (2001) and Jones and Ward (2002), which resonates closely with the analysis of state rescaling developed in this chapter. In Harvey's work, the three cuts represent progressively more sophisticated analytical lenses through which to interpret the process of crisis formation under capitalism. In the present context, by contrast, each of the cuts corresponds to a particular stage within the institutional and scalar evolution of RCSRs, as well as to theoretical efforts to decipher the latter. However, the third-cut analysis of RCSRs presented at the end of this chapter is speculative: it focuses not upon a new developmental formation of RCSRs, but upon the prospects—currently bleak—for a progressive transformation of the current, second-cut formation.

Unstable state spaces: regulatory deficits of urban locational policies

> The logic of interurban competition [...] turns cities into accomplices of their own subordination [...] The public subsidy of zero-sum competition at the inter-urban scale rests on the economic fallacy that every city can win, shored up by the political reality that no city can afford principled noninvolvement in the game.
>
> Jamie Peck and Adam Tickell (2002: 46)

> The implementation of urban policy is frequently associated with crises, which are diffused—temporarily [...]—through a centrally orchestrated state apparatus, to reappear at a later date and require 'new' urban policies that, in turn, create further contradictions and crisis.
>
> Martin Jones and Kevin Ward (2002: 128)

As outlined in the preceding chapter, urban locational policies—and, by implication, RCSRs—are premised upon spatially polarizing institutional innovations and regulatory initiatives. In neoliberalized political systems, such policies are justified through the contention that stable macroeconomic growth will be secured as local and regional economies are forced to compete on the basis of their supranational market positions. By contrast, in national and regional contexts in which social- and christian-democratic traditions have remained more robust, intra-national territorial inequalities are usually viewed as an unavoidable consequence of global and European economic integration. The polarization of territorial development is seen as an undesirable but necessary side-effect of political initiatives to maintain national economic competitiveness. In both instances, however, it is assumed that the place-specific competitive advantages of city-regions will not be threatened by rising levels of intra-national sociospatial polarization. More generally, it is assumed that the benefits of urban economic dynamism—both within and beyond the city-regions that are targeted for development initiatives—will offset any detrimental political-economic consequences that might flow from the new territorial polarization.

In practice, however, such assumptions have proven to be thoroughly problematic. For, as noted in the opening chapter of this book, while uneven spatial development may present certain fractions of capital with new opportunities for profit-making, it may also undermine the socioeconomic and territorial preconditions upon which the accumulation process as a whole depends (Harvey 1982; Massey 1985). As numerous urban scholars have suggested, a number of regulatory failures and crisis-tendencies have become evident across the western European urban system during the last two decades, as national, regional, and local state institutions have mobilized urban locational policies in the absence of a comprehensive regulatory framework for containing their territorially polarizing consequences.[3] Such policies have proven contradictory in the sense that, in channeling public resources towards the goal of enhancing urban territorial competitiveness, they have simultaneously contributed to a destabilization of urban, regional, and national economic development. To be sure, the patterns of regulatory failure and crisis formation induced by urban locational policies have been articulated in nationally, regionally, and locally specific forms. For instance, the macrogeographical impacts of offensive, social-democratic approaches to urban locational policy have been less destructive, destabilizing, and polarizing than defensive, neo-liberal approaches (Leborgne and Lipietz 1991). Nonetheless, as Harvey (1989a: 10–11) recognized in the late 1980s, urban locational policies (in his terms, 'entrepreneurial' forms of urban governance) cause urban systems to become more 'vulnerable to the uncertainties of rapid change' and thus trigger 'all manner of upward and downward spirals of urban growth and decline' (ibid.). The following are among the major regulatory failures and crisis-tendencies that have been generated through the widespread mobilization of urban locational policies in post-1980s western Europe:

- *Inefficiency and waste.* Urban locational policies enhance competitive pressures upon subnational administrative units to offer favorable terms to potential investors. As these policies have been diffused, the potential disadvantages of a failure or refusal to introduce them have escalated (Leitner and Sheppard 1998). Despite this, there is currently little evidence that urban locational policies generate positive-sum, supply-side gains for local economies, for instance, by upgrading locally embedded industrial capacities. More frequently, such initiatives have entailed public subsidies to private firms, leading to a zero-sum redistribution of capital investment among competing locations within the EU (Cheshire and Gordon 1998, 1996; Dunford 1994). In this manner, urban locational policies may induce inefficient allocations of public resources as taxpayer revenues are channeled towards the promotion of private accumulation rather than towards the general conditions of production or social expenditures. Hence, as Cheshire and Gordon (1995: 122) conclude, 'much territorial competition [among cities] is pure waste'.
- *Short-termism.* The proliferation of urban locational policies has encouraged 'the search for short-term gains at the expense of more important longer-term investments in the health of cities and the well-being of their residents' (Leitner and Sheppard 1998: 305). Even though some cities have managed to acquire short-term competitive advantages through the early adoption of urban locational policies, such advantages have generally been eroded as analogous policies have been diffused among similarly positioned cities within the European spatial division of labor (Leitner and Sheppard 1998). In

---

[3] See e.g. Cheshire and Gordon 1996; Dunford 1994; Eisenschitz and Gough 1998, 1996; Jones 2001; Keating 1991; Lovering 1995; MacLeod 2000; Peck and Tickell 1995, 1994; Leitner and Sheppard 1998.

this sense, while urban locational policies have helped unleash short-term bursts of economic growth within some cities and regions, they have proven far less effective in sustaining that growth over the medium or long term (Peck and Tickell 1995, 1994).

• *'Glocal enclavization'*. Urban locational policies entail the targeting of strategic, globally connected urban regions, or specific locations therein, as the engines of national economic dynamism. Such policies are premised upon the assumption that enhanced urban territorial competitiveness will benefit the broader regional and national space-economies in which cities are embedded. In practice, however, urban locational policies have contributed to the establishment of technologically advanced, globally connected urban enclaves that generate only limited spillover effects into their surrounding territories. This tendency towards 'glocal enclavization' is being articulated at a local scale, as advanced infrastructural hubs and high-technology production centers are delinked from adjoining neighborhoods, and at supralocal scales, as globally competitive agglomerations are delinked from older industrial regions and other marginalized spaces within the same national territory (Graham and Marvin 2001). The resultant intensification of national and local sociospatial polarization may undermine macroeconomic stability; it may also breed divisive, disruptive political conflicts (see below).

• *Regulatory undercutting*. Particularly in their defensive, neoliberal forms, urban locational policies have encouraged a race to the bottom in social service provision as national, regional, and municipal governments attempt to reduce the costs of capital investment within their territorial jurisdictions. This process of regulatory undercutting is dysfunctional on a number of levels: it aggravates rather than alleviates municipal fiscal and regulatory problems; it worsens life-chances for significant segments of local and national populations; and it exacerbates entrenched inequalities within national urban hierarchies (Eisenschitz and Gough 1998; Peck and Tickell 1995). These outcomes tend to downgrade national economic performance (Cheshire and Gordon 1996; Hudson 2001).

• *Uneven spatial development and territorial conflicts*. The aforementioned regulatory problems may assume more moderate forms in conjunction with offensive, social-democratic forms of urban locational policy. Nonetheless, offensive forms of urban locational policy are likewise prone to significant crisis-tendencies (Eisenschitz and Gough 1996, 1993; Gough and Eisenschitz 1996; Leborgne and Lipietz 1991). First, like defensive approaches to urban locational policy, offensive approaches 'operate . . . as a strategy for strengthening some territories vis-à-vis other territories and other nations' (Leborgne and Lipietz 1991: 47); they thus 'increase the profitability of strong economies more than the weak', and intensify uneven development beyond the territorial zones in which they are deployed (Eisenschitz and Gough 1996: 444). The macroeconomic instability that subsequently ensues may undermine the very localized socioeconomic assets upon which offensive urban locational policies depend (Leborgne and Lipietz 1991). Second, even more so than defensive forms of urban locational policy, offensive approaches to urban economic development suffer from serious problems of politicization. Their effectiveness hinges upon being confined to locally delineated areas; yet the apparent successes of such strategies at a local scale generate intense distributional pressures as other localities and regions within the same national territory strive to replicate the 'recipe' or to reap some of its financial benefits (Eisenschitz and Gough 1996).

• *Problems of interscalar coordination.* The proliferation of place-specific strategies of local economic development exacerbates coordination problems within and among national, regional, and local state institutions. First, because urban locational policies enhance the geographical differentiation of state regulatory activities without embedding subnational competitive strategies within an encompassing national policy framework, they have undermined the organizational coherence and functional integration of state institutions. For, as Goodwin and Painter (1996: 646) explain, the increasing geographical differentiation of state regulatory activities induced through local economic development policies is 'as much a hindrance as a help to regulation'. Second, this lack of supranational or national regulatory coordination in the field of urban policy may exacerbate the economic crisis-tendencies discussed above: it enhances the likelihood that identical or analogous growth strategies may be replicated serially across the European urban system, thus accelerating the diffusion of zero-sum forms of interlocality competition (Amin and Malmberg 1994).

• *Democratic accountability and legitimation problems.* Finally, the proliferation of urban locational policies has generated new conflicts regarding democratic accountability and political legitimation. Many of the new, highly fragmented institutional forms established to implement urban locational policies are dominated by non-elected government bureaucrats, technical experts, property developers, and corporate elites who are not accountable to the populations that are most directly affected by their activities (Swyngedouw, Moulaert, and Rodriguez 2002). While this lack of political accountability may enable regulatory agencies to implement urban locational policies more efficiently, it systematically undermines their ability to address broader social needs and to maintain territorial cohesion (Eisenschitz and Gough 1998). The institutional fragmentation of statehood induced through urban locational policies thus constrains the capacity of state institutions, at various spatial scales, to address many of the dysfunctional side-effects of such policies, both within and beyond the cities in which they are deployed. This fragmentation may also generate serious legitimation deficits if oppositional social forces are able to politicize the negative socioeconomic consequences of urban locational policies or their undemocratic character.

These regulatory problems and crisis-tendencies are of considerable significance to the present analysis, not only because they illustrate the internally contradictory character of urban locational policies. They also provide a theoretical basis on which to decipher the institutional and scalar evolution of RCSRs during the 1990s and early 2000s. Drawing upon Offe's (1984) approach to crisis theory, Hudson (2001: 66) has recently suggested that state institutions may transform their own internal structures and modes of operation as they attempt to 'reconcile the contradictions inherent to [their] involvement in the economy and society'. Building upon this insight, I suggest that a crisis-induced recalibration of RCSRs has been unfolding since the mid-1990s, as the disruptive, dysfunctional consequences of urban locational policies have become more apparent. Under these circumstances, a rescaled layer of state spatial projects and state spatial strategies has been forged within RCSRs whose purpose is to confront some of the major regulatory failures that have been generated through urban locational policies. State rescaling has thus come to operate not only as a political strategy for promoting local economic development, but also as a form of crisis-management designed to manage the regulatory deficits, dislocations, and conflicts induced through earlier rounds of state spatial restructuring (Jones and Ward 2002; Brenner 2003*a*). These rescaled strategies of crisis-management have not challenged the growth-driven, competitiveness-oriented logic of urban locational policy. Nonetheless, such strategies have entailed the construction of institutional flanking mechanisms through which state institutions are attempting to monitor, manage, and alleviate some of the most destructive political-economic consequences of such policies. The institutional and scalar architectures of RCSRs have been qualitatively modified through the interaction of this new, scale-sensitive politics of crisis-management with inherited, post-Keynesian approaches to urban governance.

In order to explore this latest round of state rescaling, and thus develop a second-cut interpretation of RCSRs, I shall consider three scale-specific forms of regulatory experimentation that have been mobilized since the early 1990s—neighborhood-based anti-exclusion initiatives, metropolitan reform initiatives, and interurban networking initiatives. The political form, institutional shape, and scalar configuration of each of these crisis-management strategies have varied not only by national, regional, and local context, but also in relation to the specific types of urban locational policy that were previously mobilized within those contexts. For it is in relation to the endemic regulatory failures of such policies that the alleged need for a recalibration or extension of state rescaling processes has been perceived, politicized, and acted upon in specific politico-institutional settings. Despite their otherwise divergent institutional forms, scalar foci, and regulatory aims, these three forms of state rescaling share several common features:

- they have been oriented towards the place- and scale-specific political-economic conditions of urban regions;

- they have attempted, through spatially selective state projects and state strategies, to alleviate the new forms of uneven development that have emerged within and between European cities during the last two decades;
- they have attempted, through a further scalar differentiation of state space, to counteract some of the regulatory failures associated with earlier approaches to urban locational policy;
- they have reintroduced a concern with territorial cohesion back into debates on the urban question, often on the basis of claims that such an emphasis is not only compatible with, but conducive to, the pursuit of territorial competitiveness.

In interpreting the latest round of state rescaling as a form of crisis-management, I am not suggesting that state spatial configurations evolve automatically and coherently in response to inherited policy failures, or that they effectively resolve the latter. Recent rescaling initiatives in European city-regions have emerged through the combined impacts of deliberate design, institutional learning, trial-and-error regulatory experimentation, chance discoveries, and political compromises, as diverse social forces, political coalitions, and territorial alliances have struggled to reshape the field of urban governance and, more generally, to influence the trajectory of state spatial restructuring. As I argue below, the capacity of these rescaled forms of crisis-management to resolve the regulatory deficits within RCSRs remains highly problematic at the present time; and these crisis-management strategies have also generated new conflicts and crisis-tendencies of their own. In each case, therefore, the rescaling of state space has served at once as the basis on which a particular form of crisis-management has been launched and as the source of new regulatory dislocations within RCSRs.

I shall not attempt here to provide a comprehensive survey of each of these rescaling initiatives. As in the preceding two chapters, this meso-level account aims to illuminate the general, pan-European features of the institutional shifts and policy realignments in question, and on that basis, to specify their cumulative implications for urban governance, the regulation of uneven spatial development, and the evolving scalar geographies of western European statehood.

Rescaling (further) downward: neighborhood-based anti-exclusion initiatives

A number of scholars have drawn attention to the intensification of socio-spatial polarization within major European cities during the last three decades.[4] Increasingly, the neighborhood scale is recognized as a major site

---

[4] See e.g. Andersen and van Kempen 2001; Geddes and Benington 2001; Madanipour, Cars, and Allen 1998; Mingione 1996; Musterd and Ostendoorf 1998; O'Loughlin and Friedrichs 1996; and Sassen 1993, 1991.

at which new social and territorial inequalities have been articulated, as disadvantaged populations (including the long-term unemployed, recent immigrants, the elderly poor, and welfare recipients) and social problems (such as unemployment, poverty, crime, and homelessness) have been concentrated within inner-city areas and outlying housing estates (Andersen and van Kempen 2003). Of course, class- and ethnicity-based forms of urban residential segregation have a long lineage in the history of European urbanism (Hohenberg and Lees 1995). Accordingly, the scholarship on the 'new' urban exclusion has attempted to disaggregate the impacts of recent global shifts (such as geoeconomic integration), inherited national institutions (such as welfare state regimes), and emergent local struggles (regarding, for instance, the form of urban governance) on the sociospatial fabric of European cities (Marcuse and van Kempen 2001; C. Hamnett 1996). Given the multiple political-economic forces underlying contemporary urban sociospatial polarization, it would be problematic to view the latter as a direct outcome of urban locational policies. Nonetheless, because such policies have facilitated the reorientation of urban governance away from socially and spatially redistributive goals, they have contributed to an intensification of intra-urban territorial inequalities during the post-1980s period. In a number of western European national states, and also at a European scale, the problem of urban sociospatial polarization has been met with qualitatively new, rescaled regulatory responses during the course of the 1990s (Geddes and Bennington 2001; Andersen and van Kempen 2003). Three aspects of these strategies to counteract urban sociospatial polarization deserve emphasis here—their scalar selectivity; their regulatory goals; and their institutional configuration:

1. *Urban policy at a neighborhood scale.* The policies in question target specific, clearly delineated areas and neighborhoods for multifaceted forms of policy intervention. These urban districts are generally delineated strictly such that 'anything that is not located inside the selected area will be excluded from the programmes' (H. T. Andersen 2001: 241). Although the urban renewal policies of the Fordist-Keynesian period likewise targeted specific urban zones, the area-based urban policies of the 1990s 'widen the scope of intervention to include not just physical upgrading but also social relations', including social networks, labor-market participation, educational opportunities, and so forth (H. T. Andersen 2001: 242). In each case, therefore, policies are devised and implemented with reference to the place-specific socioeconomic conditions and perceived problems of disadvantaged neighborhoods.

2. *Social exclusion as a threat to economic competitiveness.* The goal of neighborhood-based urban policies is to combat the problem of social 'exclusion', conceived not only in terms of economic factors such as income levels and job availability, but also in explicitly social terms, with reference to the social networks, institutional environments, and life chances of local inhabitants. Moreover, in contrast to earlier welfarist policies oriented towards urban

problems such as poverty, crime, and unemployment, anti-exclusion policies are justified as a means to enhance urban territorial competitiveness. For, as Harloe (2001: 895–6) notes, 'social exclusion is seen as potentially or actually having negative consequences for competitiveness and cohesion; conversely, social inclusion or cohesion is seen as likely to have positive consequences for competitiveness'. In this sense, neighborhood-based anti-exclusion policies may be understood as a significant extension and fine-tuning of urban locational policies. Anti-exclusion policies acknowledge explicitly that territorial inequalities—in this case, those that emerge *within* cities—may undermine urban competitiveness. The new urban social policies are thus promoted less as an alternative to urban locational policies than as a stabilizing complement to the latter.

3. *A multilayered but localized institutional structure.* Neighborhood-based anti-exclusion policies generally entail the interaction of multiple tiers of state organization, as well as the involvement of various non-state actors, such as neighborhood- and community-based associations, private business alliances, and quasi nongovernmental organizations (Quangos). However, while national state institutions, and in some cases, the European Commission, have figured crucially in initiating and funding such area-based regulatory experiments, the latter have exhibited a strongly localized character: their specific politico-institutional forms have been conditioned above all by place- and scale-specific political-economic circumstances, coalitions, and struggles rather than by top-down policy directives. Thus, in contrast to postwar anti-poverty policies, which were nationally formulated and locally implemented, the new approaches to social exclusion 'are more likely to be organized by, and [to] take their direction from, local forms of regulation' (Le Galès 2002: 215). They often involve 'partnerships', 'contracts', and 'covenants' between national state institutions and various local and neighborhood-level institutions in which the objectives, eligible participants, and time-frames for specific policy programs are specified. They also generally involve systematic efforts, at various scales of state power, to integrate previously distinct spheres of policy in the context of concerted neighborhood-level interventions (Andersen and van Kempen 2003; H. T. Andersen 2001).

As Box 6.1 (overleaf) indicates, a number of major western European national states, along with the European Commission, mobilized neighborhood-based anti-exclusion policies during the 1990s. The statements quoted in Box 6.1 underscore the ways in which, across several national contexts, such policies have been justified not only as a means to alleviate intra-urban inequalities, but also as a basis for protecting and upgrading urban competitive advantages.

Neighborhood-based anti-exclusion policies have also had important implications for the geographies of western European statehood. On the one hand, as Fig. 6.1 indicates, neighborhood-based initiatives have entailed an

Box 6.1. Neighborhood-based anti-exclusion initiatives: selected western European examples

---

The concentration of poor [inhabitants] in Copenhagen municipality is seen as a burden in the context of attracting investments in competition with Berlin, Hamburg, Stockholm and other European cities. Changing Copenhagen's social geography has thus become a primary strategy for developing its competitiveness.

(Hansen, Andersen, and Clark 2001: 865)

The [urban revitalization] policy [in the Netherlands] to help disadvantaged groups catch up with the rest of society was legitimated with reference to the presumably negative effect that deprived neighborhoods would have on the economic base of urban amenities and on the attractiveness of the city as a prime location for economically robust companies and households.

(Vermeijden 2001: 222)

The urban problem [in the United Kingdom] has been redefined in terms of a supposed lack of social cohesion, leading ultimately to social and economic exclusion. This new concept embraces some old issues—including poverty, crime and quality of life—but now cast less as symptoms of urban failure than as potential obstacles to competitive success, both for the cities themselves and for the national economies that increasingly rely on them. The political agenda for cities is thereby defined as the search for institutions and policies that might reconcile competitiveness and cohesion goals.

(Harloe 2001: 889–90)

Key examples of neighborhood-based anti-exclusion policies in contemporary western Europe include the following:

- *Kvarterløft Program, Denmark.* The Danish national government founded an 'Urban Commission' in the early 1990s in order to promote social and economic improvements within 500 housing estates. The Commission provided financial support for a variety of neighborhood-based initiatives, including physical upgrading, rent reductions, and other social programs. Subsequently, the national government introduced the 'Urban Area Improvement Program' (*Kvarterløft-programmet*) which focused on seven large neighborhoods located in Copenhagen and several other Danish cities. Through the establishment of localized governance networks and public–private partnerships, this program was intended to enhance labor-market participation, public safety, and social vitality in disadvantaged neighborhoods (Kristensen 2001; Andersen and van Kempen 2003).

- *Grote Steden Beleid, Netherlands.* In the Dutch context, urban renewal policies were decentralized during the 1990s (Altes 2002; Vermeijden 2001). Emblematic of these changes, the Big Cities Policy (*Grote Steden Beleid*—GSB) was introduced in 1996; its overarching goal was to stimulate local governance networks that could address 'the aggravating problems [that] threatened to put a spoke in the wheel of the motors of the economy: the major cities' (van den Berg, Braun, and van der Meer 1998: 265). One of the key goals of the GSB has been to promote an integrated approach to urban regener-

ation in which multiple national governmental ministries, along with diverse local institutions, associations, and actors, would collaborate to confront social problems such as
long-term unemployment, environmental degradation, and crime. The GSB allotted
public funds to rejuvenate marginalized neighborhoods within the major Dutch cities,
whose socioeconomic vitality was now viewed as a key precondition for national
economic prosperity. While the GSB was initially oriented towards the four 'motors' of
the Dutch national economy—the 'G-4' of Amsterdam, Rotterdam, Utrecht, and the
Hague—it has subsequently been expanded to include the so-called 'G-15' and the 'G-
6', two additional clusters of medium-sized towns that likewise manifested serious
problems of sociospatial polarization (Torrance 2002; Premius, Boelhouwer, and Kruythoff 1997).

- *Contrats de Ville, France.* The so-called *Politique de la Ville* was introduced in France during
  the late 1970s in order to confront the social problems of deprived areas within the
  French urban system (Body-Gendrot 2000). Such urban social policies were expanded
  during the 1980s, first through the *Développement Social des Quartiers* (1984–8), which
  targeted 148 neighborhoods, and then through the *Développement Social Urbain*
  (1988–92), which increased the number of targeted areas to 540. These programs
  were further expanded in the early 1990s through the *Contrats de Ville* program,
  which was oriented towards employment, crime, and education in over 1,200 disadvantaged urban areas. The *Contrats* perpetuated, in a more comprehensive form, the anti-
  exclusion agendas of previous approaches to *Politique de la Ville*, while also introducing
  new forms of collaboration among diverse institutions, including the national government, regional and local authorities, and, in many cases, private bodies (Jacquier 2001).
  Additional area-based state policies were also mobilized during the 1990s—for instance,
  the Concerted Program for Urban Development (*PACT urbains*); and the Large-Scale
  Urban Projects (*Grands Projects Urbains*) (Le Galès and Loncle-Moriceau 2001; Sallez
  1998; Body-Gendrot 2000).

- *City Challenge and Single Regeneration Budget, United Kingdom.* Following the market-
  oriented transformation of British urban policy under the Thatcher government, area-
  based forms of urban social policy were mobilized across the UK in the 1990s (Wilks-Heeg
  1996). Aside from their explicit focus on marginalized urban neighborhoods, these new
  urban social policies have been characterized by (a) competitive regimes of resource
  allocation, in which local authorities must bid against one another for access to public
  funds; (b) an emphasis on localized governance networks, community-based initiatives,
  and public–private partnerships, and (c) an orientation towards a range of urban socioeconomic issues, from labor markets, housing, environmental conditions, and education
  to crime, recreation, and economic competitiveness (Parkinson 1998; Jones and Ward
  2002). The City Challenge Program was introduced in 1992; it allocated £37.5 million to
  thirty-one local partnerships during a five-year period. City Challenge focused on so-
  called 'areas of concentrated disadvantage' with the goal of promoting localized economic growth and enhancing the social integration of marginalized populations
  (Davoudi and Healey 1995). This program was expanded in 1994, through the Single
  Regeneration Budget (SRB), which amalgamated resources from various governmental
  departments and twenty urban policy initiatives into a single urban social fund (Ward
  1997).

- *URBAN Programme, European Commission.* Since 1994, neighborhood-based anti-exclusion policies have been mobilized by the European Commission, above all through the
  URBAN program. URBAN has drawn upon, and has to some extent been coordinated

with, the aforementioned, nationally specific urban social initiatives; its goals have paralleled those of the latter, and it has, in many cases, provided additional financial resources for nationally, regionally, and locally initiated regeneration projects. In its initial phase, URBAN focused upon 110 depressed neighborhoods and commanded a budget of 880 million, derived from the Structural Funds (CEC 1998; Le Galès 2002: 101–3). However, the future of the URBAN initiative remains uncertain; it is currently being debated in the context of broader struggles regarding EU enlargement and the reform of the Structural Funds.

extension and deepening of post-1980s forms of state spatial restructuring. Indeed, much like urban locational policies, so too have neighborhood-based anti-exclusion policies contributed to the consolidation of decentralized, territorially customized state spatial configurations and localized, place-specific forms of state intervention. Yet, as Fig. 6.1 also indicates, the state spatial projects and state spatial strategies associated with neighborhood-based anti-exclusion programs have tendentially modified the geographical architecture of RCSRs in at least two ways. First, such localized anti-exclusion initiatives have attempted to introduce a new scalar niche and territorial arena within RCSRs—namely, the urban neighborhood, district, or *quartier*. In this manner, the neighborhood has become a key spatial and institutional forcefield for post-Keynesian regulatory experiments. Second, neighborhood-based anti-exclusion initiatives have attempted to alleviate, at a highly localized scale, some of the polarizing sociospatial consequences of previous rounds of political-economic restructuring, including those induced through urban locational policies. By confronting the problem of uneven spatial development in place- and scale-specific ways, local anti-exclusion programs have entailed a significant evolutionary modification within RCSRs: they have expanded the problematic of territorial competitiveness to include a variety of cohesion-related issues, such as employment, housing, education, and crime, that had not previously been addressed within the parameters of urban locational policy. Neighborhood-based anti-exclusion policies may thus be viewed as an important new flanking mechanism through which one of the major regulatory deficits of urban locational policies is being addressed, albeit exclusively within the confines of particular urban districts.

Neighborhood-based anti-exclusion policies have helped to reinvigorate public debates on the problem of territorial inequality in western European cities. However, their highly localized scalar focus also appears to represent a significant structural limitation. While the neighborhood-level orientation of these anti-exclusion policies enables them to be customized according to place-specific conditions, most of the social problems they aim to confront are not, in fact, confined to the targeted areas. Consequently, selecting appropriate

	STATE SPATIAL PROJECTS	STATE SPATIAL STRATEGIES
SCALAR DIMENSION	Through neighborhood-level 'partnerships', 'contracts', and 'covenants', new forms of regulatory coordination are established among European, national, and local state agencies as well as community-based associations and private institutions This extends the decentralization and localization of state space, while also enhancing interscalar linkages among supranational, national, and local state institutions	New, area-based forms of state intervention are mobilized in order to address social problems that have crystallized with particular intensity at a neighborhood scale. Although such policies are not oriented directly towards territorial competitiveness, they are frequently justified as a means to protect or upgrade the latter by maintaining urban social cohesion In this manner, such policies reinforce the strategic role of cities and city-regions as targets and arenas for accumulation strategies
TERRITORIAL DIMENSION	Certain disadvantaged urban districts or suburban areas within national urban systems are selected for specific types of institutional reform and policy innovation. In these cases, neighborhood-specific regulatory arrangements are superimposed upon inherited, city-wide administrative structures This contributes to a further customization and differentiation of state space according to place-specific conditions and priorities	The mobilization of neighborhood-specific social policies entails the establishment of strictly defined territorial enclaves into which public funding allotments are channeled. The policies, and their associated funding streams, are applicable only within the boundaries of the targeted districts This contributes to a further territorial differentiation of state space, as a patchwork of divergent policy regimes, funding schemes, and modes of state intervention is established not only among major regional and local administrative units, but also within urban regions

Fig. 6.1. Neighborhood-based anti-exclusion initiatives and the evolution of RCSRs

spatial targets—particularly if they are required to be neighborhood-based—remains highly problematic: for 'selecting only areas with the biggest problems might mean that areas with a score that is slightly better on the variables such as unemployment, crime and quality of life do not get any attention' (Andersen and van Kempen 2003: 82–3). Relatedly, many area-based urban social policies engender the unintended but dysfunctional consequence of displacing social problems from the targeted areas into other zones of a metropolitan region. In this scenario, such policies redistribute the spatial expressions of social exclusion among different locations within an urban agglomeration, rather than addressing their underlying political-economic causes. Insofar as localized, neighborhood-level anti-exclusion policies are adopted as a means to address social problems that are actually metropolitan-wide or even national, they may obscure the supralocal institutional contexts in which territorial inequalities are generated (Andersen and van Kempen 2003: 83). Finally, many neighborhood-based anti-exclusion initiatives are not coherently integrated into European or national frameworks of spatial, regional, and urban policy; they thus exacerbate the fragmentation of state space by generating a patchwork of localized, place-specific regulatory enclaves. While some recent urban policy initiatives, such as the URBAN program of the European Commission, the British Single Regeneration Budget, and the French *Contrats de Ville*, are more explicitly attuned to the need for interscalar coordination and meta-governance, the problem of institutional fragmentation is endemic to localized, area-based approaches to urban regeneration (H. T. Andersen 2001). Thus, even under the most favorable political circumstances, the integration of area-based initiatives into metropolitan-wide or national developmental strategies poses major regulatory challenges.

This pessimistic assessment is not intended to deny the possibility that neighborhood-based initiatives might play a stabilizing, progressive role in processes of urban regeneration. For, as Moulaert (2000) has argued, such local social policies may contain considerable potential to establish alternatives to growth-oriented, competition-based models of urban development—but only if they are systematically linked to, and integrated within, a broader European and national redistributive political agenda. In the absence of such a macrogeographical project of territorial equalization, I would suggest, the aforementioned limitations of neighborhood-based social policies are likely to remain chronic ones. Under current geoeconomic and European conditions, therefore, neighborhood-based anti-exclusion policies operate primarily to address some of the most destructive effects of urban locational policies within self-enclosed urban districts; they do little to alleviate those effects at supralocal scales, to confront their underlying political-economic causes, to integrate the targeted districts into the broader metropolitan fabric, or to counteract the competitiveness-driven, growth-oriented logic upon which post-Keynesian urban governance is grounded.

Rescaling (back) upward: metropolitan reform initiatives

Like urban neighborhoods, metropolitan regions have become important sites of scale-specific transformations of statehood since the early 1990s. As indicated in the preceding chapter, comprehensive, large-scale approaches to metropolitan governance were undermined or abolished during the 1980s in conjunction with the crisis of North Atlantic Fordism and the resultant retrenchment of Keynesian welfare national states. Following the collapse of spatial Keynesianism, urban locational policies were diffused within a reterritorialized institutional landscape in which inherited regulatory controls on metropolitan-wide spatial development were significantly compromised. However, this apparent institutional vacuum in the field of metropolitan governance proved to be short-lived. Soon after the high-profile abolitions of the Greater London Council and Rotterdam's *Rijnmond* in the 1980s, local, regional, and national political coalitions across the western European urban system began to advocate a renewal of metropolitan governance—albeit in significantly different politico-institutional forms than those that had prevailed under spatial Keynesianism.

Since the early 1990s, debates on the installation of new metropolitan institutions have proliferated, in many cases leading to significant changes in regional territorial administration, spatial planning, and economic governance. In contrast to the hierarchical-bureaucratic frameworks of metropolitan service delivery that prevailed during the Fordist-Keynesian period, the metropolitan institutional reforms of the 1990s have been grounded upon a new model of public action that 'highlights values of negotiation, partnership, voluntary participation and flexibility in the constitution of new structures' (Lefèvre 1998: 18). These metropolitan institutional reforms have not been designed according to a single recipe or imposed from above, but have generally emerged 'as a product of the system of actors as the process [of institutional reform] unfolds' (Lefèvre 1998: 18). In some city-regions, such as London, Bologna, Stuttgart, Hannover, Frankfurt, and Copenhagen, new metropolitan institutional arrangements have been constructed in which multiple planning, administrative, and regulatory competencies are concentrated. In other major European urban regions, informal frameworks for metropolitan cooperation have been superimposed upon inherited political geographies and have provided a new institutional basis for intra-regional negotiations regarding diverse policy issues—including economic development, place-marketing, infrastructural planning, suburban sprawl, environmental sustainability, and democratic accountability. Faced with these recent institutional changes and regulatory experiments, several commentators have suggested that a renaissance of metropolitan regionalism is currently under way throughout western Europe.[5] Figure 6.2 (pp. 276–80) provides an overview of some of the major metropolitan reform initiatives that have emerged in the European urban system since the early 1990s.

---

[5] See e.g. Barlow 1997; Brenner 2003a; *DISP* 2003; Heinz 2000; Herrschel and Newman 2002; Jouve and Lefèvre 1999a; Keating 1998; Lefèvre 1998; Salet, Thornley, and Kreukels 2003a, b; and *STANDORT* 2000. The current round of metropolitan institutional reform has been promoted primarily by (a) modernizing national governments; (b) political elites within central cities; and (c) local and regional business elites, industrialists, and other 'boosterists'. The most vocal opponents of such reforms have generally included (a) representatives of middle-tier or provincial governmental agencies that perceive powerful metropolitan associations as a threat to their administrative authority; (b) representatives of wealthy suburban towns that fear central city dominance or reject external claims on the local tax base; and (c) residents within large cities that fear a loss of democratic accountability and local political control (Heinz 2000: 21–8).

	Form of metropolitan regionalism in the 1990s	Organizational embodiment(s)	Major political-economic forces behind metropolitan regionalism
Greater London (Thornley 2003; Newman and Thornley 1997; Syrett and Baldcock 2003)	Centrally imposed under the Blair government during the early 2000s Oriented towards enhancing London's competitive strength in global and European markets Linked to new 'third-way' discourses regarding democratic renewal and a national project of administrative devolution	Greater London Authority (GLA) (from 2000) London Development Agency (LDA) (from 2000) South East Development Agency (SEEDA) East of England Development Agency (EEDA) Various public–private partnerships and informal governance networks at regional and local scales	British national state Local and regional political elites in the London region Large business organizations in the South East of England Diverse local advocates of democratic renewal and 'third way' ideology
Greater Manchester (Deas and Ward 2002, 2000; Tickell, Peck, and Dicken 1995)	Centrally imposed during the early 2000s but also closely linked to new locally articulated regional economic development strategies within Greater Manchester Oriented towards the goal of marketing the North West of England as well as Greater Manchester as integrated, competitive locations for capital investment	North West Regional Association (NWRA); North West Development Agency (NWDA); North West Partnership Invest North West Agency for Regional Development (INWARD) City Pride Partnership Manchester Investment and Development Agency (MIDAS) Marketing Manchester	UK national state Large business organizations in the North West of England and in the Greater Manchester region Local and regional political elites in Manchester, its suburbs, and surrounding towns

Fig. 6.2A. The new metropolitan regionalism in western Europe: an overview of recent trends

As Figure 6.2 indicates, the current renaissance of metropolitan regionalism in western Europe has been multifaceted. Metropolitan reform initiatives have interacted in place-specific ways with inherited institutional frameworks, leading to the establishment of 'a more bewildering tangle of municipalities, governmental and regional organizations and institutions, and public, private, or informal cooperative approaches with differing

	Form of metropolitan regionalism in the 1990s	Organizational embodiment(s)	Major political-economic forces behind metropolitan regionalism
Greater Lyon (Bardet and Jouve 1998; Mabrouk and Jouve 1999; Motte 1997)	Transforms earlier, centrally imposed regional institutions into instruments of local and regional economic development strategy Grounded upon region-wide strategic economic planning initiatives, place-marketing campaigns, and infrastructural investment programs	Communauté Urbaine de Lyon (COURLY) Région Urbaine de Lyon (RUL) Logistical Alliance for the Urban Region of Lyon Economic Development Plan (1997) Council of Development (within the COURLY as of 2001)	DATAR (French national government) Lyon municipality Entrepreneurial local political elites (led by 'mayor-entrepreneur' Michel Noir) Local and regional business organizations in the Lyon region Participants in an emergent regional growth machine
Lille Metropolis (Newman and Thornley 1995; Moulaert, Salin, and Werquin 2001)	Transforms earlier, centrally imposed regional institutions into instruments of local and regional economic development strategy Aims to position Lille strategically in European transportation networks Tied to cross-border cooperative initiatives with Flanders (Belgium) and Kent (UK)	Communauté Urbaine de Lille (CUDL) Regional Economic Development Agency Lille Metropolitan Area Economic Promotion Agency (APIM) Lille Metropolitan Agency for Economic Development and Urban Planning (1990) Lille-Roubaix-Tourcoing Chamber of Commerce	DATAR (French national government) Lille municipality Entrepreneurial local political elites (led by Lille mayor Pierre Mauroy) Local and regional business organizations in the Lille region Participants in an emergent regional growth machine

Fig. 6.2B. (*continued*)

actors, functions, and jurisdictions' (Heinz 2000: 27). For this reason, much like the neighborhood-based anti-exclusion policies discussed above, each instance of metropolitan institutional restructuring must be understood with reference to the nationally and locally specific administrative-constitutional system and political-economic landscape in which it has emerged. Nonetheless, I suggest that the current round of metropolitan reform in western European city-regions can be deciphered, in more general terms, as a simultaneous extension and modification of previous approaches to urban locational policy.

	Form of metropolitan regionalism in the 1990s	Organizational embodiment(s)	Major political-economic forces behind metropolitan regionalism
Bologna Metropolitan City (Jouve and Lefèvre 1999b, 1997; Van den Berg, Braun, and van der Meer 1997)	Enabled in 1990 through national legislation to establish 'Metropolitan Cities' in major Italian urban agglomerations Aims to transform Bologna and its suburbs into an integrated, competitive 'Eurocity' through strategic planning projects and place-marketing campaigns	Metropolitan City Agreement (1994) Metropolitan Conference Metropolitan Economic Consultation (from 1996) Metropolitan Master Plan (from 1996)	Italian national government Bologna municipality Entrepreneurial local and regional political elites (led by mayor Walter Vitali) Selected fractions of local and regional capital in Bologna and Emilia-Romagna
Stuttgart Region (Benz and Frenzel 1999; Heeg 2003)	Enabled through a *Land* governmental initiative Aims to bundle economic capacities through the development of a coordinated regional growth strategy Combines regional approaches to infrastructural planning, spatial planning, and industrial policy	Stuttgart Regional Agency (VRS) (from 1994) Stuttgart Regional Economic Development Corporation	*Land* government of Baden-Württemberg Stuttgart municipality Local political elites in Stuttgart, selected suburbs, and various surrounding counties Major regional and local business organizations in Stuttgart and Baden-Württemberg
Hannover Region (Droste, Fiedler, and Schmidt 1997; Fürst and Rudolph 2003; Priebs 1997)	Goal is to enhance the efficiency of public administration and to develop a regionally coordinated strategy of economic development, place-marketing, and infrastructural planning	Greater Hannover Association of Municipalities (KGH) Hannover Regional County (from November 2001)	*Land* government of Lower Saxony Hannover municipality Political elites in Hannover and its suburban hinterland Major local and regional business organizations in Hannover and Lower Saxony

Fig. 6.2C. (*continued*)

	Form of metropolitan regionalism in the 1990s	Organizational embodiment(s)	Major political-economic forces behind metropolitan regionalism
Frankfurt/ Rhine-Main Region (Freund 2003; Scheller 1998; Ronneberger and Keil 1995; Brenner 1999c)	Emerges following recurrent debates on the inadequacies of earlier frameworks of city-suburban cooperation Aims to minimize zero-sum forms of inter-municipal competition within the region, to develop a coordinated strategy of regional economic development, and to enhance regional locational synergies	Greater Frankfurt Association (abolished in 2001) Frankfurt/Rhine-Main Regional Planning Association (from 2001) Council of the Region (from 2001) Rhine-Main Economic Development Corporation (from 1995) Metropolitana Frankfurt/Rhine-Main (from 2001)	Social Democratic Party of southern Hessen Local and regional political elites in Frankfurt, some of its suburbs, and some of its surrounding counties Frankfurt/Rhine-Main chamber of commerce Other major local and regional business organizations in Frankfurt and southern Hessen
Copenhagen metropolitan area (Andersen and Jørgensen 2004; Bruun 1995; Jørgensen, Kjærsdam, and Nielsen 1997)	Enabled through new national political initiatives to promote Copenhagen as a major European metropolis Combines new forms of regional planning, infrastructural investment, and place-marketing with selected institutional changes Tied to cross-border cooperative programs with Malmö and Lund (Sweden)	National Planning Strategy for Territorial Development to the Year 2018 (1992) Various 'Grand Projects' to channel infrastructural investments into the city core and strategic suburban locations (such as Ørestad) Greater Copenhagen Authority (from July 2000) Copenhagen Industrial Forum Copenhagen Capacity	Danish national government Copenhagen municipality Local and regional political elites in Copenhagen and some of its suburbs Major local, regional, and national business organizations Diverse advocates of expanded cross-border links to Malmö and Lund

Fig. 6.2D. (*continued*)

In most western European city-regions, proposals to reconfigure inherited frameworks of metropolitan governance have been justified as a means to strengthen urban locational policies by transposing them onto a regional scale. In contrast to the 1960s and 1970s, in which debates on metropolitan regionalism focused on the issues of administrative efficiency, local service

	Form of metropolitan regionalism in the 1990s	Organizational embodiment(s)	Major political-economic forces behind metropolitan regionalism
Greater Rotterdam (Hendriks and Toonen 1995; Kreukels 2003, 2000; Verges 1999)	Emerges following a failed attempt by the Dutch national government to establish a Rotterdam City-Province (1995) Promotes new forms of informal coordination among extant institutional forms and diverse public and private agencies in the Randstad's southern wing Goal is to develop a region-wide strategy of economic development and to coordinate spatial planning and infrastructural investment, particularly in the seaport zone	Rotterdam Administrative Board (OOR) (until 1996) Stadsregio Rotterdam (from 1996) Rotterdam Forum Regional Economic Board	Dutch national government Rotterdam municipality Local and regional political elites in Rotterdam and some of its suburbs Major local and regional business organizations in Rotterdam region (including seaport-related interests)
Greater Amsterdam (Salet 2003; Terhorst and van de Ven 1995; Van der veer 1997; Brenner 1999c)	Emerges following a failed attempt by the Dutch national government to establish an Amsterdam City-Province (1995) Promotes new forms of informal coordination among extant institutional forms and diverse public and private agencies in the Randstad's northern wing Aims to promote coordinated regional economic development, spatial planning, and infrastructural investment	Amsterdam Regional Agency (ROA) Amsterdam Regional Cooperation (RSA) Coordinating Commission (CoCo) Regional Economic Development Strategy (RES) Amsterdam Regional Business Platform (ORA)	Dutch national government Amsterdam municipality Local and regional political elites in Amsterdam and some of its suburbs Amsterdam chamber of commerce Other major local and regional business organizations in Greater Amsterdam

Fig. 6.2E. (*continued*)

provision, and territorial equalization, the current round of metropolitan institutional reform has been oriented towards the promotion of regional economic competitiveness in a context of intensified European interspatial competition. Metropolitan governance has thus been redefined from a vertical, coordinative, and redistributive relationship within a national administrative hierarchy into a horizontal, competitive, and developmentalist relationship between urban regions competing at European and global scales to attract external capital investment. Crucially, however, these regionalized approaches to locational policy have also entailed concerted efforts to enhance intra-regional territorial cohesion, which is now seen as a basic precondition for regional economic competitiveness. From this point of view, excessive inter-locality competition within an urban region is thought to undermine the region's capacity to compete for capital investment at supraregional scales. Region-wide forms of inter-organizational cooperation, coordination, planning, and governance are thus promoted as key components of regional economic development strategies. In essence, then, the metropolitan region-alisms of the 1990s have mobilized new forms of cooperation within urban regions as a basis for engaging still more aggressively in territorial competition against other urban regions at European and global scales (Prigge and Ronne-berger 1996). Box 6.2 presents several typical justifications for this new approach to metropolitan governance, with its combined emphasis on intra-regional political cooperation and supraregional territorial competition.

Box 6.2. Cooperation and competition in the new metropolitan regionalism

---

If the central cities agree to play the game [of metropolitan cooperation], it is because they are now aware that they need the peripheries in order to develop, or quite simply to keep their place, in the ranks of world cities [. . .] The globalization of the economy has once again meant that the economy and functional considerations are factors which make the intro-duction of metropolitan governments necessary, no longer to provide urban services, but infrastructures and facilities that a 'world' metropolis, a 'Euro-pean town', must have if it wishes to continue to play a major international role. Whether it be a question of land for facilities and housing, financial resources for building, or political agreements to bring an area-wide policy to a successful conclusion, the central cities need their peripheries to keep their place in international competition. In this respect, the metropolitan territory has become the scale on which the central cities reason. To do so, they must free themselves and go beyond their administrative limits. The metropolitan government is to them, both a necessary instrument and an advantage in attaining their objective.

(Lefèvre 1998: 22)

With the disappearance of national borders within Europe [. . .] urban regions (cities and suburbs) are competing internationally with other urban regions. This expanding scale [of competition] occurs in conjunction with a concentration and specialization of economic activities in various realms. In this context, it is of considerable importance to the Dutch econ-omy that the Dutch urban regions maintain a strong position. A unified [external] presentation and the coordination of policies on a supralocal level has a central importance in this competition.

(from a national law on metropolitan institutional
reform in the Netherlands; MBZ 1994: 10)

[One goal of regional economic strategy is] to strengthen the international business climate. The future of the region as a national gateway to the world economy depends to a large degree upon international industry. However, none of the municipalities within the region can alone maintain this international business climate. The latter is more than the sum of its parts. Therefore, mutual cooperation [among municipalities] as well as with surrounding regions within the Randstad is of major importance.

(from a draft statement of a regional economic development strategy for Greater Amsterdam, drafted by the regional association of chambers of commerce; Gemeente Amsterdam 1997: p. ii)

The European competition for capital investment intensifies the need for supramunicipal cooperation [. . .] The synergies that can be achieved through cooperation enhance the locational attractiveness of the entire region.

(from the German government's annual report on spatial planning; BMBau 1993*b*: 32)

On a European scale, not only individual cities but entire regions are competing with one another. Regional cooperation—in the areas of economic development and labor market policy, housing policy, and environmental policy—is therefore an urgent task for spatial planning in the future.

(from a law on inter-municipal cooperation in Stuttgart; quoted Scheller 1998: 14)

The municipalities of the Rhine-Main region must recognize and accept the fact that they are not competing with one another to influence the locational decisions of firms. Rather, they compete as a single region (*Gesamtraum*) with other European metropolitan locations. In the future, the region must become stronger than the sum of its municipalities in this international competition.

(statement by the Director, Department of Urban Planning, City of Frankfurt; Wentz 1994: 14)

On pain of being irrevocably outdistanced by other European urban areas, Bologna is presented as being unable to do without the Metropolitan City. Such an institution becomes a fundamental element in the economic success of international cities [. . .] Adaptation to the market is presented as inevitable [. . .] Bologna must become a hub which can withstand competition from Amsterdam, Zurich and Frankfurt.

(Jouve and Lefèvre 1997: 97)

The metropolitan reform initiatives of the 1990s have contributed to the further consolidation of RCSRs, albeit in a restructured institutional and scalar form (Fig. 6.3). Like many other post-Keynesian state spatial projects, the current round of metropolitan institutional reorganization has enhanced the regulatory significance of subnational scales of state power, while further differentiating state regulatory arrangements according to localized, place-specific political-economic conditions. Concomitantly, like many other post-Keynesian state spatial strategies, metropolitan reform initiatives have

	STATE SPATIAL PROJECTS	STATE SPATIAL STRATEGIES
SCALAR DIMENSION	Creation of new forms of state institutional organization and governance at a metropolitan scale This enhances the organizational density and regulatory responsibilities of subnational tiers of state power	New, regionally specific forms of state intervention are mobilized in order to enhance economic competitiveness and to maintain territorial cohesion within major urban regions This consolidates the role of metropolitan regions as targets and arenas for accumulation strategies.
TERRITORIAL DIMENSION	Place- and region-specific patterns of metropolitan institutional organization and economic governance are established in major urban agglomerations within each national territory This contributes to the further entrenchment of customized, place-specific institutional arrangements and regulatory configurations across each national territory	The new metropolitan regionalism promotes regionally specific development regimes oriented towards internal (interlocal) cooperation and external (interregional) competition This contributes to the further concentration of advanced socioeconomic assets and infrastructural investments within major metropolitan regions. It also contributes to a further differentiation of urban and regional developmental pathways across each national territory

Fig. 6.3. Metropolitan reform initiatives and the evolution of RCSRs

generated locally customized forms of state intervention that actively target urban regions as the geographical engines of economic development. The metropolitan reform initiatives of the 1990s have thus reinforced the major trends of state spatial restructuring that were triggered through the initial wave of urban locational policies during the preceding decade.

At the same time, much like the neighborhood-based anti-exclusion policies discussed above, metropolitan reform initiatives have contributed to at least two significant evolutionary transformations within RCSRs. First, metropolitan reform initiatives have helped consolidate the regional scale as a key focal point and target for territorial competitiveness strategies. Indeed, a key goal of newly established metropolitan institutions is to amalgamate local economies into larger, regionally configured territorial units, which are in turn promoted as integrated, competitive geographical locations for external capital investment. Urban locational policies have not been superseded by this trend, but they are increasingly being embedded within broader, metropolitan-wide approaches to economic development and territorial competitiveness. Metropolitan reform initiatives have thus established new, regionalized scalar niches and territorial enclaves for locational policies within the already differentiated subnational geographies of RCSRs. Second, by introducing new forms of regulatory coordination among the major administrative units within urban regions, metropolitan reform initiatives have attempted to counteract some of the crisis-tendencies of urban locational policies. While these new strategies of region-wide regulatory coordination have varied contextually, they have frequently been associated with territorial redistribution programs designed to minimize intra-regional sociospatial polarization; with new approaches to regional economic planning and place-marketing intended to minimize zero-sum interlocality competition within the region; and with new forms of intergovernmental cooperation and partnership oriented towards the establishment of integrated, region-wide approaches to metropolitan territorial development. Thus, like neighborhood-based anti-exclusion policies, the metropolitan reform initiatives of the 1990s have introduced an expanded approach to economic competitiveness that is attuned to the problem of maintaining territorial cohesion at a particular spatial scale. In this sense, the metropolitan regionalisms of the 1990s have promoted the regional scale not only as an institutional platform for new types of locational policy, but also as a focal point for crisis-management strategies designed to counteract the destructive intra-regional effects of such policies.

Like neighborhood-level anti-exclusion policies, metropolitan reform initiatives have added momentum to debates on the intensification of territorial inequalities within post-Keynesian western Europe, in this case at the spatial scale of entire urban regions. Despite this explicit emphasis on territorial cohesion, the consolidation of a new, metropolitan scale of regulatory activity within RCSRs has reproduced rather than alleviated the major crisis-tendencies associated with earlier forms of urban locational policy. Across national and local contexts, metropolitan reform initiatives have exacerbated the regulatory deficits of RCSRs in at least two ways. First, insofar as metropolitan reform initiatives channel institutional resources towards the mobilization of regional locational policies, they intensify interspatial competition, and thus macrogeographical instability, at supraregional scales. For, beyond their own circumscribed territorial and scalar parameters, newly established metropolitan institutions lack the regulatory capacity and political authority to counteract the destabilizing, destructive effects of locational policies. Consequently, while the new metropolitan regionalisms may provisionally ameliorate sociospatial polarization within an urban region, they share with urban locational policies the tendency to erode the socio-territorial preconditions for sustainable economic development at both national and European scales. Second, despite their attention to problems of intra-regional territorial cohesion, newly established metropolitan institutions exacerbate the coordination problems that ensue within RCSRs as subnational institutional landscapes become increasingly complex, tangled, and differentiated. Metropolitan institutional reforms may enhance intergovernmental synergies, policy coordination, and meta-governance capacities within individual urban regions, but they intensify the tendency within RCSRs to spread public funds ever more thinly among diverse, scale- and place-specific development initiatives. This increasing geographical differentiation of subnational regulatory arrangements and development regimes complicates the task of maintaining an organizationally coherent, functionally integrated and operationally unified framework for state economic intervention (Jessop, Nielsen, and Pederson 1993). It also exacerbates market failures within local economies while undercutting the capacity of state institutions, at any spatial scale, to alleviate them.

In addition to their role in aggravating the regulatory failures of inherited forms of urban locational policy, metropolitan reform initiatives generate a variety of destabilizing political conflicts and territorial fissures of their own. Particularly when powerful social and economic interests are tied closely to extant levels of state territorial organization, the project of metropolitan institutional reform generates intense struggles between opposed class fractions, political coalitions, and territorial alliances regarding issues such as jurisdictional boundaries, institutional capacities, democratic accountability, fiscal relays, and intergovernmental linkages. Relatedly, even when new frameworks of metropolitan governance are successfully established, any number of unresolved tensions permeate the project of formulating a coherent strategy of regional economic development. In most western European city-regions, the agenda of enhancing regional distinctiveness stands in tension with the perceived need to reduce production costs through regulatory downgrading and direct subsidies to capital. Meanwhile, the project of enhancing regional institutional flexibility is frequently at odds with the equally powerful need for continued fiscal support and administrative coordination from superordinate tiers of the state, including regional and national governments. The balance that obtains among these opposed regulatory priorities within a given urban region is thus a matter of intense sociopolitical contestation at a range of spatial scales (Jones 2001; Keating 1998, 1997). As such conflicts intensify, both within and beyond the urban regions in which metropolitan reform initiatives are mobilized, established patterns of economic governance may be disrupted. This may in turn destabilize the accumulation process at various spatial scales.

In sum, the metropolitan regulatory experiments that have proliferated during the 1990s appear to have differentiated the scalar architectures of RCSRs while further destabilizing urban and regional economies. As with neighborhood-based anti-exclusion policies, the scalar configuration of metropolitan reform initiatives represents, simultaneously, their basic condition of possibility and their most significant structural limitation. On the one hand, by introducing new forms of region-wide intergovernmental coordination, and thus partially counteracting the destructive consequences of unfettered interlocality competition within metropolitan regions, such experiments have begun to address a serious regulatory deficit of urban locational policies. In this manner, metropolitan reform initiatives would appear to open up new possibilities for regulatory experimentation, political compromise, and territorial redistribution at the scale of major urban regions. At the same time, these initiatives to enhance territorial cohesion within metropolitan regions have been promoted in direct conjunction with growth-driven, competitiveness-oriented, and exocentric strategies of regional economic development. Such regionalized locational policies transpose the regulatory deficits and crisis-tendencies of urban locational policies onto a larger spatial scale, rather than substantively alleviating them. In effect, the new metropolitan regionalism instrumentalizes intra-regional cooperation in order to intensify the process of interspatial competition at supraregional scales. For this reason, despite their apparently stabilizing emphasis on regional territorial cohesion, there is little evidence at the present time to suggest that recent metropolitan reform initiatives in western Europe will engender sustainable forms of economic regeneration or a less polarized pattern of territorial development, at any spatial scale, in the medium or long term.

Rescaling outward: interurban networking initiatives

Whereas recent metropolitan reform initiatives have promoted new forms of institutional coordination among geographically contiguous municipalities, there has also been an expansion of cooperative relationships among geographically noncontiguous cities and regions. In these cases, formal or informal collaborative networks have been established, generally across national borders, among cities and regions in dispersed geographical locations. Some of these new transnational interurban networks have been forged through bottom-up collaborative initiatives. However, the quantity, organizational density, and regulatory significance of interurban networks have been expanded since the early 1990s due to the facilitating role of the EU, which has provided localities with financial incentives to engage in cooperative projects. In particular, the RECITE program (Regions and Cities for Europe) was initiated in 1991 by DGXVI (the Directorate-General for Regional Policy and Cohesion) to encourage transnational interurban networking; the RECITE II framework provided a second round of EU-sponsored funding for interurban networking during the 1995–9 period.[6]

[6] The intensification of EU-sponsored and other forms of interurban networking during the last decade has been documented extensively by urban scholars. On the history of European interurban

In the western European context, interurban networks have emerged in three main forms (Benington and Harvey 1998). First, *sectoral* networks involve cooperation among localities that are specialized in similar industries and thus confronted with analogous patterns of industrial restructuring. Typical examples include EURACOM (European Action for Mining Communities), MILAN (Motor Industry Local Authority Network), and FINE (Fashion Industry Network). Second, *spatial* networks involve cooperation among similar types of cities (for instance, medium-sized cities) or among cities located in the same broad geographical context (for instance, cross-border regions, the Atlantic Arc, or the Baltic Sea region). Examples include METREX (the Network of European Metropolitan Regions and Areas) which represents metropolitan regions containing more than 500,000 inhabitants; Eurocities, which represents the major European second-tier cities; the Edge Cities Network, which represents municipalities situated on the fringes of major European urban agglomerations; the Commission des Villes, which represents small- and medium-sized European cities; and INTERREG, which represents municipalities situated in cross-border regions. Third, and partially overlapping with the aforementioned types, *thematic* networks involve cooperation among cities with reference to specific policy issues—for instance, unemployment, social welfare, poverty, or technological change. Examples of this type of interurban network include *Quartiers en Crise* (Neighborhoods in Crisis), which is concerned with the problem of urban decay and concentrated urban poverty; Telecities, which is concerned with the dissemination of telematics technology; EUROGATEWAY, which is concerned with the promotion of small business infrastructures; and POLIS, which is oriented towards the alleviation of urban traffic congestion.

As the preceding examples suggest, interurban networks have often been formed to share information and problem-solving methods among cities confronted with similar regulatory dilemmas—whether due to their industrial specializations, their spatial characteristics, their geographical locations, or their socioeconomic problems. The major aim, in these contexts, is to exchange 'best-practice experiences in order to improve the problem-solving capacity and performance in the cooperating metropolitan regions' (Heeg, Klagge, and Ossenbrügge 2003: 150). This aspect of interurban networking has contributed to a process of 'mimetic institutionalization' in which certain generic local policy frameworks, management strategies, governance practices, and place-marketing techniques have been replicated across the western European city-system (Le Galès 2002: 107–8). An additional agenda of transnational interurban networks has been to promote city-oriented lobbying activities at the European scale. The Eurocities network, which has been led

networks, see Sellers 2003. On more recent interurban networking programs, see, among other works, Benington and Harvey 1998; Dawson 1992; Parkinson 1992; Graham 1995; Heeg, Klagge, and Ossenbrügge 2003, 2000; Lavergne and Mollet 1991; Leitner 2004; Leitner and Sheppard 2002; Leitner, Pavlik, and Sheppard 2002; and Phelps, McNeill, and Parsons 2002.

by prominent political officials in many of Europe's largest cities, has played a significant role in influencing the development of EU urban policy since the late 1980s. Other, more specialized interurban networks have likewise attempted to pool local resources in order to attract EU funding and to influence specific aspects of European governance. Finally, the European Commission has supported networks in order to further its own policy goals. As Leitner, Pavlik, and Sheppard (2002: 293–4) explain:

The stated goals of [interurban] networks promoted by the Directorate-General for Regional Policy and Cohesion are as follows: improving local response to challenges posed by an increasingly European and global economy; achieving a more efficient use of resources; facilitating the spread of innovative practices in economic development; and strengthening economic and social cohesion [...] These goals match and mirror larger EU policy concerns, namely: enhancing economic growth and the competitiveness of European cities and regions; reducing waste of public resources resulting from competitive bidding of cities for businesses and investment; and developing best practices for economic development, while at the same time reducing economic and social disparities within the EU territory.

In many cases, moreover, interurban networks are viewed both by municipalities and by the European Commission as a means to circumvent national governments in pursuit of their own regulatory agendas. Thus, through such networks, European municipalities attempt to establish transnational lobbying platforms without directly involving their respective national governments. Concomitantly, the European Commission attempts to capitalize upon such networks in order to influence local development outcomes without the direct mediation of national state institutions (Leitner, Pavlik, and Sheppard 2002). Box 6.3 presents brief excerpts from the mission statements of several prominent European interurban networks; these are intended to illustrate the diversity of political concerns that have been articulated through such networks, as well as some of their shared regulatory goals in a European and global context.

Interurban networking initiatives have contributed, in distinctive ways, to the consolidation and evolution of RCSRs. As state spatial projects, interurban networking initiatives have extended the role of localized, territorially customized, and place-specific regulatory arrangements within RCSRs. Meanwhile, as state spatial strategies, interurban networks have provided municipalities with additional institutional capacities through which to promote local economic development within their boundaries, as well as to influence EU-level funding streams and policy frameworks. In these ways, much like neighborhood-based anti-exclusion policies and metropolitan reform programs, interurban networking initiatives have further enhanced the significance of urban regions as arenas for regulatory experimentation and accumulation strategies within RCSRs (Fig. 6.4, p. 291). However, as Fig. 6.4 also indicates, interurban networking initiatives have modified the inherited institutional and scalar architectures of RCSRs in several ways.

Box 6.3. Interurban networking initiatives: selected western European examples

Economic interaction, the exchange of best practice policy and resource lobbying has, in recent years, led to inter-urban co-operation and an explosion of interest and participation in networks of cities throughout Europe. These institutionalised urban 'clubs' often aim to subdue the increasing intensity of city rivalry by stimulating collaboration rather than competition.

(Dawson 1992: 7)

Networks provide an alternative route for exploration which may soften the economic fragmentation and social polarisation which derive from the crude dictates of 'marketised' territorial competition.

(Graham 1995: 518)

METREX—The Network of European Metropolitan Regions and Areas

(*Source*: http://www.eurometrex.org)

METREX is a Network of practitioners—that is, politicians, officials and their advisers—with a common interest in spatial planning and development at the metropolitan level. The twin purposes of the Network:

- to promote the exchange of knowledge between practitioners on strategic issues of common interest.
- to contribute to the metropolitan dimension to planning at the European level.

EUROCITIES

(*Source*: http://www.eurocities.org)

EUROCITIES wants to ensure that urban affairs are placed high on the European Union's policy agenda: Most decisions taken at EU level affect cities and their citizens. We take the lead to make their voices heard.

- EUROCITIES wants to promote transnational cooperation projects between its member cities across Europe: we facilitate their coordination and help provide access to EU-funding.
- EUROCITIES wants to foster a networking spirit amongst Europe's large cities: whilst having different cultural, socio-economic and political realities they share common challenges and solutions. We encourage our members to exchange their expertise, and to be proactive in shaping national and EU policy.

Quartiers en Crise / Neighborhoods in Crisis

(*Source*: http://www.styrax.com/demons/ QECOnline/en/index_html)

Quartiers en Crise is a network of towns promoting the integrated approach to the revitalisation of disadvantaged areas, with the involvement of politicians, technicians and local residents in that process. Its objectives are 'to further ... local and national policies and initiatives for the regeneration of neighbourhoods in crisis, in particular through the promotion and dissemination, in cities, regions, States and the European Commission, of methodologies for integrated urban social development'.

European Edge Cities Network

(*Source*: http://www.edgecities.com/)

The Edge Cities Network [. . .] brings together towns and cities on the edge of the major capitals of Europe. These municipal authorities have all identified that they face common economic and social challenges due to their location. The Partners have been collaborating to exchange knowledge, ideas and experience in addressing these challenges, including joint projects and activities.

POLIS (Cities and regions networking for innovative transport solutions)

(*Source*: http://www.polis-online.org/)

The primary objective of Polis is to support European cities and regions in improving quality of life through innovative measures for reducing congestion, enhancing safety, lowering polluting emissions, and offering better and equal access to transport services. Polis aims to foster co-operation and partnership across Europe, to make research and innovation accessible to cities and regions, to represent the voice of cities and regions at EU level, and to provide decision-makers appropriate information and tools for the development of sustainable mobility.

TELECITIES

(*Source*: http://www.telecities.org)

TeleCities is the major European network of cities committed to leadership in the Information and Knowledge Society [. . .] TeleCities is open to democratically elected city governments as well as to business and scientific partners. TeleCities provides a platform of over 100 local authorities from 20 different European countries, sharing experience and developing practical solutions achieving an Inclusive Information and Knowledge Society, both at European and local level. Its aim is to promote 'eCitizenship' at local level to ensure that all citizens can equally gain from the benefits of the Information and Knowledge Society. To achieve this aim, TeleCities actively works for its members to:

- Influence the European Agenda to ensure that the interests of cities are taken into account in policy making
- Foster exchange of experience and knowledge transfer amongst cities. Co-operation and networking with South European and CEE cities is also pursued to contribute to the enlargement goals of the European Union
- Inform members on policies, programmes and initiatives at EU and local level
- Facilitate and support the development of EU funded projects relevant to the members and the network.

Websites accessed 17 Feb. 2004.

First, rather than focusing upon the territorial competitiveness of a single, circumscribed urban or metropolitan location, interurban networking initiatives promote an entire network of cities over and against 'less "networked" neighbors' (Phelps, McNeill, and Parsons 2002: 214). In this manner, such initiatives introduce a more complex spatial referent—a flexible, multinodal network rather than a self-enclosed urban or metropolitan area—in terms of

	STATE SPATIAL PROJECTS	STATE SPATIAL STRATEGIES
SCALAR DIMENSION	Creation of new, transnational networks of interurban cooperation among groups of European cities confronting similar problems This extends the decentralization and localization of state space, while also enhancing the organizational density and regulatory significance of interlocal linkages across national borders	Newly established interurban networks provide municipalities with new institutional capacities through which to promote local economic development within their boundaries, to acquire EU funding, and to influence EU policies This further enhances the role of cities as targets and arenas for accumulation strategies
TERRITORIAL DIMENSION	The institutional structure of each interurban network is customized according to the priorities of its local participants. This facilitates the consolidation of customized, place-specific regulatory arrangements across each national territory The proliferation of crossborder, interurban linkages tends to puncture inherited, territorialized political geographies. As multiple, horizontally articulated interurban networks crosscut each national territory, the institutional architecture of RCSRs is further differentiated	Interurban networking initiatives contribute to the establishment of place- and jurisdiction-specific regulatory enclaves within European cities. This contributes to the further divergence of local and regional developmental pathways across each national territory Interurban networking initiatives also generate new geographies of territorial competition within RCSRs: competition among individual cities is now paralleled by competition among multinodal, interurban networks. This re-inforces the institutionalized promotion of uneven spatial development and territorial competition within RCSRs

Fig. 6.4. Interurban networking initiatives and the evolution of RCSRs

which territorial competitiveness is to be promoted. Under these circumstances, 'Competition is not eliminated [. . .] but is simply shifted to a higher spatial scale. It is no longer single cities and regions, but networks of cities and regions, that promote their economic development interests and compete with one another' (Leitner and Sheppard 1999: 240). Interurban networking initiatives have thus superimposed a new, horizontally articulated framework for the mobilization of urban locational policies upon the vertically rescaled institutional hierarchies of RCSRs.

Second, like neighborhood-based anti-exclusion programs and metropolitan reform projects, interurban networking initiatives have partially modified the entrepreneurial, competition-based model of urban governance that prevails within RCSRs. In the case of interurban networks, the goal is not to alleviate social exclusion within disadvantaged neighborhoods, or to enhance territorial cohesion at the scale of metropolitan regions, but rather, to establish cooperative institutional linkages among groups of cities dispersed across the European urban system. In this context, information pooling, cost sharing, joint lobbying, collaborative planning, and the dissemination of 'best practices' are viewed as a means to enhance the economic development capacities and geopolitical weight of the network as a whole, while counteracting some of the destabilizing, spatially polarizing consequences of previous approaches to urban locational policy. A major agenda of these cooperative interurban networks, then, is to soften the cut-throat, 'beggar-thy-neighbor' form of interspatial competition that has dominated RCSRs since their initial consolidation in the 1980s. Interurban networks pursue this goal by introducing cooperation-based interlocal relays into the volatile, spatially polarized urban landscapes of the post-Keynesian period.

Third, interurban networks have superimposed a new, horizontally articulated pattern of governance onto the splintered political geographies of RCSRs. The geographical configuration of RCSRs was defined above with reference to the rescaling of inherited national state spaces in conjunction with broader processes of scale relativization. While interurban networks have contributed to this rescaling of statehood, they have also modified the territorial framework within which this process has been unfolding. Interurban networks are scalar insofar as they are premised upon scaled units (in this case, cities) that are interconnected at a broader spatial scale (in this case, that of the western European urban system, or some part thereof). However, in contrast to territorialized regulatory forms, which assert control over political space by enclosing it within delineated boundaries, networked forms of governance are premised upon the attempt to 'span space' by establishing horizontal interlinkages among geographically dispersed nodal points (Leitner 2004: 248). The geographies of networks thus 'tend to leapfrog over space, connecting spatially separated territorial units as members of a network of interaction and exchange' (Leitner, Pavlik, and Sheppard 2002: 297). Moreover, while political territoriality is grounded upon relatively stable jurisdictional boundaries, 'the spatial surface spanned by networks is [...] fluid and unstable' insofar as (*a*) the degree of connectivity among network nodes may fluctuate; (*b*) patterns of network membership may fluctuate; and (*c*) multiple networks may overlap, interpenetrate, and crosscut one another (Leitner 2004: 248–9). In light of these distinctive features of networked forms of governance, interurban and otherwise, it is evident that their proliferation within the institutional landscapes of RCSRs has entailed the insertion of a qualitatively new dimension into inherited geographies of state regulation. In effect, interurban networks have opened up an additional parameter of state space—defined by nodal connectivity rather than by territorial enclosure or interscalar articulation—within which state spatial projects and state spatial strategies may be articulated. Contrary to some scholarly predictions (e.g. Castells 2004), networked forms of governance appear unlikely, at the present time, to supersede the territorialized institutional architecture of modern statehood. Nonetheless, governance networks are arguably being embedded within territorialized political spaces, and intermeshed with ongoing rescaling processes, in increasingly complex, conflictual, and contradictory ways (Ansell 2000; Leitner and Sheppard 2002). For this reason, the proliferation of networked approaches to urban governance represents an important evolutionary development within the political geographies of RCSRs.[7]

Like neighborhood-based anti-exclusion initiatives and metropolitan reform projects, interurban networking initiatives may be interpreted as political responses to the uncertain geoeconomic conditions and unstable regulatory landscapes in which contemporary European cities are situated. Because interurban networks are grounded upon cooperative institutional relays, they would appear to disrupt the ruthlessly competitive logic of post-Keynesian urban governance and, more generally, to provide a political opening for the establishment of a less polarizing formation of state spatial regulation. In practice, however, such interpretations amount to a 'triumph of hope over experience' (Dawson 1992: 9). For, as with neighborhood-based anti-exclusion programs and metropolitan reform projects, the distinctive scalar configuration of interurban networks systematically limits their capacity to transform the interscalar rule-regimes upon which RCSRs are grounded. The central problem, in this context, is that interurban networks modify the geographical structure of territorial competition, but do little to alleviate its polarizing, destructive socioeconomic consequences (Leitner and Sheppard 1999: 240). Indeed, despite their internally cooperative institutional logic, many networking initiatives have generated a *de facto* intensification of territorial

---

[7] I am not suggesting that networked forms of urban governance did not exist prior to the current period. On the contrary, the Hanseatic League, the World Association of Cities and Local Authorities, and the Federation of United Cities represent only a few among many interesting examples of interurban networks that emerged during previous phases of capitalist development (Sellers 2003). My claim here, rather, is that the organizational density and regulatory significance of interurban networks have markedly intensified in contemporary western Europe due to ongoing processes of scale-relativization and state rescaling. The relationship between contemporary interurban networks and the restructuring of political space in western Europe has been analyzed with considerable theoretical sophistication by Leitner 2004; Leitner, Pavlik, and Sheppard 2002; and Leitner and Sheppard 2002, 1999. Further consideration of networked forms of state spatial regulation would complicate the analytical grids depicted in Figs. 3.9, 3.10, and 3.11 (pp. 97, 102, and 104): it would entail the addition of a third axis on which state spatial projects and state spatial strategies could be articulated, defined by the broad parameters within which 'reticulation' processes (as opposed to territorialization processes and scaling processes) evolve. The concept of reticulation was suggested by Bob Jessop (personal communication).

competition by transposing urban locational policies onto the larger scale of interurban networks. In this manner, the regulatory failures and crisis-tendencies of such policies are upscaled onto a new institutional-geographical matrix rather than being alleviated.

These destabilizing, polarizing tendencies within interurban networking initiatives may in turn generate additional regulatory deficits. First, even within interurban networks that are not oriented directly towards economic development, cooperative impulses may be undermined due to 'hidden competition between internal members and between members and nonmembers' (Graham 1995: 520). To the extent that cities are embedded within a Europe-wide interscalar rule-regime in which territorial competition has been pervasively institutionalized, cooperative interurban initiatives will continue to rest upon tenuous foundations. Second, the transnational diffusion of 'best practices' in urban governance via interurban networks may unsettle rather than rejuvenate the process of urban development. The prospect of gaining access to the 'best practices' of public administration, place-marketing, and socioeconomic policy may offer a glimmer of hope to many municipal governments that are confronted with deeply rooted fiscal, economic, and social crises. However, such urban policy prototypes are often derived from apparent local 'success stories' that are extremely difficult, if not impossible, to replicate in other institutional and geographical settings. Consequently, interurban networks may serve less as a basis for enhancing territorial solidarity among cities, than as a mechanism of 'fast policy transfer' that homogenizes urban governance repertoires according to a narrowly market-based, neoliberal logic (Leitner and Sheppard 2002; Peck 2002; Peck and Theodore 2001).

In sum, despite their apparently stabilizing emphasis on cooperation, inter-urban networking initiatives have not, in practice, generated an alternative basis for urban governance that transcends the competitive logic of urban locational policies. While interurban networking initiatives have facilitated the insertion of a new, cooperation-based layer of state regulatory activities and governance practices into RCSRs, they have simultaneously reinforced a Europe-wide interscalar rule-regime grounded upon the pervasive institutionalization of interspatial competition and unfettered uneven development. At the present time, therefore, interurban networking initiatives operate primarily to rescale the regulatory deficits and crisis-tendencies of previous forms of urban locational policy.

Concluding reflections on the future(s) of new state spaces: from a second- to a third-cut interpretation of RCSRs?

> The 'future of space' [...] must be understood in terms of both worldwide social evolution [...] and also the manner in which existent space already limits and conditions that social evolution. The relationship between space and the social process is thus the central outstanding illustration of Marx's thesis, constant from the *Theses on Feuerbach* through the *18th Brumaire*, and according to which: mankind makes its own history, but on the basis of what is inherited from the past [...] The 'future of space' is not a simple projection mapped by the future of society. Society will evolve and recreate itself only because it is already rooted and made material in terrain: it already exists as a form of territory. Human space is therefore a constraint for future society (as well as a starting point for it). The contradictions between these *existing spaces* (between those forming civilization materially as we know it today) and those *'projected spaces'* (the materialization of development models competing for the future) will also have to be regulated.
>
> Alain Lipietz (1992a: 104–5; italics added)

The concept of the Rescaled Competition State Regime (RCSR) was introduced at the outset of this chapter to synthesize this book's major arguments—it served as our first-cut interpretation of the transformed form of statehood in contemporary western Europe. The analysis of alternative rescaling strategies developed in the preceding sections complicates and differentiates that first-cut characterization. For, as this discussion has revealed, RCSRs are unstable, dynamically evolving institutional and scalar configurations: they are premised upon state spatial projects and state spatial strategies that engender disruptive, dysfunctional consequences, at various geographical scales, for processes of accumulation and regulation. However, rather than signaling their imminent collapse, the regulatory deficits and crisis-tendencies within RCSRs serve as a powerful impetus for their further institutional and scalar evolution. It is in this context that the three alternative rescaling strategies examined in this chapter must be understood. Neighborhood-based anti-exclusion policies, metropolitan reform initiatives, and interurban network-ing programs can be interpreted as attempts to alleviate some of the major regulatory failures of RCSRs—in significant measure through a further rescal-ing of inherited approaches to urban locational policy. In this manner, each of these political strategies has helped to catalyze a further round of state rescaling in which new, tangled scalar layerings of institutional organization and regulatory experimentation have been superimposed upon the already extensively scale-differentiated political geographies of RCSRs. It is the consolidation of these new layers of crisis-management mechanisms within European cities and regions that necessitates a second-cut interpretation of

	Neighborhood-based anti-exclusion policies	Metropolitan reform initiatives	Interurban networking programs
Political and institutional animateurs	European Commission; national, regional, and local state institutions; community-based associations	Selected national governments; regional growth coalitions; selected municipal governments; local and regional chambers of commerce	European Commission; local state institutions; local growth coalitions
Geographical targets	Disadvantaged, marginalized neighborhoods	The regional or metropolitan scale of large urban agglomerations	Major European cities or selected parts thereof, interlinked via horizontal networks
Implications for urban governance	Channels fiscal resources into disadvantaged neighborhoods and establishes new, area-based partnerships: goal is to combat social exclusion and to enhance socio-territorial cohesion at an urban scale	Establishes new, region-wide forms of metropolitan institutional organization and regulatory coordination: goals are to prevent zero-sum interlocality competition within an urban region, to establish regionally coordinated economic development strategies, and to enhance socio-territorial cohesion at a metropolitan scale	Establishes new forms of cooperation among cities that share common concerns: goals are to promote information sharing, to disseminate knowledge about 'best practices' for urban governance, to influence EU urban and regional policies, and to acquire EU funding for local initiatives. These are viewed, cumulatively, as a means to enhance the economic development capacities of network members

Fig. 6.5A. Alternative rescaling strategies and the 'second-cut' interpretation of RCSRs: synthesis

RCSRs, which at once builds upon and extends the first-cut interpretation introduced previously. Figure 6.5 (pp. 296–8) synthesizes the key elements of this second-cut interpretation of RCSRs.

The point of this second-cut interpretation is not to suggest that these alternative rescaling strategies have effectively resolved the contradictions of urban locational policies. On the contrary, as the bottom row of Fig. 6.5C indicates (p. 298), these rescaling strategies have altered the political geographies of crisis formation within cities and regions, but without eradicating the underlying sources of economic instability and regulatory failure within RCSRs. For this reason, the proliferation of alternative rescaling strategies during the last decade must be viewed as a symptom of continued institutional and spatial disorder within RCSRs, rather than as embryonic evidence for their

	Neighborhood-based anti-exclusion policies	Metropolitan reform initiatives	Interurban networking programs
Implications for uneven spatial development	May partially alleviate uneven spatial development among neighborhoods within major urban areas: disadvantaged zones are provided with new public resources for addressing localized social problems	May partially alleviate uneven spatial development among major cities and towns within large urban agglomerations: zero-sum forms of inter-locality competition are discouraged; in some cases, intra-regional redistributive mechanisms are introduced	May partially alleviate uneven spatial development within the European urban system: informal and/or formal cooperative relays are established among localities that otherwise compete directly for external capital investment and public funds
Implications for state spatial selectivity	Establishes new, hyper-localized scalar niches and territorial enclaves within RCSRs: this further consolidates the splintering of state space induced through the previous round of state rescaling This also entails the creation of new, intra-urban redistributive relays within the already differentiated geographies of RCSRs	Establishes new regionalized scalar niches and territorial enclaves within RCSRs: this further consolidates the splintering of state space induced through the previous round of state rescaling This also entails the creation of new, regionally focused but place-specific forms of locational policy and political-economic coordination within the already differentiated geographies of RCSRs	Establishes new interlocal policy networks throughout the European state system: this further consolidates the role of localized, customized, and place-specific policy regimes and institutional forms within RCSRs The transnational, cross-border expansion of horizontal linkages among local political institutions also contributes to the puncturing of inherited, nationalized formations of state territoriality

Fig. 6.5B. (*continued*)

tendential stabilization. Indeed, the increasingly haphazard displacement of persistent governance problems among the different scalar units and territorial niches within RCSRs further exacerbates the crisis-tendencies of urban locational policies. This new scalar politics of crisis-displacement may also contribute to an exhaustion of policy repertoires in which state institutions recycle ineffectual regulatory methods, often cloaked in optimistic predictions of an imminent 'urban renaissance', in a vain effort to maintain political legitimacy and social control within their territorial jurisdictions, even in the absence of sustainable forms of economic development.

	Neighborhood-based anti-exclusion policies	Metropolitan reform initiatives	Interurban networking programs
Major regulatory deficits and crisis-tendencies	Addresses the problem of territorial inequality within specific urban zones, while neglecting the supralocal scales on which such inequalities are generated. Social problems may thus be spatially redistributed among different neighborhoods within an urban region rather than being alleviated Affirms the growth-first logic of urban locational policy insofar as anti-exclusion policies are justified with reference to the goal of enhancing local competitiveness Thus, while these policy initiatives directly address one of the major regulatory deficits of urban locational policies, they reproduce the broader interscalar framework within which such deficits are generated	The institutional form and political content of metropolitan governance are an object and stake of intense conflicts at various spatial scales of state power. Such conflicts may undermine the capacity of metropolitan institutions to confront region-wide political-economic problems Focuses on the problem of territorial inequality within metropolitan regions, but affirms the logic of interspatial competition at inter-regional scales The limitations and crisis-tendencies of urban locational policy are thus transposed onto a larger spatial scale rather than being alleviated. For this reason, metropolitan reform projects reinforce the competition-based, growth-driven interscalar rule-regime of the post-1980s period	Introduces new forms of cooperation within the European urban system, but interurban networks are still instrumentalized to enhance the competitive positions of network members The units of interspatial competition are thus altered—from individual cities to interurban networks—but the large-scale patterns of sociospatial polarization generated by that competition are not addressed The limitations and crisis-tendencies of urban locational policy are thus transposed onto large-scale interurban networks rather than being alleviated. For this reason, interurban networking initiatives reinforce the competition-based, growth-driven interscalar rule-regime of the post-1980s period

Fig. 6.5C. (*continued*)

The reinvigorated concern with territorial cohesion and interscalar cooperation in many European city-regions has been intertwined with a widespread 'depoliticization of previously contested economic policy fields' under the current global regime of 'roll-out' neoliberalism (Tickell and Peck 2003: 177). Consequently, the question of whether, and in what form, urban locational policies should be mobilized is increasingly positioned 'off-limits' to political debate; it is thereby 'dissociated' (Keil 1998*b*) from other, more explicitly contested aspects of urban policy. In this manner, the putative need for

growth-first, competitiveness-oriented approaches to local economic development has acquired 'the privileged status of a taken-for-granted or foundational
policy orientation' (Peck and Tickell 2003: 42). Each of the three alternative
rescaling strategies discussed in this chapter has contributed to this depoliticization of urban locational policy: each treats urban economic development
as a technocratic matter to be managed by local, regional, or national political-
economic elites, while refocusing mainstream political debate on the question
of how to manage the polarizing socioeconomic consequences of the new
interspatial competition. The neighborhood, the metropolitan region, and
the interurban network are thus promoted as privileged scalar and institutional
arenas in which the regulatory dislocations of contemporary capitalism may be
alleviated—even as uneven development is further institutionalized in a realm
of post-Keynesian statecraft that has been, for the moment at least, insulated
from direct political contestation. By presenting the erosion of territorial cohesion within European city-regions as an ineluctable consequence of global
economic forces, such crisis-management strategies help conceal the continued culpability of (rescaled) state institutions in generating the very regulatory dislocations they have ostensibly been mobilized to resolve.[8]

This bleak scenario of unfettered interlocality competition, rising levels of
sociospatial polarization, and deepening macroeconomic instability was an-
ticipated at the outset of Ch. 5, with reference to Petrella's (2000) pessimistic
vision of an 'Archipelago Europe' and Veltz's (1996) analogous notion of an
'archipelago economy'. At this stage of our analysis, it has become apparent
that the geographies of the contemporary archipelago economy have been
produced not only through worldwide processes of industrial restructuring,
financial speculation, and corporate reorganization, but also through concerted *political strategies* that have actively promoted and institutionalized
uneven development at all spatial scales. The more recent crystallization of
second-cut RCSRs has reinforced, not counteracted, this regressive politics of
uneven development within Archipelago Europe.

We thus arrive at the following result: despite their destabilizing consequences for accumulation and regulation, RCSRs have continued to develop
along evolutionary pathways that reinforce the primacy of urban locational
policies and, by implication, unfettered interspatial competition, in the institutional dynamics of urban governance. Processes of regulatory experimentation, institutional searching, and scalar reorganization continue unabated
within RCSRs, triggered through the very crisis-tendencies they have generated within local, regional, and national economies. Yet, even as their institutional and scalar architectures continue to evolve, RCSRs currently appear to
be 'locked in' to developmental trajectories that do not, and arguably cannot,

---

[8] For an elaboration of this line of analysis, in various institutional and geographical contexts see,
among other works, Keil 1998*b*; Peck and Tickell 2002; Tickell and Peck 2003; Swyngedouw, Moulaert, and Rodriguez 2003, 2002; Swyngedouw 2000*a, b*; and Brenner and Theodore 2002*b*.

engender either a sustainable regime of economic growth or a territorially cohesive framework of political regulation at any spatial scale.[9]

What are the prospects that this apparent evolutionary lock-in of urban locational policies, and their associated crisis-tendencies, might be broken or at least loosened? How might the trajectories of state spatial restructuring in contemporary western Europe be rechanneled to facilitate the creation of alternative political-economic geographies, at both urban and supra-urban scales, grounded upon more progressive objectives such as territorial redistribution, democratic empowerment, and sociospatial justice? These questions must lie at the heart of any third-cut analysis of RCSRs. Our first-cut account of RCSRs explored their initial consolidation following the crisis of spatial Keynesianism; our second-cut analysis of RCSRs underscored their regulatory deficits and crisis-tendencies, and traced their subsequent institutional and scalar evolution. Building upon these mappings, the central task for a third-cut analysis of RCSRs is to explore the possibility that urban policy—and more generally, political strategies to regulate uneven development—might be fundamentally transformed so as to contribute to the establishment of a more stable, cohesive, democratic, and socially just interscalar rule-regime.

In light of the foregoing analysis of state spatial restructuring, the prospects for such an evolutionary transformation—and thus, for a third-cut analysis of RCSRs—may appear limited at the present time. However, as Peck (2002) cautions, the continued reproduction of regressive regulatory arrangements and political-economic geographies should not be misconstrued as evidence for their structural stability. On the contrary, contemporary 'networks of interscalar regulatory relations are more fragile than they may seem at first, being partly designed to mystify and obfuscate the regime's serial vulnerability to local policy failure and the continuing political culpability of national states' (Peck 2002: 357). It is crucial, therefore, for progressive political forces to demarcate the institutional arenas, territorial niches, and policy relays within the current interscalar rule-regime in which hegemonic control

---

[9] Although it is not possible to develop this argument here, this situation could be plausibly explained through the principle of 'increasing returns', as developed in the literature on path-dependence in technological and institutional development (Arthur 1994; North 1990; Pierson 2000). According to Pierson (2000: 252), increasing returns ensue when 'the *relative* benefits of the current activity compared with other possible options increase over time'; concomitantly, 'the costs of exit—of switching to some previously plausible alternative—rise'. I would argue that the evolutionary development of RCSRs during the last two decades represents an excellent illustration of this principle. In this case, a sub-optimal institutional configuration has been maintained because, under geoeconomic conditions in which urban locational policies have been diffused ever more broadly, it is considered more effective to maintain them, even as their regulatory deficits and dysfunctional consequences have become increasingly manifest. Concomitantly, the perceived costs of abandoning urban locational policies are considered to rise prohibitively as they have been adopted ever more pervasively across the western European urban system (see Leitner and Sheppard 1998). A more systematic elaboration of this type of 'increasing returns' argument, with specific reference to the emergence and consolidation of RCSRs, could help explain how and why, as Peck and Tickell (2002: 46) have noted, 'The logic of interurban competition [. . .] turns cities into accomplices of their own subordination.'

appears weakest, and therefore, most vulnerable to being captured and re-shaped through counterhegemonic initiatives.

In this context, it is also worth recalling the strategic-relational conceptual-ization of institutional change upon which this analysis of state spatial re-structuring has been grounded. From this point of view, even though the process of state spatial restructuring is path-dependent, and thus susceptible to the tendency towards institutional lock-in, inherited regulatory geograph-ies cannot fully determine the shape of newly emergent regulatory strategies. Indeed, inherited formations of state spatiality may be qualitatively rearticu-lated as new layerings of state spatial projects and state spatial strategies are superimposed upon them (see Fig. 3.13, p. 109). A key task, therefore, for progressive political alliances is to locate strategic openings within the insti-tutional landscapes of RCSRs in which to launch 'path-shaping' regulatory initiatives (Nielson, Jessop, and Hausner 1995). In order to counteract the regulatory deficits and crisis-tendencies within RCSRs, such path-shaping ini-tiatives would need to mobilize *upscaled*, *recentralized* state spatial projects and state spatial strategies, and thus to promote the establishment of a reinvented 'big government' committed to the pursuit of sociospatial justice at all geo-graphical scales (Lake 2002).[10]

As our discussion of recent policy initiatives to combat social exclusion and to enhance territorial cohesion in European city-regions has indicated, many political projects that are ostensibly oriented towards such institutional alter-natives may be assimilated into the very interscalar rule-regimes they were intended to challenge. Yet, even if such path-shaping regulatory initiatives are constrained by inherited institutional configurations, they may still be har-nessed, at minimum, to expose the regressive social consequences of contem-porary spatial policies. Building upon this role, if they can be still further channeled towards a *repoliticization* of urban economic development in any local, regional, or national context, contemporary European debates on social exclusion and territorial cohesion may help to lay the foundations for a broader challenge to urban locational policies. For this reason, notwithstand-ing the pessimistic interpretation developed previously, neighborhood-based anti-exclusion policies, metropolitan reform initiatives, and interurban net-working programs may contain untapped progressive political potential.

Beyond the sphere of urban governance on which this book has focused, the European Commission represents another vibrant institutional arena in which

---

[10] Even if such a transformation of statehood were successfully accomplished, the endemic problem of uneven spatial development would presumably generate new regulatory failures and crisis-tendencies, leading to further rounds of regulatory experimentation and state spatial restruc-turing. The point of exploring the possibility for a third-cut transformation of RCSRs, therefore, is not to suggest that the problem of uneven development—or, for that matter, the basic tension between deterritorialization and reterritorialization—could ever be transcended within a capitalist space-economy. Rather, in pursuing this somewhat speculative line of analysis, my intention is to consider the possibility that these endemic regulatory problems might be confronted through more progressive political strategies than those which currently prevail in the western European context.

potentially transformative, path-shaping regulatory experiments have been emerging. Here, too, however, the project of challenging the predominant, competition-based interscalar rule-regime is permeated by deep ambiguities. As we have seen, the process of European integration (and, more recently, that of eastward enlargement) has been grounded upon an orthodox neoliberal agenda that has institutionalized market-based territorial competition, across the European space-economy, at all geographical scales (Agnew 2001; Gill 1998*a*). Nonetheless, from the early 1990s, the European Commission has also attempted to strengthen several policy programs that are ostensibly oriented towards the goal of enhancing territorial cohesion. In particular, the Structural Funds have allotted considerable financial resources towards the promotion of economic development in disadvantaged, marginalized cities and regions among the EU member states. Concomitantly, in 1999, the newly introduced European Spatial Development Perspective (ESDP) embraced the goal of promoting a balanced, polycentric pattern of spatial development across the entire EU. In practice, however, neither of these EU spatial policies has posed much of a threat to the prevalent competition-based, competitiveness-oriented model of European interscalar relations and territorial development.

• Despite their emphasis on the need for territorial cohesion, the Structural Funds have been aligned more closely with the 'supply-side orientation of the neo-liberal orthodoxy' (Amin and Tomaney 1995*a*: 177). Rather than guaranteeing socioeconomic resources and automatic fiscal transfers to marginalized regions, this program has attempted to upgrade local industrial infrastructures so that even the most peripheralized zones within the EU may be equipped to compete effectively within particular niches of the global economy and the Single European Market (Amin and Tomaney 1995*b*). This orientation has been further entrenched through Agenda 2000, which has revised the eligibility criteria for financial assistance under the Structural Funds in preparation for eastward enlargement.

• A directly analogous conclusion may be derived from the ESDP which, despite its much-publicized embrace of polycentricity, proposes to differentiate European economic space among various 'global economic integration zones' anchored by internationally competitive metropolitan regions (Map 6.1). The project of promoting polycentric territorial development is thus designed not to redistribute socioeconomic assets towards structurally disadvantaged areas, but to position European local and regional economies strategically in the competitive worldwide race to attract external capital investment (S. Krätke 2001; Atkinson 2001; Waterhout 2002).

Consequently, neither the Structural Funds nor the ESDP can be construed as genuinely compensatory, territorially redistributive policy instruments, in the classical sense associated with postwar spatial Keynesianism. Rather, like the alternative rescaling strategies discussed earlier in this chapter, the Structural Funds and the ESDP serve to reinforce the supply-side, competition-based

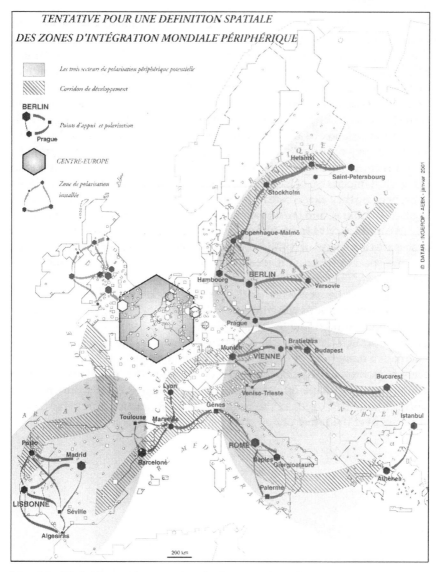

Map 6.1. 'Global integration zones' in the European Spatial Development Perspective: a basis for 'polycentric' development?

Source: Waterhout (2002: 98).

logic of locational policy, in this case at both European and regional scales. They thus provide an additional set of examples in which apparently transformative, path-shaping policy innovations, oriented towards territorially redistributive goals, function not as a counterbalance to locational policies, but rather as an instrument for their further entrenchment.

In sum, while a variety of recent regulatory experiments appear to point beyond the currently dominant interscalar framework of institutionalized uneven development, none have succeeded, in practice, in loosening, much less transcending, the persistent lock-in of locational policies, either within or beyond cities. Meanwhile, the regulatory deficits and crisis-tendencies of such policies persist, causing the landscape of contemporary statehood to be still further rescaled, reterritorialized, redifferentiated—and destabilized. This is the central paradox of the new state spaces we have explored in this study. Insofar as they continually assimilate alternative, opposing political projects, RCSRs seem to permit no alternative; they demand compliance to the grim categorical imperative of globalizing capitalism, 'Compete or die'. At the same time, because they exacerbate rather than alleviate the economic dislocations, regulatory failures, and territorial inequalities of post-Keynesian urbanization, RCSRs cannot survive in their current institutional and scalar forms. New state spaces are thus spaces of conflict, crisis, and contradiction; for this reason, they are also spaces of incessant regulatory experimentation and dynamic institutional searching.

It remains to be seen whether the process of state spatial restructuring in European urban regions will continue to institutionalize a regressive politics of unfettered territorial inequality and sociospatial polarization, or whether—perhaps through the dislocations and crisis-tendencies we have explored—an alternative framework of interscalar rules, based upon a substantive commitment to territorial redistribution and sociospatial justice, might eventually be established. The shape of a third-cut interpretation of RCSRs thus remains open. It must be forged, in the realm of political practice, through ongoing struggles over the future of new state spaces.

REFERENCES

Abu-Lughod, J. (1999) *New York, Chicago, Los Angeles: America's Global Cities*. Minneapolis: University of Minnesota Press.

Agnew, J. (2001) How many Europes? The European Union, eastward enlargement and uneven development, *European Urban and Regional Studies*, 8, 1, 29–38.

—— (1997) The dramaturgy of horizons: geographical scale in the 'reconstruction of Italy' by the new Italian political parties, 1992–1995, *Political Geography*, 16/2: 99–121.

—— (1995) The hidden geographies of social science and the myth of the 'geographic turn', *Environment and Planning D: Society and Space*, 13: 378–80.

—— (1994) The territorial trap: the geographical assumptions of international relations theory, *Review of International Political Economy*, 1/1: 53–80.

—— (1993) Representing space: space, scale and culture in social science. In J. Duncan and D. Ley, eds., *Place/Culture/Representation*. London: Routledge, 251–71.

Agnew, J., and Corbridge, S. (1994) *Mastering Space*. New York: Routledge.

Albert, M., Jacobson, D., and Lapid, Y., eds. (2001) *Identities, Borders, Orders*. Minneapolis: University of Minnesota Press.

Albrechts, L., and Swyngedouw, E. (1989) The challenges for regional policy under a flexible regime of accumulation. In L. Albrechts et al., eds., *Regional Policy at the Crossroads*. London: Jessica Kingsley, 67–89.

Albritton, R., Itoh, M., Westra, R., and Zuege, A., eds. (2001) *Phases of Capitalist Development*. New York: Palgrave.

Albrow, M. (1996) *The Global Age*. Oxford: Polity.

—— (1990) Introduction. In M. Albrow and E. King, eds., *Globalization, Knowledge and Society*. London: Sage, 1–14.

—— (1972) Regional intervention. In S. Holland, ed., *The State as Entrepreneur*. White Plains, NY: International Arts and Sciences Press, 165–83.

Allen, J., Massey, D., and Cochrane, A. (1998) *Rethinking the Region*. New York, Routledge.

Allen, K., and MacLennan, M. C. (1970) *Regional Problems and Policies in Italy and France*. Beverly Hills: Sage.

Altes, W. K. K. (2002) Local government and the decentralization of urban regeneration policies in the Netherlands, *Urban Studies*, 39/8: 1439–52.

Altvater, E. (1992) Fordist and post-Fordist international division of labor and monetary regimes. In M. Storper and A. J. Scott, eds., *Pathways to Industrialization and Regional Development*. New York: Routledge, 21–45.

Altvater, E., and Mahnkopf, B. (1995) *Die Grenzen der Globalisierung*. Münster: Westfälisches Dampfboot.

Amin, A. (2002) Spatialities of globalization, *Environment and Planning A*, 34, 385–99.

—— (1994) Post-Fordism: models, fantasies and phantoms of transition. In A. Amin, ed., *Post-Fordism: A Reader*. Cambridge, Mass.: Blackwell.

Amin, A., and Malmberg, A. (1994) Competing structural and institutional influences on the geography of production in Europe. In A. Amin, ed., *Post-Fordism: A Reader*. Cambridge, Mass.: Blackwell, 227–48.

Amin, A. and Thrift, N., eds. (1994) *Globalization, Institutions and Regional Development in Europe*. New York: Oxford University Press.
—— (1992) Neo-Marshallian nodes in global networks, *International Journal of Urban and Regional Research*, 16/4: 571–87.
Amin, A., and Tomaney, J. (1995a) The regional dilemma in a neo-liberal Europe, *European Urban and Regional Studies*, 2/2: 171–88.
—— eds. (1995b) *Behind the Myth of the European Union*. New York: Routledge.
Amin, S. (1986) *La Déconnexion, pour sortir du système mondial*. Paris: La Découverte.
—— (1979) *Accumulation on a World Scale*. Hassocks, Sussex: Harvester Press.
Anastassopoulos, J.-P. (1981) The French experience: conflicts with government. In R. Vernon and Y. Aharoni, eds., *State-Owned Enterprises in the Western Economies*. New York: St Martin's Press, 99–116.
Andersen, H. T. (2001) The new urban politics of Europe: the area-based approach to regeneration policy. In H. T. Andersen and R. van Kempen, eds., *Governing European Cities*. Aldershot: Ashgate, 233–53.
Andersen, H. T., and Jørgensen, J. (2004) Rescaling Cophenhagen government. In A. Harding, ed. *Rescaling European Urban Policy*. Boston and Oxford: Blackwell, forthcoming.
—— (1995) City profile: Cophenagen, *Cities*, 12/1: 13–22.
Andersen, H. T., and van Kempen, R. (2003) New trends in urban policies in Europe: evidence from the Netherlands and Denmark, *Cities*, 20/2: 77–86.
—— eds. (2001) *Governing European Cities*. Aldershot: Ashgate.
Andersen, J. (2003) Gambling politics or successful entrepreneurialism? The Orestad project in Copenhagen. In F. Moulaert, A. Rodriguez, and E. Swyngedouw, eds., *The Globalized City*. Oxford and New York: Oxford University Press, 91–106.
—— (1996) The shifting stage of politics: new medieval and postmodern territorialities? *Environment and Planning D: Society and Space*, 14, 133–53.
Ansell, C. (2000) The networked polity: regional development in western Europe, *Governance*, 13/3: 303–33.
Appadurai, A. (1996) *Modernity at Large*. Minneapolis: University of Minnesota Press.
Armstrong, P., Glyn, A., and Harrison, J. (1991) *Capitalism since 1945*. 2nd edn. Cambridge, Mass.: Blackwell.
Arrighi, G. (1994) *The Long Twentieth Century*. New York: Verso.
Arthur, C. (1994) *Increasing Returns and Path Dependence in the Economy*. Ann Arbor: University of Michigan Press.
Ashcroft, B. (1982) The measurement of the impact of regional policies in Europe, *Regional Studies*, 16/4: 287–305.
Atkinson, R. (2001) The emerging 'urban agenda' and the European Spatial Development Perspective, *European Planning Studies*, 9/3: 385–406.
Bade, F.-J. (1998) Möglichkeiten und Grenzen der Regionalisierung der regionalen Strukturpolitik, *Raumforschung und Raumordnung*, 56/1: 3–8.
Badie, B. (1995) *La Fin des territoires*. Paris: Fayard.
Bagnasco, A., and Oberti, M. (1998) Italy: le 'trompe-l'œil' of regions. In P. Le Galès and C. Lequesne, eds., *Regions in Europe*. New York: Routledge, 150–65.
Bairoch, P. (1988) *Cities and Economic Development*. Chicago: University of Chicago Press.
Balducci, A. (2001) New tasks and new forms for comprehensive planning in Italy. In L. Albrechts, J. Alden, and A. de Rosa Pires, eds., *The Changing Institutional Landscape of Planning*. Aldershot: Ashgate, 158–77.

Bardet, F., and Jouve, B. (1998) Defining a new territory as a means of building a political stronghold: the invention of the Région Urbaine de Lyon, *Space & Polity*, 2/2: 127–44.

Barlow, M. (1997) Administrative systems and metropolitan regions. *Environment and Planning C: Government and Policy*, 15: 399–411.

——(1991) *Metropolitan Government*. New York: Routledge.

Bassand, M., et al., eds. (1986) *Self-reliant Development in Europe*. Gower: Aldershot.

Bauman, Z. (1998) On glocalization: or globalization for some, localization for some others, *Thesis Eleven*, 54: 37–49.

Beaverstock J., Smith, R., and Taylor, P. J. (2000) World city network: a new metageography?, *Annals of the Association of American Geographers*, 90/1 (March): 123–34.

Beck, U. (2000) *What is Globalization?* Malden, Mass.: Polity.

Begg, I. (1999) Cities and competitiveness, *Urban Studies*, 36/5–6: 795–810.

Benington, J., and Harvey, J. (1998) Transnational local authority networking within the European Union. In D. Marsh, ed., *Comparing Policy Networks*. philadelphia, Pa.: Open University Press, 149–66.

Benko, G., and Dunford, M., eds. (1991) *Industrial Change and Regional Development*. London: Belhaven.

Benko, G., and Lipietz, A. (2002) From the *régulation* of space to the space of *régulation*. In R. Boyer and Y. Saillard, eds., *Régulation Theory: The State of the Art*. New York: Routledge, 190–6.

Benko, G., and Strohmayer, U., eds. (1991) *Space and Social Theory*. Cambridge, Mass.: Blackwell.

Bennett, R. J., ed. (1993) *Local Government in the New Europe*. London: Belhaven.

——ed. (1989) *Territory and Administration in Europe*. London: Pinter.

Benz, A. (1998) Rediscovering regional economic policy: new opportunities for the Länder in the 1990s. In C. Jeffery, ed., *Recasting German Federalism*. London: Pinter, 177–96.

Benz, A., and Frenzel, A. (1999) Les Politiques institutionnelles dans un état fédéral: la création du 'Verband Region Stuttgart'. In B. Jouve and C. Lefèvre, eds., *Villes, métropoles: les nouveaux territoires du politique*. Paris: Anthropos, 223–49.

Berger, S., and Dore, R., eds. (1996) *National Diversity and Global Capitalism*. Ithaca, NY: Cornell University Press.

Biarez, S. (1994) Urban policies and development strategies in France, *Local Government Studies*, 19/2: 190–207.

Blacksell, M. (1981) West Germany. In H. Clout, ed., *Regional Development in Western Europe*. London: John Wiley & Sons, 211–39.

Block, F. (1994) The roles of the state in the economy. In N. Smelser and R. Swedberg, eds., *The Handbook of Economic Sociology*. Princeton, NJ: Princeton University Press, 691–710.

Blomley, N., Delaney, D., and Ford, R., eds. (2001) *The Legal Geographies Reader*. Boston: Blackwell.

BMBau, Bundesministerium für Raumordnung, Bauwesen und Städtebau (1996) *Raumordnung in Deutschland*. Bonn. Bundesministerium für Raumordnung, Bauwesen und Städtebau.

——(1995) *Raumordnungspolitischer Handlungsrahmen*. Beschluß der Ministerkonferenz für Raumordnung in Düsseldorf am 8 März 1995. Bonn: Bundesministerium für Raumordnung, Bauwesen und Städtebau.

BMBau, Bundesministerium für Raumordnung, Bauwesen und Städtebau (1993*a*) *Raumordnungspolitischer Orientierungsrahmen*. Bonn: Bundesministerium für Raumordnung, Bauwesen und Städtebau.

——(1993*b*) *Raumordnungsbericht 1993*, Bonn: Bundesministerium für Raumordnung, Bauwesen und Städtebau.

Boddy, M., and Fudge, C., eds. (1984) *Local Socialism? Labour Councils and New Left Alternatives*. London: Macmillan.

Body-Gendrot, S. (2000) *The Social Control of Cities? A Comparative Perspective*. Cambridge, Mass.: Blackwell.

Boudeville, J.-R. (1966) *Problems of Regional Economic Planning*. Edinburgh: Edinburgh University Press.

Bourdieu, P. (1996) *Acts of Resistance: Against the Tyranny of the Market*. New York: New Press.

Boyer, R. (1996) State and market: a new engagement for the twenty-first century? In R. Boyer and D. Drache, eds., *States Against Markets: The Limits of Globalization*. London: Routledge, 84–116.

——(1990) *Regulation Theory: An Introduction*. New York: Oxford University Press.

Boyer, R., and Drache, D., eds. (1996) *States Against Markets: The Limits of Globalization*. London: Routledge.

Boyer, R., and Hollingsworth, J. R. (1997) From national embeddedness to spatial and institutional nestedness. In J. R. Hollingsworth and R. Boyer, eds., *Contemporary Capitalism: The Embeddedness of Institutions*. New York: Cambridge University Press, 433–84.

Boyer, R., and Saillard, Y., eds. (2002) *Régulation Theory: The State of the Art*. New York: Routledge.

Bozzi, C. (1995) Policies for territorial competition: the case of Milan. In P. Cheshire and I. Gordon, eds., *Territorial Competition in an Integrating Europe*. Aldershot: Avebury, 267–94.

Braudel, F. (1984) *The Perspective of the World*. Berkeley: University of California Press.

Brenner, N. (2004*a*) Urban governance and the production of new state spaces in western Europe, 1960–2000, *Review of International Political Economy*, 11/3, in press.

——(2004*b*) Rescaling state space in western Europe: urban governance and the rise of 'Glocalizing' Competition State Regimes. In M. Berezin and M. Shain, eds., *Europe without Borders*. Baltimore: Johns Hopkins University Press, 140–66.

——(2003*a*) Metropolitan institutional reform and the rescaling of state space in contemporary western Europe, *European Urban and Regional Studies*, 10: 297–325.

——(2003*b*) 'Glocalization' as a state spatial strategy: urban entrepreneurialism and the new politics of uneven development in western Europe. In J. Peck and H. Yeung, eds., *Remaking the Global Economy*. London and Thousand Oaks: Sage, 197–215.

——(2001*a*) The limits to scale? Methodological reflections on scalar structuration, *Progress in Human Geography*, 15/4: 525–48.

——(2001*b*) World city theory, globalization and the comparative-historical method: reflections on Janet Abu-Lughod's interpretation of contemporary urban restructuring, *Urban Affairs Review*, 36/6: 124–47.

——(2001*c*) State theory in the political conjuncture: Henri Lefebvre's 'Comments on a new state form', *Antipode* 33/5: 783–808.

——(2000*a*) The urban question as a scale question: reflections on Henri Lefebvre, urban theory and the politics of scale, *International Journal of Urban and Regional Research*, 24/2: 361–78.

—— (2000*b*) Building 'Euro-regions': locational politics and the political geography of neoliberalism in post-unification Germany, *European Urban and Regional Studies*, 7/4: 317–43.

—— (1999*a*) Beyond state-centrism? Space, territoriality and geographical scale in globalization studies, *Theory and Society*, 28/2: 39–78.

—— (1999*b*) Globalization as reterritorialization: the re-scaling of urban governance in the European Union, *Urban Studies*, 36/3: 431–51.

—— (1999*c*) Global Cities, 'Glocal' States: State Re-scaling and the Remaking of Urban Governance in the European Union. Unpublished Ph.D. dissertation, Department of Political Science, University of Chicago.

—— (1998*a*) Between fixity and motion: accumulation, territorial organization and the historical geography of spatial scales, *Environment and Planning D: Society and Space*, 16: 459–81.

—— (1998*b*) Global cities, 'glocal' states: global city formation and state territorial restructuring in contemporary Europe, *Review of International Political Economy*, 5/1: 1–37.

—— (1997*a*) State territorial restructuring and the production of spatial scale: urban and regional planning in the Federal Republic of Germany, 1960–1990, *Political Geography*, 16/4: 273–306.

—— (1997*b*) Global, fragmented, hierarchical: Henri Lefebvre's geographies of globalization, *Public Culture*, 10/1: 137–69.

Brenner, N., and Theodore, N. (2002*a*) Cities and the geographies of 'actually existing neoliberalism'. In N. Brenner and N. Theodore, eds., *Spaces of Neoliberalism: Urban Restructuring in North America and Western Europe*. Oxford and Boston: Blackwell, 2–32.

—— eds. (2002*b*) *Spaces of Neoliberalism: Urban Restructuring in North America and Western Europe*. Oxford and Boston: Blackwell.

Brenner, N., Jessop, B., Jones, M., and MacLeod, G., eds. (2003*a*) *State/Space: A Reader*. Boston: Blackwell.

—— (2003*b*) State space in question. In N. Brenner, B. Jessop, M. Jones, and G. MacLeod, eds., *State/Space: A Reader*. Boston: Blackwell, 1–26.

Brown, A. J. (1972) *The Framework of Regional Economics in the United Kingdom*. London: Cambridge University Press.

Brownill, S. (1999) Turning the East End into the West End: the lessons and legacies of the London Docklands Development Corporation. In R. Imrie and H. Thomas, eds, *British Urban Policy: An Evaluation of the Urban Development Corporations*. 2nd edn. London: Sage, 43–63.

—— (1993) The Docklands experience: locality and community in London. In R. Imrie and H. Thomas, eds., *British Urban Policy and the Urban Development Corporations*. London: Paul Chapman, 41–57.

Brunet, R. (1989) *Les Villes 'européennes'*. Paris: DATAR.

—— (1973) Structure et dynamisme de l'espace français: schéma d'un système, *L'Espace géographique*, 1/4: 249–54.

Bruun, F. (1995) Dilemmas of size: the rise and fall of the Greater Copenhagen council. In L. J. Sharpe, ed., *The Government of World Cities: The Future of the Metro Model*. New York: John Wiley & Sons, 57–76.

Budd, L. (1998) Territorial competition and globalisation: Scylla and Charybdis of European cities, *Urban Studies*, 35/4: 663–85.

Bullmann, U., ed. (1994) *Die Politik der dritten Ebene*. Baden-Baden: Nomos.

Bullmann, U., and Gitschmann, P. (1985) *Kommune als Gegenmacht*. Hamburg: VSA.

Bundesministerium für Raumordnung, Bauwesen und Städtebau (1996) *Raumordnung in Deutschland*. Bonn: Burdesministerium etc.

Burgel, G. (1997) Paris: city of opposites. In C. Jensen-Butler, A. Shachar, and J. van Weesep, eds., *European Cities in Competition*. Aldershot: Avebury, 103–31.

Burtenshaw, D., Bateman, M., and Ashworth, G. (1981) *The European City*. New York: Halsted Press.

Camagni, R. (2002) On the concept of territorial competitiveness: sound or misleading?, *Urban Studies*, 39/13: 2395–411.

Cameron, A., and Palan, R. (1999) The imagined economy: mapping transformations in the contemporary state, *Millennium*, 28/2: 267–88.

Cameron, G. (1970) Growth areas, growth centres and regional conversion, *Scottish Journal of Political Economy*, 17 (Feb.): 19–38.

Caporaso, J. (1997) The European Union and forms of state: Westphalian, regulatory or post-modern?, *Journal of Common Market Studies*, 34/1: 29–52.

Casper, U. (1979) Background notes to regional incentives in the Federal Republic of Germany. In K. Allen, ed., *Balanced National Growth*. Lexington, Mass.: Lexington Books, 97–130.

Castells, M. (2004) *The Power of Identity*. 2nd edn. Oxford: Blackwell.

—— (1996) *The Rise of the Network Society*. Cambridge, Mass.: Blackwell.

—— (1994) European cities, the informational society and the global economy, *New Left Review*, (Mar.–Apr.): 18–32.

—— (1983) *The City and the Grassroots*. Berkeley: University of California Press.

—— (1977 [1972]) *The Urban Question*. Cambridge, Mass.: MIT Press.

—— (1976) Is there an urban sociology? In C. G. Pickvance, ed., *Urban Sociology: Critical Essays*. New York: St Martin's Press, 33–59.

Castells, M., and Godard, F. (1974) *Monopolville*. Paris: Mouton.

CEC, Commission of the European Communities (1998) *Towards an Urban Agenda in the European Union*. Brussels: European Commission.

—— Commission of the European Communities (1997) *The EU Compendium of Spatial Planning Systems and Policies*. Brussels and Luxembourg: European Commission.

—— Commission of the European Communities (1994) *Europe 2000+. Cooperation for European Territorial Development*. Brussels and Luxembourg: European Commission.

—— Commission of the European Communities (1992) *Urbanisation and the Functions of Cities in the European Community*. Brussels and Luxembourg: Directorate General for Regional Policies.

—— Commission of the European Communities (1991) *The Regions in the 1990s: Fourth Periodic Report on the Social and Economic Situation and Development of the Regions in the Community*. Brussels: European Commission.

—— Commission of the European Communities (1977) *Report of the Study Group on the Role of Public Finance in European Integration*. Vol. 1 and 2. Brussels: European Commission.

Cerny, P. (1997) Paradoxes of the competition state, *Government and Opposition*, 32/3: 251–74.

—— (1995) Globalization and the changing logic of collective action, *International Organization*, 49/4: 595–625.

Chandler, A. (1977) *The Visible Hand*. Cambridge, Mass.: Harvard University Press.

Champion, T., Mønnesland, J., and Vandermotten, C. (1996) The new regional map of Europe, *Progress in Planning*, 46: 1–89.

Cheshire, P. (1999) Cities in competition: articulating the gains from integration, *Urban Studies*, 36/5–6: 843–64.

Cheshire, P. and Gordon, I. (1998) Territorial competition: some lessons for policy, *Annals of Regional Science*, 32: 321–46.

—— (1996) Territorial competition and the predictability of collective (in)action, *International Journal of Urban and Regional Research*, 20/3: 383–99.

—— eds. (1995) *Territorial Competition in an Integrating Europe*. Aldershot: Avebury.

Chisholm, M. (1990) *Regions in Recession and Resurgence*. London: Unwin Hyman.

Christalles, W. (1950) *Das Grunderüst der Räumlichen Ordnung in Europa*. Frankfurt am Main: W. Kramer.

Clark, D. (1997) Local government in Europe: retrenchment, restructuring and British exceptionalism, *West European Politics*, 20/3: 134–63.

Clout, H. (1981a) *Regional Development in Western Europe*. 2nd edn. Chichester: John Wiley.

—— (1981b) Population and urban growth. In H. Clout, ed., *Regional Development in Western Europe*. 2nd edn. Chichester: John Wiley & Sons, 35–59.

—— (1975) France. In H. Clout, ed., *Regional development in Western Europe*. London: John Wiley & Sons, 113–38.

Cohen, R. B. (1981) The new international division of labor, multinational corporations, and urban hierarchy. In M. Dear and A. J. Scott, eds., *Urbanization and Urban Planning in Capitalist Society*. London: Methuen, 287–315.

Collinge, C. (1999) Self-organization of society by scale: a spatial reworking of regulation theory, *Environment and Planning D: Society and Space*, 17: 557–74.

—— (1996) Spatial articulation of the state: reworking social relations and social regulation theory. Centre for Urban and Regional Studies, University of Birmingham. Unpublished manuscript.

Constandse, A. K. (1978) New towns on the bottom of the sea. In G. Golany, ed., *International Urban Growth Policies: New-town Contributions*. New York: John Wiley & Sons, 53–74.

Cooke, P., and Morgan, K. (1998) *The Associational Economy*. New York: Oxford University Press.

Coriat, B., and Petit, P. (1991) Deindustrialization and tertiarization: towards a new economic regime? In A. Amin and M. Dietrich, eds., *Towards a New Europe? Structural Change in the European Economy*. Aldershot: Edward Elgar, 18–48.

Coronil, F. (1998) *The Magical State*. Chicago: University of Chicago Press.

Courchene, T. (1995) Glocalization: the regional/international interface, *Canadian Journal of Regional Science*, 18/1: 1–20.

Cox, K. (2002) *Political Geography: Territory, State and Society*. Cambridge, Mass.: Blackwell.

—— ed. (1997) *Spaces of Globalization*. New York: Guilford.

—— (1992) The politics of globalization: a sceptic's view, *Political Geography*, 11/5: 427–9.

—— (1990) Territorial structures of the state: some conceptual issues, *Tijdschrift voor Economische en Sociale Geografie*, 81/4: 251–66.

Cox, R. (1987) *Production, Power and World Order*. New York: Columbia University Press.

Crouch, C., and Marquand, D., eds. (1989) *The New Centralism: Britain Out of Step in Europe?* Oxford: Blackwell.

Crouch, C., and Streeck, W., eds. (1997) *Political Economy of Modern Capitalism.* London: Sage.

Crouch, C., Le Galès, P., Triglia, C., and Voelzkow, H., eds. (2001): *Local Production Systems in Europe: Rise or Demise?* Oxford: Oxford University Press.

Daniels, P. W., and Lever, W. F., eds. (1996) *The Global Economy in Transition.* Essex: Longman.

Darwent, D. F. (1975) Growth poles and growth centers in regional planning: a review. In J. Friedmann and W. Alonso, eds., *Regional Policy: Readings in Theory and Application.* Cambridge, Mass.: MIT Press, 539–65.

DATAR (1989) Les Villes 'européenes'. Paris: La Documentation Française, 79.

Davoudi, S., and Healey, P. (1995) City Challenge: sustainable process or temporary gesture? *Environment and Planning C: Government and Policy,* 13: 79–95.

Dawson, J. (1992) Experiments in trans-national urban collaboration, *The Planner* (10 Jan.): 7–9.

DB, Deutscher Bundestag (1994) *Raumordnungsbericht 1993.* Drucksache 12/2143 (24 Feb.).

Deakin, N., and Edwards, J. (1993) *The Enterprise Culture and the Inner City.* London: Routledge.

Deas, I., and Ward, K. (2002) Metropolitan manœuvres: making Greater Manchester. In J. Peck and K. Ward, eds., *City of Revolution: Restructuring Manchester.* Manchester: University of Manchester Press, 116–32.

——(2000) From the 'new localism' to the 'new regionalism'?, *Political Geography,* 19: 273–92.

Delaney, D., and Leitner, H. (1997) The political construction of scale, *Political Geography,* 16/2: 93–7.

Dematteis, G. (2000) Spatial images of European urbanization. In A. Bagnasco and P. Le Galès, eds., *Cities in Contemporary Europe.* New York: Cambridge University Press, 48–73.

Der Derian, J. (1990) The (s)pace of international relations: simulation, surveillance and speed, *International Studies Quarterly,* 34: 295–310.

Dézert, B. (1999) La décentralisation industrielle et les grands projects. In Foundation Charles de Gaulle and Association Georges Pompidou, ed., *L'Amenagement du territoire, 1958–1974.* Paris: Éditions L'Harmattan, 187–97.

Dicken, P. (1998) *Global Shift: the Internationalization of Economic Activity.* 3rd edn. New York: Guilford Press.

——(1994) Global–local tensions: firms and states in the global space economy, *Economic Geography,* 70/2: 101–28.

Dicken, P., and Öberg, S. (1996) The global context: Europe in a world of dynamic economic and population change, *European Urban and Regional Studies,* 3/2: 101–20.

Dicken, P., Tickell, A., and Peck, J. (1997) Unpacking globalization. In R. Lee and J. Wills, eds., *Geographies of Economies.* London: Arnold, 158–67.

Dicken, P. Kelly, P., Olds, K., and Yeung, H. W. (2001) Chains and networks, territories and scales: towards a relational framework for analysing the global economy, *Global Networks,* 1/2: 89–112.

Dickinson, R. E. (1964) *City and Region: A Geographical Interpretation.* London: Routledge & Kegan Paul.

Dieleman, F., and Musterd, S., eds. (1992) *The Randstad: A Research and Policy Laboratory.* Dordrecht: Kluwer.

DiGaetano, A., and Klemanski, J. (1999) *Power and City Governance.* Minneapolis: University of Minnesota Press.

DISP (2003) Special issue on Metropolregionen in Westeuropa, *DISP*, Netzwerk Stadt und Landschaft, ETH Zürich, 152/1.

Droste, H., Fiedler, J., and Schmidt, V. (1997) Region Hannover. In Kommunalverband Großraum Hannover, ed., *Hannover Region 2001.* Blue Paper Appendix.

Duncan, S., and Goodwin, M. (1989) *The Local State and Uneven Development.* London: Polity.

Duncan, S., Goodwin, M., and Halford S. (1988) Policy variations in local states: uneven development and local social relations, *International Journal of Urban and Regional Research*, 12/1: 107–28.

Dunford, M. (1995) Metropolitan Polarization, the North-South Divide and Socio-Spatial Inequality in Britain: A Long-Term Perspective, *European Urban and Regional Studies*, 2/2: 145–70.

——(1994) Winners and losers: the new map of economic inequality in the European Union, *European Urban and Regional Studies*, 1/2: 95–114.

——(1988) *Capital, the State and Regional Development.* London: Pion.

Dunford, M., and Kafkalas, G., eds. (1992) *Cities and Regions in the New Europe.* London: Belhaven.

Dunford, M., and Perrons, D. (1994) Regional inequality, regimes of accumulation and economic development in contemporary Europe, *Transactions of the Institute of British Geographers*, 19: 163–82.

Dutt, A., and Costa, F. (1985) *Public Planning in the Netherlands.* New York and London: Oxford University Press.

Dyson, K. (1982) *The State Tradition in Western Europe.* New York: Oxford University Press.

Eisenschitz, A., and Gough, J. (1998) Theorizing the state in local economic governance, *Regional Studies*, 32/8: 759–68.

——(1996) The contradictions of neo-Keynesian local economic strategy, *Review of International Political Economy*, 3/3: 434–58.

——(1993) *The Politics of Local Economic Development.* New York: Macmillan.

Eisenschitz, A., and North, D. (1986) The London industrial strategy: socialist transformation or modernising capitalism?, *International Journal of Urban and Regional Research*, 10/3: 419–40.

Elden, S. (2004) *Henri Lefebvre: Introduction to the Possible.* New York: Continuum.

Esser, J. (1989) Does industrial policy matter? *Land* governments in research and technology policy in Federal Germany. In C. Crouch and D. Marquand, eds., *The New Centralism: Britain Out of Step in Europe?* Cambridge, Mass., Blackwell, 94–108.

Esser, J., and Hirsch, J. (1989) The crisis of Fordism and the dimensions of a 'postfordist' regional and urban structure, *International Journal of Urban and Regional Research*, 13/3: 417–37.

Essig, F. (1979) *DATAR. Des Régions et des hommes.* Paris: Stanké.

Evans, P. (1997) The eclipse of the state?, *World Politics*, 50: 62–87.

Evans, P., Rueschemeyer, D., and Skocpol, T., eds. (1985) *Bringing the State Back In?* New York: Cambridge University Press.

Evers, A. (1974) Agglomerationsprozess und Staatsfunktionen. In R. R. Grauhan, ed., *Lokale Politikforschung 1*. Frankfurt: Campus, 41–100.

Fainstein, S. (2001) *The city builders: property, politics and planning in London and New York*. 2nd edn. Lawrence: University of Kansas Press.

——(1994) *The City Builders: Property, Politics and Planning in London and New York*. Cambridge, Mass.: Blackwell.

Fainstein, S., Gordon, I., and Harloe, M., eds. (1992) *Divided Cities: New York and London in the Contemporary World*. Cambridge, Mass.: Blackwell.

Faludi, A. (1991) Fifty years of Dutch national physical planning: introduction, *Built Environment*, 17/1: 5–13.

Faludi, A., and van der Valk, A. (1994) *Rule and Order: Dutch Planning Doctrine in the 20th Century*. Dordrecht: Kluwer.

Feagin, J., and Smith, M. P. (1989) Cities and the new international divison of labor: an overview. In M. P. Smith and J. Feagin, eds., *The Capitalist City*. Cambridge, Mass.: Blackwell, 3–36.

Featherstone, M., ed. (1990) *Global Culture*. London: Sage.

Federal Ministry for Regional Planning, Building and Urban Development (1993) *Guidelines for Regional Planning* (Eng. version of *Raumordnungs politischer Orientierungsrahmen*). Bonn: Federal Ministry for Regional Planning, Building and Urban Development.

Ferguson, Y., and Jones, R. J., eds. (2002) *Political Space*. Albany, NY: SUNY Press.

Florida, R., and Jonas, A. (1991) U.S. urban policy: the postwar state and capitalist regulation. *Antipode*, 23/4: 349–84.

Flyvbjerg, B., Bruzelius, N., and Rothengatter, W. (2003) *Megaprojects and Risk*. New York and London: Cambridge University Press.

Fox Przeworski, J. (1986) Changing intergovernmental relations and urban economic development, *Environment and Planning C: Government and Policy*, 4/4: 423–39.

Freund, B. (2003) The Frankfurt/Rhine-Main region. In W. Salet, A. Thornley, and A. Kreukels, eds., *Metropolitan Governance and Spatial Planning*. London: Spon Press, 125–44.

Friedmann, J. (1995) Where we stand: a decade of world city research. In P. Knox and P. Taylor eds., *World Cities in a World-System*. New York: Cambridge University Press, 21–47.

——(1986a) The world city hypothesis, *Development and Change*, 17: 69–83.

——(1986b) Regional development in industrialized countries: endogenous or self-reliant? In M. Bassand, ed., *Self-Reliant Development in Europe*. Brookfield, Vt., Gower, 203–16.

Friedmann, J., and Bloch, R. (1990) American exceptionalism in regional planning, 1933–2000, *International Journal of Urban and Regional Research*, 14/4: 576–601.

Friedmann, J., and Weaver, C. (1984) *Territory and Function: The Evolution of Regional Planning*. Berkeley and Los Angeles: University of California Press.

Friedmann, J., and Wolff, G. (1982) World city formation: an agenda for research and action, *International Journal of Urban and Regional Research*, 6: 309–44.

Friedrichs, J., Häuaermann, H., and Siebel, W., eds. (1986) *Süd-Nord-Gefälle in der Bundesrepublik?* Opladen: Westdeutscher Verlag.

Frieling, D. (1994) Development of a multi-centered metropolis: from physical planning to investment strategy, *Tijdschrift voor Economische en Sociale Geografie*, 85/2: 171–5.

Fürst, D., and Rudolph, A. (2003) The Hanover metropolitan region. In W. Salet, A. Thornley, and A. Kreukels, eds., *Metropolitan Governance and Spatial Planning*. London: Spon Press, 145–62.

Gaffikin, F., and Warf, B. (1993) Urban policy and the post-Keynesian state in the United Kingdom and the United States, *International Journal of Urban and Regional Research* 17/1: 67–83.

Galantay, E. (1980) Definitions and typology: goals, policies and strategies, In Working Party 'New Towns', ed., *New Towns in National Development*. Milton Keynes: Open University, 13–28.

Galland, B. (1996) De l'urbanisation à la 'glocalisation', *Terminal*, 7/1–2: 71–88.

Galle, M., and Modderman, E. (1997) VINEX: national spatial planning policy in the Netherlands during the 1990s, *Netherlands Journal of Housing and the Built Environment*, 12/1: 9–35.

Garofoli, G. (2002) Local development in Europe: theoretical models and international comparisons, *European Urban and Regional Studies*, 9/3: 225–39.

Gay, F. (1981) Benelux. In H. Clout, ed., *Regional Development in Western Europe*. 2nd edn. Chichester: John Wiley & Sons, 179–210.

Geddes, M., and Benington, J., eds. (2001) *Local Partnerships and Social Exclusion in the European Union*. New York: Routledge.

Gemeente Amsterdam (1997) *Gebundelde Kwaliteit: Economische Ontwikkelingsstrategie voor de regio Amsterdam*. Amsterdam: Gemeente Amsterdam.

Gertler, M. (1992) Flexibility revisited: districts, nation-states and the forces of production, *Transactions, Institute of British Geographers*, 17: 259–78.

Giddens, A. (1990) *The Consequences of Modernity*. Stanford: Stanford University Press.

—— (1984) *The Nation State and Violence*. Berkeley: University of California Press.

Gill, S. (2003) *Power and Resistance in the New World Order*. London: Palgrave.

—— (1998*a*) European governance and new constitutionalism: economic and monetary union and alternatives to disciplinary neoliberalism in Europe, *New Political Economy*, 3/1: 5–26.

—— (1998*b*) New constitutionalism, democratisation and global political economy, *Pacifica Review*, 10/1: 23–38.

—— (1995) Globalisation, market civilisation and discipinary neoliberalism, *Millennium*, 24/3: 399–423.

Golany, G., ed. (1978) *International Urban Growth Policies: New-Town Contributions*. New York: John Wiley & Sons.

Goodwin, M., and Painter, J. (1996) Local governance, the crises of Fordism and the changing geographies of regulation, *Transactions of the Institute of British Geographers*, 21: 635–48.

Gordon, I. (1999) Internationalization and urban competition, *Urban Studies*, 36/5–6: 1001–16.

—— (1995) *London: World City*—political and organisational constraints on territorial competition. In P. Cheshire and I. Gordon, eds., *Territorial Competition in an Integrating Europe*. Aldershot: Avebury, 295–311.

Goswami, M. (2004) *Producing India: From Colonial Space to National Economy*. Chicago: University of Chicago Press.

Gottdiener, M. (1989) Crisis theory and socio-spatial restructuring: the US case. In M. Gottdiener and N. Komninos, eds., *Capitalist Development and Crisis Theory*. New York: St Martin's Press, 365–90.

—— (1985) *The Social Production of Urban Space*. Austin: University of Texas Press.

Gottmann, J. (1983) *The Significance of Territory*. Charlottesville: University of Virginia Press.

Gough, J. (2004) Changing scale as changing class relations, *Political Geography*, 23: 185–211.

—— (2002) Neoliberalism and socialisation in the contemporary city: opposites, complements and instabilities. In N. Brenner and N. Theodore, eds., *Spaces of Neoliberalism*. Boston: Blackwell, 58–79.

—— (2000) Changing scale as changing class relations. Paper presented at the Annual Meetings of the Institute of British Geographers, University of Sussex, Jan.

Gough, J. and Eisenschitz, A. (1996) The construction of mainstream local economic initiatives: mobility, socialization and class relations, *Economic Geography*, 72/2: 178–95.

Graham, S. (2000) Constructing premium network spaces: reflections on infrastructure networks and contemporary urban development, *International Journal of Urban and Regional Development*, 24/1: 183–200.

—— (1999) Global grids of glass: on global cities, telecommunications and planetary urban networks, *Urban Studies*, 36/5–6: 929–49.

—— (1997) Cities in the real-time age: the paradigm challenge of telecommunications to the conception and planning of urban space, *Environment and Planning A*, 29: 105–27.

—— (1995) From urban competition to urban collaboration? The development of inter-urban telematics networks, *Environment and Planning C: Government and Policy*, 13: 503–24.

Graham, S. and Marvin, S. (2001) *Splintering Urbanism*. New York: Routledge.

—— (1996) *Telecommunications and the City*. New York: Routledge.

—— (1995) More than ducts and wires: post-Fordism, cities and utility networks. In Patsy Healey et al., eds., *Managing Cities: The New Urban Context*. London: Wiley, 169–90.

Gramsci, A. (1971) *Prison Notebooks*. New York: International Publishers.

Grassini, F. (1981) The Italian enterprises: the political constraints. In R. Vernon and Y. Aharoni, eds., *State-Owned Enterprises in the Western Economies*. New York: St Martin's Press, 70–84.

Gregory, D., and Urry, J., eds. (1985) *Social Relations and Spatial Structures*. London, Macmillan.

Gualini, E. (2003) The region of Milan. In W. Salet, A. Thornley, and A. Kreukels, eds., *Metropolitan Governance and Spatial Planning*. London: Spon, 264–83.

—— (2001) 'New programming' and the influence of transnational discourses in the reform of regional policy in Italy, *European Planning Studies*, 9/6: 755–71.

Guillén, M. (2001) Is globalization civilizing, destructive or feeble? A critique of five debates in the social science literature, *Annual Review of Sociology*, 27: 235–60.

Gupta, A., and Ferguson, J. (2002) Spatializing states: toward an ethnography of neoliberal governmentality, *American Ethnologist*, 29/4: 981–1002.

—— eds. (1997) *Culture, Power, Place*. Durham, NC: Duke University Press.

Hadjimichalis, C., and Sadler, D., eds. (1995) *Europe at the Margins. New Mosaics of Inequality*. Chichester: Wiley.

Hahne, U. (1985) *Regionalentwicklung durch Aktivierung intraregionaler Potentiale*. Schriften des Instituts für Regionalforschung der Universität Kiel, 8. Munich: Florenz.

Häkli, J. (2001) In the territory of knowledge: state-centered discourses and the construction of society, *Progress in Human Geography*, 25/3: 403–22.

Halkier, H. (2001) Regional policy in transition, *European Planning Studies*, 9/3: 323–38.

Hall, P. ed. (1989) *The Political Power of Economic Ideas: Keynesianism Across Nations*. Princeton, NJ: Princeton University Press.

Hall, P., and Castells, M. (1994) *Technopoles of the World*. New York: Routledge.

Hall, P., and Pfeiffer, U., eds. (2000) *Urban Future 21. A Global Agenda for Twenty-First Century Cities*. London: Spon.

Hall, P., and Soskice, D. (2001) *Varieties of Capitalism*. New York: Oxford University Press.

Hall, T., and Hubbard, P., eds. (1998) *The Entrepreneurial City: Geographies of Politics, Regime and Representation*. London: Wiley.

——(1996) The entrepreneurial city: new politics, new urban geographies, *Progress in Human Geography*, 20/2: 153–74.

Hamnett, C. (1996) Social polarisation, economic restructuring and welfare state regimes, *Urban Studies*, 33/8: 1407–30.

——(1994) Social polarisation in global cities: theory and evidence, *Urban Studies*, 31: 401–24.

Hamnett, S. (1982) The Netherlands: planning and the politics of accommodation. In D. MacKay, ed., *Planning and Politics in Western Europe*. New York: St Martin's Press, 111–43.

Hanesch, W. (1997) Konzeption, Krise und Optionen der sozialen Stadt. In W. Hanesch, ed., *Überlebt die soziale Stadt?* Opladen: Leske + Budrich, 21–56.

Hansen, A. L., Andersen, H. T., and Clark, E. (2001) Creative Cophenhagen: globalization, urban governance and social change, *European Planning Studies*, 9/7: 851–69.

Hansen, N. (1968) *French Regional Planning*. Bloomington: Indiana University Press.

Harding, A. (1997) Urban regimes in a Europe of the cities? *European Urban and Regional Studies*, 4/4: 291–314.

——(1994) Urban regimes and growth machines: towards a cross-national research agenda, *Urban Affairs Quarterly*, 29/3: 356–82.

——(1989) Central control in British urban economic development programs. In C. Crouch and D. Marquand, eds., *The New Centralism: Britain Out of Step in Europe?* Oxford: Blackwell, 21–38.

Harding, A., Dawson, J., Evans, R., and Parkinson, M., eds. (1994) *European Cities towards 2000*. Manchester : Manchester University Press.

Hardt, M., and Negri, A. (2001) *Empire*. Cambridge, Mass.: Harvard University Press.

Harloe, M. (2001) Social justice and the city: the new 'liberal formulation', *International Journal of Urban and Regional Research*, 25/4: 889–97.

Harvey, D. (1996) *Justice, Nature and the Geography of Difference*. Cambridge, Mass.: Blackwell.

——(1995) Globalization in question, *Rethinking Marxism*, 8/4: 1–17.

——(1989*a*) From managerialism to entrepreneurialism: the transformation in urban governance in late capitalism, *Geografiska Annaler*, B, 71/1: 3–18.

——(1989*b*) *The Urban Experience*. Baltimore: Johns Hopkins University Press.

——(1989*c*) *The Condition of Postmodernity*. Cambridge, Mass.: Blackwell.

——(1985) The geopolitics of capitalism. In D. Gregory and J. Urry, eds., *Social Relations and Spatial Structures*. London: Macmillan, 128–63.

Harvey, D. (1982) *The Limits to Capital*. Chicago: University of Chicago Press.

—— (1978) The urban process under capitalism: a framework for analysis, *International Journal of Urban and Regional Research*, 2: 101–31.

—— (1973) *Social Justice and the City*. Baltimore: Johns Hopkins University Press.

Haüßermann, H. (1991) The relationship between local and federal government in the Federal Republic of Germany. In C. Pickvance and E. Preteceille, eds., *State Restructuring and Local Power: A Comparative Perspective*. London: Pinter, 89–121.

Healey, P. (1998) The place of 'Europe' in contemporary strategy making, *European Urban and Regional Studies*, 5/2: 139–53.

Healey, P., Khakee, A., Motte, A., and Needham, B., eds. (1997) *Making Strategic Spatial Plans: Innovation in Europe*. London: UCL Press.

Heeg, S. (2003) Governance in the Stuttgart metropolitan region. In W. Salet, A. Thornley, and A. Kreukels, eds., *Metropolitan Governance and Spatial Planning*. London: Spon, 163–74.

—— (2001) *Politische Regulation des Raumes. Metropolen, Regionen, Nationalstaat*. Berlin: Edition Sigma.

Heeg, S., Klagge, B., and Ossenbrügge, J. (2003) Metropolitan cooperation in Europe: theoretical issues and perspectives for urban networking, *European Planning Studies*, 11/2: 139–53.

—— (2000) *Kooperation zwischen Metropolregionen*. Hamburg: Gutachten im Auftrag der Senatskanzlei der Freien und Hansestadt Hamburg.

Heinz, W., ed. (2000) *Stadt & Region—Kooperation oder Koordination? Ein internationaler Vergleich*. Schriften des Deutschen Instituts für Urbanistik, 93. Stuttgart, Berlin, and Köln: Verlag W. Kohlhammer.

Held, D. (1995) *Democracy and the Global Order*. London: Polity.

Held, D., McGrew, A., Goldblatt, D., and Perraton, J. (1999) *Global Transformations*. Stanford: Stanford University Press.

Helleiner, E. (1994) *States and the Reemergence of Global Finance*. Ithaca, NY: Cornell University Press.

Hendriks, F., and Toonen, T. A. J. (1995) The rise and fall of the Rijnmond authority: an experiment with metro government in the Netherlands. In L. J. Sharpe, ed., *The Government of World Cities: The Future of the Metro Model*. New York: John Wiley & Sons, 147–75.

Herod, A. (1997) Labor's spatial praxis and the geography of contract bargaining in the US east coast longshore industry, 1953–1989, *Political Geography*, 16/2: 145–69.

Herrigel, G. (1996) *Industrial Constructions: The Sources of German Industrial Power*. New York: Cambridge University Press.

Herrschel, T., and Newman, P. (2002) *Governance of Europe's City Regions. Planning, Policy, Politics*. New York: Routledge.

Hesse, J. (1991) Local government in a Federal State: the Case of West Germany. In J. J. Hesse, ed., *Local Government and Urban Affairs in International Perspective*. Baden-Baden: Nomos, 353–85.

—— (1987) The Federal Republic of Germany: from co-operative federalism to joint policy-making, *West European Politics*, 10/4: 70–87.

Hirsch, J. (1995) *Der nationale Wettbewerbsstaat*. Berlin and Amsterdam: Edition ID-Archiv.

Hirsch, J., and Roth, R. (1986) *Das neue Gesicht des Kapitalismus*. Hamburg: VSA.

Hirschman, A. (1958) *The Strategy of Economic Development*. New Haven: Yale University Press.

Hitz, H., Keil, R., Lehrer, U., Ronneberger, K., Schmid., C., and Wolff, R., eds. (1995) *Capitales Fatales: Urbanisierung und Politik in den Finanzmetropolen Frankfurt und Zürich*. Zürich: Rotpunktverlag.

Hocking, B. (1998) Patrolling the 'frontier': globalization, localization and the 'actorness' of non-central governments, *Regional and Federal Studies*, 9/1: 17–31.

Hohenberg, P., and Lees, L. H. (1995) *The Making of Urban Europe, 1000–1994*. Cambridge, Mass.: Harvard University Press.

Holland, S. (1976*a*) *The Regional Problem*. New York: St Martin's Press.

—— (1976*b*) *Capital Versus the Regions*. London: Macmillan.

—— (1974) Europe's new public enterprises. In R. Vernon, ed., *Big Business and the State: Changing Relations in Western Europe*. Cambridge, Mass.: Harvard University Press, 25–42.

—— ed. (1972*a*) *The State as Entrepreneur*. White Plains, NY: International Arts and Sciences Press.

—— (1972*b*) Adoption and adaptation of the IRI formula. In S. Holland, ed., *The State as Entrepreneur*. White Plains, NY: International Arts and Sciences Press, 242–65.

Hollingsworth, J. R. (1998) New perspectives on the spatial dimensions of economic coordination: tensions between globalization and social systems of production, *Review of International Political Economy*, 5/3: 482–507.

Hollingsworth, J. R., and Boyer, R., eds. (1997) *Contemporary Capitalism: The Embeddedness of Institutions*. New York: Cambridge University Press.

Hondrich, K. O. (1992) World societies versus niche societies. In H. Haferkamp and N. Smelser, eds., *Social Change and Modernity*. Berkeley: University of California Press, 351–66.

Howitt, R. (1998) Scale as relation: musical metaphors of geographical scale, *Area*, 30/1: 49–58.

Hudson, R. (2001) *Producing Places*. New York: Guilford.

—— (1994) Institutional change, cultural transformation and economic regeneration: myths and realities from Europe's old industrial areas. In A. Amin and N. Thrift, eds., *Globalization, Institutions and Regional Development in Europe*. New York: Oxford University Press, 196–216.

Hudson, R., and Sadler, D. (1986) Contesting works closures in Western Europe's old industrial regions: defending place or betraying class? In A. J. Scott and M. Storper, eds., *Production, Work, Territory*. Boston: Allen & Unwin, 172–93.

Hudson, R., and Williams, A. (1989) *Divided Britain?* London: Belhaven.

Hull, C. (1979) Background notes to regional incentives in France. In K. Allen, ed., *Balanced National Growth*. Lexington, Mass.: Lexington Books, 55–96.

IAURIF (Institute d'Aménagement et d'Urbanisme de la Région d'Île de France) (1993) *France, Île de France: tendances et perspectives. Une contribution au debat sur l'aménagement du territoire*. Paris: Conseil Regional Île-de-France.

Jacquier, C. (2001) Urban fragmentation and revitalization policies in France. In H. T. Andersen and R. van Kempen, eds., *Governing European Cities*. Aldershot: Ashgate, 321–46.

Jameson, F. (1992) *Postmodernism, or, the Cultural Logic of Late Capitalism*. Durham, NC: Duke University Press.

Jeffery, C., ed. (1998) *Recasting German Federalism: The Legacies of Unification*. London: Pinter.

Jensen-Butler, C., Shachar, A., van Weesep, J., eds. (1997) *European Cities in Competition*. Aldershot: Avebury.

Jessop, B. (2002) *The Future of the Capitalist State*. London: Polity.

—— (2001) Bringing the state back in (yet again): reviews, revisions, rejections, redirections, *International Review of Sociology*, 11/2: 149–73.

—— (2000) The crisis of the national spatio-temporal fix and the ecological dominance of globalizing capitalism, *International Journal of Urban and Regional Research*, 24/2: 323–60.

—— (1999*a*) Narrating the future of the national economy and the national state: remarks on remapping regulation and reinventing governance. In G. Steinmetz, ed., *State/Culture: State Formation after the Cultural Turn*. Ithaca, NY, Cornell University Press, 378–405.

—— (1999*b*) Globalization and the national state: reflections on a theme of Poulantzas. In S. Aaronowitz and P. Bratisis, eds., *Rethinking the State: Miliband, Poulantzas and State Theory*. Minneapolis: University of Minnesota Press, 185–220.

—— (1999*c*) Globalization and its (il)logic(s). In Kris Olds et al., eds., *Globalization and the Asia-Pacific*. London: Routledge, 19–38.

—— (1998) The narrative of enterprise and the enterprise of narrative: place-marketing and the entrepreneurial city. In T. Hall and P. Hubbard, eds., *The Entrepreneurial City*. London: John Wiley & Sons, 77–102.

—— (1997) Survey article: the regulation approach, *Journal of Political Philosophy*, 5/3: 287–326.

—— (1995) The regulation approach, governance and post-Fordism: alternative perspectives on economic and political change?, *Economy and Society*, 24/3: 307–33.

—— (1993) Towards a Schumpeterian Workfare State? Preliminary Remarks on Post-Fordist Political Economy, *Studies in Political Economy*, 40: 7–40.

—— (1992) Fordism and post-Fordism: a critical reformulation. In M. Storper and A. J. Scott, eds., *Pathways to Industrialization and Regional Development*. New York: Routledge, 46–69.

—— (1990*a*) *State Theory*. University Park, Pa: Pennsylvania State University Press.

—— (1990*b*) Regulation theories in retrospect and prospect, *Economy and Society*, 19/2: 153–216.

—— (1982) *The Capitalist State*. New York: New York University Press.

Jessop, B., and Sum, N. J. (2001) Pre-disciplinary and post-disciplinary perspectives, *New Political Economy*, 6/1 (Mar.): 89–101.

Jessop, B., Nielsen, K., and Pederson, O. (1993) Structural competitiveness and strategic capacities: rethinking state and international capital. In J. Hausner, B. Jessop, and K. Nielsen, eds., *Institutional Frameworks of Market Economies*. Brookfield, Vt.: Avebury, 23–44.

Jessop, B., Bonnett, K., Bromley, S., and Ling, T. (1988) *Thatcherism*. Cambridge: Polity.

Jewson, N., and MacGregor, S., eds. (1997) *Transforming Cities: Contested Governance and New Spatial Divisions*. London: Routledge.

Jonas, A. (1994) The scale politics of spatiality, *Environment and Planning D: Society and Space*, 12/3: 257–64.

Jones, B., and Keating, M., eds. (1995) *The European Union and the Regions*. Oxford: Clarendon Press.

Jones, M. (2001) The rise of the regional state in economic governance: 'partnerships for prosperity' or new scales of state power?, *Environment and Planning A*, 33: 1185–211.

—— (1999) *New Institutional Spaces*. London: Jessica Kingsley.

—— (1997) Spatial selectivity of the state? The regulationist enigma and local struggles over economic governance, *Environment and Planning A*, 29: 831–64.

Jones, M., and Ward, K. (2002) Excavating the logic of British urban policy: neoliberalism as the 'crisis of crisis management'. In N. Brenner and N. Theodore, eds., *Spaces of Neoliberalism*. Oxford and Boston: Blackwell, 126–47.

Jørgensen, I., Kjœrsdam, F., and Nielsen, J. (1997) A plan of hope and glory: an example of development planning in Denmark after Maastricht. In P. Healey, A. Khakee, A. Motte, and B. Needham, eds., *Making Strategic Spatial Plans: Innovation in Europe*. London. UCL, 39–58.

Jørgensen, J., and Andersen, H. T. (2002) Institutional change in globalizing cities: urban politics between growth and welfare. Department of Geography, University of Copenhagen. Unpublished manuscript.

Jouve, B., and Lefèvre, C., eds. (1999*a*) *Villes, métropoles: les nouveaux territoires du politique*. Paris: Anthropos.

—— (1999*b*) La Cité métropolitaine de Bologne: de la 'troisième Italie' à la deuxième république? In B. Jouve and C. Lefèvre, eds., *Villes, métropoles: les nouveaux territoires du politique*. Paris: Anthropos, 45–71.

—— (1997) Where territorial political culture makes urban institution: the 'metropolitan city' of Bologna, *Environment and Planning C: Government and Policy*, 15.

Kaldor, N. (1970) The case for regional policy, *Scottish Journal of Political Economy*, 17: 337–48.

Katznelson, I. (1992) *Marxism and the City*. New York: Oxford University Press.

Keating, M. (1998) *The New Regionalism in Western Europe*. Cheltenham: Edward Elgar.

—— (1997) Size, efficiency, and democracy: consolidation, fragmentation and public choice. In G. Stoker and H. Wolman, eds., *Theories of Urban Politics*. London: Sage, 117–34.

—— (1991) *Comparative Urban Politics: Power and the City in the United States, Canada, Britain and France*. Aldershot: Edward Elgar.

Keeble, D. (1986) The changing spatial structure in the United Kingdom. In H.-J. Ewers, J. Goddard, and H. Matzerath, eds., *The Future of the Metropolis*. Berlin: Walter de Gruyter, 171–99.

Keil, R. (1998*a*) Globalization makes states: perspectives of local governance in the age of the world city, *Review of International Political Economy*, 5/4: 616–46.

—— (1998*b*) Toronto in the 1990s: dissociated governance?, *Studies in Political Economy*, 56: 151–67.

Kelly, P. (1999) The geographies and politics of globalization, *Progress in Human Geography*, 23/3: 379–400.

Kickert, W. J. M. (1996) Administrative reforms and public sector governance in the Netherlands. In C. Reichard and H. Wollman, eds., *Kommunalverwaltung im Modernisierungsschub?* Basle: Birkhäuser, 320–50.

King, A. D. (1991) *Urbanism, Colonialism and the World-Economy*. New York: Routledge.

King, R. (1975) Italy. In H. Clout, ed., *Regional Development in Western Europe*. London: John Wiley & Sons, 81–112.

Kipfer, S., and Keil, R. (1995) Urbanisierung und Technologie in der Periode des globalen Kapitalismus. In H. Hitz, et al., eds., *Capitales fatales: Urbanisierung und Politik in den Finanzmetropolen Frankfurt und Zürich*. Zürich: Rotpunktverlag, 61–89.

Kitschelt, H., Lange, P., Marks, G., and Stephens, J., eds. (1999) *Continuity and Change in Contemporary Capitalism*. New York: Cambridge University Press.

Knox, P., and Agnew, J. (1995) *The Geography of the World Economy*. 2nd edn. London: Edward Arnold.

Knox, P., and Taylor, P., eds. (1995) *World Cities in a World-System*. New York: Cambridge University Press.

Kobrin, S. (1998) Back to the future: neomedievalism and the postmodern economy, *Journal of International Affairs* (Spring): 361–86.

Kraidy, M. (1999) The global, the local and the hybrid: a native ethnography of glocalization, *Critical Studies in Mass Communication*, 16: 456–76.

Krätke, M. (1999) Globalisierung und Standortkonkurrenz, *Leviathan*, 2: 202–32.

Krätke, S. (2001) Strengthening the polycentric urban system in Europe: conclusions from the ESDP, *European Planning Studies*, 9/1: 105–16.

—— (1995) *Stadt, Raum, Ökonomie*. Basle: Birkhäuser.

—— (1993) Stadtsystem im internationalen Kontext und Vergleich. In R. Roth and H. Wollmann, eds., *Kommunalpolitik*. Opladen: Leske, 176–93.

—— (1991) *Strukturwandel der Städte*. Frankfurt: Campus.

Krätke, S., and Schmoll, F. (1987) Der lokale Staat—'Ausführungsorgan' oder 'Gegenmacht'?, *Prokla*, 68: 30–72.

Krätke, S., Heeg, S., and Stein, R. (1997) *Regionen im Umbruch*. Frankfurt: Campus.

Kreukels, A. (2003) Rotterdam and the south wing of the Randstad. In W. Salet, A. Thornley, and A. Kreukels, eds., *Metropolitan Governance and Spatial Planning*. London: Spon, 189–202.

—— (2000) Interkommunale Kooperation in den Niederlanden. In W. Heinz, ed., *Stadt & Region—Kooperation oder Koordination? Ein internationaler Vergleich*. Schriften des Deutschen Instituts für Urbanistik, 93. Stuttgart, Berlin, and Köln: W. Kohlhammer, 423–96.

—— (1992) The restructuring and growth of the Randstad cities: current policy issues. In F. Dieleman and S. Musterd, eds., *The Randstad: A Research and Policy Laboratory*. Dordrecht: Kluwer, 237–62.

Kreukels, A., and Spit, T. (1990) Public–private partnership in the Netherlands, *Tijdschrift voor Economische en Sociale Geografie*, 81/5: 388–92.

—— (1989) Fiscal retrenchment and the relationship between national government and local administration in the Netherlands. In S. Clarke, ed., *Urban Innovation and Autonomy*. London: Sage, 153–81.

Kristensen, H. (2001) Urban policies and programmes against social exclusion and fragmentation: Danish experiences. In H. T. Andersen and R. van Kempen, eds., *Governing European Cities*. Aldershot: Ashgate, 255–96.

Krugman, P. (1994) Competitiveness: a dangerous obsession, *Foreign Affairs* (Mar.–Apr.): 28–44.

Kunzmann, K. (1998) World city regions in Europe: structural change and future challenges. In Fu-chen Lo and Yue-man Yeung, eds., *Globalization and the World of Large Cities*, Tokyo: United Nations University Press, 37–75.

Kunzmann, K., and Wegener, M. (1991) The pattern of urbanization in western Europe, *Ekistics*, 350: 282–91.

Lake, R. (2002) Bring back big government, *International Journal of Urban and Regional Research*, 26/4: 815–22.

Läpple, D. (1986) Trendbruch in der Raumentwicklung, *Informationen zur Raumentwicklung*, 11–12: 909–20.

—— (1985) Internationalization of capital and the regional problem. In J. Walton ed., *Capital and Labour in the Urbanized World*. London: Sage, 73–5.

—— (1978) Gesellschaftlicher Reproduktionsprozeß und Stadtstrukturen. In M. Mayer, R. Roth, and V. Brandes, eds., *Stadtkrise und soziale Bewegungen*. Frankfurt am Main: Europäische Verlagsanstalt, 23–54.

Larner, W., and Walters, W. (2002) The political rationality of 'new regionalism': toward a genealogy of the region, *Theory and Society*, 31: 391–432.

Lash, S., and Urry, J. (1987) *The End of Organized Capitalism*. Madison: University of Wisconsin Press.

Lavergne, F., and Mollet, P. (1991) The international development of intermediate sized cities in Europe: strategies and networks, *Ekistics*, 58/350–1: 68–81.

Law, C. (1980) *British Regional Development since World War 1*. London: David & Charles.

Leborgne, D., and Lipietz, A. (1991) Two social strategies in the production of new industrial spaces. In G. Benko and M. Dunford, eds., *Industrial Change and Regional Development: The Transformation of New Industrial Spaces*. London: Belhaven, 27–49.

Lefebvre, H. (2003a [1978]) Space and the state. In N. Brenner, B. Jessop, M. Jones, and G. MacLeod, eds., *State/Space: A Reader*. Boston: Blackwell, 84–100

—— (2003b [1970]) *The Urban Revolution*. Minneapolis: University of Minnesota Press.

—— (2003c [1978]) The worldwide experience. S. Elden, E. Lebas, and E. Kofman, eds., *Henri Lefebvre: Key Writings*. New York: Continuum, 199–205.

—— (2001 [1979]) Comments on a new state form, *Antipode*, 33/5: 769–82.

—— (1996 [1968]) The right to the city. In Eleonore Kofman and Elizabeth Lebas, eds., *Henri Lefebvre: Writings on Cities*. Cambridge, Mass.: Blackwell, 63–184.

—— (1991 [1974]) *The Production of Space*. Cambridge, Mass.: Blackwell.

—— (1979) Space: social product and use value. In J. W. Frieberg, ed., *Critical Sociology: European Perspectives*. New York: Irvington Publishers, 285–96.

—— (1978) *De l'État, iv. Les Contradictions de l'État moderne*. Paris: Union Générale d'Éditions.

—— (1977) *De l'État, iii. Le Mode de production étatique*. Paris: Union Générale d'Éditions.

—— (1976a) *De l'État, ii. De Hegel à Marx par Staline*. Paris: Union Générale d'Éditions.

—— (1976b) *De l'État, i. l'État dans le monde moderne*. Paris: Union Générale d'Éditions.

—— (1976c [1973]) *The Survival of Capitalism*. New York: St Martin's Press.

Lefèvre, C. (2003) Paris–Île-de-France region. In W. Salet, A. Thornley, and A. Kreukels, eds., *Metropolitan Governance and Spatial Planning*. London: Spon, 287–300.

—— (1998) Metropolitan government and governance in western countries: a critical overview. *International Journal of Urban and Regional Research*, 22/1: 9–25.

Le Galès, P. (2002) *European Cities: Social Conflicts and Governance*. New York: Oxford University Press.

Le Galès, P., and Lequesne, C., eds. (1998) *Regions in Europe*. New York: Routledge.

Le Galès, P., and Loncle-Moriceau, P. (2001) Local partnerships and social exclusion in France. In M. Geddes and J. Benington, eds., *Local Partnerships and Social Exclusion in the European Union*. New York: Routledge, 70–91.

Le Galès, P., and Voelzkow, H. (2001) Introduction: the governance of local economies. In C. Crouch, P. Le Galès, C. Triglia, and H. Voelzkow, eds., *Local Production Systems in Europe: Rise or Demise?* Oxford: Oxford University Press, 1–24.

Leitner, H. (2004) The politics of scale and networks of spatial connectivity: transnational interurban networks and the rescaling of political governance in Europe. In E. Sheppard and R. McMaster, eds., *Scale and Geographic inquiry.* Oxford: Blackwell, 236–55.

——(1990) Cities in pursuit of economic growth, *Political Geography Quarterly*, 9/2: 146–70.

Leitner, H., and Sheppard, E. (2002) 'The city is dead, long live the net': harnessing European interurban networks for a neoliberal agenda. In N. Brenner and N. Theodore, eds., *Spaces of Neoliberalism*. Oxford: Blackwell, 148–71.

——(1999) Transcending interurban competition: conceptual issues and policy alternatives in the European Union. In A. E. G. Jonas and D. Wilson, eds., *The Urban Growth Machine. Critical Perspectives, Two Decades Later.* Albany: State University of New York Press, 227–46.

——(1998) Economic uncertainty, inter-urban competition and the efficacy of entrepreneurialism. In T. Hall and P. Hubbard, eds., *The Entrepreneurial City.* Chichester: Wiley, 285–308.

Leitner, H., Pavlik, C., and Sheppard, E. (2002) Networks, governance and the politics of scale: inter-urban networks and the European Union. In A. Herod and M. Wright, eds., *Geographies of Power: Placing Scale.* Oxford: Blackwell, 274–303.

Lever, W. (1999) Competitive cities in Europe, *Urban Studies*, 36/5–6: 1029–44.

——(1996) The European regional dimension. In W. Lever and A. Bailly, eds., *The Spatial Impact of Economic Changes in Europe*. Aldershot: Avebury, 178–203.

——(1993) Competition within the European urban system, *Urban Studies*, 30/6: 935–48.

Levine, (1994) The transformation of urban politics in France: the roots of growth politics and urban regimes, *Urban Affairs Quarterly*, 29/3: 383–410.

Leyshon, A., and Thrift, N. (1995) European financial integration: the search for 'an island of monetary stability' in the seas of global financial turbulence. In S. Hardy et al., eds., *An Enlarged Europe. Regions in Competition?* London: Jessica Kingsley, 109–44.

Lipietz, A. (2001) Fortunes and misfortunes of post-Fordism. In R. Albritton, M. Itoh, R. Westra, and A. Zuege, *Phases of Capitalist Development*. New York: Palgrave, 17–36.

——(1995) Avoiding megapolization. The battle of Île-de-France, *European Planning Studies*, 3/2: 143–54.

——(1994) The national and the regional: their autonomy vis-à-vis the capitalist world crisis. In R. Palan and B. Gills, eds., *Transcending the State-Global Divide*. Boulder: Lynne Rienner 23–44.

——(1993) The local and the global: regional individuality or interregionalism?, *Transactions of the Institute of British Geographers*, 18: 8–18.

—— (1992a) A regulationist approach to the future of urban ecology, *Capitalism, Nature, Socialism*, 3/3: 101–10.

—— (1992b) *Towards a New Economic Order*. Polity: London.

—— (1987) *Mirages and Miracles*. New York: Verso.

—— (1977) *Le Capital et son espace*. Paris: Maspero.

Lipschutz, R. (1992) Restructuring world politics: the emergence of global civil society, *Millennium*, 21: 389–421.

Logan, J., and Molotch, H. (1987) *Urban Fortunes. The Political Economy of Place*. Berkeley and Los Angeles: University of California Press.

Logan, J., and Swanstrom, T., eds. (1990) *Beyond the City Limits*. Philadelphia: Temple University Press.

Lojkine, J. (1977) *Le Marxisme, l'état et la question urbaine*. Paris: Presses Universitaires de France.

Lourau, R. (1974) *L'Analyseur Lip*. Paris: Union Générale d'Éditions.

Lovering, J. (1999) Theory led by policy: the inadequacies of the 'new regionalism', *International Journal of Urban and Regional Research*, 23/2: 379–96.

—— (1995) Creating discourses rather than jobs: the crisis in the cities and the transition fantasies of intellectuals and policy makers. In P. Healey, S. Cameron, S. Davoudi, S. Graham, and A. Madani-Pour, eds., *Managing Cities: The New Urban Context*. London: Wiley, 109–26.

LPAC, London Planning Advisory Committee (1991) *London. World City Moving into the 21st Century*. London: HMSO.

Mabrouk, T. B., and Jouve, B. (1999) La Difficile Émergence de la région urbaine de Lyon. In B. Jouve and C. Lefèvre, eds., *Villes, métropoles: les nouveaux territoires du politique*. Paris: Anthropos, 103–31.

McGrew, A. (1992) A global society? In S. Hall, ed., *Modernity and its Futures*. Cambridge: Open University Press, 61–116.

MacIntosh, M., and Wainwright, H., eds. (1987) *A Taste of Power: The Politics of Local Economics*. London: Verso.

MacKay, R. R. (1995) Non-market forces, the nation state and the European Union, *Papers in Regional Science*, 74/3: 209–31.

—— (1994) Automatic stabilizers, European union and national unity, *Cambridge Journal of Economics*, 18: 571–85.

MacKinnon, D. (2001) Regulating regional spaces: state agencies and the production of governance in the Scottish highlands, *Environment and Planning A*, 33: 823–44.

MacLeod, G. (2001) New regionalism reconsidered: globalization, regulation and the recasting of political economic space, *International Journal of Urban and Regional Research*, 25/4, in press.

—— (2000) The learning region in an age of austerity: capitalizing on knowledge, entrepreneurialism and reflexive capitalism, *Geoforum*, 31: 219–36.

—— (1997) Globalizing Parisian thought-waves: recent advances in the study of social regulation, politics, discourse and space, *Progress in Human Geography*, 21/4: 530–53.

MacLeod, G., and Goodwin, M. (1999) Space, scale and state strategy: rethinking urban and regional governance, *Progress in Human Geography*, 23/4: 503–27.

McMichael, P. (1996) *Development and Social Change*. Thousand Oaks, Calif.: Sage.

—— (1987) State formation and the construction of the world market, *Political Power and Social Theory*, 6: 187–237.

MacMillan, J., and Linklater, A. (1995) *Boundaries in Question*. London: Pinter.

McNeill, D. (2001) Embodying a Europe of the cities: geographies of mayoral leadership, *Area*, 22/4: 353–9.

Madanipour, A., Cars, G., and Allen, J., eds. (1998) *Social Exclusion in European Cities*. London: Jessica Kingsley.

Magnusson, W. (1996) *The Search for Political Space*. Toronto: University of Toronto Press.

Maier, C. (2000) Consigning the twentieth century to history: alternative narratives for the modern era, *American Historical Review*, 105/3: 807–31.

Majone, G. (1994) The rise of the regulatory state in Europe, *West European Politics*, 17/3: 77–102.

Malkki, L. (1992) National geographic: the rooting of peoples and the territorialization of national identity among scholars and refugees, *Cultural Anthropology*, 7/1: 24–44.

Mann, M. (1997) Has globalization ended the rise and rise of the nation-state?, *Review of International Political Economy*, 4/3: 472–96.

——(1993) *The Sources of Social Power*, ii. *The Rise of Classes and Nation-States*. New York: Cambridge University Press.

——(1988) The autonomous power of the state: its origins, mechanisms and results. In M. Mann, *States, War and Capitalism*. Cambridge, Mass: Blackwell, 1–32.

Marcuse, P., and van Kempen, R., eds. (2001) *Globalizing Cities*. Cambridge, Mass.: Blackwell.

Marden, P. (1997) Geographies of dissent: globalization, identity and the nation, *Political Geography*, 16/1: 37–64.

Marglin, S., and Schor, J., eds. (1990) *The Golden Age of Capitalism: Reinterpreting the Postwar Experience*. New York: Oxford University Press.

Marston, S. (2000) The social construction of scale, *Progress in Human Geography*, 24/2: 219–42.

Martin, R. (1989) The new economics and politics of regional restructuring: the British experience. In L. Albrechts et al., eds., *Regional Policy at the Crossroads*. London: Jessica Kingsley, 27–51.

——(1988) The political economy of Britain's north-south divide, *Transactions, Institute of British Geographers*, 13: 389–418.

Martin, R., and Rowthorn, B., eds. (1986) *The Geography of De-industrialisation*. London: Macmillan.

Martin, R., and Sunley, P. (1997) The post-Keynesian state and the space economy. In R. Lee and J. Wills, eds., *Geographies of Economies*. London: Arnold, 278–89.

Martinelli, F., and Schoenberger, E. (1991) Oligopoly is alive and well: notes for a broader discussion of flexible accumulation. In G. Benko and M. Dunford, eds., *Industrial Change and Regional Development*. London: Belhaven, 117–33.

Marx, K. (1973 [1857]) *Grundrisse. Foundations of the Critique of Political Economy*. Trans. Martin Nicolaus. New York: Penguin.

Maskell, P., and Törnqvist, G. (2000) *Building a Cross-Border Leaning Region: Emergence of the North European Øresund Region*. Copenhagen: Copenhagen Business School Press.

Massey, D. (1995) Reflections on debates over a decade. In D. Massey, *Spatial Divisions of Labor*. 2nd edn. London: Macmillan, 296–354.

——(1994) Politics and space/time. In D. Massey, *Space, Place, Gender*. Minneapolis: University of Minnesota Press, 249–72.

——(1986) The legacy lingers on: the impact of Britain's international role on its internal geography. In R. Martin and B. Rowthorn, eds., *The Geography of De-industrialisation*. London: Macmillan, 31–52.

——(1985) *Spatial Divisions of Labour*. London: Macmillan.

Mayer, M. (1994) Post-Fordist city politics. In A. Amin, ed., *Post-Fordism: A Reader*. Cambridge, Mass.: Blackwell, 316–37.

——(1993) The career of urban social movements in West Germany. In R. Fischer and J. Kling, eds., *Mobilizing the Community*. London: Sage, 149–70.

——(1992) The shifting local political system in European cities. In M. Dunford and G. Kafkalas, eds., *Cities and Regions in the New Europe*. New York: Belhaven, 255–76.

——(1991) Politics in the post-Fordist city, *Socialist Review*, 1: 105–24.

——(1990) Lokale Politik in der unternehmerischen Stadt. In R. Borst, ed., *Das neue Gesicht der Städte*. Basle: Birkhäuser, 190–208.

MBZ, Ministerie van Binnenlandse Zaken (1994) *Kaderwet bestuur in verandering: Tekst en uitleg*. The Hague: Ministerie van Binnenlandse Zaken.

——(1990) *Bestuur en stedelijke gebieden: Bestuur op niveau*. The Hague: Ministerie van Binnenlandse Zaken.

——(1989) *Rapport van de Externe Commissie Grote Stedenbeleid: Grote steden grote kansen*. The Hague: Ministerie van Binnenlandse Zaken.

Mény, Y., and Wright, V., eds. (1985) *Centre–Periphery Relations in Western Europe*. London: Allen & Unwin.

Merlin, P. (1971) *New Towns: Regional Planning and Development*. Trans. M. Sparks. London: Methuen.

Messner, D. (1997) *The Network Society*. London: Frank Cass.

Meyer, J. (1999) The changing cultural content of the nation-state: a world society perspective. In G. Steinmetz, ed., *State/Culture: State Formation after the Cultural Turn*. Ithaca, NY: Cornell University Press.

Meyer, J., Boli, J., Thomas, G., and Ramirez, F. (1997) World Society and the Nation-State, *American Journal of Sociology*, 103/1: 144–81.

Milward, A. (2000) *The European Rescue of the Nation State*. 2nd edn. New York: Routledge.

Mingione, E. (1996) *Urban Poverty and the Underclass: A Reader*. Cambridge, Mass.: Blackwell.

Mittleman, J. (2000) *The Globalization Syndrome*. Princeton, NJ: Princeton University Press.

——ed. (1997) *Globalization: Critical Perspectives*. Boulder: Lynne Rienner.

MoE, Ministry of the Environment (1992) *Denmark Towards the Year 2018: The Spatial Structuring of Denmark in the Future Europe*. Copenhagen: Ministry of the Environment, Denmark.

Moody, K. (1996) *Workers in a Lean World*. New York: Verso.

Moore, B., Rhodes, J., and Tyler, P. (1986) *The Effects of Government Regional Economic Policy*. London: Department of Trade and Industry.

Motte, A. (1997) Building strategic urban planning in France. The Lyon urban area, 1981–93 experiments. In P. Healey, A. Khakee, A. Motte, and B. Needham, eds., *Making Strategic Spatial Plans: Innovation in Europe*. London. UCL, 59–76.

Moulaert, F. (2000) *Globalization and Integrated Area Development in European Cities*. New York: Oxford University Press.

Moulaert, F. (1996) Rediscovering spatial inequality in Europe: building blocks for an appropriate 'regulationist' analytical framework, *Environment and Planning D: Society and Space*, 14: 155–79.

Moulaert, F., and Demazière, C. (1995) Local economic development in post-Fordist Europe: survey and strategy reflections. In C. Demazière and P. Wilson, eds., *Local Economic Development in Europe and the Americas*. London: Mansell, 2–28.

Moulaert, F., Rodriguez, A., and Swyngedouw E., eds. (2003) *The Globalized City*. Oxford and New York: Oxford University Press.

Moulaert, F., Salin, E., and Werquin, T. (2001) Euralille: large-scale urban development and social polarization, *European Urban and Regional Studies*, 8/2: 145–60.

Moulaert, F., Swyngedouw, E., and Wilson, P. (1988) Spatial responses to Fordist and post-Fordist accumulation and regulation, *Papers of the Regional Science Association*, 64: 11–23.

Mouritzen, P. E., ed. (1991) *Managing Cities in Austerity*. London: Sage.

Müller, W., and Wright, V. (1994) Reshaping the state in Western Europe: the limits to retreat, *West European Politics*, 17/3: 1–11.

Musterd, S., and Ostendorf, W., eds. (1998) *Urban Segregation and the Welfare State*. New York: Routledge.

MVROM, Ministerie van Volkshuisvesting, Ruimtelijke Ordening en Milieubeheer (1991) *Vierda nota over de ruimtelijke ordening Extra*, Tweede Kamer der Staten-Generaal, 1990–1, 21879, nos. 1–2. The Hague: SDU.

——(1988) *Vierda nota over de ruimtelijke ordening*, Tweede Kamer der Staten-Generaal, 1987–8, 20490, nos. 1–2. The Hague: SDU.

Myrdal, G. (1957) *Rich Lands and Poor*. New York: Harper & Bros.

Nevins, J. (2002) *Operation Gatekeeper*. New York: Routledge.

Newman, D., ed. (1999) *Boundaries, Territory and Postmodernity*. London: Frank Cass.

Newman, D., and Paasi, A. (1998) Fences and neighbors in the postmodern world, *Progress in Human Geography*, 22/2: 186–207.

Newman, P., and Thornley, A. (1997) Fragmentation and centralisation in the governance of London, *Urban Studies*, 34/7: 967–88.

——(1996) *Urban Planning in Europe*. London: Routledge.

——(1995) Euralille: 'boosterism' at the centre of Europe, *European Urban and Regional Studies*, 2/3: 237–46.

Nielsen, K., Jessop, B., and Hausner, J. (1995) Institutional change in post-socialism. In J. Hausner, B. Jessop, and K. Nielsen, eds., *Strategic Choice and Path-Dependency in Post-Socialism*. London: Edward Elgar, 3–46.

Nijkamp, P. (1993) Towards a network of regions: the United States of Europe, *European Planning Studies*, 1/2: 149–68.

Nilsson, J.-E., and Schamp, E. (1996) Restructuring of the European production system, *European Urban and Regional Studies*, 3/2: 121–32.

North, D. (1990) *Institutions, Institutional Change and Economic Performance*. London and New York: Cambridge University Press.

O'Brien, R. (1992) *Global Financial Integration: The End of Geography*. London: Pinter.

OECD (1991) *Historical Statistics, 1960–1989*. Paris: OECD.

——(1976) *Regional Problems and Policies in OECD Countries*. Paris: Organization for Economic Cooperation and Development.

Offe, C. (1984) 'Crisis of crisis management': elements of a political crisis theory. In *Contradictions of the Welfare State*. Cambridge, Mass.: MIT Press, 35–64.

—— (1974) Structural problems of the capitalist state: class rule and the political system, *German Political Studies*, 1: 31–57.

Ohmae, K. (1995) *The End of the Nation State: The Rise of Regional Economies*. New York: Free Press.

—— (1990) *The Borderless World*. New York: Harper.

Ollman, B. (1993) *Dialectical Investigations*. New York: Routledge.

O'Loughlin, J., and Friedrichs, J., eds. (1996) *Social Polarization in Post-Industrial Metropolises*. New York and Berlin: Walter de Gruyter.

O'Riain, S. (2000) States and markets in an era of globalization, *Annual Review of Sociology*, 26: 187–213.

Osborn, F., and Whittick, A. (1977) *New Towns: Their Origins, Achievements and Progress*. 3rd edn. London: Leonard Hill.

Overbeek, H., ed. (1991) *Restructuring Hegemony in the International Political Economy*. New York: Routledge.

Paasi, A. (1996) *Territories, Boundaries and Consciousness*. Chichester: John Wiley.

Painter, J. (1991) Regulation theory and local government, *Local Government Studies* (Nov./Dec.): 23–44.

Painter, J., and Goodwin, M. (1995) Local governance and concrete research: investigating the uneven development of regulation, *Economy and Society*, 24/3: 334–56.

Palat, R. A. (1996) Fragmented visions: excavating the future of area studies in a post-American world, *Review*, 19/3: 269–315.

Panitch, L. (1994) Globalization and the state. In R. Miliband and L. Panitch, eds., *Socialist Register 1994*. London: Merlin, 60–93.

Panitch, L., and Gindin, S. (2003) American imperialism and EuroCapitalism: the making of neoliberal globalization, *Studies in Political Economy*, 71–2: 7–38.

Parkinson, M. (1998) The United Kingdom. In L. van den Berg, E. Braun, and J. van der Meer, eds., *National Urban Policies in the European Union*. Aldershot: Ashgate, 402–33.

—— (1992) City links, *Town & Country Planning* (Sept.): 235–6.

—— (1991) The rise of the entrepreneurial European city: strategic responses to economic changes in the 1980s, *Ekistics*, 350: 299–307.

Parr, J. B. (1973) Growth poles, regional development and central place theory, *Papers of the Regional Science Association*, 73: 173–212.

Parris, H., Pestieau, P., and Saynor, P. (1987) *Public Enterprise in Western Europe*. London: Croom Helm.

Parsons, T. (1971) *The System of Modern Societies*. Englewood Cliffs, NJ: Prentice Hall.

Peck, J. (2003), Geography and public policy: mapping the penal state, *Progress in Human Geography*, 27/2: 222–32.

—— (2002) Political economies of scale: fast policy, interscalar relations and neoliberal workfare, *Economic Geography*, 78/3 (July): 332–60.

—— (2001a) Neoliberalizing states: thin policies/hard outcomes, *Progress in Human Geography*, 25/3: 445–55.

—— (2001b) *Workfare States*. New York: Guilford.

—— (1998) Geographies of governance: TECs and the neo-liberalisation of 'local interests', *Space & Polity*, 2/1: 5–31.

Peck, J., and Theodore, N. (2001) Exporting workfare/importing welfare-to-work: exploring the politics of Third Way policy transfer, *Political Geography*, 20: 427–60.

Peck, J. and Tickell, A. (2002) Neoliberalizing space. In N. Brenner and N. Theodore eds., *Spaces of Neoliberalism*. Boston: Blackwell, 33–57.

—— (1995) The social regulation of uneven development: 'regulatory deficit', England's South East, and the collapse of Thatcherism, *Environment and Planning A*, 27: 15–40.

—— (1994) Searching for a new institutional fix. In A. Amin, ed., *Post-Fordism: A Reader*. Cambridge, Mass.: Blackwell, 280–315.

Peet, R. (2003) *Unholy Trinity: The IMF, WTO and World Bank*. London: Zed.

Perkmann, M., and Sum, N.-L., eds. (2002) *Globalization, Regionalization and Cross-Border Regions*. London: Palgrave.

Perroux, F. (1955) Note sur la notion de 'pôle de croissance', *Cahiers de l'Institute de Science Economique Appliquée*, D, 8.

—— (1950) Economic space, theory and applications, *Quarterly Journal of Economics*, 64.

Peterson, M. J. (1992) Transnational activity, international society and world politics, *Millennium*, 21/3: 171–92.

Petit, P. (1999) Structural forms and growth regimes of the post-Fordist era, *Review of Social Economy*, 57/2: 220–43.

Petrella, R. (2000) The future of regions: why the competitiveness imperative should not prevail over solidarity, sustainability and democracy, *Geografiska Annaler*, 82B/2: 67–72.

Phelps, N., McNeill, D., and Parsons, N. (2002) In search of a European edge urban identity: trans-European networking among edge urban municipalities, *European Urban and Regional Studies*, 9/3: 211–24.

Pickvance, C. (1991) The difficulty of control and the ease of structural reform: British local government in the 1980s. In C. Pickvance and E. Preteceille, eds., *State Restructuring and Local Power: A Comparative Perspective*. London and New York: Pinter, 48–90.

—— (1990) Introduction: the institutional context of local economic development. In M. Harloe, C. G. Pickvance, and J. Urry, eds., *Place, Policy and Politics: Do Localities Matter?* London: Unwin Hyman, 1–41.

Pickvance, C., and Preteceille, E., eds. (1991*a*) *State Restructuring and Local Power: A Comparative Perspective*. London and New York: Pinter.

—— (1991*b*) Conclusion: towards a comparative analysis of state restructuring and local power. In C. Pickvance and E. Preteceille, eds., *State Restructuring and Local Power: A Comparative Perspective*. London and New York: Pinter, 196–224.

Pierson, P. (2000) Increasing returns, path dependence and the study of politics, *American Political Science Review*, 94/2: 251–68.

Pletsch, C. (1981) The three worlds, or the division of social scientific labor, circa 1950–1975, *Comparative Studies of Society and History*, 23/4: 565–90.

Polanyi, K. (1957) *The Great Transformation*. Boston: Beacon.

Pollack, M. (1998) Beyond left and right? Neoliberalism and regulated capitalism in the treaty of Amsterdam, *Working Paper Series in European Studies*, European Studies Program, University of Wisconsin-Madison, 2/2: 1–16.

Porter, M. (1990) *The Competitive Advantage of Nations*. New York: Free Press.

Postone, M. (1993) *Time, Labor and Social Domination: A Reinterpretation of Marx's Critical Theory*. New York: Cambridge University Press.

Poulantzas, N. (1978) *State, Power, Socialism*. London: New Left Books.

Pounds, N. (1985) *An Historical Geography of Europe, 1800–1914*. Cambridge University Press.

Premius, H. (1997) Market-oriented housing policy: a contradiction in terms: recent Dutch experiences, *International Journal of Urban and Regional Research*, 21/1: 133–42.

—— (1994) Planning the Randstad: between economic growth and sustainability, *Urban Studies*, 31/3: 509–34.

Premius, H., and van der Wusten, H., eds. (1995) *Bestuurlijke en ruimtelijke inrichting van de Randstad*. Delft: Delft University Press.

Premius, H., Boelhouwer, P., and Kruythoff, H. (1997) Dutch urban policy: a promising perspective for the big cities, *International Journal of Urban and Regional Research*, 21/4: 677–90.

Preteceille, E. (1991) From centralization to decentralization: social restructuring and French local government. In C. Pickvance and E. Preteceille, eds., *State Restructuring and Local Power: A Comparative Perspective*. London and New York: Pinter, 123–49.

—— (1975) *Équipements collectifs, structures urbaines et consommation sociale: introduction théorique et méthodologique*. Paris: Centre de sociologie urbaine.

Priebs, A. (1997) Der Reformvorschlag 'Region Hannover': Modell für die zukünftige Regionalverwaltung, *Raumforschung und Raumordnung*, 55/3: 219–21.

Prigge, W., and Ronneberger, K. (1996) Globalisierung und Regionalisierung—Zur Auflösung Frankfurts in die Region, *Österreichische Zeitschrift für Soziologie*, 21/2: 129–38.

Radice, H. (2000) Responses to globalisation: a critique of progressive nationalism, *New Political Economy*, 5/1: 5–20.

—— (1999) Taking globalization seriously. In L. Panitch and C. Leys, eds., *Global Capitalism versus Democracy: Socialist Register 1999*. New York: Monthly Review, 1–28.

—— (1998) 'Globalization' and national differences, *Competition and Change*, 3: 263–91.

—— (1984) The national economy: a Keynesian myth?, *Capital and Class*, 22: 111–40.

Reich, R. (1991) *The Work of Nations*. New York: Knopf.

Rhodes, M. (1995) 'Subversive liberalism': market integration, globalization and the European welfare state, *Journal of European Public Policy*, 2/3: 384–406.

Rhodes, M., Heywood, P., and Wright, V., eds. (1997) *Development in West European Politics*. New York: St Martin's Press.

Robertson, R. (1994) Globalisation or glocalisation, *The Journal of International Communication*, 1/1: 33–51.

—— (1992) *Globalization*. London: Sage.

Rödenstein, M. (1987) Durchstaatlichung der Städte? Krisenregulierung durch die kommunale Selbstverwaltung. In W. Prigge ed., *Die Materialität des Städtischen*. Basel: Birkhäuser Verlag, 107–123.

Rodríguez-Pose, A. (1998) *The Dynamics of Regional Growth in Europe*. Oxford: Clarendon Press.

Rokkan, S., and Urwin, D., eds. (1982) *The Politics of Territorial Identity*. London: Sage.

Ronneberger, K., and Keil, R. (1995) Ausser Atem—Frankfurt nach der Postmoderne. In H. Hitz et al., eds., *Capitales Fatales: Urbanisierung und Politik in den Finanzmetropolen Frankfurt und Zürich*. Zürich: Rotpunktverlag, 208–84.

Ronzani, S. (1979) Background notes to regional incentives in Italy. In K. Allen, ed., *Balanced National Growth*. Lexington, Mass.: Lexington Books, 131–56.

Rose, R. (1985) From government at the centre to nationwide government. In Y. Mény and V. Wright, eds., *Centre–Periphery Relations in Western Europe*. London: Allen & Unwin, 13–32.

Rosenberg, J. (2000) *The Follies of Globalization Theory*. New York: Verso.

Ross, G. (1998) European integration and globalization. In R. Axtmann, ed., *Globalization and Europe*. London: Pinter, 164–83.

Ross, G., and Cohen, S. (1975) The politics of French regional planning. In J. Friedmann and W. Alonso, eds., *Regional Policy: Readings in Theory and Application*. Cambridge, Mass.: MIT Press, 727–50.

Röttger, B. (1997) *Neoliberale Globalisierung und eurokapitalistische Regulation*. Münster: Westfälisches Dampfboot.

Rubenstein, J. (1978) French new-town policy. In G. Golany, ed., *International Urban Growth Policies: New-Town Contributions*. New York: John Wiley, 75–103.

Ruggie, J. (1993) Territoriality and beyond: problematizing modernity in international relations, *International Organization*, 47/1: 139–74.

—— (1982) International regimes, transactions and change: embedded liberalism in the postwar economic order, *International Organization*, 36/2: 379–415.

Ruigrok, W., and van Tulder, R. (1995) *The Logic of International Restructuring*. New York: Routledge.

Sabel, C. (1994) Flexible specialisation and the re-emergence of regional economies. In A. Amin, ed., *Post-Fordism: A Reader*. Cambridge, Mass.: Blackwell, 101–56.

Sablowski, T. (1998) *Italien nach dem Fordismus*. Münster: Westfälisches Dampfboot.

Sack, R. (1986) *Human Territoriality. Its Theory and History*. New York: Cambridge University Press.

Salet, W. (2003) Amsterdam and the north wing of the Randstad. In W. Salet, A. Thornley, and A. Kreukels, eds., *Metropolitan Governance and Spatial Planning*. London: Spon, 175–88.

Salet, W., Thornley, A., and Kreukels, A. (2003*a*) Institutional and spatial coordination in European metropolitan regions, *Metropolitan Governance and Spatial Planning*. London: Spon, 3–19.

—— eds. (2003*b*) *Metropolitan Governance and Spatial Planning*. London: Spon.

Salin, E., and Moulaert, F. (1999*a*) Lille-France. Euralille development project. Contribution to *Urban Development and Social Polarisation in the City* project. Accessed at: http://www.ifresi.univ-lille1.fr/PagesHTML/URSPIC/Index.htm, accessed 3 March 2004.

—— (1999*b*) Euralille and the urban policy challenge in France. Contribution to *Urban Development and Social Polarisation in the City* project. Accessed at: http://www.ifresi.u-niv-lille1.fr/PagesHTML/URSPIC/Index.htm, accessed 3 March 2004.

Sallez, A. (1998) France. In L. van den Berg, E. Braun, and J. van der Meer, eds., *National Urban Policies in the European Union*. Aldershot: Ashgate, 97–131.

Sassen, S. (1996) *Losing Control? Sovereignty in an Age of Globalization*. New York: Columbia University Press.

—— (1993) *Cities in the World Economy*. London: Sage.

—— (1991) *The Global City*. PrincetonNJ: Princeton University Press.

Saunders, P. (1985) *Social Theory and the Urban Question*. 2nd edn. New York: Routledge.

—— (1979) *Urban Politics: A Sociological Interpretation*. London: Penguin.

Savitch, H., and Kantor, P. (2002) *Cities in the International Marketplace*. Princeton, NJ: Princeton University Press.

Sawers, L., and Tabb, W., eds. (1984) *Sunbelt/Snowbelt: Urban Development and Regional Restructuring*. New York: Oxford University Press.

Sayer, A. (1999) *Long Live Postdisciplinary Studies! Sociology and the Curse of Disciplinary Parochialism/Imperialism*. Department of Sociology, Lancaster University. Available at: http://www.comp.lancs.ac.uk/sociology/soc025as.html, accessed 16 Jan. 2004.

Scargill, I. (1983) *Urban France*. Beckenham: Croom Helm.

Scharpf, F. (1999) *Governing in Europe*. New York: Oxford University Press.

Scharpf, F., and Schmidt, V., eds. (2000) *Welfare and Work in the Open Economy*. New York: Oxford University Press, i.

Scheller, J. (1998) *Rhein-Main—eine Region auf dem Weg zur politischen Existenz*. *Materialien 25*. Frankfurt: Institut für Kulturgeographie, Stadt- und Regionalforschung der Johann Wolfgang Goethe-Universität.

Schikora, A. (1984) *Die Eignung des Konzeptes der 'endogenen Entwicklungspotentiale' zur Herstellung gleichwertiger Lebensbedngungen*. Munich: Florenz.

Schmidt, H. (1985) *Sozialphilosophie des Krieges. Staats- und subjekttheoretische Untersuchungen zu Henri Lefebvre und Georges Bataille*. Essen: Klartext.

Schmidt, V. (2002) *The Futures of European Capitalism*. New York: Oxford University Press.

——(1988) Industrial management under the Socialists in France: decentralized dirigisme at the national and local levels, *Comparative Politics*, 21/1: 53–72.

Schmitter, P. (1999) The future of democracy: could it be a matter of scale? *Social Research*, 66/3: 933–58.

Scholte, J. A. (2000) *Globalization: A Critical Introduction*. London: Palgrave.

——(1997) Global capitalism and the state, *International Affairs*, 73/3: 427–52.

——(1996) The geography of collective identities in a globalizing world, *Review of International Political Economy*, 3/4: 565–608.

Schwartz, H. (1994) *States and Markets*. New York: St Martin's Press.

Scott, A. J., ed. (2001) *Global City-Regions*. New York: Oxford University Press.

——(1998) *Regions and the World Economy*. London: Oxford University Press.

——(1996) Regional motors of the global economy, *Futures*, 28/5: 391–411.

——(1988) *New Industrial Spaces*. London: Pion.

Scott, A. J., and Storper, M. (2003) Regions, globalization, development, *Regional Studies*, 37/6–7: 579–93.

——(1992) Industrialization and regional development. In M. Storper and A. J. Scott, eds., *Pathways to Industrialization and Regional Development*. New York: Routledge.

——ed. (1986) *Production, Work, Territory*. Boston: Allen & Unwin.

Selan, V., and Donnini, R. (1975) Regional planning in Italy. In J. Hayward and M. Watson, eds., *Planning, Politics and Public Policy*. New York: Cambridge University Press, 269–84.

Sellers, J. (2003) Transnational urban associations and the state in contemporary Europe: a rebirth of the Hanseatic League?, *Jahrbuch für europäische Verwaltungsgeschichte*, 15, 289–308.

——(2002) *Governing from Below: Urban Regions in the Global Economy*. New York: Cambridge University Press.

Sengenberger, W. (1993) Local development and international economic competition, *International Labour Review*, 132/3: 313–29.

Shachar, A. (1996) European world cities. In W. Lever and A. Bailly, eds., *The Spatial Impact of Economic Changes in Europe*. Aldershot: Avebury, 145–77.

Sharpe, L. J., ed. (1995*a*) *The Government of World Cities: The Future of the Metro Model*. New York: John Wiley.

—— (1995*b*) The future of metropolitan government, *The Government of World Cities: The Future of the Metro Model*. New York: John Wiley, 11–31.

—— ed. (1993) *The Rise of Meso Government in Europe*. London: Sage.

Shaw, M. (2000) *Social Theory of the Global State*. New York: Cambridge University Press.

—— (1992) Global society and global responsibility: the theoretical, historical and political limits of international society, *Millennium*, 21: 421–34

Sheppard, E. (2002) The spaces and times of globalization: place, scale, networks and positionality, *Economic Geography*, 307–30.

Sites (2003) *Remaking New York: Primitive Globalization and the Politics of Urban Community*. Minneapolis: University of Minnesota Press.

Skocpol, T. (1977) Wallerstein's world capitalist system: a theoretical and historical critique, *American Journal of Sociology*, 82/5: 1075–102.

Smith, N. (2004) Scale bending and the fate of the national. In E. Sheppard and R. McMaster, eds., *Scale and Geographic Inquiry*. Oxford: Blackwell, 192–212.

—— (2002) New globalism, new urbanism: gentrification as a global urban strategy. In N. Brenner and N. Theodore, eds., *Spaces of Neoliberalism*. Boston: Blackwell, 80–103.

—— (1996) Spaces of vulnerability: the space of flows and the politics of scale, *Critique of Anthropology*, 16/1.

—— (1995) Remaking scale: competition and cooperation in prenational and postnational Europe. In H. Eskelinen and F. Snickars, eds., *Competitive European Peripheries*. Berlin: Springer, 59–74

—— (1993) Homeless/global: scaling places. In J. Bird, B. Curtis, T. Putnam, G. Robertson, and L. Tickner, eds., *Mapping the Futures. Local Cultures, Global Change*. New York: Routledge, 87–119.

—— (1992) Geography, difference and the politics of scale. In J. Doherty, E. Graham, and M. Malek, eds., *Postmodernism and the Social Sciences*. New York: St Martin's Press, 57–79.

—— (1990) *Uneven Development*. 2nd edn. Cambridge, Mass.: Blackwell.

Soja, E. (2000) *Postmetropolis*. Cambridge, Mass.: Blackwell.

—— (1996) *Thirdspace*. Cambridge, Mass.: Blackwell.

—— (1989) *Postmodern Geographies*. New York: Verso.

—— (1985) Regions in context: spatiality, periodicity, and the historical geography of the regional question, *Environment and Planning D: Society and Space*, 3: 175–90.

—— (1980) The socio-spatial dialectic, *Annals of the Association of American Geographers*, 70: 207–55.

Speer, A. (2000) Zielvorstellung für die Gestaltung des engeren Verdichtungsraums Rhein-Main bis zum Jahr 2000. Unpublished mimeograph, Albert Speer & Partner, Frankfurt.

Spruyt, H. (1994) *The Sovereign State and Its Competitors*. Princeton, NJ: Princeton University Press.

Spybey, T. (1996) *Globalization and World Society*. Oxford: Polity.

Staalduine, J. van, and Drexhage, B. (1995) The state of the nation after five years of national spatial planning, *Tijdschrift voor Economische en Sociale Geografie*, 86/2: 191–6.

STANDORT (2000) *Neubau der Region*. Special issue of *STANDORT—Zeitschrift für Angewandte Geographie*, 2/2.

Steinacher, B. (2000) Zukunftsperspektiven für die Region Stuttgart, *STANDORT—Zeitschrift für Angewandte Geographie*, 2: 18–24.

Steinmetz, G., ed. (1999) *State/Culture: New Approaches to the State in the Social Sciences*. Ithaca, NY: Cornell University Press

Stöhr, W. (1990) Synthesis. In. W. Stöhr, ed., *Global Challenge and Local Response*. London: United Nations University, 1–19.

—— (1986) Changing external conditions and a paradigm shift in regional development strategies? In M. Bassand et al., eds., *Self-reliant Development in Europe*. Gower: Aldershot, 59–76.

Stöhr, W., and Taylor, D. R. (1981) *Development from above or below? The dialectics of regional planning in developing countries*. New York: Wiley.

Storper, M. (1996) *The Regional World*. New York: Guilford.

Storper, M., and Salais, R. (1997) *Worlds of Production*. Cambridge, Mass.: Harvard University Press.

—— (1989) The geographical foundations and social regulation of flexible production complexes. In J. Wolch and M. Dear, eds., *The Power of Geography*. Boston: Unwin Hyman, 19–40.

Storper, M., and Walker, R. (1989) *The Capitalist Imperative*. Cambridge, Mass.: Blackwell.

Strange, S. (1996) *The Retreat of the State*. New York: Cambridge University Press.

Swyngedouw, E. (2000a) Authoritarian governance, power and the politics of rescaling, *Environment and Planning D: Society and Space*, 18: 63–76.

—— (2000b) Elite power, global forces and the political economy of 'glocal' development. In G. Clark, M. Feldman, and M. Gertler, eds., *The Oxford Handbook of Economic Geography*. New York: Oxford University Press, 541–58.

—— (1997) Neither global nor local: 'glocalization' and the politics of scale. In K. Cox, ed., *Spaces of Globalization*. New York: Guilford, 137–66.

—— (1996) Reconstructing citizenship, the re-scaling of the state and the new authoritarianism: closing the Belgian Mines, *Urban Studies*, 33/8: 1499–521.

—— (1992a) The Mammon quest: 'Glocalisation', interspatial competition and the monetary order: the construction of new scales. In M. Dunford and G. Kafkalas, eds., *Cities and Regions in the New Europe*. London: Belhaven, 39–68.

—— (1992b) Territorial organization and the space/technology nexus, *Transactions, Institute of British Geographers*, 17: 417–33.

—— (1989) The heart of the place: the resurrection of locality in an age of hyperspace, *Geografiska Annaler*, B, 71/1: 31–42.

Swyngedouw, E., Moulaert, F., and Rodriguez, A. (2003) 'The world in a grain of sand': large-scale urban development projects and the dynamics of 'glocal' transformations. In F. Moulaert, A. Rodriguez, and E. Swyngedouw, eds., *The Globalized City*. Oxford and New York: Oxford University Press, 9–28.

—— (2002) Neoliberal urbanization in Europe: large-scale urban development projects and the new urban policy. In N. Brenner and N. Theodore, eds., *Spaces of Neoliberalism*. Oxford and Boston: Blackwell, 195–229.

Syrett, S., and Baldock, R. (2003) Reshaping London's economic governance, *European Urban and Regional Studies*, 10/1: 69–86.

Taylor, P. J. (2003) Radical political geographies. In J. Agnew, K. Mitchell, and G. Toal, *A Companion to Political Geography*. Boston: Blackwell, 47–58.

Taylor, P. J. (2000) *Metageographical Moments*. Research Bulletin 33, Globalization and World Cities Study Group and Network, University of Loughborough. Available at: http://www.lboro.ac.uk/gawc/rb/rb33.html, accessed 3 March 2004.

—— (1996) Embedded statism and the social sciences: opening up to new spaces, *Environment and Planning A*, 28/11: 1917–28.

—— (1995) World cities and territorial states: the rise and fall of their mutuality. In P. Knox and P. J. Taylor, eds., *World Cities in a World-System*. New York: Cambridge University Press, 48–62.

—— (1994) The state as container: territoriality in the modern world-system, *Progress in Human Geography*, 18/2: 151–62.

—— (1993) *Political Geography: World-Economy, Nation-State and Locality*. 3rd edn. New York: Longman.

Taylor, P. J., and Hoyler, M. (2000) The spatial order of European cities under conditions of contemporary globalization, *Tijdschrift voor Economische en Sociale Geografie*, 91/2: 176–89.

Terhorst, P., and van de Ven, J. C. L. (1995) The national urban growth coalition in the Netherlands, *Political Geography*, 14/4: 343–61.

Thomas, D. (1975) United Kingdom. In H. Clout, ed., *Regional Development in Western Europe*. Chichester: John Wiley, 191–210.

Thornley, A. (2003) London: institutional turbulence but enduring nation-state control. In W. Salet, A. Thornley, and A. Kreukels, eds., *Metropolitan Governance and Spatial planning*. London: Spon, 41–56.

Thrift, N. (1987) The fixers: the urban geography of international commercial capital. In J. Henderson and M. Castells, eds., *Global Restructuring and Territorial Development*. London: Sage, 203–33.

Tickell, A., and Peck, J. (2003) Making global rules: globalization or neoliberalization? In J. Peck and H. W. C. Yeung, eds., *Remaking the Global Economy*. London: Sage, 163–81.

—— (1995) Social regulation after Fordism: regulation theory, neo-liberalism and the global-local nexus, *Economy and Society*, 24/3: 357–86.

Tickell, A., Peck, J., and Dicken, P. (1995) The fragmented region: business, the state and economic development in North West England. In M. Rhodes, ed., *The Regions in the New Europe*. Manchester and New York: Manchester University Press, 247–72.

Tilly, C. (1990) *Coercion, Capital and European States*. Cambridge, Mass.: Blackwell.

Tömmel, I. (1992) Decentralization of regional development policies in the Netherlands—a new type of state intervention?, *Western European Politics*, 15/2: 107–25

Toninelli, P. A., ed. (2000) *The Rise and Fall of State-Owned Enterprise in the Western World*. New York: Cambridge University Press.

Toonen, T. A. J. (1993) Dutch provinces and the struggle for the meso. In L. J. Sharpe, ed., *The Rise of Meso Government in Europe*. London: Sage, 117–53.

—— (1991) Change in continuity: local government and urban affairs in the Netherlands. In J. J. Hesse, ed., *Local Government and Urban Affairs in International Perspective*. Baden-Baden: Nomos, 291–331.

—— (1990) A country without regions and the Committee of the Regions: the case of the Netherlands. In H. J. Hesse, ed., *Regions in Europe*. Baden-Baden: Nomos, 75–99.

—— (1987) The Netherlands: a decentralized unitary state in a welfare society, *West European Politics*, 10/4: 108–29.

Töpfer, K. (1998) Die Zukunft der Stadtregionen. In Bundesministerium für Raumordnung, Bauwesen und Städtebau, ed., *Die Zukunft der Stadtregionen. Dokumentation eines Kongresses in Hannover am 22. und 23. Oktober 1997*. Bonn.

Torfing, J. (1999) Towards a Schumpeterian workfare postnational regime: path-shaping and path-dependency in Danish welfare state reform, *Economy and Society*, 28/1: 369–402.

Torrance, M. (2002) Soft neoliberal influence on urban policy making in the USA and the Netherlands. Case studies of Chicago and Rotterdam. Masters Thesis, Department of Geography, University of Utrecht.

Tweede Kamer der Staten-Generaal (1987–8) *Vierda nota over de ruimtelijke ordening*, 20490, nos. 1–2.

Urry, J. (2000) *Sociology beyond Societies. Mobilities for the 21st Century*. New York: Routledge.

van den Berg, L., Braun, E., and van der Meer, J. (1998) The Netherlands. In L. van den Berg, E. Braun, and J. van der Meer, eds., *National Urban Policies in the European Union*. Aldershot: Ashgate, 254–89.

—— eds. (1997) *Metropolitan Organising Capacity: Experiences with Organising Major Projects in European Cities*. Aldershot: Ashgate.

van der Veer, J. (1997) *Omstreden Stadsgrenzen: een eeuw besluitvorming over annexaties en regionale besturen rond Amsterdam en Eindhoven*. Delft: Uitgevereij Eburon.

Väth, W. (1980) *Raumplanung. Probleme der räumlichen Entwicklung und Raumordungspolitik in der Bundesrepublik Deutschland*. Königstein: Hain.

Veltz, P. (2000) European cities in the world economy. In A. Bagnasco and P. Le Galès, eds., *Cities in Contemporary Europe*. New York: Cambridge University Press, 1–32.

—— (1997) The dynamics of production systems, territories and cities. In F. Moulaert and A. J. Scott, eds., *Cities, Enterprises and Society on the Eve of the 21st Century*. London: Pinter, 78–96.

—— (1996) *Mondialisation, villes et territoires*. Paris: Presses Universitaires de France.

Verges, V. (1999) Le Grand Rotterdam: entre territorialité locale et uniformité nationale. In B. Jouve and C. Lefèvre, eds., *Villes, métropoles: les nouveaux territoires du politique*. Paris: Anthropos, 191–222.

Vermeijden, B. (2001) Dutch urban renewal, transformation of the policy discourse, 1960–2000, *Journal of Housing and the Built Environment*, 16: 203–32.

Vernon, R. (1974) Enterprise and government in western Europe. In R. Vernon, ed., *Big Business and the State*. Cambridge, Mass.: Harvard University Press, 3–24.

Virilio, P. (1984) *Speed and Politics*. New York: Semiotexte.

Wacquant, L. (1999) How penal common sense comes to Europeans, *European Societies*, 1: 319–52.

Wade, R. (1996) Globalization and its limits: reports of the death of the national economy are greatly exaggerated. In S. Berger and R. Dore, eds., *National Diversity and Global Capitalism*. Ithaca, NY: Cornell University Press, 60–88.

Walker, R. (1997) California rages: regional capitalism and the politics of renewal. In R. Lee and J. Wills, eds., *Geographies of Economies*. London: Arnold, 345–56.

Walker, R.B.J. (1993) *Inside/outside: International Relations as Political Theory*. New York: Cambridge University Press.

Wallerstein, I. (2000) Globalization or the age of transition?, *International Sociology*, 15/2: 249–65.

Wallerstein, I. ed. (1996) *Open the Social Sciences*. Stanford: Stanford University Press.

—— (1991) A call for a debate about the paradigm, *Unthinking Social Science*. Cambridge, Mass.: Polity, 237–56.

—— (1989) *The Modern World System*. New York: Academic Press, iii.

—— (1988) Inventions of TimeSpace realities, *Geography*, 73/4: 289–97.

—— (1984) *The Politics of the World-Economy*. New York: Cambridge University Press.

—— (1983) *Historical Capitalism*. New York: Verso.

—— (1980) *The Modern World System*. New York: Academic Press, ii.

—— (1979) The rise and future demise of the world capitalist system, *The Capitalist World-Economy*. New York: Cambridge University Press, 7–19.

—— (1974) *The Modern World-System*. New York: Academic Publishers, i.

Wannop, U. (1995) *The Regional Imperative*. London: Jessica Kingsley Publishers.

Wapner, P. (1995) Politics beyond the state: environmental activism and world civic politics, *World Politics*, 47: 311–40.

Ward, K. (1997) The single regeneration budget and the issue of local flexibility, *Regional Studies*, 31/1: 78–81.

Waterhout, B. (2002) Polycentric development: what is behind it? In A. Faludi, ed., *European Spatial Planning*. Cambridge, Mass.: Lincoln Institute of Land Policy, 83–103.

Waters, M. (1995) *Globalization*. New York: Routledge.

Webber, M., and Rigby, D. (1996) *The Golden Age Illusion*. New York: Guilford.

Weber, M. (1946) *Essays from Max Weber*. London: Routledge & Kegan Paul.

Wegener, M. (1995) The changing urban hierarchy in Europe. In J. Brotchie et al., eds., *Cities in Competition*. Brisbane: Longman Australia, 139–60.

Weiss, L. ed. (2003) *States in the Global Economy*. New York: Cambridge University Press.

—— (1998) *The Myth of the Powerless State*. New York: Polity.

—— (1989) Regional economic policy in Italy. In C. Crouch and D. Marquand, eds., *The New Centralism: Britain out of Step in Europe?* Oxford: Blackwell, 109–24.

Weiss, L., and Hobson, J. (1995) *States and Economic Development*. London: Polity.

Wentz, M., ed. (1994) *Region. Die Zukunft des Städtischen Frankfurter Beiträge Band 5*. Frankfurt: Campus.

Whitfield, D. (2001) *Public Services or Corporate Welfare*. London: Pluto.

Wilks-Heeg, S. (1996) Urban experiments limited revisited: urban policy comes full circle? *Urban Studies*, 33/8: 1263–79.

Wright, V. (1998) Intergovernmental relations and regional government in Europe: a sceptical view. In P. Le Galès and C. Lequesne, eds., *Regions in Europe*. New York: Routledge, 39–49.

—— (1994) Reshaping the state: the implications for public administration, *West European Politics*, 17/3: 102–37.

WRR, Wetenschappelijke Raad voor het Regeringsbeleid (1990) *Van de stad en de rand. Rapporten aan de Regering 37*. The Hague: SDU.

Yeung, H. W. C. (2002) The limits to globalization theory: a geographic perspective on global economic change, *Economic Geography*, 78/3: 285–305.

—— (1998) Capital, state and space: contesting the borderless world, *Transactions, Institute of British Geographers*, 23: 291–309.

Yuill, D. (1979) Background notes to regional incentives in Britain. In K. Allen, ed., *Balanced National Growth*. Lexington, Mass.: Lexington Books, 35–54.

Zielinski, H. (1983) Regional development and urban policy in the Federal Republic of Germany, *International Journal of Urban and Regional Research*, 7/1: 72–92.

Zonneveld, W. (1989) Conceptual complexes and shifts in post-war urban planning in the Netherlands, *Built Environment*, 15/1: 40–8.

INDEX

law
  bourgeois 85
  labor 125
'layered' regulation 81, 107–11
lean production *see* flexible/lean production
  systems
Leborgne, D. 14, 208, 263, 264, 265
Lees, L. H. 119, 120, 268
Lefebvre, H. v, vii, 24, 25, 36, 69, 73, 75, 99, 111,
  114, 135, 136, 257
  on 'explosion of spaces' 1, 5
  on the production of space 32, 42–3, 66, 79,
    123, 246
  on the question of scale 8, 10
  on state mode of production 124–6
  on uneven spatial development 121, 130–1
  on urbanization 117, 118
Lefèvre, C. 157, 158, 217, 240, 275, 278, 281,
  282
Le Galès, P. 205, 255, 269, 271, 272, 287
Leitner, H. 9, 15, 205, 218, 219, 263, 264, 288,
  291, 292, 293, 294
Lenin, V. I. 41 n.
Lever, W. F. 5, 180, 207
Leyshon, A. 127, 167
Lille Metropolis 277
Linklater, A. 71
Lipietz, A. 14, 70, 107, 127, 174, 203, 217, 240,
  254, 263, 264, 265, 294–5
Livingstone, K. 243
local economic initiatives 218–19, 226, 265
local government 152–4, 157, 218–27
  endogenous development strategies 194–8
  expenditure 194, 225
  reorganization of 135, 217
localization 3, 4, 6, 7, 45, 54, 58, 62, 213, 214,
  215, 218–27
  see also neighborhood-based anti-exclusion
    initiatives
locational policies 202–3
  see also urban locational policies
Loncle-Moriceau, P. 271
London 240, 242–3, 276
London Docklands 250–1, 252
London Docklands Development Corporation
  (LDDC) 250–1
London Planning Advisory Committee
  (LPAC) 242
Lourau, R. 197
Lovering, J. 165, 208
Luxemburg, R. 41 n.
Lyon 277

Maastricht Treaty, Social Charter (1991) 200
Mabrouk, T. B. 277
MacDougall Report (1977) 146
MacIntosh, M. 197
MacKay, R. R. 136, 145, 146
MacKinnon, D. 79, 110
MacLennan, M. C. 148
MacLeod, G. 90
McMichael, P. 41, 42, 203
MacMillan, J. 71
McNeill, D. 255, 290
macroeconomic policy 60, 163, 175
macroeconomic theory 39

Madrid Metropolitan Area Planning and
  Coordinating Commission 157
Maier, C. 5, 41, 54, 123, 128
mainports 234, 251–2
Malkki, L. 39
Malmberg, A. 16, 167, 181, 201, 265
managerialism, urban 137, 151–4, 219
Manchester 276
Mann, M. 41, 81, 92, 95, 123
manufacturing 119, 162, 178
  decentralization of 120, 121, 134
  decline of 164–5, 166, 170, 178, 179
  employment 162, 164, 178, 179
  flexible production methods in 165
Marcuse, P. 21, 268
marginalized zones 184, 258
Marglin, S. 127
Marquand, D. 219, 226
Marshall Plan 129
Martin, R. 2, 15, 115, 129, 132, 133, 136, 151,
  186, 187, 210, 247
Martinelli, F. 164
Marvin, S. 16, 100, 120, 124, 244, 248, 251, 253,
  264
Marx, K. 33, 41 n.
Marxist theory 83
Maskell, P. 249
mass consumption 127, 130, 131, 152–3
mass production 120, 127, 130, 131, 134, 161,
  164–5, 166, 178
Massey, D. 10, 14, 29, 108, 109–10, 121, 187,
  262
Mauroy, P. 249
Mayer, M. 135, 152, 168, 196, 201, 204, 217,
  219, 221
mega-projects, urban 219, 243–53
Mény, Y. 135, 152
mergers and acquisitions 167, 181, 200
Merlin, P. 136, 156
meso level analysis 19, 20, 21, 22
Messner, D. 193, 219, 226, 254
METREX (Network of European Metropolitan
  Regions and Areas) 287, 289
metropolitan government vi, 135, 157–9,
  200–1, 224, 225
metropolitan reform initiatives 26, 217, 261,
  266, 274–86, 295, 296, 298
metropolitan regionalism 180–1, 187, 190,
  227–43, 275–86
metropolitan regions, transnational links
  between 168
Meyer, J. 53
migration
  labor 5
  see also immigration
Milan 239
MILAN (Motor Industry Local Authority
  Network) 287
military defense 77
military technology 54
Milward, A. 129
Mittleman, J. 3, 6, 61
Modderman, E. 234, 243
monetarism 162, 175, 199
monetary integration 167, 199, 201
monetary markets 54

state spatiality (*Cont*):
  as political strategy 82–94
  polymorphic character of 77–80
  processual conceptualization of 66, 74, 75–7,
    82, 89, 103, 111, 257
  scalar articulation of 95, 97, 98, 99–100, 101,
    102, 104, 106
  territorial articulation of 95, 97, 98–9, 100–1,
    102, 104, 106
state strategies 86, 87, 88, 91
state-centrism 29–30, 37–43, 44, 64, 66, 70,
    73–4
  and conceptualizations of global space
    47–54
statehood 4, 92
steel industry 139, 149
Stein, R. 187
Steinmetz, G. 24
Stöhr, W. 193, 195, 196
Storper, M. 6, 13, 21, 96, 118, 120, 121, 165,
    178, 180, 188, 208, 218
Strange, S. 1
strategic alliances 59, 167
strategic selectivity 87–9, 89, 90, 91
strategic-relational state theory 25, 72, 82–94,
    111, 300–1
Structural Funds 302
structural selectivity 87, 88, 89
Stuttgart Region 278
Stuttgart Regional Association 157
subcontracting 165
subnational scale 44, 45, 46, 67
subnational spaces 3, 59, 100, 260
suburbanization 154–7
Sum, N.-L. 6, 23, 71
Sunley, P. 2, 15, 115, 129, 132, 133, 136, 151,
    210
supply-side economics 60, 169, 175
supranational institutions 2, 4, 6–7, 59, 61, 62,
    66, 100
supranational scale 44, 45, 46, 67
supraterritoriality 55, 65
surplus value 84
Sweden 148, 151
Swyngedouw, E. 7, 9, 58, 59, 127, 128, 129, 137,
    164, 175, 215, 218, 219, 246, 248
systemic crises 50

Tabb, W. 184
taxation 136, 145
  local 194, 220
Taylor, D. R. 195, 196
Taylor, P. J. 29, 37, 39, 41, 42, 70, 73, 77, 122,
    182, 183, 187
technological change 36, 118
technopoles 58, 59
Telecities 287, 290
Terhorst, P. 224, 280
territorial articulation of state space 95, 97,
    98–9, 100–1, 102, 104, 106
territorial conflicts, and urban locational
    policy 264–5
territorial differentiation, internal 13, 78, 80,
    92, 93, 102, 103, 104, 106–7
territorial fixity 42
territorial reform initiatives 135

territorialism
  global 47–54
  methodological 38, 53, 70, 74
territoriality, national state 28–30, 36–47,
    54–68, 69–72, 76–7, 80, 92
  decline of 55–6, 60, 65, 70
  and global space 47–54, 56, 65
  historicity of 56, 63–4, 65
  processual conceptualization of 76–7
territorialization 36–7, 40, 42–3, 44, 45, 46, 47,
    55, 65
Theodore, N. 5, 169, 175, 200, 294
Thornley, A. 220, 227, 240, 242, 249, 276, 277
Thrift, N. 127, 166, 167, 182
Tickell, A. 127, 161, 174, 205, 212, 262, 276, 298
  on globalization 31, 45, 200, 297
  on uneven development 14, 18
Tilly, C. 18
time-space compression 33, 42
Tomaney, J. 180, 302
Tömmel, I. 234
Toninelli, P. A. 129
Toonen, T. A. J. 158, 222, 223, 224, 280
Töpfer, K. 233
Törnqvist, G. 249
Torrance, M. 271
tourism 185
trade 6, 59
  international regulation of 161; liberalization
    of 5, 31, 41, 166, 199
trade theory 39
transnational corporations 12, 31, 54, 57, 60,
    66, 167, 168, 181, 182, 183, 184, 258
transportation 5, 31, 36, 42, 54, 117, 119, 120,
    124, 125, 134, 137, 151, 152, 168, 183,
    244
Treaty of Westphalia (1648) 40, 76

unemployment 161, 164, 178, 179, 192, 199
uneven development 12–17, 19, 34, 35, 64,
    96–8, 117–26, 163, 170, 172, 178–92,
    257–61, 262, 297, 299
  alleviation of *see* equalization of
    socioeconomic activities; spatial
    Keynesianism
  as basis for macroeconomic growth 169, 170
  and interurban networking programs 297
  and metropolitan reform initiatives 297
  and neighborhood-based anti-exclusion
    programs 297
  urban locational policies and 213–15, 232–4,
    259, 264–5
uniformity, administrative 2, 97, 98–9, 102,
    103, 104, 105, 106, 132, 134, 135, 170
United Nations 212 n.
United States 175
  hegemony of 114, 129, 130, 163
  industrial restucturing 184
Urban Development Corporations 217–18, 226,
    241, 242, 250
urban hierarchies, transnational 181–3, 190,
    191
urban locational policy 16–17, 26, 176, 202–56,
    261, 269, 295–6, 297–9, 299–300
  advanced infrastructural systems as
    mechanism of 246

Lightning Source UK Ltd.
Milton Keynes UK
UKOW03f0044090714

234761UK00002B/5/P